CAREERS OF COUPLES IN CONTEMPORARY SOCIETIES

Careers of Couples in Contemporary Societies

From Male Breadwinner to Dual Earner Families

EDITED BY

Hans-Peter Blossfeld

and

Sonja Drobnič

OXFORD
UNIVERSITY PRESS

OXFORD
UNIVERSITY PRESS

Great Clarendon Street, Oxford OX2 6DP

Oxford University Press is a department of the University of Oxford.
It furthers the University's objective of excellence in research, scholarship,
and education by publishing worldwide in

Oxford New York

Athens Auckland Bangkok Bogotá Buenos Aires Cape Town
Chennai Dar es Salaam Delhi Florence Hong Kong Istanbul Karachi
Kolkata Kuala Lumpur Madrid Melbourne Mexico City Mumbai
Nairobi Paris São Paulo Shanghai Singapore Taipei Tokyo Toronto Warsaw

and associated companies in Berlin Ibadan

Published in the United States
by Oxford University Press Inc., New York

British Library Cataloguing in Publication Data

Data available

Library of Congress Cataloging in Publication Data

Careers of couples in contemporary societies: From male breadwinner
to dual earner families / edited by Hans-Peter Blossfeld and Sonja Drobnič.
p. cm.
Includes bibliographical references.
1. Dual Earner families—Cross-cultural studies.
I. Blossfeld, Hans-Peter.   II. Drobnič, Sonja.
HQ518.C367 2001   306.3′6—dc21   2001021220
ISBN 0–19–924491–X

1 3 5 7 9 10 8 6 4 2

Typeset by Hope Services (Abingdon) Ltd.
Printed by T.J. International Ltd.
Padstow, Cornwall

PREFACE

This book concerns the transformation of couples' careers in contemporary societies. During recent decades, a remarkable shift has taken place in industrialized countries from the traditional male breadwinner to the dual-earner family model. However, the timing, speed, and pattern of this transition varies significantly across countries, and it is still unclear what has and what has not changed for couples in various countries due to women's greater involvement in paid employment. This volume presents the findings of an internationally comparative study on careers of couples in twelve countries. We use the more general term 'couples' instead of 'spouses' because in some of the countries studied in this volume the process of family formation and the structure of households have changed to such an extent that the distinction between marital and cohabitational unions has become blurred (see for example the chapter on Sweden). The focus of the book, however, is on husbands' and wives' coupled transitions between full-time or part-time work and unpaid housework over the life course, beginning with the time of entry into the marital union. The distinction between full-time and part-time jobs makes it possible to evaluate the relationship of primary and secondary earners over time. Our life-course approach explicitly recognizes the dynamic nature of family roles and circumstances as partners move through their life paths, the interdependence of lives and life choices among family members, the situational imperatives confronting families in different countries, and the cumulation of advantages and disadvantages experienced by individual members of the family.

The initial idea for this cross-national comparative project was stimulated by research findings from an event-history analysis carried out on West Germany. This research clearly indicated that the process of equalization of gender roles has been much slower than was originally expected based on the predictions of the economic theory of the family or the resource-bargaining approach. Despite substantial improvement in German women's educational attainment and career opportunities, the dimensions of role specialization in German couples has been surprisingly stable. In particular, housework and childcare remained primarily 'women's work'; husbands seemed to insist on the provider role, even if their wives had a higher income potential at the time of marriage. Thus, gender role change within the family has generally been asymmetric in Germany, with a greater movement of women into the traditional male sphere than vice versa. In addition, we found that, in Germany, men with higher occupational resources suppressed their wife's participation in paid employment, which dampens the speed of diffusion of dual-earner families.

The primary interest in our twelve-nation comparison was to check the generality of our findings and interpretations for Germany. Taking into account the inevitable constraints of data availability and expertise, we tried to include countries varying widely in important characteristics, such as industrial development and culture, political system and its history, differentiation of the family system, role of the state, and extent to which the roles of men and women have undergone a progressive transformation. The countries included in our comparison are Germany, the Netherlands, the Flemish part of Belgium, Italy, Spain, Great Britain, the United States, Sweden, Denmark, Poland, Hungary, and China.

In the course of our comparative project, two features of the transformation of careers of couples in contemporary societies have become clear to us: (1) that the change in gender roles has been quite asymmetrical across all countries; and (2) that a country's timing, speed, and pattern of change from the traditional male breadwinner to the dual-earner family model is closely linked to its type of welfare state regime. In particular, the impact of men's resources on their female partners' employment careers matches nicely with a typology of welfare-state regimes. These context effects demonstrate that theories which try to explain the decision-making processes concerning the division of labour within couples as independent of institutional arrangements and cultural settings within which these decisions are made are highly vulnerable.

As editors of the book and organizers of the cross-national research project, we would like to thank all the contributors for their fruitful co-operation and for the enormous effort they put into their analyses and manuscripts. We tried to use comparable data and made a commitment to apply a common research design to study the changes in careers of couples. However, the contributors did not simply help us carry out a previously designed analysis. As clearly indicated by the wealth of information in the country-specific chapters, much of the work in this book represents the creative contributions of our collaborators.

All the chapters in the book were peer-reviewed by the members of the international group and revised several times. They were also evaluated by two anonymous Oxford University Press reviewers. We are very grateful for their thoughtful comments and constructive suggestions which tremendously improved the quality of this book.

The major financial support for the comparative project, in particular for the joint workshop held in Bremen, was a grant from the German Research Foundation (Deutsche Forschungsgemeinschaft) for the Sfb–186 research project 'Household Dynamics and Social Inequality' at the University of Bremen. During the final stages of preparation of this book, partial support was also provided by a grant from the Volkswagen Foundation (Volkswagen Stiftung) for the GLOBALIFE project at the University of Bielefeld.

Our thanks go to the colleagues at the University of Bremen for their superb collegial support. In particular, we wish to thank Katherine Bird who, as native speaker, copy-edited the entire manuscript with great sensitivity. We also thank Julie Winkler-Vinjukova, who helped us organize the workshop, and improved the English of several chapters with great care. In various stages of the project, our student assistants, Cathleen Cramm, Thorsten Schneider, and Ruben van Gaalen, supported us with commitment and professionalism in co-ordinating the project and preparing the typescript. Finally, we are grateful to the copy-editor of Oxford University Press, Jane Robson, for bringing our manuscript in its final shape.

H.-P. B.
University of Bielefeld

S. D.
University of Bremen

CONTENTS

List of Figures   xi
List of Tables   xiii
Contributors   xvi

I. INTRODUCTION

1. A Cross National Comparative Approach to Couples' Careers   1
   HANS-PETER BLOSSFELD AND SONJA DROBNIČ

2. Theoretical Perspectives on Couples' Careers   16
   HANS-PETER BLOSSFELD AND SONJA DROBNIČ

II. THE 'CONSERVATIVE' WELFARE STATE REGIME

3. Spouses' Employment Careers in (West) Germany   53
   HANS-PETER BLOSSFELD, SONJA DROBNIČ, AND GÖTZ ROHWER

4. Couples' Labour-Market Participation in the Netherlands   77
   JOHN HENDRICKX, WIM BERNASCO, AND PAUL M. DE GRAAF

5. Couples' Careers in Flanders   98
   MARTINE CORIJN

III. THE 'MEDITERRANEAN' WELFARE STATE REGIME

6. The Employment Behaviour of Married Women in Italy   121
   FABRIZIO BERNARDI

7. Spouses' Employment Careers in Spain   146
   MARÍA JOSÉ GONZÁLEZ-LÓPEZ

IV. THE 'LIBERAL' WELFARE STATE REGIME

8. Married Women's Employment Patterns in Britain   175
   ANDREW MCCULLOCH AND SHIRLEY DEX

9. Coupled Careers: Pathways Through Work and Marriage in the
United States   201
SHIN-KAP HAN AND PHYLLIS MOEN

V. THE 'SOCIAL DEMOCRATIC' WELFARE STATE REGIME

10. Earnings as a Force of Attraction and Specialization in Sweden   233
URSULA HENZ AND MARIANNE SUNDSTRÖM

11. Work Careers of Married Women in Denmark   261
SØREN LETH-SØRENSEN AND GÖTZ ROHWER

VI. THE (FORMER) 'STATE SOCIALIST' REGIME

12. Employment Patterns of Married Women in Poland   281
SONJA DROBNIČ AND EWA FRĄTCZAK

13. Employment Patterns in Hungarian Couples   307
PÉTER RÓBERT, ERZSÉBET BUKODI, AND RUUD LUIJKX

14. Job-Shift Patterns of Husbands and Wives in Urban China   332
XUEGUANG ZHOU AND PHYLLIS MOEN

VII. RESULTS OF CROSS-NATIONAL COMPARISONS

15. Careers of Couples and Trends in Inequality   371
SONJA DROBNIČ AND HANS-PETER BLOSSFELD

Subject Index   387
Author Index   390

LIST OF FIGURES

3.1. Density of occupational prestige score differences, first job   58
3.2. Transition from full-time employment to housemaking   64
3.3. Transition from full-time employment to housemaking   65
3.4. Transition from full-time employment to housemaking   67
5.1. Occupational status of women at specific family events, by
     birth cohort   110–11
6.1. Distribution of difference in education   130
6.2. Distribution of status score difference   131
7.1. Probability of experiencing a transition from full-time
     employment to homemaking (married or cohabiting women)   159
7.2. Modes of gender contracts in partnerships: transitions from
     full-time employment to homemaking (married or cohabiting
     women)   162
8.1. Husband's Hope–Goldthorpe score minus wife's
     Hope–Goldthorpe score for not previously married couples
     where both partners were employed at BHPS Wave 1 in 1991   181
8.2, *a*, *b*. Mean Hope-Goldthorpe score plotted against month after
     marriage for men and women with long and short career breaks
     for marriage cohorts 1965–74 and 1975–84   183
8.3. Percentage of women in five marriage cohorts who were in
     housework, plotted against month after marriage   189
8.4. Percentage of women in five marriage cohorts who were in
     part-time work, plotted against month after marriage   193
8.5. Percentage of women in five marriage cohorts who were in
     part-time work, plotted against month after marriage   194
9.1. Breadwinner-homemaker   203
9.2. The second shift   204
9.3. Two-career couple   205
9.4. Coupled careers: double interface over the life course   207
9.5. Sequence data: an example   210
9.6. Career pathway type: age profiles   212
9.7. Marital stability by pathway type and gender   220
9.8. Multiple interfaces in two-career couples   225
10.1. Distribution of earnings in the year of first birth   242
10.2. Average earnings by year of first birth   243
10.3. Earnings differences within couples (male minus female
     earnings)   243
11.1. Women 1980 and 1994 by participation in the labour market   262
11.2. Women 1980 and 1994 retired/out of labour force   263

11.3. Women 1980 and 1994 by status in family　　　　　264
12.1. Female employment rates, by age groups　　　　　286
12.2. Male employment rates, by age groups　　　　　287
12.3. Educational homogamy among married couples　　　　　297
14.1. Hazard rate of the timing of marriage, by cohorts　　　　　344
14.2. Proportion of men and women not in the labour force,
　　　　1949–1994　　　　　345
14.3. Joint distribution of occupational status between spouses
　　　　during marriage　　　　　348
14.4. Joint distribution of organizational status between spouses
　　　　during marriage　　　　　349

LIST OF TABLES

2.1.	Classification of welfare state regimes	41
3.1.	Gender-specific employment transitions for couples	60
3.2.	Women's employment status at the time of marriage, for various marriage cohorts	61
3.3.	Effects on the transition rate from employment to homemaking	62
3.4.	Effects on the transition rate from homemaking to employment	70
4.1.	Division of paid labour between husbands and wives in the Netherlands	79
4.2.	Hypotheses with regard to the main types of transitions	81
4.3.	Transitions in wife's labour-market status	82
4.4.	Transition from full-time employment to part-time employment or housekeeping	87
4.5.	Housekeeping versus part-time work, for women leaving full-time employment	89
4.6.	Transition from part-time employment to housekeeping	91
4.7.	Re-entry into the labour market	92
4.8.	Full-time versus part-time employment, for women re-entering the labour market	94
5.1.	Gender-specific employment transitions of married couples	108
5.2.	Effects on the wife's rate of employment exit	109
5.3.	Effects on the wife's rate of employment re-entry	114
6.1.	Patterns of employment trajectories: married women aged 30 to 50	129
6.2.	Effects on the transition rate from employment to housekeeping	134–5
6.3.	Effects on the transition rate from housekeeping to employment	138
7.1.	Estimates for logit models predicting the probability of a married or cohabiting woman changing from full-time employment to full-time homemaker	156–7
7.2.	Estimates for logit models: change from part-time employment to full-time homemaker	163–4
7.3.	Estimates for logit models: change from homemaking to full-time employment	166–7
8.1.	BHPS 1991: husband's and wife's employment status	181
8.2.	Employment transitions for couples, from marriage to interview in 1992	184

8.3.	British women's employment status at the time of marriage for various marriage cohorts	186
8.4.	Effects on the transition rate from full-time work to housekeeping	187
8.5.	Effects on the transition rate from part-time work to housekeeping	190
8.6.	Effects on the transition rate from housekeeping to full-time work	193
8.7.	Effects on the transition rate from housekeeping to part-time work	196
9.1.	Five pathway types and their characteristics	214–5
9.2.	Marital history by gender	218
9.3.	Gender, career pathway, and marital history	219
9.4.	Marital history by pathway type	221
9.5.	Marital history by pathway type by gender	221
9.6.	Gender, career pathway, and spouse's work history	223
9.7.	Spouse's work history by pathway type	224
10.1.	Number of selected labour-market transitions for women and men	241
10.2.	Effects of own and spouse's earnings on women's labour-market transitions	249
10.3.	Parameter estimates for women's transitions from part-time to full-time work	250
10.4.	Parameter estimates for women's transitions from full-time to part-time work	251
10.5.	Parameter estimates for women's transitions from full-time and part-time work to non-employment	252
10.6.	Parameter estimates for women's re-entry into the labour market	253
10.7.	Parameter estimates for women's transitions from leave to part-time work, only first leave episodes	255
10.8.	Parameter estimates for women's transitions from leave to part-time work, only second leave episodes	256
10.9.	Parameter estimates for women's transitions from leave to full-time work, only first leave episodes	257
10.10.	Parameter estimates for women's transitions from leave to full-time work, only second leave episodes	258
11.1.	Characteristics of various transitions for married women	271
11.2.	Transitions for married women working full-time	272–3
11.3.	Transitions for married women working part-time to full-time employment	276
11.4.	Transitions for married women out of the labour market to full-time employment	276
12.1.	Time use of women and men in selected activities	290

12.2. Women's employment status at the time of marriage, for various marriage cohorts 297

12.3. Parameter estimates for rate models of transitions from employment to non-employment and vice versa for married women in Poland 298–9

13.1. Husband' and wives' status characteristics 316

13.2. Women's employment status at time of marriage 317

13.3. Effects on transition rate from work to maternity leave and housekeeping 318–9

13.4. Effects on transition rate from maternity leave and housekeeping to work 322–3

13.5. Employment pattern after marriage by marriage cohort 325

13.6. Employment pattern after marriage by wife's and husband's characteristics 326

14.1. Descriptive statistics for variables used in the analysis, selected years 342–3

14.2. Parameter estimates of exponential event-history model of job shifts by periods: 1949–1979, 1980–1994 351

14.3. Parameter estimates of exponential event-history model for husband's job-shift patterns by periods: 1949–1979, 1980–1994 354–5

14.4. Parameter estimates of exponential event-history model for wife's job-shift patterns by periods: 1949–1979, 1980–1994 358–9

14.5. Parameter estimates of exponential event-history model for couples' job shifts, by periods: 1949–1979, 1980–1994 362–3

15.1. Summary of main results 376

CONTRIBUTORS

Fabrizio Bernardi has been an assistant professor in the Faculty of Sociology at the University of Bielefeld (Germany) since 1998. He holds a Ph.D. in sociology and social research from the Faculty of Sociology, at the University of Trento (Italy). He is a member of the GLOBALIFE research group that studies the effects of globalization on individual life courses and social inequalities. His current research focuses on the transition from school to work and early employment careers. His recent publications include: 'Does the Husband Matter? Married Women and Employment in Italy', *European Sociological Review*, 15/3 (1999), 285–300, and 'Who Exits Unemployment? Macroeconomic Factors, Institutional Features, Individual Characteristics and Chances of Getting a Job: A Comparison of Great Britain and Italy', (together with R. Layte, A. Schizzerotto, and S. Jacobs), in D. Gallie and S. Paugam (eds.), *Welfare Regimes and the Experience of Unemployment* (Oxford: Oxford University Press).

Wim Bernasco works at the Netherlands Institute for the Study of Criminality and Law Enforcement, where he is involved in research on the geographical dispersion and movement of crime. Besides criminology, his research interests include labour-market dynamics and family sociology. He combined the latter two interests in his 1994 dissertation 'Coupled Careers'. Major publication: *Coupled Careers; The Effects of Spouse's Resources on Success at Work* (Amsterdam: Thesis Publishers).

Hans-Peter Blossfeld is Professor of Sociology (chair in theory and empirical analysis of social structures and economic systems) at the University of Bielefeld. He was full professor of sociology and political sciences at the European University Institute in Florence (1989–92) and professor of sociology (chair in social statistics and sociological research methods) at the University of Bremen (1992–8). Since 1990 he has been editor of the *European Sociological Review*. He has published eleven books and over 100 articles on social inequality, youth, family, and educational sociology, labour-market research, demography, social stratification and mobility, the modern methods of quantitative social research, and statistical methods for longitudinal data analysis. He directs the Sfb–186 project 'Household Dynamics and Social Inequality' at the University of Bremen (together with Sonja Drobnič) and the GLOBALIFE project at the University of Bielefeld. His books include *Techniques of Event History Analysis* (with Götz Rohwer, 1995); *Between Equalization and Marginalization* (edited with Catherine Hakim, 1997); and *Rational Choice Theory and Large-Scale Data Analysis* (edited with Gerald Prein, 1998).

Erzsébet Bukodi is a researcher at the Department of Social Statistics of the Hungarian Central Statistical Office. She is also a Ph.D. student at the University of Economics in Budapest. Her thesis focuses on marriage homogamy in Hungary. She has published about social mobility and educational inequalities in Hungarian journals and recently started work on the new project of social indicators in the Central Statistical Office.

Martine Corijn is currently manager of the Fertility and Family Survey Project at the Population Activities Unit (United Nations/Economic Commission for Europe) in Geneva. Until 1999 she worked as a senior researcher at the Centre for Population and Family Studies of the Flemish Government (CBGS) in Brussels. Her research interests are the fertility and family formation and the transition to adulthood. Together with Erik Klijzing she edited a book on the *Transitions to Adulthood in Europe: From a Matter of Standard to a Matter of Choice* (Dordrecht: Kluwer Academic Publishers, forthcoming).

Shirley Dex is currently Principal Research Fellow a the Judge Institute for Management Studies, University of Cambridge. She formerly held post as Research Professor at the University of Essex, and Reader in Economics at the University of Keele. Her main research interests are in women's employment, flexible working arrangements in organizations, cross-national and longitudinal studies. Shirley Dex is the author of many books and articles on the theme on work–family issues. Her latest books include *Flexible Employment: The Future of Britain's Jobs* (Basingstoke: Macmillan, 1997, with Andrew McCulloch), and an edited collection *Families and the Labour Market: Trends Pressures and Policies*, (York: Joseph Rowntree Foundation, York Publishing Services, 1999).

Sonja Drobnič is a researcher at the Institute for Empirical and Applied Sociology (EMPAS) and the Special Research Centre 186 (Sfb–186) at the University of Bremen, where she directs a research project 'Household Dynamics and Social Inequality' (together with Hans-Peter Blossfeld). Her main research interests include life-course research and gender, in particular employment dynamics of couples and retirement in a household context, as well as issues in social stratification, comparative research, and longitudinal research methods. Recent articles were published in *European Sociological Review, Journal of Marriage and the Family, Zeitschrift für Soziologie*, and *Revue française de sociologie*.

Ewa Frątczak is an academic teacher and researcher at the Institute of Statistics and Demography, Warsaw School of Economics—SGH. Her main research interests are statistical methods and demography. She has published extensively on demographic issues and the application of longitudinal data analysis.

María José González-López is a researcher in the Centre of Demographic Studies at the Autonomous University of Barcelona. Her main areas of interest are the sociology of the family, gender, and demographic analysis. Her recent publications include (edited with T. Jurado and M. Naldini), *Gender Inequalities in Southern Europe: Women, Work and Welfare in the 1990s* (London: Frank Cass Journals, 2000) and (with M. Solsona) 'Households and Families: Changing Living Arrangements and Gender Relations', in S. Duncan and B. Pfau-Effinger (eds.), *Gender, Work and Culture in the European Union* (London: Routledge, 2000).

Paul M. de Graaf is associate professor of sociology at Nijmegen University. He works on topics in social stratification and the sociology of the family. Recent articles have been published in *Sociology of Education*, *European Sociological Review*, and *American Journal of Sociology*.

Shin-Kap Han is Assistant Professor of Sociology at the University of Illinois at Urbana-Champaign and faculty associate at the Cornell Employment and Family Careers Institute. He is co-author (with Phyllis Moen) of 'Clocking Out: Temporal Patterning of Retirement', *American Journal of Sociology*, 105/1 (1999), 191–236. He is currently at work on two projects: one on coupled careers and the other on the network structure of decision-making process in the US Supreme Court.

John Hendrickx works at the Nijmegen Business School at the University of Nijmegen. His research interests include social stratification, labour-market studies, and statistical methodology, particularly with respect to categorical data. Recent articles were published in *European Sociological Review* and *Netherlands' Journal of Social Sciences*.

Ursula Henz currently works at King's College in London. Her research interests are family sociology, social stratification, and quantitative methods. Major publications are 'Family formation and participation in higher education: crosscutting life-course events?', in Jan O. Jonsson and Colin Mills (eds.), *The Dynamics of Life Courses: Social Inequality and Social Change in Postwar Sweden* (forthcoming), and *Intergenerationale Mobilität. Methodische und empirische Analysen* (Intergenerational Mobility. Methodological and Empirical Analyses) (Berlin: Max-Planck-Institut für Bildungsforschung, 1996).

Søren Leth-Sørensen is a sociologist employed as Senior Adviser at Statistics Denmark in Copenhagen. Currently his office is located at the University of Aarhus. His responsibilities include management of the IDA database, established by the Bureau of Statistics. He has published on labour-market issues, women's employment, as well as family and fertility changes in Denmark.

Ruud Luijkx is a lecturer at the Department of Methodology of the Faculty of Social and Behavioural Sciences at Tilburg University (Netherlands). His main interests focus on comparative research on social and career mobility and categorical data analysis.

Andrew McCulloch is Senior Research Officer, Institute for Social and Economic Research, University of Essex, Colchester, CO4 3SQ. His research interests are measurement of deprivation, child outcomes, school-to-work transitions, and multilevel models. Recent publications are A. McCulloch, R. D. Wiggins, H. Joshi, and D. Sachdev, 'Internalizing and Externalizing

Children's Behaviour Problems in Britain and the U.S.: Relationships to Family Resources', *Children and Society* 14 (2000), 368–83; 'Teenage Child-Bearing in Great Britain and the Spatial Concentration of Poverty Households', *Journal of Epidemiology and Community Health* (forthcoming); and (with H. Joshi) 'Neighbourhood and Family Influences on the Cognitive Ability of Children in the British National Child Development Study', *Social Science and Medicine* (forthcoming).

Phyllis Moen is The Ferris Family Professor of Life Course Studies and Professor of Human Development and of Sociology at Cornell University. She is director of the Cornell Employment and Family Careers Institute (funded by the Alfred P. Sloan Foundation) and co-director of Cornell Gerontology Research Institute (funded by the National Institute on Aging). Moen is currently a fellow at the Radcliffe Institute for Advanced Study at Harvard University. Phyllis Moen is the author or co-author of five books, most recently *A Nation Divided: Diversity, Inequality, and Community in American Society* (Cornell University Press, 1999). Her articles on careers, gender, retirement, the life course, families, and policy have appeared in a number of leading journals. Her research focuses on work and family career paths and passages and their implications for men, women, and couples throughout the life course.

Péter Róbert is Associate Professor of Eötvös Lóránd University in Budapest. He is also Senior Researcher at the Social Research Centre (TÁRKI), Budapest. His research interests comprise social stratification and mobility, life course analysis, educational inequalities. He is the Hungarian co-ordinator of the International Social Survey Programme (ISSP). In addition to his Hungarian publications, he has published in *European Sociological Review* and in *Research in Social Stratification and Mobility*.

Götz Rohwer is professor for methods of social research and statistics at the Ruhr-Universität Bochum (Germany). He is a co-author (together with Ulrich Pötter) of the statistical package TDA (Transition Data Analysis) and a co-author (together with Hans-Peter Blossfeld) of *Techniques of Event History Analysis* (1995).

Marianne Sundström is associate professor of economics at the Swedish Institute for Social Research, Stockholm University. Her research interests lie mainly in family and labour-market dynamics and male–female wage differentials. Her publications include books and articles in *Journal of Human Resources* and *Journal of Population Economics*.

Xueguang Zhou is professor of sociology at Duke University, Durham, NC, USA. His research interests are in the areas of social stratification and the sociology of organizations. His recent publications on social stratification processes in urban China appeared in *American Sociological Review* and *American Journal of Sociology*. In addition, he also conducts research on the transformation of Chinese firms in the reform era.

I

Introduction

1

A Cross-National Comparative Approach to Couples' Careers

HANS-PETER BLOSSFELD AND SONJA DROBNIČ

THIS book discusses the relationship between class and gender inequality or, more precisely, the intersection of social class and gender within the employment careers of couples. Not only are the employment patterns of couples different in various societies and across historical periods, but our theoretical frameworks have also changed dramatically over the last four decades and shape what we perceive and how we analyse it.

Early Stratification Literature and Research on Male Family Heads

Theories of social inequality, whether influenced by Durkheim, Marx, or Weber, traditionally defined social class as a market relationship and considered the family as the key unit of social stratification. In this conceptual approach, conjugal families were regarded as collective entities in which family members share the rewards gained by the family head through relationships within labour markets and production units and, as primary agents of socialization and institutions channelling social and economic inheritance, which transmitted privilege as well as power and prestige to the next generation (Davis 1949; Hyman 1953; Coser 1973). It is therefore not surprising that until the early 1980s intra- and intergenerational social mobility studies (Goldthorpe 1980) as well as status attainment research (see e.g. Blau and Duncan 1967; Sewell and Hauser 1975) regarded the variation in the social position of male family heads as the key dependent variable to be explained. Measuring the effects of a father's education and occupation on his son's education and occupational attainment dominated stratification research for many years. When these social mobility models were extended to married women, it was not women's own resources that were studied, but the education and occupation of women's fathers were compared with those of their husbands (see e.g. Handl *et al.* 1977; Goldthorpe 1983, 1984).

The focus of this early stratification research on male family heads reflected the historical dominance of the traditional family model and the breadwinner–homemaker template of the so-called 'golden age of the family' in the 1950s and 1960s. For this historical period, stratification studies provided valuable insights into the basic relationships between social origin, education, occupation, and income among men, but clearly excluded other important forms of inequality (Curtis 1986). In particular, the division of work between husbands and their wives, the inequality between spouses, and the power structures within the family were almost completely ignored.

Labour-Market Research and the Individualistic Perspective

As married women's paid employment has increased (see Blossfeld and Hakim 1997) and the share of family income contributed by wives has steadily risen in modern societies (see e.g. Sørensen and McLanahan 1987; Sweeney 1997), this pervasive 'male bias' in the stratification literature has increasingly been criticised (see e.g. Acker 1973; Huber and Spitze 1983; Dex 1990; Sørensen and McLanahan 1987). A growing stream of research suggested that in empirical studies women should be treated just like men, and that individuals and not families should be the units of analysis in inequality studies. Subsequently, the focus gradually shifted from traditional stratification research to labour-market research and from household heads to individual women and men in the market-place, largely ignoring their family or household context, their income-sharing within the family, and their social security or other benefits enjoyed through family relationships.

It is interesting that this individualistic turn of inequality research was nurtured by quite different, even contradictory, labour-market theories, which not only treated gender as a status characteristic or individual attribute in their empirical analyses, but also led to the firm belief that equality between the sexes could be easily achieved by policy interventions in the educational system and the labour market. On the one hand, supply-oriented labour-market approaches, such as human capital studies, attempted to show that much of the sex differentials in earnings and job opportunities could in fact be explained by productivity differences, which in turn were seen as a result of differential investments in general and job-specific human capital by men and women (see e.g. Polachek 1981; Mincer and Polachek 1974; Mincer and Ofek 1982). Thus, this approach suggested that education and training are the strategic variables for change, and that equality between the sexes could be achieved by women investing more in their human capital. On the other hand, demand-oriented studies of labour-market segmentation tried to demonstrate that the labour market could be divided into relatively closed partial markets. Primary and internal labour markets were not equally accessible to equally productive women because employers, implementing mechanisms of statistical discrimination, simply believed women, on average, to be less committed and stable employees (see e.g. Phelps 1972; Arrow 1972; Cain 1976). Thus, based on this approach, the central policy route to gender equality would clearly be an increase in women's labour-force participation over the life course. Finally, many 'feminist' labour-market studies tried to establish that women's paid work, female labour-force participation, and women's income opportunities were the result of universal discriminating practices by union officials and employers (Madden 1973, 1975; Hartmann 1976). From this perspective, the implementation of equal opportunities legislation would seem to be the key variable to reduce male power and dominance and achieve equality between working men and women.

If one reviews the empirical results of these individual, work-centred labour-market studies from the last two decades, one can conclude that—although women seem to have made some slow progress in their job opportunities, upward career mobility, and earnings across birth cohorts in most modern societies—the picture is dominated by persistent inequalities between individual men and women in the labour market across industrialized societies (see e.g. Blossfeld 1987; Huber 1988; Reskin and Roos 1990; Rubery and Fagan 1993; Blau 1999). This enduring feature of the labour market in different countries is, however, quite surprising in the light of individualistic labour-market approaches. From their perspective, one would have expected that, through massive social changes in the educational and employment systems in the last decades, sex differences in all important work-related aspects would have declined much more strongly than they actually have. First, because educational expansion has led to the virtual disappearance of the differentials in educational attainment levels of men and women leaving school in nearly all modern societies (Shavit and Blossfeld 1993; Erikson and Jonsson 1996). Second, because married women's labour-force participation has risen virtually everywhere, due to the decline in the propensity of women to withdraw permanently from the labour market on marriage or after the birth of their first child, and with the declining number of children in modern families (see e.g. Blossfeld and Hakim 1997; Rubery *et al.* 1999). Third, because employers who discriminate against women have to pay an economic premium for hiring men, and should therefore—at least in the long run—suffer from a severe competitive disadvantage. And, finally, because the implementation of equal opportunities laws and policies in most of the industrialized countries are increasingly ensuring that jobs must remain formally open to all applicants. In other words, in these individualistic approaches, the mechanisms by which gender inequalities have been maintained over decades and continue to be both an individual and an institutional practice remain a puzzle.

The Role of Women's Rising Labour-Force Participation in Various Countries

A major conceptual limitation of individualistic approaches would seem their failure to acknowledge the degree to which work and family are linked, and that the interactions that take place within the family and in the labour market are embedded in a much broader system of social and cultural inequalities between the sexes. In particular, proponents of individualistic approaches would seem to have inadequately understood what the increased workforce participation of women has, and has not, entailed (Blossfeld and Hakim 1997). First, in most contemporary societies, women's primary responsibilities for children and the home seem to remain fairly unchanged, despite women's gains in the occupational sphere (Bielby and Bielby 1988; Moen 1992; Brines 1993, 1994). Secondly, the impression that women in many countries now constitute almost half the workforce, which is based on a headcount basis of labour-market statistics, is misleading because the integration of married women into the labour market has been quite specific and quite different in volume, nature, and pattern (see Blossfeld and Hakim 1997).

For example, in Northern European countries such as Germany (Blossfeld and Rohwer 1997), the Netherlands (de Graaf and Vermeulen 1997) or Britain (Burchell *et al*. 1997; Hakim 1998) part-time or even marginal work is particularly characteristic for married women with children. The majority of these female marginal workers and part-timers still seem to regard breadwinning as the primary (but not exclusive) responsibility of men, and women as secondary earners whose primary (but not exclusive) responsibility is domestic work and homemaking (Hakim 1996: 181).

In the Southern European countries, such as Italy, Spain, or Greece, women's employment as a proportion of working-age population at work is still relatively low, and part-time work is quite uncommon (Addabbo 1997; Esping-Andersen 1999; Symeonidou 1997). There are two main reasons for this situation (Blossfeld and Hakim 1997). These countries did not experience such a strong transformation of labour markets, family systems, and welfare states in the 1960s and early 1970s, as was the case in the capitalist societies of Northern Europe during the period of the 'post-war boom'. Also, these countries have suffered much more from excessively high unemployment rates in the last two decades (Jurado and Naldini 1996). Consequently, Southern European countries have to rely much more on family solidarity (Rhodes 1996) and seem to stick more to the traditional male-breadwinner, female-housewife model.

In the special case of the former socialist countries of Central and Eastern Europe, the integration of women into paid work was considered a vital strategy to achieve gender equality in socialism (Drobnič 1997; Einhorn 1993). This policy resulted in a comparatively high female full-time labour-force participation rate and a quick re-entry of mothers into full-time work after childbirth. However, not even socialist reforms seem to have generally altered the sexual segregation of paid labour and women's primary family responsibilities at home. A similar situation can be observed in the Scandinavian countries such as Denmark and Sweden (Moen 1989; Leth-Sørensen and Rohwer 1997; Sundström 1997). Although these countries have proactively tried to integrate married women with children into the labour force via full-time work, reduced full-time work, and part-time work, 'the wife's role as a supplementary worker has hardly changed' (Bernhardt 1993). It is generally acknowledged that Scandinavian women are less dependent on their husbands or partners in financial terms than women in many other Western European countries, but they, by and large, still suppress their own long-term job opportunities, earnings profiles, and other job-related interests when they raise young children (Bernhardt 1993; Kalleberg and Rosenfeld 1990; Singelmann et al. 1996).

Finally, in the United States, the growth rates of women's full-time and part-time employment were fairly balanced for decades until the end of the 1970s. Since then, married women's full-time employment started growing faster than part-time employment (Drobnič and Wittig 1995, 1997). However, since American women, regardless whether they are employed or not employed, or work full-time or part-time, continue to perform a far greater share of family and household work than men (Moen 1992; Han and Moen 1999; Presser 1994; South and Spitze 1994), their family obligations spill over into their paid work with the result that women's employment continues to be defined and limited by gender (Moen 1992; Moen and Forest 1999).

In summary, this admittedly simplified comparison shows the difficulties faced by working mothers in various countries today. Just like forty years ago, it seems that neither labour-market structures nor marriage roles have accommodated themselves to women's increasing labour-force participation.

The Family as a Unit of Stratification

In fact, not only are gender roles deeply entrenched in all social relations, but work–family linkages are of fundamental importance if we are going to understand why the increase in labour-force participation of women varies across countries and, further, what has, and has not, changed for men and women due to women's greater involvement in paid employment. Thus, we have to consider the family context when examining individual life courses. This allows us to study how unequal access to resources can be created, exacerbated, reduced, modified, or perpetuated by social organizations such as families. Erikson and Goldthorpe, who refer to the family as the appropriate unit of class composition, introduce the following considerations:

First, in so far as members of a family live together, or constitute a household, a broad similarity may be expected to prevail not only in their material conditions of life as these exist at any one time but further in a wide range of their future life-chances. The family is, in other words, the unit of class 'fate'. Secondly, the economic decision-making in which family members engage, in regard to both consumption and 'production'—especially, of course, work-force participation—is typically of a joint or interdependent kind. The family is, at the 'micro' level, a key unit of strategic action pursued within the class structure. (Erikson and Goldthorpe 1992: 233; see also Sørensen and McLanahan 1987)

Using the family as the unit of class composition does, however, not require that it be seen as an entity of an egalitarian, non-hierarchical kind (Erikson and Goldthorpe 1992); nor that some of its members, usually the husbands, do not have the power or authority to influence other family members, usually the wives and the children, through the process of interpersonal non-economic exchange (Blau 1964, 1994; Walby 1986; Huber 1988); nor that goods and rewards gained by the family through relationships within labour markets and production units are necessarily distributed within the family according to solidarity principles or in equal shares (Curtis 1986; Vogler and Pahl 1994; Roman and Vogler 1999). The implication would rather be that the interdependent decision-making processes within married or cohabiting couples have to become the focus of analysis. The fundamental drawback of the individualistic line of thought is that, by ignoring familial and household roles, or by not explicitly taking them into account, it is implicitly suggested that men and women are all alike, that there are no differences between families and households, and that employment decisions within the family are based on gender-free considerations.

This chapter, and the book as a whole, therefore starts from the premise that neither the traditional concentration on male household heads nor the more recent individualistic approach towards labour-market behaviour of 'atomized' men and women is appropriate if we want to understand how social inequalities between men and women are produced and reproduced in the labour market. Rather, the interdependent decision-making processes of men and women from different social classes within families and households have to become an issue of major interest. Families as collective entities send their male and female members out to work, assign household tasks, and share wages and resources (Moen and Forest 1999).

Cross-Sectional versus Longitudinal Data

Unfortunately, empirical research on the labour supply of families has been strongly dominated by studies focusing only on women and using cross-sectional data. Based on the classical family life-cycle concept (Glick 1947, 1977), a set of ordered stages, primarily defined by variations in family composition, age of children, and family size, has been distinguished, and then used to determine the availability of women for paid work outside the home with cross-sectional data. The implicit assumption of this approach has been that what happens to different women in various phases in the family cycle at one point in time is similar to the pattern that women experience when they make these transitions in their life course over time. In other words, these empirical studies have focused on structure rather than process and on the study of particular states (for example, stages in the family cycle) and levels (for example, income) rather than on events or transitions between these states and level changes over time. This practice, however, is problematic and has been increasingly criticized on methodological grounds. First, because entries and exits from labour market and family states are highly variable over time (for example, over the life course, historical period, and across cohorts). Secondly, because there is the well-known problem that individuals and families often fail to conform to the assumption of a single progression through a given number of stages in a predetermined order. At least three reasons for this may exist (Murphy 1991): (1) the chronology of timing of events may not conform to the ideal model, for example, childbearing may start before marriage; (2) many stages are not reached, for example, by never-married persons; and (3) the full set of stages may be truncated by events such as death or marital breakdown. In sum, these complex constellations between the family cycle and women's labour-force participation, which are changing rapidly over historical time and across birth cohorts, can hardly be meaningfully described or studied on the basis of cross-sectional data (Blossfeld and Rohwer 1995). Thus, the issue of the interdependence of husbands' and wives' careers that we address in this book has for the most part remained unstudied because the longitudinal data required for serious analysis were not available.

Only recently have scholars started to explore empirically the dynamic interrelationships between spouses with life-history data and longitudinal statistical models. And, indeed, these few dynamic studies have drawn attention to the fact that families and households, characterized by the male breadwinner, are not all the same, and that changes in family and household relatioships over time influence the labour-market behaviour of their individual members in an interdependent way (see e.g. Sørensen and McLanahan 1987; Krüger and Born 1991; Krüger 1993; Erzberger 1993; Lauterbach 1994; Bernasco 1994; Han and Moen 1999). However, these studies focus on single countries and do not attempt to explore the role of general societal factors in producing differences in the patterns of couples' careers across countries. Furthermore, there are major methodological differences between the studies, in the definition and measurement of key variables, that hinder a systematic comparison of results. Thus, the issue of coupled careers clearly demands further, more systematic study, especially from a cross-societal comparative point of view which includes the impact of broader historical, cultural, and societal contexts influencing the dynamics of the work–family interface over time in a more appropriate way (Lee 1987; Aytac and Teachman 1992).

The Cross-Societal Comparative Perspective:
The Countries

This book presents the findings of twelve very similar analyses of coupled careers in twelve different countries. The countries included vary widely in important characteristics, such as industrial development and culture, the political system and its history, differentiation of the family system, the role of the state, and the extent to which the roles of men and women have undergone a progressive transformation. The countries included in this comparison are Sweden, Denmark, Great Britain, the Netherlands, the Flemish part of Belgium, the (former) Federal Republic of Germany, Italy, Spain, Hungary, Poland, the United States and China. Chapters 3 to 14 report the findings of longitudinal analyses of changes in couples' careers in each of these twelve countries. Each study was conducted by researchers who have an intimate understanding of the country in question. Most of these studies (with the exception of the United States, where data from respondents in four cities in upstate New York were used, and China, where data are based on twenty cities) employed relatively recent nationally representative data, covering couples' careers over broad historical periods. Since each of the countries represents various unique features which are important for our substantive conclusions, we did not try to completely standardize the statistical analysis. Rather, we attempted to maintain, as far as possible, a sufficient standardization to enable a systematic comparison of the results. In other words, most of the country-specific chapters follow a common set of guidelines, and at the same time explicate the important aspects specific to each country. The country-specific chapters employ panel as well as life-history data and use event-history and sequence analysis in order to study the development of husbands' and wives' careers over the life course. The longitudinal event-history analysis of couples' interdependent careers is a methodologically difficult endeavour. In these studies, the methodological issue of reverse causation arises. Reverse causation means that a spouse's career, considered from a theoretical point of view as the dependent process, has (direct or indirect) effects on the career process of the other spouse and vice versa. In this book, most of the country-specific chapters apply a 'causal approach' to the analysis of interdependent systems that was suggested by Blossfeld and Rohwer (1995).

The Aim and Plan of the Book

The aim of this book is to study the interdependent employment careers of couples with longitudinal data, and to compare these patterns across different contemporary societies. We use the more general term 'couples' instead of 'spouses' because in the specific case of Sweden the process of family formation and the structure of households have changed to such an extent that the distinction between marital and consensual unions has almost disappeared

(Hoem 1995; Blossfeld 1995). Thus, in the Swedish chapter of this book, both unmarried and married couples are included in the analysis. The focus of the book, however, is on husbands' and wives' coupled transitions between full-time work, part-time work, and unpaid housework over the life course, beginning with the time of entry into the marital union. The distinction between full-time and part-time jobs makes it possible to differentiate between primary and secondary earners. In each of the country-specific chapters, the temporal aspects of family needs and the historical and cultural contexts within which couples have to make their decisions are taken into account. This life-course approach explicitly recognizes the dynamic nature of family roles and circumstances as husbands and wives move through their life paths, the interdependence of lives and life choices among family members, the situational imperatives confronting families in different countries, and the cumulation of advantages and disadvantages experienced by the individual members of the family (Moen and Forest 1999). In particular, we are trying to better understand how employment strategies of husbands and wives from different social classes evolve over the family cycle, along with shifts in household composition, family needs, family resources, as well as country-specific constraints and opportunities. We especially hope to contribute to the following three issues:

1. To what extent are the transitions between (full-time and part-time) work and unpaid housework gendered within marital unions in different countries and how can we explain societal differences?

2. To what degree do spouses marry assortatively and how does assortative mating as well as upward and downward marriage by women (or men) affect the employment relationships of husbands and wives over the later family cycle in different countries?

3. Do class-specific differences in the division of labour between husbands and wives over the family life cycle become more or less important across marriage cohorts in different countries, and if so, how can we interpret these variations?

We begin in Chapter 2 with a theoretical discussion of why modern societies shift from the male breadwinner to the more or less traditional dual-earner family model and formulate hypotheses about how husbands and their wives affect each other in different social classes. This will then be followed by a short description of the countries studied in this book and how these country-specific contexts influence couples' careers. Chapters 3 to 14 present country reports, grouped under various welfare state regimes: the 'conservative' welfare state regime (Germany, the Netherlands, Belgium/Flanders), the 'Mediterranean' welfare state regime (Italy, Spain), the 'liberal' welfare state regime (Britain, USA), the 'social democratic' welfare state regime (Sweden, Denmark), and the (former) 'state-socialist' regime (Poland, Hungary, China). Chapter 15 synthesizes the findings, paying particular attention to the issue of couples' careers across the family life cycle, and the implications of employment patterns of couples on the system of income and social inequalities in contemporary societies.

References

Acker, J. (1973). 'Women and Social Stratification: A Case of Intellectual Sexism', *American Journal of Sociology*, 78: 936–45.

Addabbo, T. (1997). 'Part-Time Work in Italy', in H.-P. Blossfeld and C. Hakim (eds.), *Between Equalization and Marginalization: Women Working Part-Time in Europe and the United States of America* (Oxford: Oxford University Press), 113–32.

Arrow, K. (1972). 'Models of Job Discrimination', in A. H. Pascal (ed.), *Racial Discrimination in Economic Life* (Lexington, Mass.: Lexington, Heath), 83–102.

Aytac, I. A., and J. D. Teachman (1992). 'Occupational Sex Segregation, Marital Power, and Household Division of Labor', paper presented at the ASA meetings, Pittsburgh, Pa.

Bernasco, W. (1994). *Coupled Careers: The Effects of Spouse's Resources on Success at Work* (Amsterdam: Thesis Publishers).

Bernhardt, E. M. (1993). 'Fertility and Employment', *European Sociological Review*, 9: 25–42.

Bielby, D. D. and W. T. Bielby (1988). 'She Works Hard for the Money: Household Responsibilities and the Allocation of Work Effort', *American Journal of Sociology*, 93: 1031–59.

Blau, F. D. (1999). 'Women's Economic Well-Being, 1970–1995: Indicators and Trends', *Focus*, 20: 4–10.

Blau, P. M. (1964). *Exchange and Power in Social Life* (New York: Wiley).

——(1994). *Structural Contexts of Opportunities* (Chicago and London: University of Chicago Press).

——and O. D. Duncan (1967). *The American Occupational Structure* (New York: Wiley).

Blossfeld, H.-P. (1987). 'Labor Market Entry and the Sexual Segregation of Careers in the Federal Republic of Germany', *American Journal of Sociology*, 93: 89–118.

——(ed.) (1995). *The New Role of Women. Family Formation in Modern Societies* (Boulder Colo.: Westview Press).

——and C. Hakim (eds.) (1997). *Between Equalization and Marginalization: Women Working Part-Time in Europe and the United States of America* (Oxford: Oxford University Press).

——and G. Rohwer (1995). *Techniques of Event History Modeling: New Approaches to Causal Analysis* (Mahwah, NJ: Erlbaum).

——and ——(1997). 'Part-Time Work in West Germany', in H.-P. Blossfeld and C. Hakim (eds.), *Between Equalization and Marginalization: Women Working Part-Time in Europe and the United States of America* (Oxford: Oxford University Press), 164–90.

Brines, J. (1993). 'The Exchange Value of Housework', *Rationality and Society*, 5: 302–40.

——(1994). 'Economic Dependency, Gender, and Division of Labor at Home', *American Journal of Sociology*, 100: 652–88.

Burchell, B. J., A. Dale, and H. Joshi (1997). 'Part-Time Work among British Women', in H.-P. Blossfeld and C. Hakim (eds.), *Between Equalization and Marginalization: Women Working Part-Time in Europe and the United States of America* (Oxford: Oxford University Press), 210–71.

Cain, G. G. (1976). 'The Challenge of Segmented Labor Market Theories to Orthodox Theory: A Survey', *Economic Literature*, 14: 1215–57.

Coser, L. (1973). *Greedy Institutions: Patterns of Undivided Commitments* (New York: The Free Press).

Curtis, R. F. (1986). 'Household and Family in Theory of Inequality', *American Sociological Review*, 51: 168–83.

Davis, K. (1949). *Human Society* (New York: Macmillan).

Dex, S. (1990). 'Goldthorpe on Class and Gender: The Case Against', in J. Clark, C. Modgil, and S. Modgil (eds.), *John H. Goldthorpe: Consensus and Controversy* (London: Falmer Press), 135–52.

Drobnič, S. (1997). 'Part-Time Work in Central and Eastern European Countries', in H.-P. Blossfeld and C. Hakim (eds.), *Between Equalization and Marginalization: Women Working Part-Time in Europe and the United States of America* (Oxford: Oxford University Press), 71–89.

——and I. Wittig (1995). 'Vollzeit- und Teilzeiterwerbstätigkeit im Familienzyklus US-amerikanischer Frauen: Eine Längsschnittanalyse' (Full-Time and Part-Time Employment over the Family Cycle of Women in the US: A Longitudinal Study), *Zeitschrift für Soziologie*, 24/5: 374–89.

——and ——(1997). 'Part-Time Work in the United States of America', in H.-P. Blossfeld and C. Hakim (eds.), *Between Equalization and Marginalization: Women Working Part-Time in Europe and the United States of America* (Oxford: Oxford University Press), 289–314.

Einhorn, B. (1993). *Cinderella Goes to Market: Citizenship, Gender and Women's Movements in East Central Europe* (London and New York: Verso).

Erikson, R., and J. H. Goldthorpe (1992). *The Constant Flux: A Study of Class Mobility in Industrial Societies* (Oxford: Clarendon Press).

——and J. O. Jonsson (eds.) (1996). *Can Education be Equalized?* (Boulder, Colo.: Westview Press).

Erzberger, C. (1993). 'Erwerbsarbeit im Eheleben: Männlicher und weiblicher Erwerbsverlauf zwischen Dependenz und Unabhängigkeit' (Paid Work and Family Life: Male and Female Life Courses between Dependence and Independence), *Arbeitspapier* No. 16 des Sfb 186, Universität Bremen.

Esping-Andersen, G. (1999). *Social Foundations of Postindustrial Economies* (Oxford: Oxford University Press).

Glick, P. C. (1947). 'The Family Cycle', *American Journal of Sociology*, 12 (April): 164–74.

——(1977). 'Updating the Life Cycle of the Family', *Journal of Marriage and the Family*, 39/1: 5–13.

Goldthorpe, J. H. (1980). *Social Mobility and Class Structure in Modern Britain* (Oxford: Clarendon Press).

——(1983). 'Women and Class Analysis: In Defence of the Conventional View', *Sociology*, 17: 465–88.

——(1984). 'Women and Class Analysis: A Reply to the Replies', *Sociology*, 18: 491–9.

Graaf, P. de, and H. Vermeulen (1997). 'Female Labour-Market Participation in the Netherlands: Developments in the Relationship between Family Cycle and Employment', in H.-P. Blossfeld and C. Hakim (eds.), *Between Equalization and Marginalization: Women Working Part-Time in Europe and the United States of America* (Oxford: Oxford University Press), 191–209.

Hakim, C. (1996). 'Labour Mobility and Employment Stability: Rhetoric and Reality on the Sex Differential in Labour Market Behaviour', *European Sociological Review*, 12: 1–31.

——(1998). *Social Change and Innovation in the Labour Market* (Oxford: Oxford University Press).

Han, S.-K., and P. Moen (1999). 'Work and Family over Time: A Life Course Approach', *Annals of the American Academy of Political and Social Science* (March): 98–110.

Handl, J., K. U. Mayer, and W. Müller (1977). *Klassenlagen und Sozialstruktur* (Social Class and Social Structure) (Frankfurt a.M. and New York: Campus).

Hartmann, H. (1976). 'Capitalism, Patriarchy, and Job Segregation by Sex', *Signs*, 1: 137–69.

Hoem, B. (1995). 'Sweden', in H.-P. Blossfeld (ed.), *The New Role of Women: Family Formation in Modern Societies* (Boulder, Colo.: Westview Press), 35–55.

Huber, J. (1988). 'A Theory of Family, Economy, and Gender', *Journal of Family Issues*, 9: 9–26.

——and G. Spitze (1983). *Sex Stratification* (New York: Academic Press).

Hyman, H. (1953). 'The Value Systems of Different Classes', in R. Bendix and S. M. Lipset (eds.), *Class, Status and Power* (2nd edn. 1960; London: Routledge & Kegan Paul), 426–42.

Jurado, T. J., and M. Naldini (1996). 'Is the South so Different? Italian and Spanish Families in Comparative Perspective', in M. Rhodes (ed.), *South European Society and Politics, 1. Southern European Welfare States* (London: Frank Cass), 42–66.

Kalleberg, A. L., and R. A. Rosenfeld (1990). 'Work in the Family and in the Labor Market: A Cross-National Reciprocal Analysis', *Journal of Marriage and the Family*, 52: 331–46.

Krüger, H. (1993). 'Die Analyse ehepartnerlicher Erwerbsverläufe: Ansatzpunkte für modernisierungstheoretische Überlegungen' (The Analysis of Marital Employment Careers. Reference Points for Theorizing Modernization), in C. Born and H. Krüger (eds.), *Erwerbsverläufe von Ehepartnern und die Modernisierung weiblicher Lebensführung* (Employment Careers of Spouses and the Modernization of the Female Life Course) (Weinheim: Deutscher Studien Verlag), 209–26.

——and C. Born (1991). 'Unterbrochene Erwerbskarrieren und Berufsspezifik: Zum Arbeitsmarkt- und Familienpuzzle im weiblichen Lebensverlauf' (Interrupted Employment Careers and Occupations: Towards the Labor Market and Family Puzzle of Female Life Courses) in K. U. Mayer, J. Allmendinger, and J. Huinink (eds.), *Vom Regen in die Traufe* (From Bad to Worse) (Frankfurt a. M. and New York: Campus), 142–61.

Lauterbach, W. (1994). *Berufsverläufe von Frauen: Erwerbstätigkeit, Unterbrechung und Wiedereintritt* (Occupational Careers of Women: Employment, Interruption and Re-entry) (Frankfurt a.M. and New York: Campus).

Lee, G. (1987). 'Comparative Perspectives', in M. Sussman and S. Steinmetz (eds.), *Handbook of Marriage and the Family* (New York: Plenum), 59–80.

Leth-Sørensen, S., and G. Rohwer (1997). 'Women's Employment and Part-Time Work in Denmark', in H.-P. Blossfeld and C. Hakim (eds.), *Between Equalization and Marginalization: Women Working Part-Time in Europe and the United States of America* (Oxford: Oxford University Press), 247–71.

Madden, J. F. (1973). *The Economics of Sex Discrimination* (Lexington, Mass.: Lexington Bks).

——(1975). 'Discrimination: A Manifestation of Male Market Power?', in C.B. Lloyd (ed.), *Sex, Discrimination and the Division of Labor* (New York: Colombia University Press), 146–74.

Mincer, J., and H. Ofek (1982). 'Interrupted Work Careers: Depreciation and Restoration of Human Capital', *Journal of Human Resources*, 17: 3–24.

——and S. Polachek (1974). 'Family Investments in Human Capital: Earnings of Women', *Journal of Political Economy*, 82: S76–S108.

Moen, P. (1989). *Working Parents: Transformation in Gender Roles and Public Policies in Sweden* (Madison, Wis.: University of Wisconsin Press).

——(1992). *Women's Two Roles: A Contemporary Dilemma* (New York: Auburn House).

——and K. B. Forest (1999). 'Strengthening Families. Policy Issues for the Twenty-First Century', in M. Sussman, S. K. Steinmetz, and G. W. Peterson (eds.), *Handbook of Marriage and the Family* (New York: Plenum Press), 633–63.

Murphy, M. (1991). 'The Family Life Cycle' (London: London School of Economics, unpublished manuscript).

Phelps, E. (1972). 'The Statistical Theory of Racism and Sexism', *American Economic Review*, 64: 59–63.

Polachek, S. (1981). 'Occupational Self-Selection: A Human Capital Approach to Sex Differences in Occupational Structure', *Review of Economics and Statistics*, 58: 60–9.

Presser, H. B. (1994). 'Employment Schedules among Dual-Earner Spouses and the Division of Household Labor by Gender', *American Sociological Review*, 59/3: 348–64.

Reskin, B. F., and P. A. Roos (1990). *Job Queues, Gender Queues: Explaining Women's Inroads into Male Occupations* (Philadelphia: Temple University Press).

Rhodes, M. (ed.) (1996). *South European Society and Politics, 1. Southern European Welfare States* (London: Frank Cass).

Roman, C., and C. Vogler (1999). 'Managing Money in British and Swedish Households', *European Societies*, 1/3: 419–56.

Rubery, J., and C. Fagan (1993). *Occupational Segregation of Women and Men in the European Community* (*Social Europe*, Supplement 3/93; Luxembourg: OOPEC).

——M. Smith, and C. Fagan (1999). *Women's Employment in Europe: Trends and Prospects* (London and New York: Routledge).

Sewell, W. H., and R. M. Hauser (1975). *Education, Occupation and Earnings* (New York: Academic Press).

Shavit, Y., and H.-P. Blossfeld (1993). *Persistent Inequality* (Boulder, Colo.: Westview Press).

Singelmann, J., Y. Kamo, A. Acock, and M. Grimes (1996). 'Dual-Earner Families and the Division of Household Labor: A Comparative Analysis of Six Industrial Societies', *Acta Demographica (1994–1996)*, 159–78.

Sørensen, A., and S. McLanahan (1987). 'Married Women's Economic Dependency, 1940–1980', *American Journal of Sociology*, 93: 659–87.

South, S. J., and G. Spitze (1994). 'Housework in Marital and Nonmarital Households', *American Sociological Review*, 59/3: 327–47.

Sundström, M. (1997). 'Managing Work and Children: Part-Time Work and the Family Cycle of Swedish Women', in H.-P. Blossfeld and C. Hakim (eds.), *Between Equalization and Marginalization: Women Working Part-Time in Europe and the United States of America* (Oxford: Oxford University Press), 272–88.

Sweeney, M. M. (1997). *Women, Men, and Changing Families. The Shifting Economic Foundation of Marriage* (Working Paper No. 97–14; Madison, Wis.: Center for Demography and Ecology, University of Wisconsin-Madison).

Symeonidou, H. (1997). 'Full-Time and Part-Time Employment of Women in Greece: Trends and Relationships with Life-Cycle Events', in H.-P. Blossfeld and C. Hakim (eds.), *Between Equalization and Marginalization: Women Working Part-Time in Europe and the United States of America* (Oxford: Oxford University Press), 90–112.

Vogler, C., and J. Pahl (1994). 'Money, Power and Inequality within Marriage', *Sociological Review*, 42/2: 263–88.

Walby, S. (1986). *Patriarchy at Work: Patriarchal and Capitalist Relations in Employment* (Cambridge: Polity).

2

Theoretical Perspectives on Couples' Careers

HANS-PETER BLOSSFELD AND SONJA DROBNIČ

I N this chapter, we present a series of rival arguments concerning the dynamics of couples' careers, which vary widely in both the nature and extent of their theoretical grounding and often come to contradictory conclusions. Among the arguments we consider, some are older—developed in a historical period in which fathers were typically viewed as breadwinners and mothers as full-time homemakers—and pertain to the most highly developed and influential theory in this field so far available: the economic theory of the family. Others are relatively new and draw directly on the conceptual distinctions and refinements necessitated by the growing diversity in family structures and employment roles that has arisen during the last two decades. We also review previous research findings regarding the interdependence of husbands' and wives' employment and family patterns, and develop hypotheses about social class and cross-national differences that provide the frame of reference for the country-specific chapters of the book.

The Economic Theory of the Family: The Importance of Specialization

The economic theory of the family was developed by American economists (see e.g. Schultz 1974; Mincer and Polachek 1974; Becker 1981) between the early 1970s and early 1980s—a period in which women's increasing labour-force participation, the rising costs of living, and demands for gender equality began to transform women's role as full-time homemakers in America (Moen 1992). The chief concern of the proponents of this approach was that changes in women's income potential would endanger the interdependence between the sexes produced by the sexual division of labour in the family and the labour market, and destabilize the family as a social institution. This notion can also be found in the writings of Parsons, who believed that one of the main functions of the specialization of men in paid employment and women in work within the family was to prevent disruptive status competition between the spouses (Parsons 1942; Parsons and Bales 1966).

The economic theory of the family is thus an approach which relatively early drew attention to the fact that an individual's decision regarding the allocation of time and effort to paid work in the labour market and unpaid work in the home is usually not an 'isolated' act, but can best be understood within the context of the family. The type of family considered in this approach is the traditional married couple with children and a wife who is not in the paid labour force. The decisions of each spouse are viewed as interdependent with the activities and characteristics of the other family members (Mincer and Polachek 1974). In the following, we briefly review the main hypotheses of this conceptual approach and draw some conclusions for the empirical analysis of the research questions in this book.

To begin with, an interesting aspect of the economic theory of the family is that it provides an intergenerational framework. It links human capital investment decisions of each new generation of men and women to the current structure of the sex-specific division of labour in the adult population of a country. Thus, when the family's economic provider role is typically assigned to husbands and its homemaker role to wives, young women will be less likely than young men to acquire market skills as a result of both sex-specific socialization and education, as well as the decisions of employers, who only invest in workers' on-the-job training when they are sure that they will make long-term gains from their investment. It follows that the more 'conventional' or 'traditional' the family system of a country, the greater the tendency that the accumulation of earnings capacity over the early life course will induce (1) a comparative advantage of young women over young men in household work and (2) a comparative advantage of young men over young women in the labour market.

It is further claimed that it is this sex-specific specialization of labour in the early life course and the mutual dependence it produces between the prospective mates that provides the major incentive for partners to marry. Young men and women behave like trading partners who decide to marry if each partner has more to gain by marrying than by remaining single. In a traditional family system, men expect to benefit from their wives, since women have been socialized to be more oriented towards taking charge of the household and raising children; women, on the other hand, count on benefiting from husbands, since men have specialized in the goal of lifelong gainful employment. The questions of whether to marry and who to marry are therefore based on one's expectations of what will happen within the union in the future and are dependent on the following:

1. The gains from a single family utility function. In this regard, the economic theory of the family considers altruism to be an important element in the functioning of families. Altruism is common within families not only because families are small and have many interactions, but also because marriage markets

tend to 'assign' altruists to their beneficiaries. Becker (1981) referred to the altruist as 'he' and the beneficiary as 'she', in this way implicitly specifying which spouse is the altruist. The utility function of an altruist depends positively on the well-being of other individuals. In particular, he is made better off by actions that raise the family income and worse off by actions that lower it. Since family income is the sum of his own and his beneficiary's income, the altruist would refrain from actions that raise his own income if they lower the beneficiary's even more; and he would take actions that lower his own income if they raise the income of the beneficiary even more. It is held that altruism ties couples together, even if only one of the partners is altruistic. The mechanism that guarantees this is compensatory transfers from altruists to others. Thus, it is in the self-interest of a selfish beneficiary to be altruistic towards the altruist on any matters that affect the production of income or other services by the altruist. Altruists make it possible to define a single family utility function based on the altruist's preferences that everybody in the family is led to maximize. However, as England and Farkas (1986) pointed out, altruism can generate altruism. Thus, a single utility function only emerges if the altruist has power but does not use it selfishly. This is one of the difficulties with Becker's formulation: The model requires that the person who has the greatest power to withhold resources—that is, in the traditional family normally the husband—must also be inclined to altruism. Yet empirical evidence reveals that men normally have greater authority and power but women have a greater tendency to care for family members, to meet loved ones' needs, and to internalize others' feelings. In short, it seems that it is not men but women who to a greater extent include others' utility functions into their own. Thus, the single family utility function seems to be on shaky empirical ground (England and Farkas 1986). We will come back to this issue later.

2. The gains based on positive assortative mating with regard to non-market traits. Becker (1981) distinguishes the individual's traits that determine earnings capacity (income and wage potential) and individual characteristics which influence non-market productivity (intelligence, health, etc.). If the earnings capacity is held constant, the optimal sorting of most non-market traits of mates tends to be positive and strong. Thus, a 'superior' woman, *ceteris paribus*, raises the productivity of a 'superior' man and vice versa.

3. The gains based on specialization and the division of labour between the mates. If non-market traits are held constant, the utility of mates is maximized by a perfect negative assortative match with regard to their earnings capacities. This means that low-wage women tend to marry high-wage men and low-wage men tend to marry high-wage women. Men and women with lower earnings capacity will then be used extensively in household production, and those with higher earnings capacity will be used extensively in market production.

Furthermore, the economic theory of the family argues that the production and rearing of children is the main purpose of families. Families use market goods and services as well as parents' time to achieve this goal. Based on the comparative advantages of mates at the time of marriage, spouses will tend to further increase their specialization with increasing marriage duration because that is the most efficient productive strategy for the family. Only because it is typically women who have acquired a comparative advantage as caretakers of children in the more 'conventional' or 'traditional' family systems, is it mother's time that is the major part of the total cost of bearing and rearing children. In other words, in traditional family systems, it is typically the wife who schedules her work and family roles sequentially over the life course, leaving her job on marriage or at the birth of her first child, and returning to paid work when the children grow older. At the same time, the husband—the primary earner of the family—will show a fairly uninterrupted employment career over the life course. Thus, the economic theory of the family is an approach that tends to predict that one spouse (in the past normally the wife) concentrates on full-time homemaking and childrearing, while the other one (in the past normally the husband) works full-time in the market-place.

In summary, even if the economic theory of the family argues that wives normally rely on husbands as providers, and husbands mostly depend on wives for the maintenance of the home as well as for the rearing of children, it is only because young men and young women have invested differently in their earnings capacities during the early life course. Thus, the economic theory of the family holds that the sexual division of labour in the family and in the labour market is not so much based on biological sex-differences—although this aspect still remains a subject of intense debate—but is rather the result of gender-specific educational and training investments. The division of labour in the household is socially produced via inputs of time and resources into particular types of investments that are made by one sex and not by the other. These investments and the connected comparative advantages, however, could in principle be balanced (or reversed) between young men and young women.

Women's Earning Capacity and the Family Structure

Based on this model, it is possible to make predictions with regard to changes in the family and the employment behaviour of husbands and wives, as young women's earnings capacity continues to increase relative to that of young men's across birth cohorts. However, before we do that, it is important to stress that the economic theory of the family is unable to explain why these shifts happen in the younger generations. Factors responsible for these changes can therefore only be treated as exogenous in the economic theory of the family. They are related to exogenous macro processes such as educational expansion, economic growth, changes in the labour-market structure and wages, or the liberalization of sex-role attitudes. Two of these structural shifts seem to be particularly important for women's rise in earnings capacity. First, in most modern countries the differentials in educational attainment levels of men and women leaving school have almost disappeared across birth cohorts (Blossfeld and Shavit 1993; Erikson and Jonsson 1996). And secondly, the shift in the occupational structure from relatively unskilled production and service jobs to skilled service and administrative occupations with higher wages has been more pronounced for young women than for young men across cohorts (Blossfeld 1989; Esping-Andersen 1993). Thus, young women not only stay in the educational system longer than the women of older generations, but are better able than their mothers and grandmothers to turn higher education into better job and career opportunities as well as higher wages (Blossfeld and Huinink 1991), with the effect that the distributions of earnings capacity of young men and women are becoming increasingly similar across cohorts.

On the basis of this relative increase in women's earnings capacity, Becker (1981) predicts that the family as a social institution will decline because:

1. The rise in the earning power of women relative to men reduces the gain from marriage for prospective husbands and wives. Thus, the marriage rates in modern societies should strongly decline.

2. The increase in the value of women's time as a result of increases in investments in education and earning power increases the opportunity costs of children and thereby reduces the demand for children. Thus, the proportion of childless women should increase and the number of children per family should decline in modern societies.

3. Wives' increasing employment makes the division of labour between husbands and wives less advantageous, which reduces the gains from marriage and raises the risk of marital disruption.

However, these predictions are at least partly at odds with recent results from cross-national comparative studies using longitudinal data. First, this research shows that the decline in marriage clearly cannot be attributed to women's better educational attainment and increasing career opportunities (Blossfeld and Huinink 1991; Blossfeld 1995). Instead, higher educated women tend to postpone marriage mainly because they postpone the transition from youth to adulthood. The longer women remain in the educational system, the longer they delay getting marriage. After leaving the educational system, most women catch up with their less educated contemporaries. Thus, in modern societies, it is not so much the case that the incidence of marriage is declining, but that its timing has been shifting over the life course. A similar pattern occurs when the impact of women's educational attainment level and career resources on entry into first motherhood is considered from a cross-national comparative point of view. Attending school strongly delays women's propensity to have a first child (Blossfeld 1995). There are structural, institutional, and normative restraints implying that young women enrolled in education are 'not ready' to have a child. Completing education, as one of the important steps towards adult status, leads to a steep rise in motherhood for most countries (for a different institutional pattern in the former socialist German Democratic Republic see e.g. Huinink and Mayer 1995).

Support for the economic theory of the family, however, may be seen in the negative effect of income potential on entry into motherhood in most industrialized countries (Blossfeld and Huinink 1991; Blossfeld 1995). Women still take primary responsibility for childcare, even in 'modernized' family systems such as Sweden, and are still disadvantaged in their careers when they interrupt them after having a child. Women who have accumulated a high level of human capital therefore try to postpone or—to a much smaller extent—avoid the birth of a first child; and the more traditional the family system, the stronger this effect (Blossfeld 1995). This means that the conflict between a woman's accumulation of human capital and societal expectations regarding her role as a mother is especially pronounced in traditional family systems, such as the Southern European ones, leading to a strong decline in fertility in these countries (Blossfeld 1995). The mix of women's values of self-realization and economic emancipation with traditional forms of the family in particular increases the costs of children (Bettio and Villa 1998; González-López 1998). Currently, two traditional Catholic countries—Italy and Spain—have the world's lowest fertility levels, while those with the more differentiated family systems in Sweden and Denmark rank among the highest in Europe. This means that at the macro level the correlation between fertility and women's paid employment is now precisely the opposite of what one might have expected according to the economic theory of the family: the higher the rate of female employment in a country, the higher the level of fertility. Of course, this is a consequence of differences in welfare state policies which make wives' decisions to work more or less easy. However, the general decrease in fertility across cohorts in almost all modern societies allows younger married women to spend more time in the labour force prior to having their first child and also after their last child has entered school, which therefore reduces the aggregate time spent in childcare (Blossfeld and Hakim 1997).

Finally, with regard to marital breakdown, country-specific patterns also seem to be important. The negative effect of women's educational attainment level on breakdown risks is not constant across societies. It changes as family systems are transformed from 'traditional' to more (differentiated) 'modern' ones. A comparison of the gradient in the effects of women's educational level on divorce risks in Italy, West Germany, and Sweden, for example, shows that the 'liberating' impact of a woman's higher educational attainment declines strongly as the family system becomes less 'traditional', as other socially accepted living arrangements (for example, consensual unions) become more common, and as divorce becomes more acceptable for all women (Blossfeld *et al*. 1995). Thus, for example, divorce rates in Scandinavia remain at relatively high levels with little or no further growth; they even show evidence of switching back to marital stability instead. In Southern Europe divorce rates are still low but rising steeply.

In summary, there is no empirical evidence for the predicted effect of the women's rise in earnings capacity on entry into marriage. Secondly, it seems that the effect of women's rise in earnings capacity on fertility and divorce rates is dependent on the type of family system. The more traditional the family system, the stronger the effects on the family; and the more differentiated the living arrangements in a society, the weaker these effects (Blossfeld 1995). Thus, the changes in the structure of the family system itself make families increasingly less responsive towards changes in women's earnings capacity.

Comparative Advantage and the Division of Labour

According to the economic theory of the family, an increasing equalization of educational attainment levels and earning power of young men and women across cohorts should also affect the process of assortative mating and change the structure of couples' sex-specific division of labour within the family and the labour market.

1. It should lead to a decline in the proportion of men marrying downwards—or women marrying upwards—with regard to traits determining earnings capacity (or income and wage), simply because the structures of these traits are becoming more equalized across cohorts. In fact, there is empirical evidence that the incidence of these traditional marriages is declining strongly in the course of educational expansion (Blossfeld and Timm forthcoming).

2. It should raise the proportion of couples marrying homogamously because, given the increasingly gender-equalized structure of traits determining earnings capacity, the economic theory of the family predicts that mates benefit most from each other when they resemble each other as far as possible in their non-market traits (intelligence, health, education, etc.). For example, there is empirical evidence in Germany that educational homogamy is increasing across cohorts (Blossfeld *et al.* 1997; Blossfeld and Timm 1997). An important mechanism in this respect is that 'contextual effects', such as relatively homogeneous marriage markets in school systems, increase the rate of positive assortative mating (Blossfeld and Timm forthcoming).

3. It should increase the likelihood that young women marry downwards. When young women profit more than young men from educational expansion and career resources, then, from a statistical point of view, the random probability that women marry downwards—or men upwards—with regard to traits determining earnings capacity (or income and wage) should increase for each younger cohort. Empirical studies reveal that there are significant country differences in this regard, for example, between West Germany and the United States (Timm *et al.* 1998). In West Germany, the percentage of women who married less qualified men has been small and fairly constant across cohorts. In the United States of America, on the other hand, it is larger and has been growing (Blossfeld and Timm forthcoming).

4. Finally, both an increasing number of homogamous marriages, where the relative earning power of husband and wife is uncertain, and a rising number of women marrying downwards, where the wife has a markedly

higher income potential than her husband, should increase the proportion of males who rely on wives as providers, and of wives who rely on husbands for the maintenance of the home as well as for the rearing of children. Therefore, from a life-course perspective, it should then be the husband who typically schedules his work and family roles sequentially over the life course, leaving his job when he marries or with the birth of the first child and returning to paid work when his children grow older. And, at the same time, it should be the wife who as the family's primary earner should have a fairly uninterrupted employment career over the life course.

In summary, Becker's predictions are based on the distinction between roles that complement each other; they hinge on the argument that spouses will tend to specialize within the marriage, regardless of whether it is 'traditional' or 'non-traditional', because this is the most efficient productive strategy for the family as a unit. In terms of life-course patterns, this specialization mechanism systematically produces an 'optimal' arrangement: (a) a continuous employment career over the life course for the spouse, be it husband or wife, who specializes in market work, and (b) non-employment after entry into marriage or at least a chronological sequence of work and family roles over the life course for the spouse, be it husband or wife, who focuses on non-market work.

Family and Work: Role Specialization versus Role Combination

The 'optimality' of Becker's specialization mechanism has been seriously questioned. For example, Oppenheimer (1993) argues that, although specialization may promote interdependence, it may not provide much cohesion for particular marriages. If it is relatively easy for one partner to replace the other through divorce and remarriage, then a considerable amount of marital instability is produced by specialization. In traditional families, segregated sex roles do increase the stakes in marriage but mainly for the wives who are at home, not for the husbands who go to work (England and Farkas 1986). Thus, the consequence for the integrative mechanism of gender specialization in the traditional family is economic dependency of wives on husbands (Sørensen and McLanahan 1987). Hence, specialization in traditional families may increase the 'gain' women obtain from a particular marriage by virtually eliminating other marital and non-marital options (Oppenheimer 1993).

Beyond that, specialization also means that the small nuclear family is particularly vulnerable to the temporary (through unemployment, illness) or permanent (through separation, death) loss of a unique individual who provides an essential function—at home or in the labour market. The specialization of spouses into full-time provider and full-time homemaker not only entails risks in a world characterized by unpredictable events, such as sickness, death, or unemployment, but also because of the very nature of the family as a social unit. It is an inescapable biological fact that individuals' consumption needs and productive capabilities vary markedly by age. Consequently, 'a basic feature of nuclear families is that the ratio of consumers to producers, and hence the family's standard of living can vary substantially over the family's development cycle . . . Hence, specialization involves a potentially serious loss of flexibility in dealing with changes in both a family's internal composition and the stresses posed by its environment' (Oppenheimer 1993: 24). From this perspective, wives' employment can be viewed as a highly adaptive family strategy in a modern society, rather than as a threat to the family as a social institution (Oppenheimer 1997).

The Importance of Family Power Structures

Becker not only ignored the negative consequences of 'extreme' role special-ization, in terms of families' limited flexibility and higher vulnerability, but also neglected the issue of power within families. He assumed that all family members make decisions to maximize the well-being of the family as a whole. However, as already discussed above, the single family utility function is not only on shaky empirical ground. Spouses often have conflicts of interest and hold quite different views regarding issues affecting them both. Thus, marital relationships normally make their way through situations of conflict and this raises the question of whether one spouse gets more of what he/she wants than the other, at least in areas where interests conflict. In other words, the question of who has more power or authority has to be addressed.

   Max Weber defined 'power' as the probability that an actor will be able to carry out his or her will even when opposed by others and, in a consensual context, an actor has 'authority' when there is a probability that subordinates accept his or her will as being used legitimately (Weber 1972: 28). We will briefly discuss three approaches to family power structures: (1) patriarchy models based on the idea of male solidarity and domination, (2) resource-bargaining models based on economic exchange, and (3) marital dependency models based on non-economic exchange.

Patriarchy: Male Oppression of Women

One stream of research on family power structures argues that women's heavy domestic load is the result of patriarchy (Hartmann 1976; Reskin 1988; Sokoloff 1988; Walby 1986, 1990). These writers refer to the fact that men often get women to do what they want, whether women like it or not. Men obtain power from many different sources, including control of resources, physical force, influence, manipulation of interests, strategic scheming, intimidation, and knowledge. Hartmann defines patriarchy as a 'set of social relations which has a material base and in which there are hierarchical relations between men,

[and] solidarity among them which enable them to control women. Patriarchy is thus the system of male oppression of women' (Hartmann 1976: 138). Walby's definition of patriarchy as 'a system of social structures and practices in which men dominate, oppress and exploit women' (1990: 20) is closer to the sociological structural stance since the term 'social structure' implies rejection of both biological determinism and the notion that every individual man is in a dominant position and every woman in a subordinate one. The exploitation of women at home and at work, these writers argue, augers to the benefit of men. It follows that exploitation is ubiquitous and not apt to disappear easily in the household and in the labour market, regardless of the recent trends in women's employment (Hartmann 1976, Reskin 1988; Sokoloff 1988). In fact, 'male domination' is seen to be much the same under both patriarchal capitalism and patriarchal socialism (Huber 1988).

For our own part, we would regard the 'patriarchy' approach to the family power structure as being itself problematic. Insofar as a sociological argument is advanced in this model, this would appear to rest on a fairly amorphous concept. In addition, patriarchy as an explanatory mechanism appears quite tautological: On the one hand, patriarchy is used to explain why women are subordinated to men; but on the other, the observed subordination of women to men is identified as patriarchy. Thus, the concept actually assumes what is to be proved (Curtis 1986). There is empirical evidence that discrimination of women continues in many countries, even in social democratic and socialist ones. But it does not follow that all differences between women and men can immediately be attributed to patriarchy. At this general level, patriarchy is difficult or perhaps impossible to study. More concrete explanatory mechanisms are, however, suggested by the resource-bargaining model.

The Resource-Bargaining Model: Economic Exchange

Resource-bargaining models view household work as a source of disutility, an onerous activity one wishes to 'buy out of' either through purchasing services or demanding greater spousal participation (see Hiller 1984; Lee 1987; McRae 1986; Skolnick 1987). This approach views each marital partner as pursuing his/her own utility and not the joint utility of the whole family, as maintained by the economic theory of the family. At each point in time, spouses consider the union as open to future negotiation and adjustments and these adjustments are made in response to changes in either partner's resource bundle. Most researchers who follow this argument explain husbands' power in conventional marriages in terms of economic exchange: husbands provide the income and status and thereby 'earn' an entitlement to be the principal decision-maker or the provider (Blood and Wolfe 1960; McDonald 1977; McRae 1986; Sørensen and McLanahan 1987). And indeed, empirical research seems to indicate that husbands and wives make such evaluations of each other all the time (Jasso 1988).

The basic premise of this model is that the division of household labour is an outcome of negotiations between the spouses. The individual with higher earnings, or the provider, has more resources to strike a deal in his/her best interests and will therefore do less housework than his/her less well-paid counterpart, the dependent. Thus, if wives do more paid work, they will do less housework, and husbands whose wives work more do more domestic and childcare work. However, as discussed by Curtis (1986), research on family power and authority often focuses too sharply on current economic resources as a basis for power, and pay insufficient attention to the emergence of a power structure through the process of interpersonal exchange.

The Marital Dependency Model: Non-Economic Exchange

When men and women start forming a union, they normally exchange benefits that create diffuse future obligations, or when they carry out a joint enterprise such as having and rearing a child, they must make plans about unknown events far in the future. Thus, a husband and wife cannot only rely on economic exchanges, specified in detail at the moment of exchange, as assumed by the resource-bargaining model; they must also rely on what Blau (1964) has called non-economic exchanges. These exchanges are based on favours and gifts and on the debtor's willingness to respond at some time in the future. This is to say that the purpose of a union is far too general to be conceptualized in a 'price list' that defines how much of one type of behaviour on his part is worth how much of another type of behaviour on her part. Researchers have therefore conceptualized marriage and other long-term cohabitational arrangements as implicit contracts, with many unstated and thus not formally binding agreements (England and Farkas 1986: 47). In this view, marriage generally represents the promise to reciprocate diffuse obligations at some unspecified future date (Blau 1994) and to remain in the relationship irrespective of future contingencies. However, (rising) divorce rates make it clear that such contracts can also (increasingly) be broken and partners (more and more often) fail to honour such promises.

According to the theorists of marital dependency (England and Farkas 1986; Acker 1988), it is precisely the long-term nature of marriage that makes spouses' recurrent negotiations necessary and possible. In this process, every rewarding experience engenders obligations to reciprocate, and the recurrent reciprocation promotes trust to do larger favours and strengthens the union as a marital bond (Blau 1964). Once bonds of mutual support and trust are established, it is the rewarding experience derived from the union itself that represents the prime benefit (Blau 1994).

A key argument of the theory of marital dependency is that marital power is derived not only from contributions to the marital relationship, but also from one's alternatives outside the relationship (Blau 1964; England and Farkas 1986). Both game theory and exchange theory suggest that a spouse's marital power within a union decreases the more the gains within the relationship exceed what they could receive outside the relationship. Thus, different patterns of division of labour between husband and wife in a union are likely to generate different trajectories of spouses' relative marital power over time.

If wives undertake greater relationship-specific investments in traditional marriages than their husbands, while husbands accumulate resources (primarily earning power) which are easily transferred to other relationships, unequal marital power is generated between the spouses: the difference in the alternatives available to husband and wife outside the current relationship generally leads to greater male power within it. This male advantage decreases with the increase in women's employment and should disappear when both partners have made the same amounts of relationship-specific and relationship-transferable investments.

An interesting aspect of the marital dependency model, compared to the economic theory of the family, is that it can explain why young women's earnings capacity increases across birth cohorts in modern societies. This is because the continued increase in divorce rates and decrease in fertility from generation to generation make it more important for each younger cohort of women to be better educated and employed. Wives' paid employment represents more readily transferable investments, strengthening their marital power and making them better able to cope with the consequences of a possible divorce (England and Farkas 1986). Thus, the marital dependency theory assumes a mutually reinforcing link between increasing divorce rates and women's rising educational attainment, as well as married women's rising labour-force participation across cohorts and vice versa. However, in this framework, rising divorce rates will not lead to the decline of the family as a social institution as predicted by the economic theory of the family. Instead, experiencing divorce inserts a new stage into the life course, so that for many individuals marriage becomes sequential rather than for life (England and Farkas 1986).

Based on the resource-bargaining model and the theory of marital dependency, increasing equalization of educational attainment and earning power of young men and women across cohorts should thus affect not only the process of assortative mating, but also change the structure of couples' sex-specific division of labour within the family and labour market. However, these predictions (see England and Farkas 1986) are slightly different to those made by the economic theory of the family:

1. If wives' employment and earnings continue to increase and become a major component determining the economic status of the whole family, men will tend to pay greater attention to women's earning power (Oppenheimer 1988). Thus, based on this change, one would (*a*) expect a decline in the proportion of men marrying downwards, and (*b*) predict that via competitive

processes in the marriage market the positive correlation between mates' earnings capacities will continue to converge. Consequently, conjugal unions will tend to become more homogamous across cohorts.

2. On the other hand, one would also expect an increasing propensity of young women to marry downwards, not only because the gender-specific structures of earnings potentials are becoming more equal and make such marriages statistically more common, but also because women will increasingly assign less value to men's earning power. Indeed, empirical research shows that this appears to be the case (Winkler 1998–9).

3. Since most market work generates income which can be used as 'bargaining chips' and is readily transferable to another relationship, both spouses will try to be employed in the labour market as much as possible. Thus, these models predict a strong rise in (full-time) dual-earner couples, since the earnings potential of wives, conveying marital power, will continue to increase relative to that of husbands across cohorts.

4. Since most housework is considered unpleasant and a relationship-specific investment, both spouses will try to avoid doing it or do less of it. However, within the couple, the spouse with less marital power or the one who is dependent (with less earning power that is readily transferable to another relationship) will have to do more of it because he/she has less negotiating power and more to lose in the case of divorce. Since wives' marital power will continue to increase relative to that of husbands' across cohorts, we expect that wives who do more paid work will do less housework, and husbands whose wives work more will do more of the domestic and childcare work.

In summary, and in terms of life-course patterns, bargaining mechanisms will systematically produce the tendency that both spouses will avoid the disruptive effects of leaving and re-entering employment. Thus, at all stages of their lives, these dual-earners will try to be employed as continuously as possible and as much as possible, and they will increasingly share the housework and childcare. In other words, issues of dependency and providership are becoming increasingly blurred. Furthermore, there is also a tendency to externalize onerous housework and childcare activities through market and state provision. Finally, when wives' employment and earnings continue to increase across cohorts and become a major component determining families' economic status in the inequality system, the opportunity cost of women remaining exclusively in household work is raised and mutually reinforces the trend towards (full-time) dual-earner couples.

This trend also finds support in sociological studies which indicate that marital satisfaction has increased even though specialization and role differentiation have decreased within marriage (see e.g. McRae 1986, 1990; England and Farkas 1986). These studies not only contradict the economic theory of the family, but suggest that there is a mechanism which increases marital satisfaction when spouses play similar rather than different—although complementary—roles. Simpson and England (1981) suggested that empathy and companionship, the two major predictors of marital satisfaction, are enhanced when spouses undertake similar roles. When their roles are similar, spouses can understand one another better, and they enjoy each other's company more because of their common interests. From this standpoint, marriage may be more satisfying when husbands and wives both work outside the home and share domestic responsibilities as well. This should then contribute to a stabilization or even a decline in divorce rates in modern societies.

Dual-Earners: Income Gain versus Time for the Family

It appears that gender role transformation has accelerated because macro-structural conditions have increased the incentives for women's employment; that is, they have raised the opportunity cost of wives remaining exclusively in household work. In particular, industrialization and modern technology have dramatically changed the standard of living in modern societies since the Second World War. Households have had to shift time from domestic activities to work in the market to enjoy the benefits of this tremendous growth in the standard of living (Eggebeen and Hawkins 1990). This is because the most sophisticated and diverse goods that advanced technologies can offer are not produced at home and the only way to enjoy quality goods and services is to purchase them in the market. Therefore, Eggebeen and Hawkins (1990) conclude that the need to provide basic necessities for the family has declined over time as a motive for married mothers' labour-force participation. At the same time, however, desires to achieve and maintain a higher standard of living have increased. 'Couples' choices to enjoy the fruits of a prosperous economic system and the products of a technologically advanced society, and to enjoy them at a younger age, are responsible for this important trend' (Eggebeen and Hawkins 1990: 56).

Quite different structural backgrounds explain the high full-time labour-force participation rate of wives in (former) socialist countries (Drobnič 1997). On the one hand, labour shortages in inefficient economies made employment of all able-bodied individuals possible and necessary. On the other hand, there were also a number of supply-side factors that promoted high rates of labour-force participation. Due to low wages and the official doctrine emphasizing the role of employment in gender equality, there were strong financial and ideological pressures on women to enter paid employment. For a family, an adequate standard of living could in most cases only be maintained by two wage-earners who contributed not only their income but also other benefits and services provided to the population by enterprises (Drobnič 1997).

One of the most significant changes within advanced industrial societies, whether capitalist or (former) socialist, is therefore the shift from the single- to the dual-earner family as the norm (OECD 1988). There are, of course, a variety of dual-earner couples: it is an important question whether both spouses work full-time, both work part-time, or one of them works full-time and the other part-time (Blossfeld and Hakim 1997). Since market work is normally still rigidly organized in most societies and time allocated to market employment is unavailable for other activities, including family life, full-time employment of both spouses is lost time—for the couples, for the families, and for the husbands and wives themselves (Moen 1992). Thus, time pressures from full-time work necessarily limit the amount of joint activities undertaken by the family, and this is particularly the case when parents of young children combine full-time paid work with childcare. In other words, there is often a severe conflict between families' gain in income through work and time for the family. The severity of this conflict is not only determined by the family-cycle location of the employment spells, but also by social class, that is, families' relative position within the inequality system, and by the country-specific context, that is, by a host of cultural and institutional factors, including the structural availability of various employment opportunities, prevailing wage rates, and the 'costs' of employment within a country. We will come back to these issues later.

The 'Doing Gender' Approach: Symbolic Exchange

The 'doing gender' approach starts from the assumption that gender identities have to be produced and reproduced in recurrent everyday social interaction (see e.g. West and Zimmerman 1987; Fenstermaker *et al.* 1991). Such interaction provides the stage for the enactment of gender identities (Goffman 1977). Men have to display that they are 'men' and women that they are 'women'. Thus, part of what spouses invest when they establish a marital union is a socially sanctioned arrangement offering recurrent opportunities to advance claims about the self as 'naturally' male or female.

Berk (1985: 204) maintains that housework and childcare

can become the occasion for producing commodities (for example clean children, clean laundry, and new light switches) and a reaffirmation of one's gendered relation to the work and to the world. In short, the 'should' of gender ideals are fused with the 'musts' of efficient household production. The result may be something resembling a 'gendered' household-production function.

Thus, in this view, the issue of female dependency is coupled with behavioural displays of femininity via housework and under certain conditions gender itself becomes the immediate object of purposive action via housework. But what do people regard as 'men's work'? The answer in most contemporary societies is routinely that men's work remains associated with primary providership for the family (Brines 1994).

This gender-specific association is deeply entrenched in the socio-institutional structures of many countries, and 'to the extent that these structures remain predicated on the ideal of durable heterosexual unions, institutions presume male providership just as much as they presume female dependency' (Brines

1994: 664). Accordingly, the link between dependency and housework might be derived not only from relations of economic or non-economic exchange, but from gender relations that regulate symbolic displays of masculine or feminine accountability.

The 'doing gender' model suggests that when a couple's relations of dependency and support align with normative expectations—in other words, when the wife is dependent and the husband is the main breadwinner—the exchange of housework for support poses no problem from the point of view of gender enactment. Husbands and wives do gender as they exchange resources. In this case, the 'doing gender' approach explicitly recognizes normative expectations and distributive realities regarding the gender of providers and dependants. However, when expected and actual relations of support and dependency diverge along gender lines, then husbands and wives violate the norms. In this case, the display perspective suggests that breadwinning wives and dependent husbands risk (a) social accountability, (b) negative judgements from relatives, friends, colleagues, and (c) a threat to their gender identities, so they are likely to compensate by adopting gender-traditional behaviours elsewhere in the marriage. In this framework, one would not expect couples supported economically by wives to divide 'women's work' in a manner consistent with the terms of the economic or non-economic exchange discussed above. Rather, these couples may resort to traditional housework and childcare arrangements as a means of reclaiming gender accountability in the eyes of self, partner, and others. In other words, the more severely a man's identity is financially threatened—by his wife's higher salary—the less he can afford to threaten it further by doing 'women's work' at home. The greater the degree of deviance, the greater the threat to both partner's gender accountability, and in turn, the greater the likely level of investment in compensatory traditional behaviour (Brines 1994). This situation seems an unstable solution because some domestic and childcare work that could enhance household well-being is left undone while dependent husbands realize greater leisure and the wives increasingly seem to struggle with the competing demands on their time of two 'jobs', one at home and one at work (Hochschild, with Machung 1989). Brines (1994) therefore predicts that where norms of equity compete with the terms of such a compromise, the additional strains placed on the relationship may call for another solution: that of divorce.

In sum, the 'doing gender' perspective suggests that, for providing wives and dependent husbands, social and interactional pressures conspire to limit the possibility of symmetrical change in gender roles. However, depicting rigid gender-based divisions of household labour as normative and too invariant also poses a danger. In particular, it might mask the increasing diversity among couples in modern societies and disregard exceptions to normative patterns and their change over time. Thus, to treat gender as a kind of 'cause' of household division of labour might tend to overlook its emergent character and fail to acknowledge how it is in fact implicated in precisely such routine practices (see Coltrane 1989).

The Identity-Formation Model: The Trade-Off between Roles versus Multiple Roles

Another model, developed by Bielby and Bielby (1989), suggests that the diffusion of new gender patterns and gender identities in modern societies will take a long time because work and family identity-formation processes are recurrently shaped by structural and cultural contexts which only accommodate slowly. According to this perspective, commitments to paid work and family roles are functions of one's past work and current experiences, responsibilities, and statuses at work and in the family, respectively. One is 'committed' to the extent that role behaviours become a source of meaning or identity; however, the identity is not given and invariant. As individuals become engaged in role behaviours, they develop identities linked to those roles. The question of whether husbands and wives have to trade off commitments among alternative activities or whether they can form strong commitments to multiple roles is dependent on sex-role norms.

Bielby and Bielby (1989) conclude that contemporary demands of household responsibilities and expectations surrounding the roles of 'wife' and 'mother' lead wives who are employed outside the home to balance work and family identities by trading one off against the other. Thus, culturally prescribed role structures normally require wives to sacrifice a strong work identity if they are to identify with a traditional family role—and vice versa. In contrast, for men, the normative expectations of the 'husband' and 'father' roles do not include fully shared responsibility and involvement in household and childcare activities. A husband's role in the workplace is consistent with his family obligations as a provider. A successful worker is a good provider. Accordingly, married men may not trade off one identity against the other. Rather, men have greater freedom to develop strong levels of identification with both work and family roles. In short, Bielby and Bielby (1989) expect that the differential structural and normative constraints on husbands and wives allow husbands to sustain dual work and family identities but constrain wives to forgo one to sustain the other.

Based on this model, Bielby and Bielby (1989) formulated several hypotheses about the changes in work and family identities of husbands and wives when they live in single-earner and more or less traditional dual-earner families:

1. Single-earner families. The consequence of having a spouse who is not in the paid labour force should be different for husbands and wives. For a husband, the wife is likely to be specializing in household activities in ways that facilitate his identification with a job. For a wife, the husband is more likely to be unemployed than to be specializing in household activities. Accordingly, the authors hypothesize that a spouse not in the paid labour force facilitates a husband's career identity but has no impact on a wife's. For traditional husbands, identification with family roles may be greater when the wife specializes

in household activities. In contrast, an economically inactive husband is by cultural definition an unemployed husband and is therefore likely to have a negative impact on family dynamics. Thus, Bielby and Bielby hypothesize that having a spouse who is not in the paid labour force increases family identity for the working husbands but decreases it for working wives. This is the exact opposite of the prediction made by the economic theory of the family: when the wife is working full-time and the husband is not in the labour force, he will not specialize in housework and childcare.

2. Part-time work and disrupted work histories. Part-time and part-year employment allow for more time in family roles relative to work roles and should therefore decrease work identity and increase family identity for husbands and wives. For wives, the choice of part-time versus full-time work and an interrupted work history versus a continuous one is likely to be based on a concern for balancing work and family responsibilities. Accordingly, the impacts of these employment forms are expected to be greater among wives. For men, this choice is more likely to be shaped by constraints in employment opportunities. Part-time work and a disrupted work history are unlikely to reflect a strong family orientation on the part of husbands; instead, they are more likely to reflect instability in a husband's social situation and erode commitments to the family. Thus, contrary to the predictions of the resource-bargaining model and the theory of marital dependency, husbands who have less 'bargaining chips' will not do more domestic and childcare work.

3. For dual-earner couples with well-paid spouses. For husbands and wives, having a well-paid spouse reduces the extent to which financial constraints motivate work behaviours. Bielby and Bielby (1989) therefore argue that a spouse who pursues a career despite a partner's high earning power is likely to develop greater work identification than someone who is forced to work because of the partner's lack of earnings potential. Since the 'breadwinner' role is culturally prescribed for husbands, work identity for males should be less sensitive to spouse's income than it is for women. Next, having a well-paid spouse enhances the financial resources available to sustain a family and should therefore facilitate family identification for both partners. Again, because of culturally prescribed role expectations, this effect should be greater among women than among men. Thus, even in the case where both spouses have similar 'bargaining chips', there will be a greater tendency for wives to do housework and childcare than for husbands.

Of course, such gender-specific work and family identities will have consequences for the labour market. When an individual's commitment to a family role precludes a strong identification with a career, then the traditional household division of labour could be largely responsible for gender inequalities in the workplace. This is especially the case when for these groups of (potential) workers a greater diversity of working hours, such as half-time and marginal jobs, part-time and full-time self-employment, temporary and casual jobs, is acceptable (Hakim 1998). Employers will then mainly recruit primary earners into 'male' occupations, while secondary earners are mainly recruited into 'female' occupations. 'So even if "male" and "female" occupations do not necessarily utilise specifically masculine or feminine skills and talents, they may still justify their sex-stereotyped labels by their compatibility with typically male and typically female employment histories over the life cycle' (Hakim 1998: 63). At the same time, many women may sustain high levels of commitment to work, yet find themselves disadvantaged in the workplace because of assumptions employers make about women's 'average' commitment to work roles ('theory of statistical discrimination'). This means that in many countries it is difficult for employers to predict how long a female employee will stay in a job because continuously working women are virtually impossible to identify, except *post hoc*. Thus, changes in the sexual division of work in the household and changes in the sexual segregation of work in the labour market are interdependent processes and are likely to influence each other over time.

Bielby and Bielby (1989) predict that increased parity between men and women in their workplace and household roles should contribute to a stronger work identity among women and a stronger family identity among men. However, the extent to which dual-earner couples actually have changed these roles over time is still unclear in many countries. Bielby and Bielby speculate that the increase in female labour-force participation and in the number of female-headed households may make the dual roles of 'mother' and 'provider' culturally acceptable and the dual identity more easy to sustain for working wives. On the other hand, they also acknowledge that there has been only modest reduction in sex segregation in the workplace and even less change in the household division of labour. Thus, they consider it an empirical question whether the structural and cultural context of work and family roles have changed enough to alter the identity-formation process.

Social Class and the Sex-Specific Division of Labour

The division of work between husbands and their wives in the household and in the labour market should strongly depend on social class. There is a stream of qualitative studies indicating that husbands and wives in different social classes organize the dual-earner family in different ways and develop various strategies to retain the image that husbands are the main providers.

Thoits argues that middle- and upper-class spouses are first to change their division of labour by gender if there are children, and this change filters down the social ladder (1987: 21). Working-class wives often work for financial reasons. These couples try to maintain the image of wives as secondary providers by defining the husbands' income as essential and the wives' salary for 'extras' (Zavella 1987). Ferree (1976, 1987) and Rosen (1987) show that most working-class wives in the United States of America do wage work for both economic and personal reasons. Ferree reports that, although working-class wives' jobs are often worrisome and wearisome, most working-class women take pride in their job, welcome contact with other people, and enjoy the recognition and respect that accompanies a pay-cheque. When they want to quit work, it is typically because their jobs are not good, not because they want to be full-time homemakers (Rosen 1987). However, most of these women have contradictory feelings: they think their jobs are good for themselves and their families but, at the same time, feel guilty about their homes and children (Zavella 1987). 'The realities of class mean that working-class families often find themselves dividing paid-work by gender more equitably than middle-class families, not only in terms of earnings, but also in responsibility and recognition for family provision' (Thompson and Walker 1989).

Middle-class husbands seem to have the most trouble sharing family provision with their wives (Fendrich 1984). Stanley *et al.* (1986) found that young, highly educated, and occupationally successful fathers in dual-earner marriages are less satisfied with their marriages and personal lives than similar men who are sole providers for their families. They report that these successful men feel cheated because they have no wife at home to provide full-time service. Ferree (1987) argued that, in middle-class families, husbands' earnings levels make wives' income, at best, supplemental and, at worst, unnecessary. Thus, it is easy in such families for husbands to view wives as secondary providers and their paid work as an individual privilege rather than as a contribution to the whole family. Weiss (1985, 1987) also reports that successful middle-class men believe that their wives work for their own benefit, not to contribute to the family. Market employment is seen as an opportunity for wives to get out of the house and to give them a chance to realize their potential and express themselves. Husbands tend to think that they are unselfish for supporting their wives' need to work outside of the family. Most of these husbands feel proud of their wives' success, but feel that their time on the job means diminished attention to childcare and home management.

In many upper-middle-class families, wives' efforts help husbands to succeed. However, their efforts are less visible. Pananek (1979) shows how upper-middle-class wives support their husbands' career advancement through family work: maintaining clothing, entertaining colleagues, appropriately training children, and engaging in the politics of status maintenance. Fowlkes (1987) describes how many wives of professors and physicians keep the home running, encourage their husbands, accommodate their own careers, and move when their husbands have to move. Thus, wives of professional husbands are more likely to be in intermittent part-time employment, whereas wives of non-professional husbands tend to be in intermittent full-time employment (Moen 1992).

In sum, these studies clearly indicate that, when couples are 'doing gender', the relationship between social class and normative gender structures becomes quite complex and even contradictory. On the one hand, the probability that a wife is (part-time or full-time) employed is likely to increase with her earnings potential. On the other hand, it is likely to decrease with the level of her husband's breadwinner family income, that is, with social class. Since women with higher earnings potential are typically married to men with a higher breadwinner family income, and vice versa, women's labour-force particip-ation is hard to predict. That is, upper-class wives are normally better educated with a higher earnings potential, but their husbands' family wage is relatively high, too. Thus, even if these wives have—also enhanced by their social net-works (or social capital)—good opportunities to get attractive, highly paid jobs in the labour market, they have no need to work to reach high standards of living. At the same time, upper-middle-class husbands are more likely to hold liberal attitudes towards wives' (part-time and full-time) employment because they are better educated (Bernasco 1994) and it is easier for them to view their wives as secondary providers. The reverse seems to be true for working-class wives: they have to work (often full-time) if they want to enjoy the products and services of a technologically advanced society, but when they do, they get unattractive, low-paid jobs. In addition, working-class husbands are more likely to hold traditional attitudes towards wives' employment because they are less educated and it is harder for them to maintain the image of wives as secondary providers. We consider it an empirical question what the relative strengths of these contradicting socio-economic, socio-cultural, and 'doing gender' forces are in various social classes and different countries. However, based on these complex class-specific relationships between spouses, it will often be difficult or even impossible to predict the extent and patterns of mar-ried women's labour-force participation in various countries, without taking their husbands' characteristics into account. Indeed, this is the main objection we raise against individual, work-centred labour-market studies which con-centrate on individual characteristics, such as the level of educational attain-ment or labour-force experience, and ignore the family or household contexts of women and men in the market-place.

From a theoretical point of view, the most interesting couples are those where wives have married downwards with regard to traits determining earn-ing power. In these cases, the conflict between wives' wage potential and the need to work, on the one hand, and the rules of 'doing gender', on the other, should be particularly strong—though they vary across the societies studied in this book. The question as to whether these wives or their husbands are employed (and to what extent) should depend on the extent to which these couples are 'doing gender'. Finally, for couples where wives have married upwards concerning traits determining earning power, the structural (or eco-nomic) and cultural (or normative gender) contexts of work and family roles do not contradict. But even in these traditional cases, we assume that the extent of wives' labour-force participation depends on the family wage of the husband—at least in some of the countries studied in this volume.

In sum, we assume that, in all contemporary industrialized societies, hus-bands try to work (full-time and continuously) and take over the provider role, independent of their own level of resources (educational attainment level, labour-force experience, etc.) and the resources of their wives. On the other hand, we would expect the extent of wives' labour-force participation and employment patterns over the life course to depend on wives' levels of resources relative to those of their husbands: wives work more hours and more continuously the better their education and the more labour-force experience they have already accumulated, and the lower their husbands' income potential. Thus, husbands' earnings capacity should suppress wives' employment in paid work. On the other hand, one might assume that husbands with higher earnings also have higher levels of education and therefore tend to have less traditional values (Bernasco 1994). Thus, when husbands' earnings capacity is held constant, we suggest that husbands' level of education has a positive effect on wives' labour-force participation (Bernasco *et al.* 1998).

Couples' Careers and Country Contexts

The patterns of labour-force participation of husbands and their wives are also contingent on a number of other structural influences including the national context. The twelve countries included in this book may be classified into five major groups according to their basic cultural and economic systems: (1) Western capitalist countries with 'conservative' welfare states, (West) Germany, the Netherlands, and (the Flemish part of) Belgium; (2) Southern European capitalist countries with 'familialistic' welfare states, Italy and Spain; (3) Western capitalist countries with a 'liberal' welfare state, the United Kingdom and the United States of America, (4) Western capitalist countries with a 'social democratic' welfare state: Denmark and Sweden; and (5) Central and Eastern European (formerly) socialist countries, Poland and Hungary. Finally, and in order to enrich the selection of societies examined here, we have included a study on non-Western state socialist China.

These countries do not constitute a representative sample of all contemporary societies, but do represent considerable variation in the following characteristics important for our research question: the level of industrialization/tertiarization and the standard of living (compare the United States of America, Germany, Hungary, Poland, and China); the political system (democracies versus socialist/communist regimes); the degree of decommodification by the capitalist welfare state (social democratic, conservative, liberal, familialistic); the degree to which the husband can earn a breadwinner family wage (Germany and the Netherlands versus Sweden, Denmark, the United States of America, and (former) socialist countries), the package of public policies that support maternal employment (Sweden, Denmark, (former) state socialist states versus Germany, the Netherlands); and the variation in women's full-time and part-time employment rates. Thus, this array of countries enables an evaluation of the hypotheses listed earlier in a variety of societies.

In this book, the most important insights into couples' employment careers over the last decades result from our case-study approach, showing how common trends in the division of work between husbands and their wives have been suppressed or sustained by broader structural, political, and ideological country 'packages' and hence have generated quite heterogeneous patterns and diverse changes of divisions of work between husbands and their wives. Thus, it will become clear that changes taking place in one country do not necessarily occur in the other countries and that seemingly inexorable processes in one society are in fact contingent on country-specific conditions. Although each country studied in this volume has its own patterns of couples' division of work, it is possible to formulate general hypotheses about how various structural trends and different packages of employment, family, and welfare policies foster or hinder male breadwinner families as well as more or less traditional dual-earner families.

Country-Specific Employment Structures

The employment structure of a country as a whole, and its gender-specific occupational patterns in particular, shape opportunities and constraints, and in this way influence the choices couples make. However, this is a two-way dynamic relationship where couples' choices in turn produce a renewal as well as changes of these structures. Thus, we have to understand the country-specific employment constraints and their changes within which husbands and wives operate.

   In the countries studied in this book, whether capitalist or (former) state socialist, whether Western or non-Western, men have normally been employed continuously and full-time, unless they were in school, partially retired, suffered from health problems, or were employed part-time involuntarily due to low labour demand (Rosenfeld and Birkelund 1995). Thus, nonemployment of men normally has taken the form of unemployment, and part-time employment of men (and its increase) has mainly been a matter of very specific (but growing) groups such as students or (early) retirees, and not an important phenomenon related to men's roles as husbands and fathers. In the countries studied in this book, the average proportion of part-time working men is about 3–4 per cent, with the Netherlands (16 per cent), the United States of America (11 per cent), and Denmark (10 per cent) as the exceptions (Blossfeld and Hakim 1997). From a life-course perspective, men's part-time work is concentrated at the ages of transition from school to work and from work to retirement. It follows that, in the countries studied in this book, most husbands during middle age have quite a saturated level of labour-force participation—at least as long as they do not suffer from unemployment—and are usually working in full-time 'male' occupations which makes them prone to become the providers or at least the primary earners of their families (Hakim 1998).

   On the other hand, amongst the countries analysed in this book, women show a substantial variation in the proportion of labour-force participation over the life course and the extent to which they work full- or part-time. Full-time employment levels of married women are relatively high in countries such as Sweden and Denmark (where part-time working women frequently work hours long enough to be classified as full-timers), the United States of America, and the (former) state socialist countries like Poland and Hungary, as well as China. This similarity in women's full-time participation between these countries, otherwise tremendously different, is highly significant for our cross-national comparison because full-time jobs are particularly important in breaking down sex-stereotypes and cultural barriers to women at all occupational levels. Recent labour-market studies indicate that full-time jobs normally give better access to 'male' and 'gender-mixed' occupations (Hakim 1998). In particular, the small group of 'gender-mixed' occupations which absorb a disproportionate share of service class positions (for example, the class schema developed by Erikson and Goldthorpe 1992: 38) seems to be growing rapidly as a result of the process of occupational and industrial restructuring in many countries. Thus, the best jobs in terms of earnings, status, and prestige are increasingly 'gender-mixed' occupations shared proportionately by men and women, and not male-dominated occupations (Hakim 1998). In other words, declining occupational segregation in the full-time workforce should give full-time employed wives an increasingly better lever to become equal providers or even primary earners for their families (Saltzman Chafetz 1995).

In many countries, declining occupational segregation in the full-time workforce is, however, counterbalanced and concealed by rising occupational segregation in the part-time workforce. As Hakim (1998) has noted, part-time jobs are not just diminutive versions of full-time jobs, they are jobs that mainly recruit wives who want to work as secondary earners. However, the opportunity to work part-time, as well as the composition of the part-time workforce, differs greatly in the countries studied in this book. In Italy, Spain, and in most of the (former) centrally planned economies such as Hungary, Poland, or China, very few part-time options are available. Moreover, married women of childbearing and childrearing ages are a minority among part-timers (Drobnič 1995, 1997). This means that these women either have to work full-time, as in Hungary, Poland, and China, where integrating women into paid full-time work was considered a vital strategy to achieve gender equality in the socialist/communist development. Or they have to become economically inactive, which has been the standard situation of wives in Italy and Spain.

Part-time work by married wives has grown considerably in the capitalist countries of Northern Europe since the early 1960s (Blossfeld and Hakim 1997). This is reflected in today's relatively high proportion of married women in part-time jobs in the Netherlands, West Germany, the United Kingdom, Belgium, Denmark, and Sweden. Between the late 1950s and the mid-1970s, economic growth and the overall demand for labour, accompanied by a rapid structural shift towards administrative and service jobs, led to a massive integration of wives into the part-time labour force in these countries. Part-time work was attractive for married women because it represented a convenient compromise between employment and family obligations (Blossfeld and Hakim 1997), but it hardly changed the role of part-time working wives as supplementary workers (Bernhardt 1993).

Different Welfare State Regimes

These country-specific patterns of wives' labour-force participation, as well as the extent of female full-time and part-time work, are closely (inter)related with various types of welfare state regimes. 'Regime' here refers to the typical ways in which welfare production is allocated between state, market, and households (Esping-Andersen 1990, 1999). It is important to approach the country-specific differences from such a broad theoretical perspective because husbands' and wives' employment patterns are not a matter of narrowly defined (fiscal, monetary, family, labour-market, etc.) policies. Such policies are described in detail, for example, in Dingeldey (2000), Gornick *et al.* (1997), Rubery *et al.* (1998), Stockman *et al.* (1995), Ellingsæter (1999). However, the same socio-political goals can be achieved by alternative policies, and within broader country-specific policy packages various policies can serve as functional equivalents. For example, childcare provision, which influences wives' decisions to work, can be organized primarily via public-sector provision by the state (for example, Sweden, Denmark, and (former) state socialist regimes), low-priced family care services via the market (for example, the United States), or through kinship care networks via the households (for example, Germany). The diversity of these state–market–family packages reflects cross-national differences in historical origins, cultural models, and contemporary policy goals (Gornick *et al.* 1997; Pfau-Effinger 1999).

Partly following Esping-Andersen (1990, 1999), we distinguish in this book five main clusters of regimes that are supposed to produce markedly different patterns of couples' careers: the 'conservative', the 'Mediterranean', the 'liberal', the 'social democratic', and the (former) 'state socialist' regime (see Table 2.1). We explicitly emphasize that there is no one-to-one relationship between ideal welfare regimes and individual welfare states, and a country might in some aspects significantly digress from a 'pure' welfare state regime of the form within which it is placed. Nevertheless, we believe that typologies of this kind are a useful tool to conceptualize the general contours of institutional characteristics of various societies in cross-national comparison. They also provide a theoretical orientation and facilitate the interpretation of differences and similarities found in cross-national comparisons.

The conservative welfare state in the Netherlands, West Germany, and to a lesser extent in Belgium (Flanders), supports wives and mothers who give priority to family activities (Esping-Andersen 1999). National policies are generally familialistic, in the sense that they favour wives' economic dependence on their husbands and stimulate mothers' choices for non-employment against part-time work, and part-time work against full-time employment. In other

Table 2.1. Classification of welfare state regimes

Welfare state regime	Characteristics:			Dominant locus of solidarity	Preservation of male-breadwinner family model	Effects of husband's resources on wife's employment
	egalitarian	decommodifying	defamilialistic			
Conservative: Germany, the Netherlands, Belgium (Flanders)	+	+	− −	family	++	−
Mediterranean: Italy, Spain	− −	− −	− −	family	+	−
Liberal: Great Britain, USA	− −	− −	++	market	− −	0/+
Social democratic: Denmark, Sweden	++	++	+	state	− −	++
(Former) state-socialist: Hungary, Poland, China	++	++	++	state	− −	++

Source: Adapted (and extended) from Esping-Andersen (1999).

words, this welfare state regime tends to preserve the male-breadwinner family model. The principle of subsidiarity in its present-day form means that, in these countries, a strong welfare policy guarantees the male breadwinner wage. The male-breadwinner is decommodified via income guarantees (the 'just wage'), which strengthens wives' economic dependence on their husbands and husbands' social reproduction dependency on their wives (Blossfeld and Rohwer 1997; Graaf and Vermeulen 1997). Thus, conservative welfare states typically provide low levels of childcare and day-care services (Gornick *et al.* 1997). In Germany, for example, the school day ends at lunchtime, so that only jobs with short hours in the morning become attractive to mothers. Furthermore, full-time working German dual-earner couples are punished by the tax system, which privileges wives' non-work or part-time work. Compared to the liberal welfare state, the labour market of the conservative welfare state is far more regulated and the proportion of the workforce employed in the public sector is much higher. Thus, compared to the USA or UK, most part-time jobs tend to be better protected and the proportion of marginal jobs is lower. It follows that the high part-time labour-force participation of women in the Netherlands and in Germany is basically the expression of a pervasive male breadwinner assumption (Blossfeld and Hakim 1997). Based on this welfare state regime, we assume that husbands' resources suppress wives' employment, in particular full-time employment (Table 2.1).

On almost all counts, the Mediterranean welfare states such as Italy and Spain display extremely low public provision (Esping-Andersen 1999). In fact, they have a limited focus on social assistance, and direct family benefits are truly meagre (González-López 1998). They are far less egalitarian and decommodifying than the social democratic or conservative welfare states and rather resemble the liberal welfare states. Thus, in this respect, the conservative welfare states such as West Germany or the Netherlands appear more familialistic and discourage wives' employment more than the Mediterranean model. However, the familialism of Mediterranean countries is distinct in the centrality of the family as a provider of care and ultimate responsibility-taker for its members' welfare (the subsidiarity principle) (Bettio and Villa 1998; Esping-Andersen 1999). In other words, in the Catholic familialism of Southern Europe, families are the relevant locus of social aid: parents are responsible for their children and vice versa. Thus, it is characteristic of the Mediterranean model that, with women's better education and increasing career opportunities, couples are confronted with a choice between Scylla and Charybdis: either the couple decides to follow the traditional model which is associated with the wife's economic dependency on her husband (Saraceno 1996), or it follows a dual-earner model, with both spouses working full-time and constrained fertility. In addition, the Mediterranean cohesive family model, with 'prolonged adolescence' in parental home, coupled with high youth unemployment, produced a simultaneous occurrence of low female employment participation and low fertility (Bettio and Villa 1998). In our context, given the importance of the traditional family model in the Mediterranean welfare state, we assume that the decision for wife's employment is also strongly dependent on the husband's social position (Table 2.1).

The liberal welfare states in the United Kingdom and the United States emphasize the principle of individual freedom. They accept the distributional consequences of market forces in terms of class and gender inequalities and do little to stimulate married women's labour supply by direct public policy measures in particular (Esping-Andersen 1999). Thus, on the one hand, this type of welfare state is far less egalitarian and decommodifying than the social democratic welfare state, but on the other hand, it is defamilialistic, too. Here, defamilialization is produced via market provisions. The unregulated, market-driven employment structure of the liberal welfare state produces a large pool of low-wage workers in the service sector and a declining wage rate for 'middle-class' workers, with two consequences: (1) households, especially lower-income families, increasingly have to shift time from domestic activities to market work to enjoy the benefits of the growth in the standard of living; (2) labour-intensive and cost-sensitive market services become affordable for an increasing number of households. Hence, the cheaper services, such as day-care, laundering, etc., raise the opportunity costs for families doing unpaid domestic work, particularly in the middle class. It follows that, in the United States, the cost of private care is relatively low compared to average family income, so that it is affordable at least to the 'middle class'. In other words, wives in the United States are integrated (often full-time) into the labour market via a decreasing male breadwinner market wage and the availability of inexpensive market services for the household. This implies an erosion of the male-breadwinner model and an increasing importance of wives' income for the socio-economic status of the family. Thus, at a certain point of the diffusion of the dual-earner couples, the wife's employment and income is also in the interest of the husband. We expect that the negative impact of husbands' resources on wives' employment disappears or even becomes positive.

Social democratic welfare states in Sweden and Denmark emphasize the principles of 'egalitarianism', 'de-commodification', and 'de-familialization' (Esping-Andersen 1999). The egalitarian element is expressed in that most benefits are universal in these countries. Decommodification means that the social democratic welfare state is particularly committed to comprehensive risk coverage and generous benefit levels which weaken the cash nexus. Finally, and most importantly for this study, defamilialization refers to the degree to which households' welfare and caring responsibilities are relaxed via welfare state provision. Thus, a defamilializing regime is one which seeks to unburden the household and diminish individuals' welfare dependence on kinship. The first capitalist countries to undertake a major expansion of family services—in particular childcare, residential homes, or home help for the aged—were Denmark and Sweden. 'As of today, these states remain the only welfare states meaningfully committed to a de-familialization of servicing burdens' (Esping-Andersen 1999: 55). It is now widely recognized that the compatibility of family obligations with paid (female) employment is vastly enhanced by access to care services. Thus, the social democratic welfare state radically increases women's choices in favour of (full-time and part-time) employment and decreases the economic dependence on a husband (Table 2.1). The result is an early and fast diffusion of the dual-earner model and also a relatively high fertility rate. The increase in women's employment goes hand-in-hand with an increase in public-sector jobs and growing occupational sex segregation (Esping-Andersen 1993). Since the public-sector workforce and active labour-market policies are very costly, personal tax rates are steeply progressive and relatively high. Accordingly, wives in Sweden and Denmark are integrated into the labour market by a tax system that penalizes a male breadwinner wage and offers public-sector service support to the households. Since wives' employment is ubiquitous, their income has become an important component of the family's social status, and husbands should show strong interests in their wives' labour-force participation.

Finally, the political and ideological contexts in the (former) state socialist countries such as Hungary, Poland, and China, differ profoundly from Western capitalist economies. A far-reaching redistribution of resources, egalitarian policies with regard to class and gender, and the ideology of equality of conditions were the main principles explicitly pursued by state socialist countries. In most of the former socialist countries of Central and Eastern Europe, official unemployment was non-existent or negligible, and as a rule the demand for labour exceeded the labour supply (Ferge 1992; Jackson *et al.* 1995). Work arrangements in these countries could tentatively be described as standard forms of employment, with lifelong, secure, permanent, full-time jobs for both men and women. Under state socialism, female labour-force participation was extremely high, with women accounting on average for 45–51 per cent of the total labour force in 1989–90 (Einhorn 1993). Women as a rule worked full-time; part-time work was not considered a typically female phenomenon (Drobnič 1995, 1997). These countries set up a comprehensive and relatively generous system of family benefits, including lengthy periods of paid maternity and childcare leave (Deacon *et al.* 1992; Göting 1993). The common employment pattern was based on a family model with two earners working full-time, and husband's resources should therefore have a positive effect on wife's employment (Table 2.1). After the breakdown of the socialist economies in Central and Eastern Europe, unemployment erupted, legal possibilities for fixed-term employment and part-time work have been broadened considerably, and in many respects the employment patterns in transition economies are becoming more similar to those in Western Europe. However, we do not expect that the prevailing dual-earner model will radically change, although it might be modified to some extent, depending on characteristics of individual countries.

Finally, China implemented the most determined social engineering policy aimed at eradicating the sexual division of labour in society. The principles of equality between the sexes, monogamy, freedom of choice of a marital partner, and the right to sue for divorce were laid down already in the Marriage Law of 1950. This was a radical breakaway from Confucian patriarchal values which supported a conception of the difference between the sexes, and sharply segregated roles for men and women (Stockman *et al.* 1995). In this

largest-ever real-world social experiment, . . . success was greatest in eradicating centuries-old perceptions of sex differences in ability and in the practice of male domi-nance in the household. There was also substantial success in eradicating the sexual divi-sion of labour: a low-wage full-employment policy made it necessary for all adults to work and hence for couples to share domestic work as well. (Hakim 1996: 96)

In contemporary urban China, there is a prevalence of dual full-time working among spouses and parents of young children. This is associated with a wide-spread joint conjugal sphere, with spouses sharing the domestic tasks of housework and caring for children and with greater equality in domestic deci-sion-making (Stockman *et al.* 1995: 135). China is thus unique on a number of fronts, perhaps the most important being the impact of the state on the role of the family through specific social policies (for example, the one-child pol-icy) as well as through redistributive economic institutions. It is therefore exciting to study how in this context the allocation decisions are being made and to investigate what kind of adaptive family strategies are being developed by Chinese couples.

The following country chapters have been ordered according to the classifi-cation of welfare state regimes as outlined above. They study in detail how employment strategies of husbands and wives evolve over the family life course. Given disparities in the data available for each country, only broader contrasts can be drawn between societies, and the effects of particular factors cannot be isolated and proven conclusively. None the less, comparisons of couples' careers across these dozen cases contribute a new understanding of how husbands' and wives' careers can take qualitatively different forms in dif-ferent contexts, and how the observed patterns emerge and perpetuate over the individual and the family life course.

References

Acker, J. (1988). 'Class, Gender, and the Relations of Distribution', *Signs*, 13: 473–97.

Becker, G. S. (1981). *A Treatise on the Family* (Cambridge, Mass.: Harvard University Press).

Berk, S. F. (1985). *The Gender Factory: The Apportionment of Work in American Households* (New York: Plenum Press).

Bernasco, W. (1994). *Coupled Careers: The Effects of Spouse's Resources on Success at Work* (Amsterdam: Thesis Publishers).

——P. M. de Graaf, and W. C. Ultee (1998). 'Coupled Careers: Effects of Spouse's Resources on Occupational Attainment in the Netherlands', *European Sociological Review*, 14: 15–31.

Bernhardt, E. M. (1993). 'Fertility and Employment', *European Sociological Review*, 9: 25–42.

Bettio, F., and P. Villa (1998). 'A Mediterranean Perspective on the Breakdown of the Relationship between Participation and Fertility', *Cambridge Journal of Economics*, 22: 137–71.

Bielby, W. T., and D. D. Bielby (1989). 'Family Ties: Balancing Commitments to Work and Family in Dual-Earner Households', *American Sociological Review*, 54: 776–89.

Blau, P. M. (1964). *Exchange and Power in Social Life* (New York: Wiley).

——(1994). *Structural Contexts of Opportunities* (Chicago and London: University of Chicago Press).

Blood, R. O., and D. Wolfe (1960). *Husbands and Wives: The Dynamics of Married Living* (Glencoe, Ill.: Free Press).

Blossfeld, H.-P. (1989). *Kohortendifferenzierung und Karriereprozeß: Eine Längsschnittanalyse über die Veränderung der Bildungs- und Berufschancen im Lebenslauf* (Cohort Differentiation and Career Process: A Longitudinal Analysis of the Changes in Educational and Job Opportunities over the Life Course) (Frankfurt a.M. and New York: Campus).

——(ed.) (1995). *The New Role of Women: Family Formation in Modern Societies* (Boulder, Colo.: Westview Press).

——A. DeRose, J.M. Hoem, and G. Rohwer (1995). 'Education, Modernization, and the Risk of Marriage Disruption', in K. Oppenheim Mason, and A.-M. Jensen (eds.), *Gender and Family Change in Industrialized Countries* (Oxford: Clarendon Press), 200–22.

——and C. Hakim (eds.) (1997). *Between Equalization and Marginalization: Women Working Part-Time in Europe and the United States of America* (Oxford: Oxford University Press).

——and J. Huinink (1991). 'Human Capital Investments or Norms of Role Transition? How Women's Schooling and Career Affect the Process of Family Formation', *American Journal of Sociology*, 97: 143–68.

——and G. Rohwer (1997). 'Part-Time Work in West Germany', in H.-P. Blossfeld and C. Hakim (eds.), *Between Equalization and Marginalization: Women Working Part-Time in Europe and the United States of America* (Oxford: Oxford University Press), 164–90.

——and Y. Shavit (1993). 'Persisting Barriers', in Y. Shavit and H.-P. Blossfeld (eds.), *Persistent Inequality: Changing Educational Attainment in Thirteen Countries* (Boulder, Colo.: Westview Press), 1–23.

——and A. Timm (1997). 'Der Einfluß des Bildungssystems auf den Heiratsmarkt: Eine Längsschnittanalyse der Wahl des ersten Ehepartners im Lebenslauf' (The Impact of the Educational System on the Marriage Market: A Longitudinal Analysis of First Spouse Selection), *Kölner Zeitschrift für Soziologie und Sozialpsychologie*, 49: 440–76.

——and ——(eds.) (forthcoming). *Who Marries Whom? Educational Systems as Marriage Markets in Modern Societies*.

————and F. Dasko (1997). *The Educational System as a Marriage Market: A Longitudinal Analysis of Marriage in the Life Course* (Sfb186-Working Paper, 46; Bremen: Bremen University).

Brines, J. (1994). 'Economic Dependency, Gender, and Division of Labor at Home', *American Journal of Sociology*, 100: 652–88.

Coltrane, S. (1989). 'Household Labor and the Routine Production of Gender', *Social Problems*, 36: 473–90.

Curtis, R. F. (1986). 'Household and Family in Theory of Inequality', *American Sociological Review*, 51: 168–83.

Deacon, B. M. Castle-Kanerova, N. Manning, F. Millard, E. Orosz, J. Szalai, and A. Vidinova (1992). *The New Eastern Europe: Social Policy Past, Present and Future* (Newbury Park, Calif.: Sage).

Dingeldey, I. (ed.) (2000). *Erwerbstätigkeit und Familie in Steuer- und Sozialversicherungssystemen* (Employment and Family within Tax and Social Security Systems) (Opladen: Leske + Budrich).

Drobnič, S. (1995). 'Nestandardne oblike zaposlovanja v Srednji in Vzhodni Evropi' (Non-Standard Forms of Employment in Central and Eastern Europe), *Teorija in praksa*, 32/9–10: 796–811.

——(1997). 'Part-Time Work in Central and East European Countries', in H.-P. Blossfeld and C. Hakim (eds.), *Between Equalization and Marginalization: Women Working Part-Time in Europe and the United States of America* (Oxford: Oxford University Press), 71–89.

Eggebeen, D. J., and A. J. Hawkins (1990). 'Economic Need and Wives' Employment', *Journal of Family Issues*, 11: 48–66.

Einhorn, B. (1993). *Cinderella Goes to Market: Citizenship, Gender and Women's Movements in East Central Europe* (London and New York: Verso).

Ellingsæter, A. L. (1999). 'Dual Breadwinners between State and Market', in R. Crompton, (ed.), *Restructuring Gender Relations and Employment: The Decline of the Male Breadwinner* (Oxford: Oxford University Press), 40–59.

England, P., and G. Farkas (1986). *Households, Employment, and Gender: A Social, Economic, and Demographic View* (New York: Aldine).

Erikson, R., and J. H. Goldthorpe (1992). *The Constant Flux: A Study of Class Mobility in Industrial Societies* (Oxford: Clarendon Press).

——and J. O. Jonsson (eds.) (1996). *Can Education be Equalized?* (Boulder, Colo.: Westview Press).

Esping-Andersen, G. (1990). *The Three Worlds of Welfare Capitalism* (Cambridge: Polity Press).

——(ed.) (1993). *Changing Classes: Stratification and Mobility in Postindustrial Societies* (London: Sage).

——(1999) *Social Foundations of Postindustrial Economies* (Oxford: Oxford University Press).

Fendrich, M. (1984). 'Wives' Employment and Husbands' Distress: A Meta-Analysis and a Replication', *Journal of Marriage and the Family*, 46: 871–9.

Fenstermaker, R., C. West, and D. H. Zimmerman (1991). 'Gender Inequality', in R. L. Blumberg, (ed.), *Gender, Family, and Economy: The Triple Overlap* (Newbury Park, Calif.: Sage), 289–307.

Ferge, Z. (1992). 'Unemployment in Hungary: The Need for a New Ideology', in B. Deacon (ed.), *Social Policy, Social Justice and Citizenship in Eastern Europe* (Aldershot: Avebury), 158–75.

Ferree, M. M. (1976). 'Working-Class Jobs: Housework and Paid Work as Sources of Satisfaction', *Social Problems*, 23: 431–41.

——(1987). 'Family and Job for Working-Class Women: Gender and Class Systems Seen from Below', in N. Gerstel and H. E. Gross (eds.), *Families and Work* (Philadelphia, Penn.: Temple University Press), 289–301.

Fowlkes, M. R. (1987). 'The Myth of Merit and Male Professional Careers: The Roles of Wives', in N. Gerstel and H. E. Gross (eds.), *Families and Work* (Philadelphia, Penn.: Temple University Press).

Goffman, E. (1977). 'The Arrangement between the Sexes', *Theory and Society*, 4: 301–31.

González-López, M. J. (1998). 'Do Modern Welfare States Foster Democratic Family Arrangements? Comparative Studies of Britain and Spain', *South European Society and Politics*, 3/2: 98–123.

Gornick, J. C., M. K. Meyers, and K. E. Ross (1997). 'Supporting the Employment of Mothers: Policy Variation across Fourteen Welfare States', *Journal of European Social Policy*, 7: 45–70.

Göting, U. (1993). *Welfare State Development in Post-Communist Bulgaria, Czechoslovakia, and Hungary. A Review of Problems and Responses (1989–1992)* (Working Paper 6/93; Bremen: Center for Social Policy).

Graaf, P. de, and H. Vermeulen (1997). 'Female Labour Market Participation in the Netherlands: Developments in the Relationship between Family Cycle and Employment', in H.-P. Blossfeld and C. Hakim (eds.), *Between Equalization and Marginalization: Women Working Part-Time in Europe and the United States of America* (Oxford: Oxford University Press), 191–209.

Hakim, C. (1996). *Key Issues in Women's Work: Female Heterogeneity and the Polarisation of Women's Employment* (London: Athlone Press).

——(1998). *Social Change and Innovation in the Labour Market* (Oxford: Oxford University Press).

Hartmann, H. (1976). 'Capitalism, Patriarchy, and Job Segregation by Sex', *Signs*, 1: 137–69.

Hiller, D. V. (1984). 'Power Dependence and Division of Family Work', *Sex Roles*, 10: 1003–19.

Hochschild, A., with A. Machung (1989). *The Second Shift: Working Parents and the Revolution at Home* (New York: Viking).

Huber, J. (1988). 'A Theory of Family, Economy, and Gender', *Journal of Family Issues*, 9: 9–26.

Huinink, J., and K. U. Mayer (eds.) (1995). *Kollektiv und Eigensinn: Lebensverhältnisse in der DDR und danach* (Collectivity and Subbornness: Life Conditions in the GDR and Later) (Berlin: Akademie Verlag).

Jackson, M., J. Koltay, and W. Biesbrouck (eds.) (1995). *Unemployment and Evolving Labor Markets in Central and Eastern Europe* (Aldershot: Avebury).

Jasso, G. (1988). 'Employment, Earnings, and Marital Cohesiveness: An Empirical Test of Theoretical Predictions', in M. Webster and M. Foschi (eds.), *Status Generalization: New Theory and Research* (Stanford, Calif.: Stanford University Press), 123–64.

Lee, G. (1987) 'Comparative Perspectives', in M. Sussman and S. Steinmetz (eds.), *Handbook of Marriage and the Family* (New York: Plenum Press), 59–80.

McDonald, G. W. (1977). 'Family Power: Reflection and Direction', *Pacific Sociological Review*, 20: 607–21.

McRae, S. (1986). *Cross-Class Families* (Oxford: Clarendon Press).

——(1990). 'Women and Class Analysis', in J. Clark, C. Modgil, and S. Modgil (eds.), *John H. Goldthorpe: Consensus and Controversy* (London: Falmer Press), 117–33.

Mincer, J., and S. Polachek (1974). 'Family Investments in Human Capital: Earnings of Women', *Journal of Political Economy*, 82: S76–S108.

Moen, P. (1992). *Women's Two Roles: A Contemporary Dilemma* (New York: Auburn House).

OECD (1988). 'Women's Activity, Employment and Earnings: A Review of Recent Developments', *Employment Outlook* (Paris: OECD), 129–72.

Oppenheimer, V. K. (1988). 'A Theory of Marriage Timing', *American Journal of Sociology*, 94: 563–91.

——(1993). 'Women's Rising Employment and the Fate of the Family in Modern Industrial Societies' (mimeo; Los Angeles: University of California).

——(1997). 'Women's Employment and the Gain to Marriage: The Specialization and Trading Model', *Annual Review of Sociology*, 23: 431–53.

Pananek, H. (1979). 'Family Status Production: The "Work" and "Non-work" of Women', *Signs*, 4: 775–81.

Parsons, T. (1942). 'Age and Sex in the Social Structure of the United States', *American Sociological Review*, 7: 604–16.

——and R. Bales (1966). *Family, Socialization, and Interaction Process* (New York: Free Press).

Pfau-Effinger, B. (1999). 'The Modernization of Family and Motherhood in Western Europe', in R. Crompton (ed.), *Restructuring Gender Relations and Employment: The Decline of the Male Breadwinner* (Oxford: Oxford University Press), 60–79.

Reskin, B. F. (1988). 'Men Back In: Sex Differentiation and the Devaluation of Women's Work', *Gender and Society*, 2: 58–81.

Rosen, E. I. (1987). *Bitter Choices: Blue-Collar Women in and out of Work* (Chicago, Ill.: University of Chicago Press).

Rosenfeld, R. A., and G. E. Birkelund (1995). 'Women's Part-Time Work: A Cross-National Comparison', *European Sociological Review*, 11: 111–34.

Rubery, J., M. Smith, C. Fagan, and D. Grimshaw (1998). *Women and European Employment* (London and New York: Routledge).

Saltzman Chafetz, J. (1995). 'Chicken or Egg? A Theory of the Relationship between Feminist Movements and Family Change', in K. Oppenheim Mason and A.-M. Jensen (eds.), *Gender and Family Change in Industrialized Countries* (Oxford: Clarendon Press), 63–81.

Saraceno, C. (1996) 'Family Change, Family Policies and the Restructuration of Welfare', paper presented at the OECD Conference 'Beyond 2000: The New Social Policy Agenda', Paris, OECD.

Schultz, T. W. (ed.) (1974). 'Marriage, Family Human Capital, and Fertility', *Supplement to the Journal of Political Economy*, 82.

Simpson, I. H., and P. England (1981). 'Conjugal Work Roles and Marital Solidarity', in J. Aldous (ed.), *Two Paychecks: Life in Dual-Earner Families* (Beverly Hills, Calif.: Sage),147–72.

Skolnick, A. (1987). *The Intimate Environment* (4th edn. Boston, Mass.: Little, Brown & Co).

Sokoloff, N. (1988). 'Contributions of Marxism and Feminism to the Sociology of Women and Work', in A. H. Stromberg and S. Harkess (eds.), *Women Working: Theories and Facts in Perspectives* (Mountain View, Calif.: Mayfield).

Sørensen, A., and S. McLanahan (1987). 'Married Women's Economic Dependency, 1940–1980', *American Journal of Sociology*, 93: 659–87.

Stanley, S. C., J. G. Hunt, and L.L. Hunt (1986). 'The Relative Deprivation of Husbands in Dual-Earner Households', *Journal of Family Issues*, 7: 3–20.

Stockman N., N. Boney, and Sheng Xuewen (1995). *Women´s Work in East and West: The Dual Burden of Employment and Family Life* (London: UCL).

Thoits, P. A. (1987). 'Negotiating Roles', in F. J. Crosby (ed.), *Spouse, Parent, Worker: On Gender and Multiple Roles* (New Haven, Conn.: Yale University Press), 11–22.

Thompson, L., and A. J. Walker (1989). 'Gender in Families: Women and Men in Marriage, Work, and Parenthood', *Journal of Marriage and the Family*, 51: 845–71.

Timm, A., H.-P. Blossfeld, and R. Müller (1998). 'Der Einfluß des Bildungssystems auf die Heiratsmuster in Westdeutschland und den USA: Eine vergleichende Längsschnittanalyse der Wahl des ersten Ehepartners im Lebenslauf' (The Impact of the Educational System on Marriage Patterns in West Germany and the USA: A Comparative Longitudinal Analysis of First Spouse Selection), in W. Heinz, W. Dressel, D. Blaschke, and G. Engelbrech (eds.), *Was prägt Berufsbiographien? Lebenslaufdynamik und Institutionenpolitik* (What Influences Job Biographies? Life Course Dynamic and the Polity of Institutions) (BeitrAB 215; Nuremberg, IAB: 129–66.

Walby, S. (1986). *Patriarchy at Work. Patriarchal and Capitalist Relations in Employment* (Cambridge: Polity).

——(1990). *Theorizing Patriarchy* (Oxford: Basil Blackwell).

Weber, M. (1972). *Wirtschaft und Gesellschaft* (Economy and Society) (Studienausgabe; Tübingen: Mohr).

Weiss, R. S. (1985). 'Men and the Family', *Family Process*, 24: 49–58.

——(1987). 'Men and their Wives' Work', in F. J. Crosby (ed.), *Spouse, Parent, Worker: On Gender and Multiple Roles* (New Haven, Conn.: Yale University Press), 109–21.

West, C., and D. H. Zimmerman (1987). 'Doing Gender', *Gender and Society*, 1: 125–51.

Winkler, A. E. (1998–9). 'Earnings of Husbands and Wives in Two-Earner Families', *Focus*, 20/1: 17–19.

Zavella, P. (1987). *Women's Work and Chicano Families* (Ithaca, NY: Cornell University Press).

II

The 'Conservative' Welfare State Regime

3

Spouses' Employment Careers in (West) Germany

HANS-PETER BLOSSFELD, SONJA DROBNIČ, AND GÖTZ ROHWER

Introduction

IN this chapter, we present a dynamic study on how spouses in (West) Germany[1] affect each other over the life course. Our approach is based on a symmetric perspective, trying to examine the interdependencies of husbands' and wives' transitions between full-time or part-time paid work and unpaid household work, beginning at the time of entry into marriage. What follows can therefore not be generalized for all women, all men, or women and men in non-marital unions. The extent and nature of these interdependencies within marriages, varying across the family life cycle as well as between social classes, is examined. Using data from the German Socio-Economic Panel (SOEP), an event-history analysis is used in order to consider the development of husbands' and wives' careers over the life course and across a broad range of marriage cohorts. This long-term longitudinal approach allows married couples' employment careers to be studied in the context of a changing system of social stratification. There are three specific questions that will be addressed here. (1) To what extent are the transitions between (full-time and part-time) paid market work and unpaid housework gendered within marital unions in West Germany? (2) To which degree do spouses marry assortatively and how does this affect their employment relationships over the family cycle? (3) Do class-specific differences in the division of labour between husbands and wives become more or less important across marriage cohorts?

Theoretical perspectives that guide our research are discussed in detail by Blossfeld and Drobnič in Chapter 2. Let us here briefly reiterate the main premises of the economic theory of the family that directed our empirical analysis. Economic theory argues that the partner with greater comparative

---

[1] Data refer to former West Germany only because the structure of the labour market, female employment, and family formation patterns were very different in former East Germany (Trappe and Rosenfeld 1998; Brüderl and Diekmann 1994).

advantage in the market (that is, higher wage rate) will specialize in paid work and the other partner will specialize in housework in order to maximize their shared unitary utility. This division of labour maximizes a joint utility function of the couple due to the greater resulting efficiency in the division of labour. The common preference of the spouses is guaranteed by altruism (Becker 1993).

It is important to note that the economic theory of the family predicts the division of labour between a husband and a wife on the basis of the comparative advantage and does not *per se* assign the housework to wives. This gender-neutral principle fits the empirical observations of older cohorts and can be explained by differential sex-specific investments in human capital at the beginning of marriage. However, the theory should also explain developments in the employment behaviour of husbands and wives if the earnings capacity of young people changes across birth cohorts. In West Germany, women have shown a larger increase than men at all higher levels of educational attainment across birth cohorts (Blossfeld and Shavit 1993) and their shift from relatively unskilled production and service jobs to skilled service and administration occupations has been more pronounced than that of men (Blossfeld 1987). Young German women therefore do not only stay in the educational system longer than the women of older generations, but they are better able than ever to turn higher education into better job and career opportunities (Blossfeld 1989). This growth in the earning power of younger women and their increasing labour-force experience before marriage (Blossfeld and Huinink 1991) should raise the labour-force participation of each younger cohort of married women. In combination with declining fertility across cohorts, this should allow younger married women to spend more time in the labour force prior to their first child and after the last child has entered school, and therefore reduce the aggregate time spent in childcare by young mothers. The greater number of women with better career opportunities should, however, also increase the likelihood of high-wage women marrying low-wage men. In turn, this should then lead to an increasing proportion of males relying on wives as providers, and wives relying on husbands as supplementary workers and for the maintenance of the home, as well as for the rearing of children.

In the following, we are going to assess empirically some of the hypotheses about the dynamic interrelationship of spouses over the life course in West Germany, in order to gain more insight into the basic structure of spouses' relationships and their long-term changes across marriage cohorts.

Data, Variables, and Methods

Data

Our analysis of couples' careers is based on data from the German Socio-Economic Panel (SOEP), a nationally representative longitudinal data set of persons, households, and families in the Federal Republic of Germany. The first data collection was carried out in 1984 when about 6,000 households and 12,245 individuals were interviewed, and data on their employment histories were collected retrospectively. There has been a further panel wave in every subsequent year. We used information from ten panel waves in West Germany. Since all adult members of the sample households have been interviewed individually, SOEP offers a unique opportunity to match and study couples. Since one of our aims is to study long-term changes over various cohorts and non-marital cohabitation is a relatively recent phenomenon in Germany, we limited the analysis to married couples.

For the analysis presented here, we first reconstructed individuals' employment histories from the respondent's fifteenth birthday until the time of data collection or his/her sixty-fifth year of age. Further, we extended these histories with monthly data that noted individuals' employment changes between each panel wave for the period 1983–1991. Next, we reconstructed the family histories that were recorded in the second panel wave. These data include information on the beginning and the end of (at most three) respondent's marriages in the period before 1984, as well as birth years of children for female respondents. Later, changes in marital status and childbearing history were obtained on a monthly basis from the consecutive panel waves.

Female respondents served as a basis for matching. To be included in the spouses' sample, a woman must have reported being 'married', and must have identified the person to whom she was married in at least one wave of the panel. Although theoretically it would be most appropriate to study first marriages for all cohorts, this selection criterion was abandoned in view of practical difficulties. If a person's marriage started and ended before 1984, this ex-spouse was not included in the sample and no information on him or her was available, which made the selection of the first marriage unsuitable. Therefore, the respondents' last marriages were studied. We succeeded in identifying and matching 1,289 German spouses for whom all required variables were available.

The basic spouses' data consisted of a series of respondents' employment episodes and out-of-labour-market statuses, starting with the time of marriage and ending with a right censored observation at the time of marriage dissolution or the last panel wave.

Variables

The purpose of our study is explicitly to link the dynamics of the family life course and spouses' resources with the career patterns of the family members. To be able to perform a causal analysis, we need information on underlying processes that generate the observed distribution of a person's employment statuses. Therefore, the processes of entering and leaving the labour force in the career history must be known. In the SOEP dataset, several states in respondents' employment history have been distinguished: full-time, part-time employment, housemaking, unemployed, retired, and other. Dependent variables in the analysis presented in this analysis are transition rates from (1) full-time employment to housemaking status, (2) part-time employment to housemaking, (3) housemaking status to full-time employment, and (4) housemaking to part-time employment.

There are two kinds of independent variables: time-constant, and time-varying variables which can change their states over the time of marriage. To introduce time-dependent measures into the rate equations, we used the method of episode splitting, described in detail by Blossfeld *et al.* (1989), and Blossfeld and Rohwer (1995). We split each episode in a duration of at most twelve months. For each of the sub-spells, the following pieces of information were provided: time at the beginning and end of the sub-spell as well as its location within the employment episode, values of the time-dependent covariates at the beginning of these sub-spells, whether the interval ended with an event or not, and the values of other covariates relevant for the analysis. Estimates were performed with the Transition Data Analysis (TDA) program (Rohwer 1994*a*; Rohwer and Pötter 1998).

The following sets of independent variables were included in the analysis: woman's social origin, her occupational resources, age, career history before marriage, and childrearing history, as well as her partner's occupational resources and information on marriage cohort. A more detailed description of independent variables used in the analysis can be found in the appendix to this chapter.

Methods

The longitudinal analysis of spouses' interdependent careers is a methodologically difficult endeavour because of the issue of reverse causation. Reverse causation means that one career, considered from a theoretical point of view as the dependent one, has (direct or indirect) effects on the independent covariate process(es). Reverse causation is seen as a problem in event-history analysis because the effect of a time-dependent covariate on the transition rate is confounded with a feedback effect of the dependent process on the values of the time-dependent covariate.[2]

In this analysis, we apply a 'causal approach' to the analysis of interdependent systems that was suggested and described in detail by Blossfeld and Rohwer (1995). We believe that this is a more appropriate approach for a study of spouses' careers than the normally used 'systems approach' (Tuma and Hannan 1984: ch. 9) In particular, it provides a straightforward solution to (1) the simultaneity problem of interdependent processes, (2) the identification of lags between causes and their effects, and (3) the study of temporal shapes of effects (Blossfeld and Rohwer 1995; Blossfeld *et al.* 1995). In this approach, the history and the present state of the system are seen as a condition for change in (any)

---

[2] In other words, the value of the time-dependent covariate carries information about the state of the dependent process.

one of its partial processes. Given two parallel employment careers of a husband ($Y_t{}^A$) and his wife ($Y_t{}^B$), a change in $Y_t{}^A$ at any (specific) point in time t' may depend on the history of both processes up to, but not including, t'. Or stated in another way: what happens with $Y_t{}^A$ at any point in time t' is conditionally independent of what happens with $Y_t{}^B$ at t', conditional on the history of the joint process $Y_t = (Y_t{}^A, Y_t{}^B)$ up to, but not including, t'. Of course, the same reasoning can be applied if one focuses on $Y_t{}^B$ instead of $Y_t{}^A$ as the 'dependent variable'. Blossfeld and Rohwer (1995) call this the principle of conditional independence for parallel and interdependent processes.[3]

The same idea can be developed more formally. Beginning with a transition rate model for the joint careers, $Y_t = (Y_t{}^A, Y_t{}^B)$, and assuming the principle of conditional independence, the likelihood for this model can be factored into a product of the likelihood for two separate careers: a transition rate model for $Y_t{}^A$ which is dependent on $Y_t{}^B$ as a time-dependent covariate, and a transition rate model for $Y_t{}^B$ which is dependent on $Y_t{}^A$ as a time-dependent covariate.[4] Estimating the effects of time-dependent (qualitative and metric) changes on the transition rate can easily be achieved by applying the method of episode splitting (see Blossfeld *et al.* 1989; Blossfeld and Rohwer 1995).

Results

We begin our empirical analysis of the employment careers of spouses with a description of who marries whom, then describe gender-specific employment transitions over the joint family history, and finally study the mobility between full-time or part-time work and homemaking with hazard rate models.

Assortative Mating in West Germany

In the past, research on assortative mating in Germany tended to focus on the wife's status mobility but not on that of the husband (Mayer 1977; Handl 1988; Teckenberg 1991). This is because, in conventional stratification theory, social inequality among families is thought to be determined only by the occupational attainment of the male heads of household. A woman's social status has therefore only been ascribed to her on the basis of the job position of her providers, that is, her father in the family of origin or her husband in her own family (Goldthorpe 1980, 1983). This traditional perspective is reflected in the statement that 'What a man "does" defines his status, but whom she marries defines a woman's'. The opposite perspective, that a man's social class might be affected through marriage, has therefore been widely neglected in sociological research (McRae 1986; Jones 1990). The following analysis takes a more symmetric view. It examines the job position of

---

[3] The terminology is adapted from Gardner and Griffin (1986), and Pötter (1993).
[4] The mathematical steps leading to this factorization are, in principle, very easy but unfortunately need a complex terminology. The mathematical apparatus will therefore not be given here. The mathematics can be found in Gardner and Griffin (1986), Pötter (1993), and Rohwer (1994*b*).

young men and women close to the time of marriage and compares the extent of status mobility through occupational attainment and marriage for both sexes.

Figure 3.1 shows the degree of upward and downward mobility through marriage for husbands and wives. The density of the differences between husbands' and wives' status scores clearly peaks and strongly clusters around zero. Thus, there is a great deal of endogamy and homogamy in the social statuses of spouses and most people marry within their own status group. The distribution, although slightly skewed to the right, is surprisingly symmetric. Thus, there is an upward and downward mobility through marriage for both wives *and* husbands.

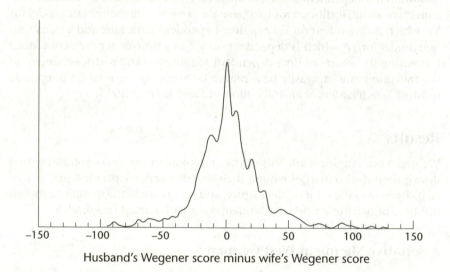

Husband's Wegener score minus wife's Wegener score

Figure 3.1. Density of occupational prestige score differences, first job

This finding raises a question about how the status of husbands and wives is measured. The occupational structure in West Germany, as in all modern societies, is highly sex-segregated (see Blossfeld 1987). The magnitude prestige scale of Wegener (1985), which certainly has a male bias, could to some degree overestimate women's social position because it could assign higher scores to occupations that are dominated by women. And a wife with a higher status than her husband, but in a female-typed occupation, may not be perceived as having a higher occupational status because the dominant feature of her occupation is not its status but its feminine identification. Thus, the 'sex-segregated labour force may provide a buffer, preventing status comparisons between spouses from being made' (Hiller and Philliber 1982). Although both of these arguments are plausible and may explain some of the differences between wives and husbands, there are many couples in our sample where the wife's status score was much higher than the husband's[5] (see Figure 3.1). Based on the economic theory of the family, one would therefore expect that within these couples, males would rely more on wives as providers, and husbands would show a tendency to specialize in the maintenance of the home and the rearing of children, as well as taking over the role of a supplementary worker. Our further analysis explores whether this is indeed the case in (West) Germany.

Another closely related issue is the intergenerational aspect of assortative mating. In Blossfeld *et al.* (1998), we plotted the status difference between father's (when the respondent was 16 years old) and daughter's or son's position (at her/his first job) against the difference in husbands' and wives' status score. Four different cases are logically possible: respondents move up occupationally when compared to their fathers and then once again through marriage; respondents move downwards occupationally, but gain in status position through marriage; respondents move up occupationally and then experience downward mobility through marriage; and finally, respondents move down occupationally and then also through marriage.

For women, all of the four logical possibilities are more or less equally distributed. However, the corresponding pattern for men indicates more intergenerational association than for women. In particular, men who have achieved a higher social position than their fathers tend to marry wives who have a social position at about the same level as their family of origin. As will be seen later on in our empirical analysis, this type of husband has the most trouble in dealing with his wife's paid employment and tends to use his wife's efforts for his own career advancement.

Employment Transitions of Husbands and Wives

In terms of occupational scores and earnings potentials of first jobs, husbands and wives show strong homogamous tendencies, which was an expected outcome of our analysis. However, a relatively large proportion of spouses also exhibit differences in their career resources, and these differences span in both directions (Figure 3.1). Not only are cases where men have considerably higher earnings potentials than their wives relatively frequent, but so are cases where women surpass their husbands in levels of career resources.

Due to high homogamy and the symmetry of the differences in earnings potentials of husbands and wives, one would expect not only a large number of wives but also a substantial number of husbands with lower earnings capacity to specialize in household production or work part-time. Thus, we were particularly interested in transitions between paid employment and out-of-the-labour-market state for both husbands and wives. However, the initial

---

[5] Empirical examples from the Socio-Economic Panel of status differences, where the scores of the wives' first jobs considerably exceed those of their husbands: the wife is a pharmacist and the husband an engine fitter; the wife is a sociologist and the husband a carpenter; the wife is a social worker and the husband an agricultural labourer; the wife is a teacher and the husband a watchmaker.

Table 3.1. Gender-specific employment transitions for couples

Origin state	Destination state	No. of events	
		Husbands	Wives
Transitions between paid work and housework:			
full-time	housemaking	25	1,243
part-time	housemaking	5	1,020
housemaking	full-time	26	465
housemaking	part-time	5	1,441
Transitions between various labour market statuses:			
full-time	part-time	136	584
part-time	full-time	133	374
full-time	unemployment	587	264
part-time	unemployment	20	172
unemployment	full-time	506	133
unemployment	part-time	22	161
unemployment	housemaking	8	262

Source: German Socio-Economic Panel.

intentions to study these moves for both spouses in parallel were swiftly abandoned after the employment trajectories for couples were examined. Table 3.1 shows how extraordinarily gender-specific the employment transitions in West Germany are. For example, among all married West German spouses that we identified in the SOEP sample, only twenty-five full-time employment episodes for husbands ended up in housemaking (Table 3.1). However, for wives, this is a common move within marriage: no less than 1,243 events of this type were recorded among the wives. Also other transitions between paid work and housemaking are very frequent for wives but negligible for husbands, so we have to conclude that employment patterns within marriages in West Germany are so gender-specific that no parallel analysis is feasible. Therefore, the following analysis will only concentrate on wives' transitions.

The crucial conclusion at this point is that the division between market work and household work among West German husbands and wives does not seem to be driven by the logic of a comparative advantage in investments in human capital. Even in those couples where wives have a much higher earnings potential than their husbands, husbands will normally work full-time and the wives—as the following analysis shows—will adjust their paid (full-time and part-time) work in response to family demands. Thus, according to the economic theory suggested by Becker (1993), the sexual division of labour within families could then only be explained by reference to biological and intrinsic differences between sexes. However, this seems to us to be a very reductionist perspective. Instead, we argue from a sociological perspective that there are pervasive gender-specific norms in the German society, as in many other modern societies, that assign the responsibility and recognition for family provision to husbands and not to wives. In addition, welfare state policies and regulations effectively support the male-breadwinner model of the family. These norms and structural support are so strong that they make comparative advantages in human capital investments meaningless for the division of work between husbands and their wives.

Transition from Full-Time Employment to Housemaking for Wives

Table 3.2 shows the 'initial' status of wives at the time of marriage across consecutive marriage cohorts. Particularly in the oldest marriage cohort, the proportion of housewives around the time of marriage is relatively high; however, this proportion falls in younger cohorts. In the 1960s and 1970s, almost three-quarters of newly married women worked full-time. This high percentage of full-timers continued for younger cohorts but has been somewhat eroded for women married in the second part of the 1980s, when unemployment seized a non-negligible share of the female labour force. In spite of that, the general pattern is that a large majority of women work full-time at the time when they marry. This makes full-time work a natural starting-point for the analysis of transitions in employment states for married women

Table 3.2. Women's employment status at the time of marriage, for various marriage cohorts (%)

	Married by 1954	Married 1955–64	Married 1965–74	Married 1975–84	Married in 1985 or later
Full-time empl.	57	73	74	70	68
Part-time empl.	5	6	4	8	6
Housewife	29	16	12	11	13
Other[a]	9	5	10	11	13
Total	100	100	100	100	100

Source: German Socio-Economic Panel.
[a] Other statuses: in school or vocational training, student, unemployed, retired, on childcare leave, other.

Table 3.3 presents the estimated effects on the hazard rate of employment exits. Piecewise constant rate models have been used to control for the duration dependence in employment. For full-time employment (Models 1 to 4), the general pattern in this transition is a low initial exit rate, which increases in the period when the woman is in employment for six to twelve months; afterwards the rate falls continuously over the time spent in employment. Since our main purpose in this analysis is to examine the effects of the family

Table 3.3. Effects on the transition rate from employment to housemaking

	Full-time employment to housemaking, N=639				Part-time employment to housemaking, N=545			
	Model 1	Model 2	Model 3	Model 4	Model 5	Model 6	Model 7	Model 8
Duration < 6 months	−2.8541**	−3.1433**	−3.3040**	−3.2719**	−5.0438**	−5.7166**	−5.8892**	−5.9363**
Duration 6–12 months	−0.9020	−1.1623**	−1.3164***	−1.2869***	−5.3273**	−5.9876**	−6.1578***	−6.1825***
Duration 1–3 years	−1.5612**	−2.0456**	−2.1948***	−2.1651***	−5.5206**	−6.1668**	−6.3338***	−6.3218***
Duration 3–5 years	−1.6155**	−2.1723**	−2.3056***	−2.2760***	−6.1013**	−6.7141**	−6.8753***	−6.7982***
Duration > 5 years	−1.7915**	−2.2761**	−2.3956***	−2.3710***	−6.9614**	−7.4712**	−7.6255***	−7.4593***
W's social origin	0.0015	0.0011	−0.0000	−0.0002	0.0025	0.0024	0.0023	0.0032*
W's education	−0.0207	−0.0084	−0.0412	−0.0382	0.0385	0.0403	0.0303	0.0279
W's occupational score	−0.0057**	−0.0057**	−0.0079***	−0.0075***	−0.0024	−0.0032	−0.0032	−0.0053*
W's full-time before marr.	0.0014	0.0010	0.0011	0.0009	−0.0001	−0.0002	−0.0002	0.0010
W's part-time before marr.	−0.0080	−0.0080	−0.0076	−0.0079	0.0015	0.0013	0.0013	0.0026
W's age	−0.1997**	−0.2283**	−0.2401**	−0.2423**	0.0269	0.0592	0.0591	0.0485
W's age sq.	0.0016**	0.0024**	0.0025**	0.0025**	−0.0002	−0.0006	−0.0006	−0.0001
W's age at marriage	0.0668**	0.0679**	0.0710**	0.0749**	−0.0020	−0.0020	−0.0003	−0.0377***
No. of children		−0.0527	−0.0280	−0.0302		0.0774*	0.0785*	0.0781*
Youngest child is								
pre-school		1.2426**	1.2457**	1.2283**		−0.0044	0.0043	−0.0469
school age		−0.0841	−0.0708	−0.0788		−0.3064**	−0.3083***	−0.3429***
18 years or older		−0.4171	−0.4240	−0.4265		−0.6317**	−0.6375***	−0.7512***
H's social origin			−0.0042**	−0.0041**			−0.0027	−0.0027
H's education			0.0666**	0.0652**			0.0413*	0.0362*
H's occupational score			0.0040*	0.0038*			−0.0023	−0.0017
Married 1955–64				−0.0455				0.0734
Married 1965–74				−0.0548				0.8701**
Married 1975–84				−0.1542				1.0105**
Married 1985–				−0.1190				1.4943**

SOEP, piecewise constant model. ** p ≤ .05; * p ≤ .10

cycle and the spouse, the specification of the baseline rate only serves for control purposes and will not be interpreted substantively.

In model 1, we first estimate wives' own characteristics on the likelihood that they will interrupt their employment: social origin, education, occupational score of their first job, employment career before marriage, and age. The effect of social origin is not statistically significant, indicating that social origin in itself does not directly explain women's behaviour in the labour market. However, higher status families typically provide better opportunities for higher educational attainment, which, in turn, increases labour-market chances and the attractiveness of paid employment. Indeed, if only social origin and education are included in model estimations, wives' schooling has a strong negative effect on employment interruptions (not shown). However, when wives' first job is included in model 1, it becomes evident that, not the abstract educational level in itself, but the market value of this education is decisive in governing their labour-market behaviour. It is only when a woman is able to translate her educational resources into a 'good' job that her attachment to the labour market within marriage increases.

Age has been included in this model in linear and quadratic form to assess the baseline rate over the life course. Age also orders multiple episodes over the life span and is in many cases a good proxy for different stages in the individual life course. The shape of the hazard rate has a decreasing tendency over the life cycle and only reverses its direction at the age of 62. Here it should be noted, however, that only married women are included in our sample and the observation starts at the time of marriage. Marriage age also has a strong statistically significant impact on wives' employment interruptions; the older the women are when they marry, the more rapidly they leave full-time employment. This is quite a surprising result and demands careful consideration.[6] Previous empirical analyses have shown that a longer participation in the educational system shifts women's entering into marriage to older ages (Blossfeld and Huinink 1991). Education thus has two contradicting effects on wives' labour-market interruptions. On the one hand, higher education results in better occupational opportunities and better jobs, which prevents women from leaving paid work. On the other, longer schooling typically increases the age at marriage (Oppenheimer 1988; Blossfeld 1995), which leads to earlier interruptions. The explanation for this may be that a woman who marries late is more likely to be in a situation where her family can afford her non-employment.

To illustrate these complex and not readily obvious results of our event-history analysis, we simulated a series of examples that should provide a more straightforward insight into the estimated effects of the independent variables on the non-observable hazard rate. Figure 3.2 presents the estimated effects of covariates on the likelihood to quit a full-time job and become a housewife for two different women. Both of them married at the age of 25; one of them is a

---

[6] A similar finding was reported for the United States (Sørensen 1983).

secretary (occupational score on the Wegener scale=65); the other is a medical doctor with the highest possible occupational score of 186.8. The fact that no information on children and partner is used is a common situation in standard labour-market analyses. In this graph, we can easily see how both women experience a falling shape in the hazard rate across the age span from 25 to 55. The secretary, with lower occupational resources, has a higher tendency to interrupt her employment; the difference is particularly large in younger ages.[7] These results corroborate hypotheses of the human capital theory.

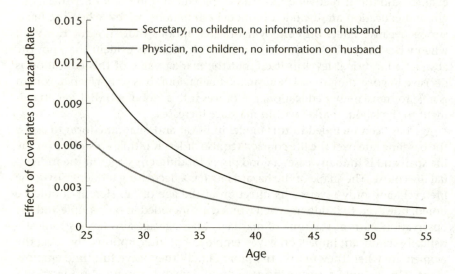

Figure 3.2. Transition from full-time employment to housemaking

At the next stage, we include information on children in the analysis. Because of the gender-specific division of labour within the family and the labour market in West Germany, wives' employment patterns are particularly affected by the number and age of children. These factors have been included in a time-varying form and the results are presented in model 2 (Table 3.3). Not surprisingly, there is a strong effect of a pre-school child in the family on the mother's transition rate to housemaking. The presence of a pre-school child increases the transition rate by 246 per cent.[8] The effect is clearly visible in Figure 3.3, where it has been assumed that both the secretary and the physician had their first child at the age of 29 and the second one at the age of 32.

---

[7] Note: the illustrative figures in this chapter do not display the actual level of the hazard rate and should therefore not be interpreted as such. The baseline rate has been omitted from our calculations in order to avoid a mingling of the covariate effects with the baseline rate which is not constant over the duration of the episodes.

[8] Since (exp(1.2426)–1)*100%=246%.

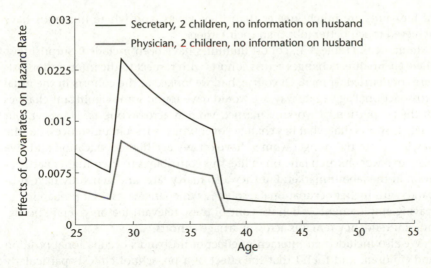

Figure 3.3. Transition from full-time employment to housemaking

Again, both women display a similar shape but the secretary with less career resources displays a higher likelihood to quit employment. The rate falls considerably only after the second child reaches school age. This is again in agreement with human capital theory.

We finally elaborate our model further to specify the extent to which wives' labour-market exits depend on their husbands' resources. In model 3 (Table 3.3), all the previous covariates that refer to women's characteristics and children remain significant, and at the same time strong effects of partners are detected. The higher the husband's education, the faster women leave their employment. This effect is additionally strengthened by a good occupational position of the husband. Overall, husband's resources have an impeding effect on wife's labour-force participation. Similar results have been found in other studies (Bernasco 1994; Ferber and Huber 1979; Erzberger 1993). The positive effect of husband's education remains a bit of a puzzle. The typical argument from the economic theories that education is an indicator of higher earnings which in effect induces specialization in the household is questionable. The effect of education also remains present when we include husbands' earnings capacity in terms of their jobs.[9]

Another interesting result that emerges shows how behaviour patterns are mediated through social relations across generations. In models 3 and 4, there is a strong significant negative effect of husband's social origin on his wife's hazard rate. This means that particularly men who come from lower status families, but themselves have succeeded in reaching good occupational positions, tend to put pressure on their wives to quit their employment. In sum, the most traditional division of labour is found in families where the resources

---

[9] Also Bernasco (1994), who directly included information on husbands' earnings in his estimation of exit rates of Dutch women, found a persistent and substantial effect of husband's education.

of husbands are much greater than their wives' and where husbands have achieved much better jobs than their fathers.

In model 4 (Table 3.3), cohort dummies have been included. Surprisingly, there are no direct changes across cohorts with respect to the interruption patterns of married women. Of course, had we looked at the cohorts in the usual cross-sectional aggregate way, we would have found some significant changes in the proportion of working married women across cohorts. However, our analysis shows that what has changed over time are the circumstances, not the baseline pattern. Younger women have on average higher education and give birth to fewer children later on in life; this contributes to their higher participation in the labour market. But they also marry later and generally have husbands with higher occupational resources, which increases their probability of leaving employment. When we control these relevant factors overall, no significant tendency remains across marriage cohorts.

We also included an interaction effect of husband's occupational position and children, and found that the effect of a pre-school child is particularly strong in families where a husband has a higher occupational status (not shown). In such families, the option of not working is more affordable for women. Also, higher education and higher income enhance the family's demand for (or ability to produce) 'child quality' (Even 1987; Gronau 1973) and increase the value of home-made goods and services (Joesch 1994).

Again, we simulated various situations to illustrate how the effects of husbands modify the transition rate of wives from full-time employment to housemaking. In Figure 3.4, upper graph, we included information on husband's schooling and job position in our example cases. A secretary and a female physician, married at the age of 25 and having two children, are now both married to a husband with eleven years of education and a rather low occupational score of 40. Neither woman is very likely to interrupt their work and the difference in the hazard rate between them becomes very small. Thus, to some extent, the wives' employment interruptions in Germany reflect the system of social inequalities. There seems to be a strong impact of the economic needs of the family on women's employment. When husbands cannot provide sufficient financial support, wives tend to stay in full-time employment and, in such a situation, the effects of small children are also moderate.

The situation would have been very different if both women were married to a physician, as shown in middle graph in Figure 3.4. Now the rate for both women increases somewhat already at the beginning of marriage and escalates—particularly for the secretary—at the time of birth of the first child. This suggestively illustrates the impact of husband's position on his wife's employment behaviour. Particularly when the husband has a much higher occupational position than his wife—that is, when the differences in resources that the couple brings into the marriage are large—there is a tremendous influence on her likelihood to become a housewife. In such households, the traditional family pattern with strict division of market work for husband and domestic work for wife is most commonly found. It is interesting to note that the impact

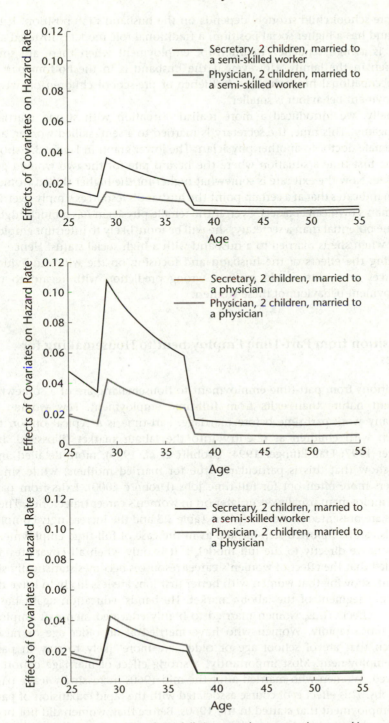

Figure 3.4. Transition from full-time employment to housemaking

of a pre-school child strongly depends on the husband's job position. If the husband has a higher social position, a traditional role model is fostered and there is a high tendency to interrupt employment when there are small children in the family. However, if the husband is in the bottom part of the occupational hierarchy, the influence of pre-school children on wives' employment behaviour is smaller.

Finally, we introduced a more realistic situation with strong marriage homogamy. This time, the secretary is married to a semi-skilled worker, and the female doctor to another physician. The lower graph in Figure 3.4 shows for the first time a situation where the hazard rate for the two women gets reversed. Now the exit rate is somewhat higher for the higher skilled woman, which indicates that at a certain point the husband's resources simply override a woman's own career assets. Even if the female physician has a much higher income potential than a secretary, she will be more likely to interrupt employment when she is married to a husband with a high social status. Hence, by omitting the effects of the husband and focusing on the wife's individual resources only, one would make a wrong prediction with regard to the employment behaviour of these women.

Transition from Part-Time Employment to Housemaking for Wives

Transitions from part-time employment to housemaking are of a somewhat different nature than exits from full-time employment. Few women in Germany work part-time before marriage. Part-time is a typical option for women with children at re-entry into the labour market (Blossfeld and Rohwer 1997; Pfau-Effinger 1994; Drobnič et al. 1999); more detailed analyses show that this is particularly true for married mothers, while single mothers more often opt for full-time jobs (Drobnič 2000). Exits from part-time employment usually occur later on in women's career trajectories. These results are presented in models 5–8 in Table 3.3 and the increasingly complex models can be followed step-by-step as in the case of full-time employment. Let us move directly to the full model 8. It is only when all covariates are included that the effect of women's career resources becomes statistically significant, showing that women with better first jobs are less likely to leave the part-time segment of the labour market. Husbands' education again has a positive effect. Thus, women married to highly educated men exit employment more rapidly. Women who have married at an older age or raised children that are of school age or older, are more likely to stay in part-time employment. Most importantly, a strong effect of marriage cohort is observed. Women who married after the mid-1960s increasingly leave part-time jobs. This effect is of course associated with the rapid expansion of part-time employment that started in the 1960s. Before that, women did not hold part-time jobs and could therefore not leave them. The result also shows that part-time work is a more transient employment form—it is often accepted and often quit.

Transition from Housemaking to Full-Time Employment for Wives

It has already been shown that no changes in the inclination to exit full-time employment occurred across cohorts, apart from changes resulting from the changed composition of the female labour force. However, the labour-force participation rate of women rose during the periods under consideration. A logical explanation for that phenomenon is that women must have been re-entering the labour force after the interruption faster and on a more massive scale. Let us first have a look at the (re)entries into full-time jobs in Table 3.4, models 1–4. The first unexpected result is that women's entry into full-time employment is independent of their educational level and career resources. However, it does depend on their husband's resources. A higher occupational status of the husband decreases the hazard rate, as shown in model 4.

A substantive change in terms of married women in full-time employment in West Germany has only come about since the mid-1980s, but this change is by no means trivial. Women in younger marriages are almost four times more likely to move from housemaking to full-time employment than women who married before the mid-1980s.[10] However, with the increased flow into the labour market, the differentiation between social classes became more pronounced, too. The rate of entering full-time employment increased for all women but was disproportionally strong for those women whose husbands have a low occupational status. Thus, full-time employment of married women seems to be fostered by the economic need of the family to a large extent. With a more massive entering into the full-time segment of the labour market, however, the household composition gains in importance. Young children play a much more important role for these women than earlier, when the group of women entering full-time jobs was small and highly selective. With full-time work becoming increasingly common, particularly in households with less resources from the husband, it also becomes more life-cycle-specific, with children having a strong inhibiting effect (see illustrative examples in Blossfeld *et al.* 1998).

Transition from Housemaking to Part-Time Employment for Wives

It has been shown that full-time employment has only recently gained in importance for married women after the family interruption. Part-time work,

---

[10] An important impetus for this development was probably the extension of the child-raising leave (*Erziehungsurlaub*). Since January 1986, a parent who cares for and brings up his/her child in the household, and is not gainfully employed or does not work full-time, is entitled to an income-tested child-raising allowance until the child is 2 years old. The person is also guaranteed a workplace if he/she returns to work within three years of the child's birth.

.Table 3.4. Effects on the transition rate from housemaking to employment

	Housemaking to full-time employment, N=242				Housemaking to part-time employment, N=762			
	Model 1	Model 2	Model 3	Model 4	Model 5	Model 6	Model 7	Model 8
Duration < 6 months	-7.1546**	-6.1942**	-6.0386**	-5.9494**	-10.3845**	-9.4911**	-9.6127**	-9.7503**
Duration 6–12 months	-7.3378**	-6.3472**	-6.1916**	-6.0698**	-11.3160**	-10.4177**	-10.5362**	-10.5998**
Duration 1–3 years	-7.5153**	-6.4578**	-6.2960**	-6.1318**	-11.5630**	-10.6424**	-10.7532**	-10.7143**
Duration 3–5 years	-7.8884**	-6.7846**	-6.6171**	-6.4076**	-12.2240**	-11.2850**	-11.3905**	-11.2694**
Duration > 5 years	-8.4071**	-7.4872**	-7.2989**	-7.0597**	-12.8159**	-11.9564**	-12.0527**	-11.6934**
W's social origin		-0.0051	-0.0035	-0.0037	0.0007	0.0006	0.0010	0.0018
W's education		0.0101	0.0439	0.0131	0.1269**	0.1316**	0.1479**	0.0994**
W's occupational score		-0.0025	-0.0001	-0.0005	0.0004	0.0009	0.0023	0.0005
W's full-time before marr.		-0.0037*	-0.0040**	-0.0031	0.0000	0.0001	-0.0002	-0.0001
W's part-time before marr.		-0.0045	-0.0050	-0.0044	0.0059**	0.0055**	0.0053**	0.0068**
W's age		0.1019**	0.1035*	0.1038*	0.3831**	0.3226**	0.3204**	0.2769**
W's age sq.		-0.0018**	-0.0018***	-0.0017**	-0.0045**	-0.0038**	-0.0037**	-0.0027**
W's age at marriage		-0.0081	-0.0019	-0.0214	-0.1030**	-0.0964**	-0.0907**	-0.1292**
No. of children		0.1274**	0.1195**	0.1197**		0.0806**	0.0748**	0.1066**
Youngest child is								
pre-school		-0.7056**	-0.6968**	-0.7925**		-0.1500	-0.1437	-0.3340**
school age		0.0471	0.0474	-0.0037		0.1691	0.1774	-0.0178
18 years or older		0.3224	0.3184	0.2287		-0.3225	-0.3114	-0.5589**
H's social origin			0.0007	-0.0000			-0.0042*	-0.0034*
H's education			-0.0525				0.0204	0.0156*
H's occupational score			-0.0052	-0.0075**			-0.0053*	-0.0047**
Married 1955–64				-0.1621				0.9958**
Married 1965–74				0.0774				1.8577**
Married 1975–84				0.2571				2.5384**
Married 1985-				1.3501**				2.9691**

SOEP, piecewise constant model. ** p ≤ .05; * p ≤ .10

on the other hand, has been the major engine of change in female employment in West Germany for decades (Table 3.4, models 5–8). In the transition from housemaking to part-time employment, women's own resources, children, the partner's resources, as well as the overall increase in the availability of part-time jobs, play an important role.

If only information on women is available, the rate of entry into part-time employment gives a smooth non-monotone shape over the life course. Women's own resources increase their attachment to the labour market. When information on children is included, the rate decreases but the shape remains basically the same. It is only when the husband's characteristics and the historic period in which the couple got married is known that the whole spectrum of variation in females' life courses becomes visible. For example, a woman with low education, with two children, married in the 1950s to a husband of either high or low social status, had an extremely low likelihood of entering part-time employment. Consequently, her household characteristics were basically unimportant. A woman in such a situation remained a housewife or perhaps entered full-time employment.

In the 1980s, circumstances changed dramatically. The woman's own educational level strongly augmented her entrance into part-time employment. In addition, the household's characteristics became very important. When a woman's own characteristics are held constant, the husband's resources play a contradictory role in the wife's employment behaviour. On the one hand, his education fosters the wife's employment (Table 3.4, model 8). Higher educated husbands perhaps recognize that employment for its own sake might be important for women, and a part-time working wife does not threaten their gender identity. However, husbands' high occupational status has a negative effect on their wives' labour-market participation, even for part-time employment. It seems that, in spite of higher education, men keep their traditional role expectations. The higher their occupational position—particularly when it is much higher relative to the wife's own career resources—the more power they wield in the bargaining position over their wives' employment.

Thus, higher status husbands decrease the likelihood of their wives' entry into part-time jobs. Also, the effects of children have become more pronounced for these younger marriage cohorts (see graphical simulations in Blossfeld *et al.* 1998). When pre-school children are present in the household, or if the couple has grown-up children, the entry rate decreases. The number of children, however, increases the entry rate. These are fairly complex patterns, which reflect household responsibilities and the time requirements of children, as well as the need for a supplementary income in larger families.

Summary and Conclusion

The purpose of this study has been to explore: (1) to which degree spouses marry assortatively and how this affects their employment patterns over the family life cycle; (2) to what extent the transitions between (full-time and part-time) paid work and unpaid household work are gendered within marital unions; (3) whether there are class-specific differences in the division of labour between husbands and wives and if yes, to what degree do they change across marriage cohorts.

In terms of career resources and earnings potentials of first jobs, spouses show strong homogamous tendencies. However, a considerable proportion of couples also exhibit differences in their career resources, and these differences span in both directions. Not only are cases where men have higher earnings potentials than their wives relatively frequent, but so are those where women surpass their husbands in their levels of career resources.

Within the marital union, this initial symmetry, which should in effect imply similar employment patterns for husbands and wives in marital unions, becomes very skewed with regard to moves between paid work and unpaid household work. This clearly contradicts the 'comparative advantage' thesis of the economic theory of the family. The moves between labour market and household work are extremely gender-specific in West Germany and can only be studied for women.

Contrary to the individualistic approaches frequently used in labour-market and social mobility studies, we have demonstrated that married women's employment behaviour can only be understood in its household context. Women who are predominantly in full-time employment at the time of marriage continue to interrupt their employment at the birth of the first child. This does not mean that women's own resources do not matter. Well-educated women with higher career resources and income potential are less likely to interrupt their careers and—had they interrupted—are more likely to re-enter the part-time segment of the labour market. This corroborated the human capital theory. In addition, there is a general trend across marriage cohorts increasingly to re-enter paid employment after the interruption. This has been true for part-time employment for a long time, and has also become more common for full-time employment in the last decade. Wives' work has become an important condition for achieving and maintaining a higher standard of living in West Germany.

However, our analysis also shows that there are strong effects of husbands on their wives' employment careers. The higher the occupational position of the husband, the stronger the impact on their wives to leave and stay out of the labour market. This is particularly pronounced in cases where the husband has considerably more earnings potential than his wife. However, even when the wife has substantial resources at her own disposal, high career resources of the husband may override her own career potential. This has been shown in our example for employment interruptions—when a highly skilled wife, married to a high-status man, had a higher interruption rate than a less-skilled woman married to a man with lower income potential.

Another interesting finding is that the husband's social origin tends to have a more distinct impact on the wife's employment behaviour than her own social origin. The most traditional family patterns, with strong specialization of the husband on market work and the wife in the domestic sphere, are found in cases where the husband comes from a lower-class family, experiences an upward mobility in the occupational hierarchy, and then marries a woman with lower career resources. This could be interpreted as a sign that upwardly mobile men need stronger support from their wives within the domestic sphere in order to succeed in their careers. Thus, these wives in particular accommodate their own careers and behave very traditionally.

Finally, a clear trend of the increasing effects of children and spouses on women at the stage of re-entry into the labour market is visible across the cohorts. In the past, married women typically interrupted their employment because of household and childcare responsibilities, and only small proportions of them re-entered the labour force. Those who re-entered either did so for financial reasons or valued other rewards of occupational achievement; in any case, the impact of the household structure and the occupational position of their husbands had little effect on the likelihood of re-entering. However, when a rising proportion of women opt for employment, their employment patterns become increasingly dependent on the household situation, that is, the number and ages of children, and the social class of their husbands. Hence, some traditional structural determinants of the life course of wives may be changing in contemporary modern societies, but at the same time new distinct gender and class structural parameters come into play.

References

Becker, G. S. (1993 [1981]): *A Treatise on the Family* (enlarged edn. Cambridge, Mass.: Harvard University Press).

Bernasco, W. (1994). *Coupled Careers: The Effects of Spouse's Resources on Success at Work* (Amsterdam: Thesis Publishers).

Blossfeld, H.-P. (1987). 'Labor Market Entry and the Sexual Segregation of Careers in the Federal Republic of Germany', *American Journal of Sociology*, 93: 89–118.

——(1989). *Kohortendifferenzierung und Karriereprozeß: Eine Längsschnittanalyse über die Veränderung der Bildungs- und Berufschancen im Lebenslauf* (Cohort Differentiation and Career Process: A Longitudinal Analysis of the Changes in Educational and Job Opportunities over the Life Course) (Frankfurt a.M.: Campus).

——(ed.) (1995). *The New Role of Women: Family Formation in Modern Societies* (Boulder, Colo.: Westview Press).

——and J. Huinink (1991). 'Human Capital Investments or Norms of Role Transition? How Women's Schooling and Career Affect the Process of Family Formation', *American Journal of Sociology*, 97: 143–68.

——and G. Rohwer (1995). *Techniques of Event History Modeling: New Approaches to Causal Analysis* (Mahwah, NJ: Erlbaum).

——and ——(1997). 'Part-Time Work in West-Germany', in H.-P. Blossfeld and C. Hakim (eds.), *Between Equalization and Marginalization: Women Working Part-Time in Europe and the United States* (Oxford: Oxford University Press), 164–90.

Blossfeld, H.-P. and Y. Shavit (1993). 'Persisting Barriers', in Y. Shavit and H.-P. Blossfeld (eds.), *Persistent Inequality: Changing Educational Attainment in Thirteen Countries* (Boulder, Colo.: Westview Press), 1–23.

——S. Drobnič, and G. Rohwer (1998). 'Les trajectoires professionnelles des couples mariés en Allemagne: Une étude longitudinale de long terme de carrières des époux en Allemagne de l'Ouest' (Occupational Trajectories of Married Couples in Germany: A Long-Term Longitudinal Analysis of Spouses' Careers in West Germany), *Revue française de sociologie*, 39/2: 305–51.

——A. Hamerle, and K. U. Mayer (1989). *Event History Analysis* (Hillsdale, NJ: Erlbaum).

——E. Klijzing, K. Pohl, and G. Rohwer (1995). 'Modellierung paralleler und interdependenter Prozesse in der Bevölkerungswissenschaft' (Modelling of Parallel and Interdependent Processes in Demography), *Zeitschrift für Bevölkerungswissenschaft*, 21: 29–56.

Brüderl, J., and A. Diekmann (1994). 'Bildung, Geburtskohorte und Heiratsalter: Eine vergleichende Untersuchung des Heiratsverhaltens in Westdeutschland, Ostdeutschland und den Vereinigten Staaten' (Education, Birth Cohort, and Marriage Age: A Comparative Study of Marriage in West Germany, East Germany and the U.S.), *Zeitschrift für Soziologie*, 23/1: 56–73.

Drobnič, S. (2000). 'Effects of Children on Married and Lone Mothers' Employment in the United States and (West) Germany', *European Sociological Review*, 6/2: 137–57.

——H.-P. Blossfeld, and G. Rohwer (1999). 'Dynamics of Women's Employment Patterns over the Family Life Course: A Comparison of the United States and Germany', *Journal of Marriage and the Family*, 61: 133–46.

Erzberger, C. (1993). *Erwerbsarbeit im Eheleben. Männlicher und weiblicher Erwerbsverlauf zwischen Dependenz und Unabhängigkeit* (Employment within Marriage: Life Courses of Men and Women between Interdependence and Independence) (Sfb 186 Arbeitspapier, 16; Bremen: University of Bremen).

Even, W. E. (1987). 'Career Interruptions Following Childbirth', *Journal of Labor Economics*, 5: 255–77.

Ferber, M., and J. Huber (1979). 'Husbands, Wives, and Careers', *Journal of Marriage and the Family*, 41/1: 315–25.

Gardner, W., and W. A. Griffin (1986). 'A Structural-Causal Model for Analyzing Parallel Streams of Continuously Recorded Discrete Events' (mimeo; University of Washington).

Goldthorpe, J. H. (1980). *Social Mobility and Class Structure in Modern Britain* (Oxford: Clarendon Press).

——(1983). 'Women and Class Analysis: In Defence of the Conventional View', *Sociology*, 17/4: 465–88.

Gronau, R. (1973). 'The Effect of Children on the Housewife's Value of Time', *Journal of Political Economy*, 81: 168–99.

Handl, J. (1988). *Berufschancen und Heiratsmuster von Frauen* (Job Opportunities and Marriage Patterns) (Frankfurt A.M. and New York: Campus).

Hiller, D. V., and W. W. Philliber (1982). 'Predicting Marital and Career Success among Dual-Worker Couples', *Journal of Marriage and the Family*, 44/1: 53–62.

Joesch, J. M. (1994). 'Children and the Timing of Women's Paid Work after Childbirth: A Further Specification of the Relationship', *Journal of Marriage and the Family*, 56: 429–40.

Jones, G. (1990). 'Marriage Partners and their Class Trajectories', in G. Payne and P. Abbott (eds.), *The Social Mobility of Women* (London: Falmer Press), 101–19.

McRae, S. (1986). *Cross-Class Families* (Oxford: Clarendon Press).

Mayer, K. U. (1977). *Statushierarchie und Heiratsmarkt* (Status Hierarchy and Marriage Market) (Universität Mannheim, Habilitationsschrift).

Oppenheimer, V. K. (1988). 'A Theory of Marriage Timing', *American Journal of Sociology*, 94/3: 946–61.

Pfau-Effinger, Birgit (1994). 'Erwerbspartnerin oder berufstätige Ehefrau: Sozio-kulturelle Arrangements der Erwerbstätigkeit von Frauen im Vergleich' (Employment Partner or Working Wife: Sociocultural Arrangements of Women's Labour Force Participation in Comparison), *Soziale Welt*, 45/3: 322–37.

Pötter, U. (1993). 'Models for Interdependent Decisions over Time', in J. Janssen and C. H. Skiadas (eds.), *Applied Stochastic Models and Data Analysis* (Singapore: World Scientific Publishers), 767–79.

Rohwer, G. (1994*a*). *TDA Working Papers* (Bremen: University of Bremen).

——(1994*b*). *Kontingente Lebensverläufe: Soziologische und statistische Aspekte ihrer Beschreibung und Erklärung* (Contingent Life Courses: Sociological and Statistical Aspects of their Description and Explanation) (Universität Bremen, Habilitationsschrift).

——and U. Pötter (1998). *TDA User's Manual. Version I* (Bochum: Ruhr-Universität Bochum).

Sørensen, A. (1983). 'Women's Employment Patterns after Marriage', *Journal of Marriage and the Family*, 45: 311–21.

Teckenberg, W. (1991). *Sozialstruktur als differentielle Assoziation* (Social Structure and Differential Association) (Universität Heidelberg, Habilitationsschrift).

Trappe, H., and R. A. Rosenfeld (1998). 'A Comparison of Job-Shifting Patterns in the Former East Germany and the Former West Germany', *European Sociological Review*, 14/4: 343–68.

Tuma, N. B. and M. T. Hannan (1984). *Social Dynamics: Models and Methods* (Orlando, Fla.: Academic Press).

Wegener, B. (1985). 'Gibt es Sozialprestige?' (Does Social Prestige Exist?), *Zeitschrift für Soziologie*, 14/3: 209–35.

APPENDIX TO CHAPTER 3: THE LIST OF INDEPENDENT VARIABLES

Variable	Variable Type	Operationalization / Measurement
Wife's stratification variables:		
Social origin	time-constant	her father's occupational status, measured by the Wegener (1985) occupational score
Education	time-constant	years of schooling
Career resources	time-constant	occupational status of first job, measured by the Wegener occupational score

Variable	Variable Type	Operationalization / Measurement
Wife's age and career history before marriage:		
Full-time work experience	time-constant	cumulative duration of her employment in full-time jobs before marriage
Part-time work experience	time-constant	cumulative duration of her employment in part-time jobs before marriage
Age	time-varying	in a linear and quadratic form
Age at marriage	time-constant	
Wife's childrearing history:		
Number of children	time-varying	
Pre-school child	time-varying dummy	youngest child is up to 6 years of age
School child	time-varying dummy	no child younger than 6 but at least one child 7–17 years of age
Child 18	time-varying dummy	no child younger than 18 but at least one child of age 18 and over
Husband's resources:		
Social origin	time-constant	his father's occupational status, measured by the Wegener occupational score
Education	time-constant	years of schooling
Career resources	time-constant	occupational status of first job, measured by the Wegener occupational score
Marriage cohorts:		
Married 1955–64	time-constant dummy	
Married 1965–74	time-constant dummy	
Married 1975–84	time-constant dummy	
Married 1985 or later	time-constant dummy	

The reference category for the children variables is 'no children'. The reference category for marriage cohorts are couples married in the period before 1955.

4

Couples' Labour-Market Participation in the Netherlands

JOHN HENDRICKX, WIM BERNASCO, AND PAUL M. DE GRAAF

Introduction

T HE Netherlands, a progressive country in many respects, has a surprisingly traditional division of labour between spouses. The husband's traditional role of breadwinner is still largely unchallenged and until recently women's participation in the labour market lagged behind neighbouring countries. In this chapter, we examine how couples organize the division of paid labour in the Netherlands and attempt to explain the variation between couples. Since there is little variation in labour-market participation of the husband—husbands overwhelmingly have full-time jobs—we will focus on the wife's participation (Kempkens 1993; Eijkhout 1995). What factors affect the wife's decision to leave paid employment? What prompts her to re-enter the labour market?

These transitions can be affected by the husband's characteristics as well as those of the wife. The better the husband's financial position, the less incentives there are for the wife to seek paid employment. The more traditional the husband is, the more likely he will be to oppose his wife having a job. We therefore pay special attention to the impact of the husband's characteristics on the wife's labour-market participation. Since characteristics of husband, wife, and household are subject to change over time, we analyse the transitions between the wife's labour-market participation status using event-history models.

In the Netherlands, women's labour-market participation is strongly associated with the process of family formation (de Graaf and Vermeulen 1997). Until the 1970s, most women stopped working after they became married. Later, many women stayed in the labour force until the arrival of children. More recently, it has also become an option to reduce the number of working hours, rather than stop working completely. In addition, many women who decide to stop working on the arrival of children re-enter the labour market once the children start going to school, often in part-time jobs. The family cycle is therefore a key factor affecting transitions between full-time work, part-time work, and outside the labour market.

Another important factor to take into account is the period in which the decision took place to reduce or increase the wife's labour-market participation. Until 1970 the Netherlands had a very low rate of participation by women in the labour force compared to neighbouring countries (Mol *et al.* 1988). Even in 1973, only 29 per cent of Dutch women were in paid employment, the lowest rate of labour-market participation of all OECD countries (OECD 1992). This was far below the participation rate in Germany (50 per cent) or Belgium (41 per cent), whereas in Scandinavian countries women's labour-market participation was over 60 per cent. An explanation for this low participation rate is the central role of religion in Dutch society in the period before 1970 (Lijphart 1968; Bax 1988). Church attendance was high and the local priest or minister was a figure of considerable authority. The prestige of church leaders was compounded by a system of separate organizations for each denominational group, as well as for the socialists. Separate political parties gave church leaders a direct say in matters of state, and separate schools, hospitals, unions, newspapers, sport clubs, etc., made religion pervasive in everyday life. In this climate, traditional family values stated that a woman's place was in the home, particularly for a married woman, and most definitely for a woman with children. Before 1960, married women were officially banned from the labour market. The role of religion also kept fertility high, which impeded women's entry into the labour market even if they were so inclined.

The influence of religion started to erode during the 1960s, and by 1970 the stoutly traditional Dutch society had become a highly liberal one. Despite a favourable climate towards working women and a growing economy in the 1960s, female labour-market participation did not increase substantially until the 1970s. One reason for this is the fertility rate, which remained high until 1970. From that point on, labour-market participation began to increase and by 1990 had reached levels comparable to those of neighbouring countries (48 per cent for the Netherlands, versus 52 per cent in Germany and 55 per cent in Belgium; OECD 1992). Not only did women participate more in the labour market, they stayed in it longer as well. In the 1970s, women remained in the labour force when they became mothers or re-entered once their children started requiring less attention.

The increased participation of women in the labour force during the 1970s and 1980s was strongly affected by the growing availability of part-time work (Hooghiemstra and Niphuis-Nell 1993; de Graaf and Vermeulen 1997). Virtually all mothers who keep working after having had children reduce the number of working hours, and virtually all women who return to the labour market after a period of housekeeping take part-time jobs. Part-time work is often seen as the most convenient arrangement in which a mother can take care of children and of other domestic work, and contribute to the family income at the same time. During the last decades, men have increased their share of domestic work to some extent (van der Lippe and Siegers 1994), but the wife still assumes most of the responsibility for the majority of everyday domestic tasks.

In the Netherlands, part-time jobs are not necessarily in the secondary labour market, where wages are low and social rights are absent. However, the focus of women on part-time work is detrimental to their careers. Women with full-time jobs accumulate human capital faster and are seen by employers as more motivated than part-time workers. Because of this, women have lower average wage rates and are underrepresented in the higher occupational groups. On the other hand, having a part-time job is much better than having no job at all. Being outside the labour market altogether for an extended period would have an even more damaging effect on women's career resources.

Table 4.1 shows the distribution of working hours for couples without and with children under the age of 12, in the year 1997. In order to avoid complication by older cohorts of women with low participation rates, the table has been limited to couples in which the wife is 40 years old or younger. The upper panel shows that in 56.8 per cent of all young couples without young children, both husband and wife have full-time jobs of more than thirty hours a week. In most of the other couples without young children the husband has a full-time job and the wife has a part-time job (twelve to thirty working hours), or the husband has a full-time job and the wife has no job or is marginally employed (none to eleven working hours). In a very limited proportion of all couples the wife has more working hours than her husband. Couples in which both husband and wife have part-time jobs are scarce (0.8 per cent).

Table 4.1. Division of paid labour between husbands and wives in the Netherlands (%)

Working hours of couples without children (N=575,000)

wife	husband			
	< 12 hours	12–30 hours	> 30 hours	all
< 12 hours	3.1	0.6	14.2	17.9
12–30 hours	1.2	0.8	17.6	19.6
> 30 hours	3.7	1.9	56.8	62.5
all	8.0	3.4	88.7	100

Working hours of couples with children (N=1,043,000)

wife	husband			
	< 12 hours	12–30 hours	> 30 hours	all
< 12 hours	4.8	0.7	49.6	55.2
12–30 hours	1.2	1.0	32.6	34.8
> 30 hours	1.4	0.5	7.7	10.0
all	7.4	2.7	90.0	100

Population estimates for 1997, for couples without and with children under 12, in which the wife is 40 years old or younger. Data collected by Netherlands' Statistics: Labor Market Survey 1997 (EBB–1997), own computations.

The lower panel of Table 4.1 for couples with children shows a completely different picture. The majority of full-time working women apparently reduce their working hours when they have children. Whereas 62.5 per cent of women with no children have full-time jobs, this percentage is only 10.0 for women with children. Even at the end of the 1990s, more than half (55.2 per cent) of women with young children have no job or marginal employment. Only a small fraction of couples distribute the working hours evenly between both partners. The modal pattern is a full-time working husband and a non-participating wife (49.6 per cent). The second highest frequency occurs for couples in which the husband has full-time work and his wife works part-time (32.6 per cent).

The low participation rate for women with children is related to the division of domestic labour within households. Although norms regarding participation in the labour market by women with children have changed enormously (Sociaal en Cultureel Planbureau 1997), the division of labour is still rather traditional. Men work full-time and women are expected to assume most of the household tasks, even if they have full-time jobs of their own (van der Lippe and Siegers 1994). Until 1988, the tax system also provided disincentives to dual-earner families, absorbing a large portion of the woman's income (WRR 1990). A further obstacle for women with small children is the difficulty and expense of finding good day-care facilities (Tijdens *et al.* 1994; van Dijk and Siegers 1996).

Although family cycle and period are important factors, the main focus of this chapter is on the effects of economic and cultural characteristics of both partners on the wife's participation in the labour force. The more human capital a woman has, the higher her wage rate and the more incentives she has to remain in the labour market. Women with higher paying jobs and with greater work experience are therefore more likely to continue working once they have children, at least in part-time jobs, whereas women with less human capital will interrupt their careers. Women with more human capital can also be expected to return more readily to the labour market after an interruption. Characteristics of the husband can affect the wife's labour-market participation as well. Economic theory has it that the husband's financial resources (income, employment stability) lower the wife's economic incentives to seek paid employment and therefore negatively affect her labour-market participation (Killingsworth 1983).

Cultural factors relate to the norms and values of the spouses. The more traditional a woman is, the more likely that she will stop working or work fewer hours once children arrive, and the less likely she is to re-enter the labour market at some point. Modern husbands will support their wives' decision to work and could facilitate this to some extent by assuming a greater portion of domestic tasks. Traditional husbands will disapprove of their wives working and, since they will tend to be more authoritarian, could exert strong pressures on the wife to remain at home.

In the analyses below, we examine which factors cause women to reduce their labour-market participation and which factors prompt them to increase their participation. With regard to the effects of economic and cultural characteristics of husbands and wives, Table 4.2 summarizes our hypotheses with regard to these main types of transitions. An important aspect of these hypotheses is the association between husbands' and wives' economic and cultural characteristics, which is likely to be very strong. Husbands with higher earnings will also have higher levels of education and will therefore also tend to have modern values. Their earnings will create disincentives for their wives to seek paid employment, whereas the liberal norms will stimulate their wives' labour-market participation. For this reason, the husband's financial characteristics and his cultural characteristics must be analysed simultaneously (Bernasco 1994; Bernasco *et al.* 1998). Since the effects of the two resource types have opposite signs, they could suppress each other if only one type were included. There will also be a strong relationship between economic and cultural characteristics for the wives as well. However, these effects are expected to have the same direction. Human capital and modern norms will go hand in hand and will lead to the decision to participate in the labour market.

Table 4.2. Hypotheses with regard to the main types of transitions

	Economic factors		Cultural factors (traditional versus modern)	
	wife	husband	wife	husband
Reduce labour-market participation	negative	positive	positive	positive
Increase labour-market participation	positive	negative	negative	negative

Data and Methods

In order to test our hypotheses, we use discrete time event history models on retrospective life-history data. To increase the statistical power, two large-scale surveys were combined, the *Netherlands Family Survey 1992–93* (*NFS92*: Ultee and Ganzeboom 1993), and *Households in the Netherlands 1995* (*HIN95*: Weesie and Ganzeboom 1995). Both surveys contain a broad range of retrospective items for both husbands and wives. The joined dataset contains 2,190 couples, 784 (36 per cent) from the *NFS92* and 1,406 (64 per cent) couples from *HIN95*. In order to test for effects of differences in formulation and sequence of the questions, a dummy variable indicating data source was included in the analysis.

We examined selected transitions between the following four states in the labour-market careers of women:

(*a*) *full-time employment*: thirty-two hours or more paid employment
(*b*) *part-time employment*: twelve to thirty-two hours paid employment

(c) *housekeeping*: less than twelve hours paid employment, adult education, unpaid work

(d) *otherwise outside the labour market*: unemployment, illness, disability

A distinction is made between 'housekeeping' and 'otherwise outside the labour market' in order to differentiate voluntary from involuntary non-employment. People become unemployed or disabled due to circumstances beyond their control, whereas leaving paid employment to become a house-keeper is usually a matter of choice. Table 4.3 shows the frequency of transitions from one month to the next between these four labour-market states in the life course of our sample of 2,190 women, separately for women with no or pre-school children only (upper panel) and for women with at least one child (lower panel). Only transitions made before the age of 55 are included in this table, in order to omit transitions which have to do with early retirement. Many transitions between the four states are available for analysis in both panels, but we decided to limit our analyses to five important events which provide insight in women's labour-market careers, especially with respect to reducing working hours in the early phase of marriage, and with respect to re-entrance into the labour market and the increase in the number of working hours when children are growing up.

The upper panel of Table 4.3 shows transitions for married (or cohabiting) women with no or pre-school children, which are the focus of our analyses of decreases in labour-market participation. In the first place we focus on the transition from full-time employment to either part-time employment or to

Table 4.3. Transitions in wife's labour-market status

For women with no or pre-school children only

Origin state	Destination state				
	Full-time	Part-time	Housekeeping	Other outside	Total
Full-time	—	401	917	129	1,447
Part-time	90	—	326	54	470
Housekeeping	226	254	—	52	532
Other outside	66	73	115	—	254
Total	382	728	1,358	235	2,703

For women with at least one child

Origin state	Destination state				
	Full-time	Part-time	Housekeeping	Other outside	Total
Full-time	—	172	509	57	738
Part-time	50	—	315	71	436
Housekeeping	113	373	—	55	541
Other outside	22	53	79	—	154
Total	185	598	903	183	1,869

the housekeeping status. To analyse this transition a two-stage decision process seems to be appropriate, since we assume that women first decide to stop working full-time, and then decide whether to work part-time or become housekeepers. In the second place we analyses transitions from part-time employment to housekeeping. The first events to be analysed are:

(1a) from full-time employment into either part-time employment or house-keeping (401 + 917 = 1,318 events);

(1b) the choice of housekeeping versus part-time employment, given a transition out of full-time work (917 events);

(2) from part-time employment into housekeeping (326 events).

In the lower panel of Table 4.3 we focus on the increase of working hours for women with children who have part-time jobs or no job at all (housekeeping and others outside labour market taken together). This is relevant to questions about re-entrance to the labour market for women who reduced their working hours after they had children. Again we model a two-stage decision process. We assume that women re-entering the labour market will first decide to seek employment, and then decide whether to work full-time or part-time. We would also have liked to analyse the determinants of transitions from part-time to full-time work when children become older, but here only fifty events are available, which is not enough to estimate multivariate models.

(3a) from housekeeping or otherwise outside the labour market into either part-time employment or full-time employment (113 + 373 + 22 + 53 = 561 events);

(3b) the choice of full-time versus part-time employment, given a re-entry into the labour market (113 + 22 = 135 events).

The analyses of the economic and cultural determinants of transitions 1a, 2, and 3a were done using discrete time event history models (Allison 1984; Yamaguchi 1991). A couple-month file was created, with a separate record for each month in which the wife was at risk of experiencing a transition. The effects are estimated by logistic regression models. For models 1b and 3b, the records were restricted to those in which a transition had taken place. A logistic regression analysis was performed to analyse the choice in question, given that a transition had occurred.

A main advantage of the use of event-history analysis is that it can take into account changes through time of the independent variables. Since life-history data were available for the independent variables, these are treated as time-varying covariates. The independent variables form three groups: time-related factors, economic factors, and cultural factors. Each group is discussed separately in the following paragraphs.

Time-Related Factors

The group 'time-related factors' consists of two variables, family cycle and period. As noted in the introduction, many women in the Netherlands stop working when they get married or when the first child is born. Many also re-enter the labour market once the children reach age 4 and start going to school. The variable 'family cycle' is based on stages of household formation and the age of the youngest child and plays a key role in our analyses. Family cycle distinguishes the following five stages:

(1) *starting houshold*: from six months before living together until six months before the birth of the first child;
(2) *youngest child 0–4*: from six months before the birth of the first child until all children older than 4;
(3) *youngest child 4–12*: no children under 4, at least one child between 4 and 12;
(4) *youngest child 12–18*: no children under 12, at least one child between 12 and 18;
(5) *empty nest*: no children under 18.

A couple enters the first stage, *starting household*, six months before they start cohabiting or become married. The period of six months before actual marriage or cohabitation is included in order to capture anticipation effects. In the past, women often left employment once definitive marriage arrange-ments had been made and these transitions should be included in our analy-ses. The next stage, *youngest child aged 0–4*, starts six months before the birth of the couple's first child. Again, the lead period of six months is included in order to take into account the effects of anticipation of childbirth on labour-market decisions. The third stage, *youngest child aged 4–12*, starts when the youngest child in the couple's household reaches the age of 4. At that age, children start attending nursery school, giving their mothers new opportun-ities to re-enter the labour market. When the youngest child in the couple's household reaches the age of 12 the couples enters the *youngest child 12–18* stage. All children are now in high school and are considered mature enough to require less adult supervision. The *empty nest* stage starts when the couple's youngest child reaches age 18. At this point, children start living on their own and in any case require (or tolerate) little supervision. Women in the empty nest phase therefore have the best opportunity to enter the labour market. On the other hand, at this stage they are relatively old and an extended period outside the labour market has strongly depreciated their human capital. Although they have the time and in many cases the desire to re-enter the labour market, finding paid employment will not be easy at this stage.

Couples need not progress smoothly from one stage to the next. Childless couples remain in the *starting household* stage throughout. In a few rather exceptional cases couples skip this stage, if their first child is born within three months after they start living together. If there is a gap of more than four years between the births of consecutive children, couples will re-enter the stage *youngest child aged 0–4* from the later stage *youngest child aged 4–12*. If the gap is large enough, couples can re-enter stage 2 from stage 4.

The second time-related factor in our analyses is period. From 1970 onward, women have become increasingly more likely to enter the labour market. As time progressed, they also tended to stay longer and were more likely to re-enter the labour market after an interruption. The retrospective data used here allow us to distinguish five periods: before 1960, the 1960s, the 1970s, the 1980s, and the 1990s. However, because part-time work only became available during the 1970s and 1980s, there were insufficient transitions for a meaningful analysis. In some of the analyses, the first two periods were therefore merged.

Economic Factors

The time-related factors can be expected to have large and important effects, but the main focus in this chapter is on the effects of economic and cultural factors of both the wife and her husband. The economic factors consist of occupational status for both husband and wife, wife's work experience, and husband's employment stability. Education is included as a cultural rather than an economic factor, although it has aspects of both. However, the economic effects of education will run via occupation. Any independent effect of education can therefore be attributed to its cultural aspects.

Husband's and wife's occupation were measured using a scale of *economic status* developed by de Graaf and Kalmijn (1995) based upon average income levels per occupational group. Research by Pollaerts *et al.* (1997) showed that this scale is better at uncovering differences between men and women than scales of occupational prestige or socio-economic status. The scale contains standardized values, with a mean of 0 and a standard deviation of 1. Occupation measures highest economic status of husband and wife, rather than current economic status. Women sometimes accept a downgrading in occupational status when re-entering the labour market or in order to work part-time. We feel that highest occupational status is a better measure of investment in human capital and motivation to remain in the labour force.

We also included the wife's number of years in a paid occupation as a measure of her labour-market experience. This variable was weighted by the number of hours in each job, using forty hours as the standard. Each unit is therefore the equivalent of a year's full-time work experience. Work experience relates to human capital accumulated on the job and should therefore decrease the probability of the wife reducing her labour-market participation and increase the probability of her increasing it. It is generally accepted that the accumulation of human capital through work experience has a curvilinear form, with diminishing returns as employees become older and less able to absorb new knowledge and skills. We therefore included a squared term of experience to capture this process. For analyses of re-entry into the labour force, we also included a variable for the *duration of non-employment*, measured in years.

Husband's employment stability represents the percentage of time that the husband has been unemployed during at most the last five years, or since entering the labour force if that was less than five years ago. The unit of measurement is 10 percentage points, in order to avoid small parameter values.

Cultural Factors

As noted above, husband's and wife's education are considered to be cultural rather than economic factors. Husbands and wives with higher levels of education will have modern values, so the wife will be more likely to increase her labour-market participation and less likely to decrease it. Education here refers to highest completed level of education and was included as a time-varying covariate. The classification scheme used in the questionnaires comprises nine levels of education ranging from primary education to post-academic degrees (Ph.D., for example). In order to obtain a better approximation of an interval level scale, we recoded this classification into 'effective years of schooling', ranging from six (primary education) to seventeen (post-academic degree).

Wife's religion is included in the analysis as an objective measure of traditional versus modern values. Religion was coded as a three-category variable, indicating whether the wife has no denomination, whether she has a denomination but does not attend church services on a regular basis (at least once per month), or whether she has a denomination and does attend services regularly. A second objective measure of the wife's cultural values used in these analyses is *mother's employment status*. This was measured by a dummy variable indicating whether the wife's mother held a paid job (1) or not (0) when the wife was a teenager.

A final indicator of cultural values is *relationship status*. This dummy variable indicates whether a couple is formally married (1) or cohabiting (0) at the time of relationship formation. Relationship formation is set at six months before the date of marriage or the start of cohabitation, in order to include transitions which occur in anticipation of marriage/cohabitation. Couples who get formally married are more traditional than couples who cohabit, even if the cohabiting couple does marry at some later date. Relationship status also has economic aspects, since married women are economically more secure than cohabiting women (Bernasco and Giesen 1997). This is not problematic, since both aspects work in the same direction by increasing the likelihood of the wife reducing her labour-market participation.

Results

Exits from Full-Time Employment

Our first model examines exits from full-time employment for women with no or pre-school children. This section contains the results of all voluntary exits, the following section examines the choice of housekeeping versus part-time employment, given a voluntary exit from full-time employment. The effects of our independent variables on exits from full-time work are presented in Table 4.4. This and ensuing tables for the event-history models contain the multiplicative effect in the first column, the linear B parameter in the second column, and the Wald statistic in the third column. If the multiplicative effect is less than 1, its inverse is given with the superscript –1. This allows for a clearer interpretation of the parameters as multiplicative effects, while avoiding the interpretation difficulties that occur when these effects are between 0 and 1. The multiplicative effects indicate by what factor the odds of the transition increases or, if the value has been superscripted, by what fraction the odds decreases, for a unit's change of the independent variable. When the baseline odds are small, this effect can also be interpreted as the change in the probability rather than the odds of a transition.

The Wald statistic in the third column is equal to the parameter divided by its standard error and then squared. Wald statistics have a chi-square distribution with 1 df for a single parameter and k df for a categorical variable with k parameters. The Wald statistic is included to provide a scale-independent measure of the strength of an effect. The critical chi-square value for 1 df is 2.7 for $p = 0.10$, 3.8 for $p = 0.05$, and 6.6 for $p = 0.01$.

Table 4.4. Transition from full-time employment to part-time employment or housekeeping

	Multiplicative effect	B	Wald
Family cycle: youngest < 4 (starting household)	4.38	1.48	571.9
Period	—	—	117.8
1960s (< 1960)	1.82^{-1}	–.60	15.9
1970s (1960s)	1.65^{-1}	–.50	25.1
1980s (1970s)	1.22^{-1}	–.20	5.7
1990s (1980s)	1.03^{-1}	–.03	.1
Education	1.05^{-1}	–.05	13.0
Occupation	1.26^{-1}	–.23	29.3
Experience	1.01^{-1}	–.01	.4
squared	1.00^{-1}	–.00	5.2
Religion	—	—	5.2
irregular attendance (no religion)	1.17^{-1}	–.16	5.2
regular attendance (no religion)	1.07^{-1}	–.07	.8
Relationship status: married (cohabiting)	2.42	.88	81.4
Mother's employment status	1.18^{-1}	–.16	2.5
Husband's education	1.02	.02	3.1
Husband's occupation	1.03	.03	.8
Husband's unemployment history	1.03^{-1}	–.03	4.8
Source of record, HIN (NFS)	1.12^{-1}	–.11	2.3
Constant	153.65^{-1}	–5.03	277.0

The results in Table 4.4 show a massive effect of family cycle on voluntary exits from full-time work. Women with pre-school children are 4.4 times more likely to leave full-time work in a given month than married women with no children. The Wald statistic shows that family cycle is by far the most important factor affecting voluntary exits. The second variable, period, uses the difference contrast. This means that each previous period is used as the reference category, rather than a fixed period. The Wald statistic for the total effect of period shows it is the second most important variable. The linear parameters for period are all negative, indicating that voluntary exits from full-time employment became less likely for each subsequent period. However, the magnitude of this effect decreases for each subsequent period and it was no longer significant for the last parameter for the 1990s versus the 1980s.

Each extra year of education reduces the probability of the wife leaving full-time employment by 5 per cent, whereas an increase of occupational status by 1 unit of standard deviation reduces the probability by 26 per cent. Effects of the economic aspects of education on leaving full-time employment will be interpreted via occupation. The independent effect of education found here can therefore be seen as a cultural effect. Women with higher levels of education will tend to have more progressive values, and feel that a woman's place is at her job. Work experience has a significant and curvilinear effect, which becomes increasingly negative as time progresses. Ten years of full-time work experience reduce the probability of leaving full-time employment by a factor of 1.4, twenty years by a factor of 3.2, thirty years by a factor of 11.5.

Religion, relationship status, and mother's employment status measure the woman's non-traditional values. Women who are religious but do not attend church are significantly less likely to leave full-time work than non-religious women. This effect is negative but non-significant for women who do attend church regularly. This is surprising, since we had expected the effect to be in the opposite direction, with religious women being most likely and non-religious women least likely to leave full-time work. We are reluctant to offer *post-hoc* explanations, but it might be that religious women working in full-time jobs are a selected group with a strong work ethic. Given that these women take a full-time job, they are very committed and therefore unlikely to abandon their employer.

Relationship status has a significant effect, with married women being more likely to leave full-time employment than cohabiting women, an effect which has also been found in Sweden (see Henz and Sundström in Chapter 10, below). This could be a cultural effect due to the fact that women who cohabit instead of marrying are less traditional and ignore norms stating that their place is in the home. The effect of relationship status could also be due to economic considerations, since married women have greater economic security.

With regard to husband's labour-market resources, only unemployment history has a significant effect. Each 10 per cent period of unemployment during the last five years decreases the probability of the wife leaving full-time employment by 3 per cent. If the husband is an unreliable provider, then the wife will hesitate to leave her full-time job. However, other characteristics of the husband have no effects.

Housekeeping versus Part-Time Work, Given an Exit from Full-Time Employment

The second step in the analysis of exits from full-time employment examines the choice of housekeeping versus part-time employment, given that a transition occurred. These results are presented in Table 4.5. The effect of family cycle is again very large, although smaller than for leaving full-time employment. Women with pre-school children are 3.5 times more likely to choose housekeeping rather than part-time work. Period is the most important factor in this analysis, judging by the Wald statistic. In each successive period, women became less likely to choose housekeeping over part-time work. This effect was strong but not significant for the 1960s compared to the pre-1960s, due to the scarcity of part-time jobs before 1970. The propensity to choose part-time work over housekeeping seems to be tapering off, as the effect for the 1990s versus the 1980s is considerably lower than for the 1980s versus the 1970s.

Table 4.5. Housekeeping versus part-time work, for women leaving full-time employment

	Multiplicative effect	B	Wald
Family cycle: youngest < 4 (starting household)	3.50	1.25	65.5
Period	—	—	81.0
1960s (< 1960)	2.36^{-1}	−.86	2.7
1970s (1960s)	2.09^{-1}	−.74	7.5
1980s (1970s)	2.28^{-1}	−.83	17.7
1990s (1980s)	1.69^{-1}	−.53	8.9
Education	1.06^{-1}	−.06	3.5
Occupation	1.06^{-1}	−.06	0.4
Experience	1.18^{-1}	−.17	11.0
squared	1.01	.01	5.8
Religion	—	—	3.1
irregular attendance (no religion)	1.05^{-1}	−.05	0.1
regular attendance (no religion)	1.33	.29	2.3
Relationship status: married (cohabiting)	1.47	.39	3.1
Mother's employment status	1.21^{-1}	−.19	0.6
Husband's education	1.01^{-1}	−.01	0.1
Husband's occupation	1.09^{-1}	−.08	1.1
Husband's unemployment history	1.00^{-1}	−.00	0.0
Source of record, *HIN* (*NFS*)	1.02^{-1}	−.02	0.0
Constant	5.19	1.65	5.5

A woman's education or occupation does not affect her choice of house-keeping versus part-time work, but her work experience does. The effects of experience are strongly curvilinear, with greater experience leading to a reduction in the likelihood that housekeeping will be chosen. This effect reaches an extreme value after fifteen years of experience, after which it becomes weaker again. At ten years full-time work experience, the odds of a woman choosing housekeeping over part-time work are reduced by a factor of 3. At twenty years, this factor is 2.9, at thirty years it has almost disappeared and is only 1.1. It is possible that life-cycle and cohort effects are being confounded here, since women with greater experience will also belong to older cohorts and therefore be more traditional.

Surprisingly, there are no effects of non-traditional values on the choice of housekeeping versus part-time work. The husband's characteristics also show no significant effects on the choice of housekeeping versus part-time work.

Exits from Part-Time Employment

The second analysis examines the transition from part-time employment to housekeeping. Table 4.6 contains the results of the event-history analysis. There is a strong effect of family cycle, although it is weaker than for leaving full-time employment. Women are 2.8 times more likely to leave a part-time job after having a child than women with no children. The effects of period as a whole are significant. Only the contrast of the 1970s with the pre-1970s is not significant, due to the scarcity of part-time work prior to 1970. The effects of period are all negative and increase in magnitude as time progresses, indicating that women are increasingly less likely to leave part-time work.

The effects of economic resources show significant effects of occupation and experience. The higher a woman's earnings potential, the less likely she is to leave part-time work, although the effect is weaker than for full-time work. Experience has significant effects which are negative until seventeen years of full-time experience. However, since experience is weighted by the number of hours that the woman worked, this is beyond the careers of women in this analysis. At ten years full-time experience, a woman is less likely to leave part-time work by a factor of 3.8. At twenty years, the factor is 5.0, but at thirty years it would be only 2.2. With regard to non-traditional values, religion shows no effects but there are significant effects of relationship status and mother's employment status. Married women are 1.8 times more likely to leave part-time work compared to cohabiting women. Women whose mothers worked when they were 15 are less likely to leave part-time employment by a factor of 1.7.

There is little to be said with regard to the effects of husband's resources on the odds of the wife leaving part-time employment. Husband's education, occupation, and unemployment history all have no effects.

Table 4.6. Transition from part-time employment to housekeeping

	Multiplicative effect	B	Wald
Family cycle: youngest < 4 (starting household)	2.77	1.02	56.5
Period	—	—	28.5
1970s(< 1970)	1.10^{-1}	−0.09	0.2
1980s (1970s)	1.39^{-1}	−0.33	4.8
1990s (1980s)	1.62^{-1}	−0.49	10.4
Education	1.00	0.00	0.0
Occupation	1.19^{-1}	−0.17	4.3
Experience	1.21^{-1}	−0.19	10.8
squared	1.01	0.01	1.1
Religion	—	—	1.8
irregular attendance (no religion)	1.05^{-1}	−0.05	0.1
regular attendance (no religion)	1.18	0.17	1.2
Relationship status: married (cohabiting)	1.81	0.60	6.2
Mother's employment status	1.70^{-1}	−0.53	5.4
Husband's education	1.01	0.01	0.1
Husband's occupation	1.10^{-1}	−0.10	2.7
Husband's unemployment history	1.01	0.01	0.2
Source of record, HIN (NFS)	1.12	0.11	0.6
Constant	202.96^{-1}	−5.31	63.6

Re-entry into the Labour Market

The next two analyses examine re-entry into the labour market for women with at least one child. This section analyses re-entry into paid employment and the following section examines the choice of full-time versus part-time work, given the decision to re-enter the labour market. The results of the first step are presented in Table 4.7. The effects of family cycle show that women with children between 4 and 12 years of age are 2.4 times more likely to re-enter the labour market than women with pre-schoolers. This effect is only slightly lower once the children are of high-school age (12 to 18), but is much lower although still significant in the empty-nest stage, when all children are over 18. Women in the empty-nest stage have more opportunities to seek employment but will be less eligible due to the depreciation of human capital. These women will also belong to older, more traditional cohorts and therefore be less inclined to re-enter the labour market. The effects of period are all positive, with a strong effect for the 1970s versus the pre-1970s and to a lesser extent the 1990s versus the 1980s. Interestingly, women in the 1980s were not significantly more likely to re-enter the labour market than women in the 1970s. This could be due to high unemployment rates, particularly in the early 1980s, which prevented women from finding work even if they were more motivated to do so.

Table 4.7. Re-entry into the labour market

	Multiplicative effect	B	Wald
Family cycle	—	—	60.3
youngest < 12 (youngest < 4)	2.35	0.85	57.9
youngest < 18 (youngest < 4)	2.23	0.80	20.9
empty nest (youngest < 4)	1.61	0.48	4.3
Period	—	—	29.6
1970s (< 1970)	2.37	0.86	12.5
1980s (1970s)	1.13	0.12	1.0
1990s (1980s)	1.33	0.28	6.5
Education	1.09	0.08	19.3
Occupation	1.04^{-1}	−0.03	0.5
Experience	1.09^{-1}	−0.08	5.3
squared	1.00	0.00	0.4
Duration of non-employment	1.06^{-1}	−0.06	51.4
Religion	—	—	18.0
irregular attendance (no religion)	1.11^{-1}	−0.10	1.0
regular attendance (no religion)	1.72^{-1}	−0.54	17.8
Relationship status: married (cohabiting)	1.93^{-1}	−0.66	13.3
Mother's employment status	1.05	0.05	0.1
Husband's education	1.01	0.01	0.9
Husband's occupation	1.09^{-1}	−0.09	4.3
Husband's unemployment history	1.01	0.01	0.2
Source of record, *HIN* (*NFS*)	1.33^{-1}	−0.28	3.4
Constant	209.96^{-1}	−5.35	128.8

Education, previous work experience, and duration of non-employment have significant effects on the decision to re-enter the labour market, but occupation does not. Interestingly, prior work experience decreases rather than increases the likelihood of re-entry into the labour market. Women with ten years prior work experience are only half as likely to re-enter the labour market. At twenty years of experience, the probability is reduced by a factor of 2.9, at thirty years experience it is reduced by a factor of 3.1. This negative effect of work experience is due to the fact that women who have their children at an early age, when they have limited labour-market experience, are more likely to re-enter the labour market at some point. On the other hand, women who have children later on tend to end their labour-market careers at that point in order to become full-time mothers. The duration of being outside the labour force decreases the likelihood of re-entry by 6 per cent for each year of non-employment.

Education increases the probability of re-entry by a factor of 9 per cent for each year of education. The values of higher education stimulate women to re-enter the labour force. Traditional women who are religious and attend church regularly are less likely to re-enter the labour market than non-religious women. This effect has the same direction but is not significant for women who do not attend church regularly. Married women are also significantly less likely to re-enter the labour market than women who were cohabiting at the time of relationship formation. On the other hand, mother's working status has no effect in this analysis.

Husband's occupation has a significant negative effect on the probability of the wife re-entering the labour market. An increase in husband's earnings potential by one standard deviation reduces the probability of the wife re-entering the labour market by 9 per cent. So although this effect is significant, it is not very strong.

Full-Time versus Part-Time Work, Given Re-entry into the Labour Market

The last analysis of this chapter regards the choice of full-time versus part-time work, given the decision to re-enter the labour market (see Table 4.8). In this case, only period has a significant effect. Until 1970, part-time work was not really an option and the positive value of the parameter for the 1970s versus the pre-1970s indicates that women tended to choose full-time work. This changed in the 1980s when part-time jobs became widely available. The parameter for the 1980s versus the 1970s is negative and significant. Women in the 1990s are even more likely to choose part-time work, but the difference to the 1980s is no longer significant. None of the other variables had significant effects on the choice of full-time versus part-time work for women re-entering the labour market.

Conclusions

In this chapter, we analysed the effects of cultural and economic characteristics of women and their husbands on the woman's participation in the labour market. Decreases in participation were analysed in the form of transitions from full-time employment into either part-time employment or housekeeping, and from part-time employment into housekeeping. Increases in participation were analysed as re-entry into full-time or part-time employment after a period of housekeeping. The analyses of decreases in participation were restricted to women with no or pre-school children, the analyses of increases were restricted to women with at least one child. Economic characteristics of the wife were hypothesized to increase participation, whereas the husband's economic characteristics would tend to decrease the wife's participation. Cultural indicators of traditional values of both husband and wife were hypothesized to decrease the wife's labour-market participation. In addition to cultural and economic characteristics of the partners, family cycle and period

Table 4.8. Full-time versus part-time employment, for women re-entering the labour market

	Multiplicative effect	B	Wald
Family cycle	—	—	0.4
youngest < 12 (youngest < 4)	1.04^{-1}	−0.04	0.0
youngest < 18 (youngest < 4)	1.07	0.07	0.0
empty nest (youngest < 4)	1.37	0.32	0.3
Period	—	—	8.4
1970s (< 1970)	1.28	0.25	0.2
1980s (1970s)	1.84^{-1}	−0.61	4.5
1990s (1980s)	1.38^{-1}	−0.33	1.2
Education	1.04	0.04	0.8
Occupation	1.19^{-1}	−0.17	1.8
Experience	1.01^{-1}	−0.01	0.0
squared	1.01^{-1}	−0.01	0.3
Duration of non-employment	1.01	0.01	0.2
Religion	—	—	1.0
irregular attendance (no religion)	1.28	0.24	0.9
regular attendance (no religion)	1.02^{-1}	−0.02	0.0
Relationship status: married (cohabiting)	1.81^{-1}	−0.59	2.1
Mother's employment status	1.94^{-1}	−0.66	2.6
Husband's education	1.05^{-1}	−0.05	1.5
Husband's occupation	1.00	0.00	0.0
Husband's unemployment history	1.01	0.01	0.0
Source of record, HIN (NFS)	1.01^{-1}	−0.01	0.0
Constant	1.97	0.68	0.4

were included to model the effects of time. In order to capture the dynamic aspects of women's participation in the labour market, the analyses were performed using event-history models.

The time-related factors, family cycle and period, had the strongest effects on women's labour-market decisions. Having a pre-school child versus no children has an enormous impact on the decision to reduce labour-market participation, and having a pre-school child versus school age or older children strongly affects increases in participation. Period also has strong effects, both because of the steady increase in women's labour-market participation from 1970 onwards, and because of the increasing prevalence of part-time work from that point on.

The main interest of these analyses was the impact of economic and cultural characteristics of both the wife and her husband on her labour-market decisions. Of the wife's own characteristics, work experience had the most consistent impact, with significant effects in all models except the choice of full-time versus part-time work for women re-entering the labour market. The more human capital a woman accumulates through work experience, the less likely she is to reduce her labour-market participation. On the other hand, experience reduces the likelihood of the women increasing her participation through re-entry into the labour market. This effect is due to the fact that women who have children at a young age are more likely to re-enter the labour market, whereas women who have children later in their careers tend to leave the labour market permanently. We found that a higher occupational status tends to keep women in the labour force, but does not induce them to re-enter the labour market once they have left.

Since the economic aspects of education are interpreted via occupation, the independent effects of education can be attributed to its cultural aspects. Education tends to reduce the likelihood of women leaving full-time, but not part-time work and does induce them to re-enter the labour market once they have children. With regard to other cultural characteristics, religion had the unexpected effect of keeping women in full-time employment, particularly if the woman did not attend church regularly. Religion also impedes women's re-entry into the labour market, which is in the expected direction. Having a mother who also worked inhibits departure from part-time work, but does not affect other transitions. Being married rather than cohabiting generally had a negative effect on participation in the labour market. This could be because cohabiting women are more modern or because married women have greater economic security.

Whereas the wife's economic and cultural characteristics had many strong effects, there were only two significant effects of the husband's characteristics on the wife's labour-market choices. First, the more the husband is unemployed, the less likely the wife is to leave full-time employment. Second, the higher the husband's earnings potential, the less likely the wife is to re-enter the labour market once she has children, which parallels the results for Germany (Chapter 3 above) but contradicts, for example, the Swedish case (Chapter 10 below). Both effects are significant, but relatively small. It is interesting to note that these are both economic factors. There were no effects of husband's education and earlier models (not presented here) showed no effects of husband's religion either. There is no evidence of enlightened husbands furthering their wives' careers.

In summary, it appears that women's decisions on leaving and re-entering the labour force are determined for the main part by their stage in the family cycle and by the historical period in which the decisions were made. Women's aspirations and opportunities are also moulded by their own human capital and norms and values, but the human capital and the norms and values of their partners do not seem to play a very important role in women's employment histories.

References

Allison, P. D. (1984). *Event History Analysis: Regression for Longitudinal Event Data* (Beverly Hills, Calif.: Sage).

Bax, E. H. (1988). *Modernization and Cleavage in Dutch Society: A Study of Long Term Economic and Social Change* (Dissertation for the Degree of Doctor of Economy; Groningen: Universiteitsdrukkerij).

Becker, G. (1981). *A Treatise on the Family* (Cambridge, Mass.: Harvard University Press).

Bernasco, W. (1994). *Coupled Careers: The Effects of Spouse's Resources on Success at Work* (Amsterdam: Thesis Publishers).

——and D. Giesen (1997). 'De strategische waarde van het huwelijk voor de arbeidsverdeling tussen levenspartners: Naar een verklaring van de relatie tussen samenleefvorm en arbeidsdeelname van vrouwen' (The Strategic Value of Marriage for the Division of Labour between Spouses: Towards an Explanation of the Relationship between Partnership Status and Women's Labour Force Participation) (*Mens en Maatschappij*, 72: 115–31.

——P. M. de Graaf, and W. C. Ultee (1998). 'Coupled Careers: Effects of Spouse's Resources on Occupational Attainment in the Netherlands', *European Sociological Review*, 14: 15–31.

Dijk, L. van, and J. J. Siegers (1996). 'The Division of Child Care among Mothers, Fathers, and Nonparental Care Providers in Dutch Two-Parent Families', *Journal of Marriage and the Family*, 58: 1018–28.

Eijkhout, M. P. (1995). 'Huishoudens en hun arbeidsmarktparticipatie 1981–1993' (Households and their Labour Participation 1981–1993), *Sociaal-Economische Maandstatistiek*, 95/2: 17–26.

Graaf, P. M. de and M. Kalmijn (1995). 'Culturele en economische beroepsstatus: Een evaluatie van subjectieve en objectieve benaderingen' (Cultural and Economic Occupational Status: An Evaluation of Subjective and Objective Approaches), *Mens en Maatschappij*, 70: 152–65.

——and H. Vermeulen (1997). 'Female Labour-Market Participation in the Netherlands: Developments in the Relationship between Family Cycle and Employment', in H.-P. Blossfeld and C. Hakim (eds.), *Between Equalization and Marginalization: Women Working Part-Time in Europe and the United States of America* (Oxford: Oxford University Press), 191–209.

Hooghiemstra, B. T. J. and M. Niphuis-Nell (1993). *Sociale atlas van de vrouw II* (Social Atlas of Women, part ii) (Rijswijk: Sociaal en Cultureel Planbureau).

Kempkens, L. (1993). 'Arbeid van paren in 1991' (Labour Participation of Pairs in 1991), *Sociaal-Economische Maandstatistiek*, 93/7: 7–8.

Killingsworth, M. R. (1983). *Labor Supply* (Cambridge, UK: Cambridge University Press).

Lijphart, A. (1968). *The Politics of Accommodation: Pluralism and Democracy in the Netherlands* (Berkeley, Calif.: University of California Press).

Lippe, T. van der, and J. J. Siegers (1994). 'Division of Household and Paid Labour between Partners: Effects of Relative Wage Rates and Social Norms', *Kyklos*, 47: 109–36.

Mol, P. W., J. C. Van Ours, and J. J. M. Theeuwes (1988). *Honderd jaar gehuwde vrouwen op de arbeidsmarkt* (A Hundred Years of Married Women's Involvement in the Labour Market) (OSA-Werkdocument W48; The Hague: Organisatie voor Strategisch Arbeidsmarktonderzoek).

OECD (1992). *Employment Outlook 1992* (Paris: Organization for Economic Co-operation and Development).

Pollaerts, H., P. M. de Graaf, and R. Luijkx (1997). 'Ontwikkelingen in intragenerationele beroepsmobilitieit gedurende de vroege carrière van Nederlandse mannen en vrouwen geboren tussen 1915 en 1967' (Developments in Intragenerational Occupational Mobility during the Early Careers of Dutch Men and Women Born between 1915 and 1967), *Mens en Maatschappij*, 72: 48–67.

Sociaal en Cultureel Planbureau (1997). *Bijlage: Opinies over emancipatie en gezin* (Supplement: Opinions about Emancipation and the Family) (Rijswijk: Sociaal en Cultureel Planbureau).

Tijdens, K., H. Maassen van den Brink, M. Noom, and W. Groot (1994). *Arbeid en zorg: Maatschappelijke effecten van strategieen van huishoudens om betaalde arbeid en zorg te combineren* (Effects of Household Strategies to Combine Paid and Care Labour), (OSA-werkdocument W124; The Hague: Organisatie voor Strategisch Arbeidsmarktonderzoek).

Ultee, W. C. and H. B. G. Ganzeboom (principal investigators) (1993). *Netherlands Family Survey 1992–93* (machine-readable dataset; Nijmegen: Department of Sociology, Nijmegen University). Codebook prepared by Harry B. G. Ganzeboom and Suzanne Rijken, Sept. 1993 edn. Changes and additions made by Harry B. G. Ganzeboom and Roland Weygold, Jan. 1995 edn.

Weesie, J., and H. B. G. Ganzeboom (principal investigators) (1995). *Households in the Netherlands 1995* (machine-readable dataset; Utrecht: Department of Sociology, Utrecht University). Codebook prepared by Matthijs Kalmijn, Wim Bernasco, and Jeroen Weesie, ISCORE paper no. 67 (1996).

WRR (1990). *Een werkend perspectief. Arbeidsparticipatie in de jaren '90* (A Working Perspective: Labour-Market Participation in the 1990s) (Rapport van de Wetenschappelijke Raad voor het Regeringsbeleid, 38; The Hague: SDU-uitgeverij).

Yamaguchi, K. (1991). *Event History Analysis* (Newbury Park, Calif.: Sage).

5

Couples' Careers in Flanders

MARTINE CORIJN

Introduction

C OUPLES (have to) make several decisions with regard to their family life and work. Theories focus on different mechanisms at work in these decisions: rational choices, structural constraints, cultural conditions (see Bernardi, in Chapter 6 below). Both stratification and mobility research and family formation studies have for a long time omitted consideration of the couple as a unit and even neglected the wife as an individual subject of a family or employment career. As decisions on the family formation usually rely upon both partners involved, characteristics of both partners are important determinants because partners constitute, to a certain degree, each other's constraints.

Aspects from the context of decision-making relevant to the family formation have recently been introduced in different ways in empirical research. Studies on the determinants of the family-formation process first analysed only the impact of men's characteristics. The increasing female labour-force participation shifted the focus towards the wife's characteristics as main determinants. In the 1990s, men were again included in the picture (see Oppenheimer *et al.* 1993; Huinink 1995). However, empirical research on the family-formation process often remains confined to characteristics of one of the partners. Recently, some studies included characteristics of both partners or of the couple. Confining the analysis to characteristics of only one partner has been justified by the partner selection process that is highly selective and results in a high degree of homogamy within couples (Kalmijn 1991). Homogamy makes it in a sense redundant to focus on characteristics of both partners. However, although particularly educational and religious homogamy are strong, homogamy is far from complete. A substantial literature analyses the consequences of couple heterogamy for marital stability and disruption (Bitter 1986; Rogler and Procidano 1989; Shehan *et al.* 1990; Tzeng 1992). Only a few studies examine its consequences for fertility (Corijn *et al.* 1996; Kalmijn 1996; Krishnan 1993; Marcum 1986; Mascie-Taylor 1986;

I am very grateful to Aart Liefbroer (NIDI) for his assistance in preparing this contribution.

Sørenson 1989). The occupational career, mostly of the wife, is considered as
an important determinant of the family-formation process (Blossfeld 1995).
Studies that take into account both the employment career and other characteristics of both partners involved are very scarce (Huinink 1995). In the study
presented in this chapter we investigate the employment career of women,
considering the family-formation process, characteristics of both the partners,
and parental resources as potential determinants.

Trends in Labour-Force Participation

Developments in the labour market (policy) offer the structural opportunities
and constraints for career decisions taken by individuals and couples. In
Belgium, the employment careers of men, particularly of young and less educated men, have been subjected mainly to periods of unemployment during
the last three decades. The employment careers of women have been influenced by several developments: the increasing female and particularly maternal labour-force participation; the unemployment crisis that affected women
more than men; the increase of (in)voluntary part-time work; the opportunities created to reconcile work and family life. During the last three decades, the
activity rates of women have been increasing strongly, particularly among
the age group 25 to 49. The female activity curve is gradually approaching the
male bell form, which indicates a career without long interruptions. The activity rates of women aged 25 to 49 were in Belgium in 1991 just above the mean
of the twelve members of the European Union (EUR12) (see CEC 1993). In the
1960s, part-time employment in Belgium initially developed within a context
of shortages in the labour market. At that time, part-time work existed almost
exclusively for women who wanted to combine family life with a limited occupational career by (re-)entering the labour market on a part-time basis. Until
1980, part-time work was an exception as regulations in labour and social
security laws had not been adapted. The unemployment crisis in the 1970s
created the conditions for a radical change in the structure of part-time work.
During the 1980s, the Belgian government promoted part-time work very
actively and pushed it as a redistributive labour measure to combat unemployment. A supplementary unemployment benefit was granted to anyone
who was unemployed, wanted to work full-time but could not find a full-time
job, and accepted a part-time job. On becoming unemployed again, one
received full unemployment benefits. The number of beneficiaries under this
scheme rose from 20,000 in 1982 to 200,000 in 1989. For the government the
substitution of full-time jobs by part-time jobs did indeed yield a surplus of
jobs. For employers, this system offered possibilities with respect to work flexibility. Employees got an additional allowance to supplement their part-time
wages. Some persons chose to remain within this scheme, even though their
part-time work was initially involuntary (Callens 1995a; Ramioul 1992). With
regard to part-time employment, Belgium approached in 1991 the EUR12

mean (CEC 1993). Under pressure from diminishing public funds, the federal government reformed this 'escape from unemployment' system considerably in 1993, making it less attractive. It is expected that this reform will slow down the growth in part-time work (Callens 1995a). Part-time work among females increased from 15 per cent in 1981 to 31 per cent in 1991. The female unemployment rate remained in that period at about 8 per cent (Van Hoof 1997).

As in other EU countries, the female activity rate in Belgium decreases at every age with the number of children. The differences in activity rates between women with no, one, or two children are relatively small; the rate is remarkably lower for women with three children (Callens et al. 2000).

Asked about how they would like to combine parenthood and employment, Flemish women aged 21 to 40 in 1991 chose 'a part-time job and one or more children' as the most favoured option (47 per cent). 'Full-time work and one or more children' held second place at 38 per cent (Van Peer and Moors 1996). Only 8 per cent of the women excluded employment from their life.

The increasing female labour-force participation yields strong inequalities in work experience. Based on data about the previous and current employment and on the employment intentions, Van Dongen et al. (1995) created for Flemish married women aged 20 to 49 a work orientation index. They found that 15 per cent of these women have a very weak work orientation (having been, being, and intending to be (mostly) housewives). Women in this group are mainly over 40 and less educated. Almost half of the women had a very strong work orientation (having been, being, and intending to be employed).

The Belgian welfare policy combines social democratic and conservative/corporative elements. In spite of a high level of industrial development and a strong welfare state, Belgium takes up only an average position as far as the economic position of women is concerned. This is mainly because both the social partners and the government have always used a traditional male-breadwinner model (Triest 1993). As far as childcare facilities are concerned, only Denmark scores higher than Belgium in the EU concerning the percentages of places for under-3s. This good position is only partly related to a social policy supporting mothers' employment, as half of the childcare for these children is a private matter (grandparents or other relatives). One-quarter of these children attend day-care centres and one-quarter go to childminders (Callens et al. 2000). With regard to policies aimed at children under 6 and more generally in giving support for families, Belgium belongs to the most generous countries (Gornick et al. 1997; Ray 1997).

Previous Research on Couples' Careers

Research introducing characteristics of the partner as possible determinants of the family-formation process is rather scarce. Mascie-Taylor (1986) finds that educationally homogamous couples have a higher rate of completed fertility than educationally heterogamous couples. Sørenson (1989) shows that the educational level of the female partner is much more important for the completed fertility rate than that of the male partner, and that, moreover, their relative importance is culture-specific. The rate of first childbirth among Flemish couples is much lower if the female partner or if both partners are highly educated. Among Dutch couples, however, this rate is lowest if both partners are highly educated. If only one of the partners is highly educated, this is somewhat higher, although still substantially lower than among couples with two less educated partners (Corijn *et al.* 1996). Kalmijn (1996) finds among Dutch couples that highly educated people have a lower first childbirth rate than less educated people. However, if data about both partners are included in the analyses the effect of the man's educational level disappears and that of the woman remains. Studying the impact of religious characteristics of spouses on fertility, Marcum (1986) finds that religious homogamy has no effect at all on recent and completed fertility. Krishnan (1993) finds a weak negative effect of religious homogamy on childlessness. In Flanders the religious commitment of the female partner is more important than that of the male partner for the timing of the first childbirth (Corijn *et al.* 1996). Some of these results suggest that, in Thomson's (1990) terminology, a 'sphere-of-interest' rule is operative as the woman's characteristics are more important than the man's for the family-formation process.

Studies including characteristics of the occupational career as determinants of the family-formation process mostly concern only women. Blossfeld (1995) concludes that women's growing economic independence has had a critical and presumably irreversible impact on the family system in modern societies, but that this impact is differentiated according to the family system. Analysing the determinants of the entry into fatherhood in Germany, Huinink (1995) takes account of parental resources, characteristics of both partners, and the employment careers of both partners involved. Within this constellation of determinants, he only finds strong negative effects of the educational level and the labour-force participation of the female partner. During the 1960s and 1970s the unemployment of women had a strong negative effect on family formation in Flanders (Impens, 1987). Using data on male and female careers, it appears that in the 1970s and 1980s the impact of employment status is gender-specific and that it operates differently for the marriage and first childbirth timing. The first-marriage rate of unemployed men is much lower than that of their employed counterparts. Unemployed women, however, have the same marriage rate as employed women. The employment status of males does not have any influence on the first childbirth rate. Among women, however, there is a very strong effect. Women who live with a partner and are not employed have their first child sooner than employed women (Corijn 1996; Liefbroer *et al.* 1996). Both full-time employment and unemployment of women have a negative impact on the birth of a third child (Callens 1995c).

Based on the Flemish FFS data there is some research on the impact of family formation on the female employment career. In the 1960s and 1970s the labour-force participation of married women, aged 20 to 45, was most strongly determined by their educational level and by their number of children. The influence of their husband's resources was less strong. An impact of the husband's income on the wife's labour-force participation was only observable in the highest income category. In this category, there no longer seemed to be any pressure for a second income. The effect of the husband's educational level was not that clear. Religious affiliation had a small effect on the wife's labour-force participation: non-Catholic wives seem to have a higher activity rate (Pauwels *et al.* 1984). A study on the labour-force participation of married women, aged 25 to 59, in Belgium confirms the negative impact of the number of children. The children's age does not seem to have any effect on the mother's probability of having a paid job. The net hourly wage of the wife has a positive effect on her labour-force participation. The net income in the household—of which the male income constitutes the largest share—has a negative effect (Henkens *et al.* 1992). As such, both studies point to the negative impact of the spouse's financial resources on the wife's occupational status. Using the Flemish FFS data, Callens (1995*a*) counts for women, aged 21 to 40 and hence entering the labour market since the 1970s, the number of person-years spent in employment in different stages of the family-formation process. Marriage does not seem to influence the involvement in full-time employment. The presence of children does. The person-years spent in full-time employment drop considerably once there is at least one child; those spent in part-time employment rise strongly from that stage on.

Callens *et al.* (2000) finds in that same survey that for women born since 1950 the involvement in employment drops from more than 80 per cent before the birth of the first child, to over 69 per cent after the birth of the first child, 58 per cent after the birth of the second child, to 45 per cent after the birth of the third child. These activity rates are particularly influenced by the wife's educational level and by her age at the births. One year after the first, the second, and the third childbirth respectively 18, 30, and 50 per cent of the mothers work part-time. These proportions increased strongly during the 1980s: from 6 to 32 per cent after the birth of the first child and from 20 to 40 per cent after the birth of the second child.

Van Dongen *et al.* (1995) asked married women, aged 20 to 49, about their motives for their employment status. Currently employed wives mainly state that they want to contribute to the family income (76 per cent) and that they have more social contacts through their job (72 per cent). For 63 per cent of the wives there is a financial necessity for a paid job. Education has a negative effect on this last motive. A financial independence of the spouse and a dislike for housework are less important motives (respectively 43 and 38 per cent). The latter one is positively related to education. The most important motives for currently being employed full-time are a more equal share in the family income (63 per cent) and the financial necessity of a paid job (50 per cent). The most important reasons for currently being employed part-time are the fact that housework is a large burden (78 per cent) and that couples prefer to raise their children themselves (76 per cent). The first motive is negatively related to education. Among this group of married women 20 per cent are full-time housewives and another 10 per cent are not employed. Housewives are particularly prevalent in the over-40 age group and more than half of the housewives have a low educational level. Asked about their motives these housewives say that they want to raise their children themselves (83 per cent) and that they love being full-time housewives (64 per cent). The second motive is less relevant among highly educated women. Only 21 per cent of the housewives want to re-enter the labour market. Those who want to re-enter are younger and more highly educated. This pattern of motives illustrates three aspects: the supplementary but necessary role of female employment, particularly for less educated women; the preference for a specialization in household work that is more relevant for less educated women; and the solutions for the childrearing task. Household income data in this same survey further illustrate the financial role of women's employment. In only 14 per cent of the households do husband and wife have an equal share in the total household income. In 6 per cent of the households the female's share is larger. Among almost half of the couples the wife's share is more than a quarter but less than half. The household income is strongly reduced only if there is no contribution by the wife, that is, if she is a housewife (Van Dongen *et al.* 1995). Asked about women's preferred employment situation for the future: 28 per cent of the employed wives want to reduce their labour time or stop working. The socio-economic profile of this group is not different from that of the others. The most important motive for this change is to have more time to raise children, a motive that becomes less important when women are older. Of all housewives, 21 per cent want to re-enter the labour market. These wives are younger, more highly educated, have more labour-force experience, and have a lower household income. Their most important motives are to have more social contacts and to have a share in the household income.

Hypotheses

In this chapter we focus on determinants of the entry into and exit out of the household work position of married women in Flanders. Using the FFS data the hypotheses have to be confined to women born since 1950, who have subsequently married, and who have been in the labour market since about 1970.

In the context of a general trend of an increasing female labour-market participation, we expect a marriage cohort effect. As housework becomes less attractive, particularly for younger women, exits to household work should become rarer and re-entries after housework periods should become more prevalent. Within the more restricted age range, being under 40, we expect age effects to be hardly observable. More labour-force participation before marriage might reflect a stronger employment orientation. As such we expect more pre-marital work experience to decrease the probability of an exit from the labour market and increase the probability of a (re)entry into the labour market.

According to Becker's theory, more human capital investment—as expressed in the educational level—should increase the wife's probability of not leaving the labour market and of (re-)entering the labour market. With regard to the impact of the husband's characteristics on the wife's employment career, authors point to contrasting effects. Bernasco *et al.* (1998) make a distinction between the financial resources and the labour-market resources that a husband offers for his wife's occupational career. Based on the social capital idea, stressing the facilitating effects of network resources on occupational attainment, they expect the husband's labour market-resources to affect positively the wife's occupational attainment. From an economic theory predicting a negative association between the spouses' level of occupational attainment due to gains from specialization between housework and paid work, they expect the husband's financial resources to negatively affect the wife's occupational attainment. Róbert *et al.* (Chapter 13 below) make a similar distinction. A clear prediction of the impact of the husbands' educational level on the wives' occupational career, in the absence of a more economic determinant, is hence impossible.

Empirical evidence supports the impact of the family-formation process—the number and the age of the children—on the (un)employment of the wife. We expect the number and the age of the children to have an impact on the exit to housework and on the (re)-entry after housework.

In line with the social mobility research tradition, one can expect an impact of social origin or parental resources on the occupational career. Blossfeld *et al.* (Chapter 3) point to opposing effects as higher status families may, on the one hand, transmit negative attitudes towards female employment, but on the other hand provide better opportunities for higher educational attainment, which in turn increase labour-market chances and attractiveness of paid employment. A clear prediction related to the impact of the parents' educational level is hard to make.

Bernardi (Chapter 6) suggests that the cultural conditioning playing a role in decisions on labour-market participation should be taken into account. An important aspect of this cultural context, originating in the parental home and related to gender identity, concerns the mother's employment behaviour. We expect a kind of housewife role inheritance, giving daughters of non-working mothers a higher probability of exiting the labour market into housework and a lower probability of (re-)entering the labour market after a period of household work.

Data, Variables, and Method

Data

The analyses presented in this study are based on the Fertility and Family Survey (FFS) in Flanders in 1991 (Callens 1995*b*) and Brussels (1992–3)

(Daelemans and Callens 1994). The sample consisted of men and women of Belgian nationality, born between 1951 and 1970. Only the Flemish-speaking people of the survey in Brussels were added as a weighed subsample to the Flemish sample. In the survey information is gathered about the occupational history and the partnership and family history (that is, partnership, civil status, living arrangements, childbearing) from age 16 on. To make the Flemish and Brussels data comparable all histories were censored in April 1991.

The basic dataset for this study consists of the employment and family-formation history of women still in their first marriage, as the available partner's characteristics concern the current partner. The analyses presented concern 1,248 men and 2,269 women.

Variables

Resources: Only the educational level and the occupational history of the respondent and his/her current partner, if any, are available. In order to try to distinguish the cultural and economic resources of the partner, we used respectively his educational level and his unemployment record. With regard to parental resources, the educational level was asked for both the woman's own parents and the current partner's parents. Selecting the educational level of only the father is a good proxy for social origin, as the educational homogamy in this parents' generation, using three levels of education, is about 75 per cent. Mother's employment during the formation years is part of the cultural resources. Among these post-war generations 59 per cent were raised by a full-time mother-housewife.

Family status: As the female employment histories revealed that the person-years spent in part-time work before marriage did not exceed 5 per cent in any cohort or in any age period (Callens 1995a), it seemed more meaningful to take into account any work experience before marriage. The data on child-bearing are drawn from the pregnancy history by selecting the live childbirths. As the upper age limit of the women is 40 years, the age range of the children involved is left skewed. It seems meaningful to look only at the presence of pre-school children. As most children in Flanders attend kindergarten from age 2.5 to 3 onwards, the limit of age 3 is used.

Time effects: Age and cohort are important indicators of changes over time. The operationalization of the independent variables can be found in the appendix to this chapter.

Dependent variable: In the occupational history only those activities which lasted for at least three consecutive months had to be dated. Where several activities were combined, only one category was recorded, according to the following hierarchical rules: (1) occupational activity comes before inactivity, (2) involuntary inactivity takes precedence over voluntary inactivity. In this study full-time employment is distinguished from part-time employment; the later being any involvement in employment that is less than 100 per cent of a full-time post or thirty-eight hours a week. In the studies by Callens, based on the same survey, part-time employment was delineated as any involvement in employment that was less than 75 per cent. We use the other distinction in order to increase the number of relevant transitions.

The dependent variables are the rates of transition from employment to housework and from housework to employment. To highlight the specific profile of determinants of these transitions, the rates of transition from full-time to part-time employment, from employment to unemployment, from part-time to full-time employment, and from unemployment to employment were also analysed. The distinction between full-time and part-time employment is included as an additional independent variable.

Method

Hazard rate models are used to analyse the timing of the transitions in the female employment career. In such models, the rate at which people experience the transition is analysed dependent on a time-related factor and other covariates. Piecewise constant models are used to control for the duration dependence. The models were calculated with the TDA software package (Rohwer 1994).

Results

The Couple as a Unit: Assortative Mating in Flanders

Using characteristics of the partner, one must take into account the degree of couple homogamy. In Flanders the educational homogamy among (married) partners belonging to post-war cohorts is about 57 per cent, when distinguishing three educational levels. Hence, for more than half of these couples the starting conditions for their parallel careers are identical. In about one-fifth of the couples one spouse has an educational level higher than that of the partner. The size of the group of couples with the wife at a disadvantage is similar to that of the couples with the husband at a disadvantage. These proportions do not seem to support Becker's ideas on the comparative advantage of human capital investments. The educational homogamy in couples and the heterogamy with highly educated wives increase across cohorts in Flanders.

The degree of homogamy with regard to religion, another strong determinant of the family-formation process in Flanders (Corijn 1996; Liefbroer et al. 1996), is even higher. In the FFS one finds a religious homogamy of about 73 per cent, using five categories of current religious affiliation/church attendance. No clear changes across post-war cohorts show up.

Full-time employment among men is almost general. In the FFS men (under age 40) spent more than 95 per cent of their time (person-years) in full-time employment after completing their education (Callens 1995a). The equity in the starting conditions, in terms of a similar educational level for more than half of the married couples, remains in a sense, as in about half of the couples (under age 40) both partners worked full-time at the time of the survey. Among a quarter of the couples the wife worked part-time. These proportions are strongly age-related.

With regard to educational mobility the FFS reveals that, using four levels of education, about 65 per cent of the adults, aged 21 to 40 years, have a less educated father and about 7 per cent have a higher educated father. Upward educational mobility is for these cohorts almost the rule. Besides the 50 per cent of educational homogamy among couples, marriage introduces about an equal degree of ascending and descending educational mobility. Combining the intergenerational association and the assortative mating, the most prevalent pattern is an educational upgrade compared with the father and an educational similarity compared with the partner.

The Female Employment Career

For women, aged 21 to 40, the FFS reveals a strong polarization in terms of the person-years women spent in employment after their completion of education. Of all women 22 per cent spent less than half of their time in (part-time or full-time) employment and 51 per cent spent more than 90 per cent of their time in employment. Since the 1970s young women, aged 20 to 24, are less involved (person-years spent) in full-time employment (from 70 to 51 per cent) and more involved in part-time employment (from 3 to 12 per cent). The first development is due to the further prolongation of educational enrolment. The latter one can be explained by part-time work being the only possible entry into the labour market. At the ages of 25 to 29, women remain across cohorts for 60 per cent of their time involved in full-time work, but increase somewhat their involvement in part-time work (from 10 to 14 per cent) (Callens 1995a).

Looking at the intentions of women aged 21 to 40 with regard to their future employment, one gets an idea of the desirability of an entry into and an exit out of the labour market. Given their current occupational status, almost three out of four women do not expect any change in their situation. The women that do expect a change are mainly the unemployed women and those with irregular positions. Among the women that do expect a change the most prevalent one is a re-entry into the labour market from a housework or unemployed position (31 per cent). A less prevalent expected change is an exit out of the labour market to unemployment or housework (12 per cent). Being employed, 19 per cent expect a reduction in number of working hours and 10 per cent expect an expansion. Combining the expectations for stability and change, housewives and unemployed women seem to have contrasting expectations. Two-thirds of the housewives expect to stay in that position and a quarter want to enter the labour market, mainly on a part-time basis.

One-third (37 per cent) of the unemployed wives expect to stay unemployed and 59 per cent expect to enter the labour market.

Looking at female employment status at the time of first marriage, two trends appear across cohorts married since the late 1960s: the increase of part-time employment and the decrease in being a housewife. The marriage cohort of the early 1980s was particularly hit by unemployment.

At the time of the FFS about 48 per cent of the married women, aged 21 to 40, were employed full-time. Married women in their twenties had higher full-time activity rates. About 25 per cent of the married women were working part-time and about 9 per cent were unemployed. Being employed part-time is less prevalent and being unemployed is more prevalent in the youngest age group entering the labour market since the 1980s. Of the married women 11 per cent were housewives. Being a housewife is strongly age-related; it shows up particularly from age 30 onwards.

Looking at the kind of transitions in the employment career of married men and women, aged 21 to 40, the gender-specificity is very obvious (Table 5.1). Prevalent transitions in the wife's employment career are employment reduction (from full-time to part-time) and the labour-market exit (to unemployment and housekeeping). Given the changes in labour-market policies, it is not clear to what degree the reduction was (in)voluntary. About one-third of part-time work was by obligation in 1987 (Eurostat 1992). Given the regulations about the (cessation of) unemployment benefit the (in)voluntary character of the labour-market exits is not clear either. About 131 labour-market exits are to career leave, a transition that is also subject to sector-specific regulations. About 300 transitions in the wife's occupational career are to or from irregular employment periods.

Table 5.1. Gender-specific employment transitions of married couples

Origin state	Destination state	N of events	
		men	women
Full-time	Part-time	15	459
Full-time	Unemployed	55	496
Full-time	Housework	2	179
Part-time	Full-time	16	210
Part-time	Unemployed	1	85
Part-time	Housework	0	48
Unemployed	Full-time	87	307
Unemployed	Part-time	5	193
Unemployed	Housework	0	75
Housework	Full-time	0	93
Housework	Part-time	1	63

Source: FFS Flanders, 1991–2, CBGS Brussels (*N* men = 1,248, *N* women = 2,269).

Among married women in Flanders full-time employment decreases and part-time employment increases across the family cycle (Figure 5.1). Particularly the birth cohort of 1961–5, entering the labour market in the 1980s, is less involved in full-time work and more involved in part-time work. Moreover, this cohort is most affected by unemployment. Housework is most popular in the oldest cohort. An increase in household work is best observable at the birth of the third child.

Determinants of the Female Labour-Market Exit

To highlight better the specific determinants of transitions in the female employment career, three kinds of exits out of the labour market are analysed: the employment reduction (being the transition from full-time to part-time employment); the transition from (full-time or part-time) employment to unemployment, and the transition from (full-time or part-time) employment to housework (Table 5.2).

Table 5.2. Effects on the wife's rate of employment exit

	Full-time employment to part-time employment	Employment to unemployment	Employment to housework
Duration < 6 months	−6.4060*	−0.8912	−2.5287
Duration 6–12 months	−5.6150*	−0.3836	−1.9702
Duration 1–3 years	−6.1314*	−0.7035	−1.1898
Duration 3–5 years	−6.0788*	−1.0310	−1.3199
Duration > 5 years	−6.0362*	−1.2110	−1.3894
Married 1976–80	0.4474*	0.3509*	−0.4876*
Married 1981–85	0.9095*	0.5633*	−1.3455*
Married after 1985	1.3189*	0.6613*	−1.8489*
W's age	−0.1745	−0.1075	−0.5694*
W's age sq.	0.0036	0.0002	0.0059
W's education	0.0701*	−0.1525*	−0.1143*
H's education	0.0560*	−0.0075	0.0097
H's unemployment	0.1005	0.3113*	−0.0741
W's social origin	−0.0075	0.0049	0.0290
H's social origin	−0.0008	0.0222	0.0226
Mother's employment	0.0083	−0.0129	−0.2296*
W's employment before marriage	−0.0008	−0.0003	0.0032
W's age at marriage	−0.0164	−0.0451	0.2719
N of children	0.2694	0.0407	0.5182
Pre-school child	0.6266	0.5034*	−0.1671
Full/part-time	—	−0.3914*	0.5788*
Number of events	411	338	88

Source: FFS Flanders, 1991–2, CBGS Brussels. Piecewise constant model. *p < .05.

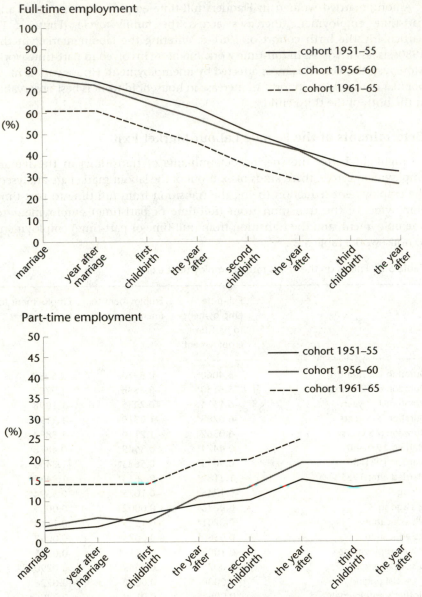

Figure 5.1. Occupational status of women at specific family events, by birth cohort. *Source*: FFS-Flanders, 1991–2, CBGS Brussels.

Housework

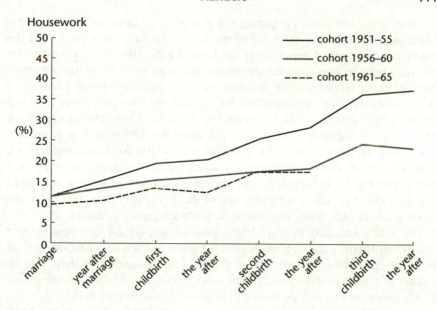

Unemployment

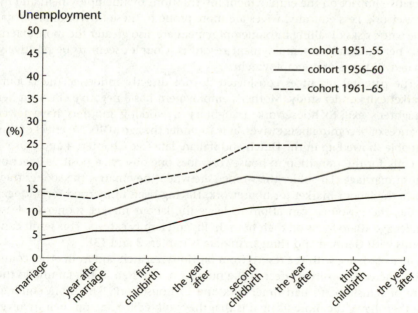

Apart from changing circumstances across time, changes remain across marriage cohorts in the exits out of the labour market. The direction of the marriage cohort effect depends on the kind of exit. The effect is positive for the transition to part-time employment: the more recently married women have a higher rate of leaving full-time work for part-time work. Changes in labour-market policy are responsible for this increase. The positive effect is less strong for the exit to unemployment. The effect is, as predicted, negative for the exit to housework: women married since the 1980s have a lower rate for leaving the labour market for housework. Part-time work, unemployment, and career leave became '(in)voluntary solutions' for the combination of work and family life. Only for the exit to housework can one observe a significant negative effect of age. Under the age of 40, it appears that, the older the women are, the less likely they are to stop working and do housework.

The wife's educational level has a positive impact on her employment reduction. Highly educated wives have a higher probability of reducing their full-time employment involvement. Only for this transition is there also an impact of the husband's educational level. Spouses of highly educated husbands can afford to reduce their employment hours. Wives' schooling has a negative impact on the employment interruptions by unemployment and by housework. Less educated wives are more prone to these (in)voluntary exits. The wife's risks of falling into unemployment are also greater the more extensive her husband's unemployment record is. Couples seem to be positively 'mated' in terms of unemployment.

The parental resources considered do not directly influence the labour-market exits under study. Mother's employment has a negative effect on her daughter's exit to housework. Daughters of working mothers have fewer chances of becoming housewives, at least under the age of 40. No effect of this variable showed up in the Dutch and Italian data (see Chapters 4 and 6).

Only for the transition to housework does one observe a positive effect of age at marriage. The older the women are when they marry, the sooner they leave the labour market for housework. Having been unmarried for a longer while, these women can afford to leave the labour market sooner (at least under age 40) to focus on their households and family careers. This result conforms with German and Hungarian data (Chapters 3 and 13).

In accordance with the results from previous research and from other countries, there is a positive effect of the number of children in the family on the rate of transition to part-time work and to housework. The more children mothers have, the more likely it is that they will reduce or stop their involvement in the labour market. This is in accordance with the motives married women mention for working part-time or being housewives (see above). The presence of at least one pre-school child almost doubles the transition rate to part-time work. The presence of at least one pre-school child also increases the transition rate to unemployment by more than 50 per cent. It is not yet clear whether personal decisions (for example, lowered motivation to prolong a contract) or regulations in the labour market are involved. It looks somewhat surprising that the presence of pre-school children does not influence the exit to housework. The rich availability of childcare facilities can partly explain these results.

The exit rate to unemployment is higher if women are working full-time compared to part-time. The exit rate to housework is higher if women are working part-time compared to full-time. The same result was found in the Italian data (see Chapter 6).

The results show that labour-market exits at relatively young ages are mainly determined by the wife's educational level and by the (number and/or age of) children. Characteristics of other persons such as the husband or the parents (-in-law) do not or only seldom directly influence the wife's occupational career. A husband's higher cultural resources (educational level) enable a wife to afford part-time work; a husband's unfavourable economic resources (unemployment record) brings a wife into unemployment. Apart from the changes in many other characteristics across time, there remains a time effect (marriage cohort effect), probably related to economic cycles and to changes in labour-market policies.

Determinants of the Female Labour-Market (Re-)entry

To better highlight the female labour market (re-)entry, three kinds of (re-)entry are distinguished: the employment expansion (being the transition from part-time to full-time employment); the re-entry to (full-time or part-time) employment after unemployment, and the re-entry to (full-time or part-time) employment after household work (Table 5.3). Only for the re-entry after a period of unemployment do some significant effects show up. Younger marriage cohorts can re-enter the labour market more quickly after a period of unemployment. The impact of the educational level is positive. Highly educated wives are more likely to re-enter the labour market after an unemployment period. They can more easily reinvest their human capital in the labour market. The effect of the partner's unemployment record is almost significant. The more extensive the husband's unemployment record, the higher the probability that the wife will re-enter the labour market after her unemployment period. There is a negative effect of age at marriage. The younger the women are at marriage, the more likely they are to re-enter the labour market after a period of unemployment. As in the case of the exit to housework, this impact of age at marriage is hard to explain as work experience before marriage is controlled for.

The number of children has a negative effect on job re-entry after unemployment. The presence of pre-school children also reduces the likelihood of becoming employed after a period of unemployment. Unemployed mothers with more children and with very young children are less favourable candidates for the labour market. It is unclear to which degree this is related to individual preferences/decisions or to rules of the labour market.

Under the age of 40, there is no significant effect of age for any of the transitions. Nor is there any direct impact of parental resources. Re-entries into the

Table 5.3. Effects on the wife's rate of employment re-entry

	Part-time to full-time	Unemployment to employment	Housework to employment
Duration < 12 months	−2.5962	−6.1835*	−0.3837
Duration 1–3 years	−1.9857	−5.7807*	−1.1811
Duration 3–5 years	−2.2622	−6.2915*	−1.7583
Duration > 5 years	−2.2967	−6.5391*	−2.1126
Married 1976–80	−0.4065	0.2551	0.4069
Married 1980–	−0.2486	0.6766*	0.3189
W's age	0.2248	0.1593	−0.4440
W's age sq.	0.0027	−0.0022	0.0069
W's education	0.0644	0.1281*	0.0133
H's education	−0.0267	−0.0129	0.0667
H's unemployment	−0.0587	0.2743	−0.2379
W's social origin	0.0369	0.0117	−0.0001
H's social origin	−0.0128	−0.0151	−0.0093
Mother's employment	0.0125	0.0764	0.0625
W's employment before marriage	−0.0066	0.0015	0.0025
W's age at marriage	0.0554	−0.0942*	0.0876
N of children	−0.2611	−0.2119*	0.2368
Pre-school child	−0.3863	−0.3302*	−0.2980
N of events	163	318	88

Source: FFS Flanders, 1991–2, CBGS Brussels. Piecewise constant model. *p < .05.

labour market after part-time work and housework are not much subjected to the factors under study. The processes underlying a re-entry to the labour market after a period of housework have not been detected in this study.

Conclusion

Despite the varying degrees of homogamy within couples with regard to characteristics that are relevant for the employment and/or family career (education, religion, employment status, income), there is not much empirical evidence for any specific contribution of the husband's characteristics to the family-formation process or to the wife's employment career. In this study we found evidence for an impact of the husband's education in case of the wife's transition from full-time to part-time employment and for an impact of the husband's unemployment record on the wife's rate of transition into and out of unemployment.

In studies on the family-formation process, but also in this study on the female employment career, there is no or only a weak direct influence of the parents' economic resources. These results suggest that decisions in the family and employment career are individual decisions. This suggestion of individualistic thinking is in line with the individualization of economic rights and obligations. The potential instability of work and family careers seems to promote a kind of 'independent' behaviour.

Factors known to play an important role in the general labour-force participation of women—being the educational level and the number and/or age of children—also seem to determine more specific transitions in the female employment career, although in a more differentiated way. The specific role of the tradition of a high female activity rate, of the steering influence of the part-time employment policy, and of the generous availability of childcare facilities in Flanders, can only become clear in comparative studies with other countries.

References

Bernasco, W., P. M. de Graaf and W. C. Ultee (1998). 'Coupled Careers: Effects of Spouse's Resources on Occupational Attainment in the Netherlands', *European Sociological Review*, 14/1: 15–32.

Bitter, R. G. (1986). 'Late Marriage and Marital Instability: The Effects of Heterogeneity and Inflexibility', *Journal of Marriage and the Family*, 48: 631–40.

Blossfeld, H.-P. (1995). *The New Role of Women: Family Formation in Modern Societies* (Boulder, Colo.: Westview Press).

Callens, M. (1995a). 'Family Life Cycle and Employment in Flanders: Results from NEGO V (1991)', in H. Van de Brekel and F. Deven (eds.), *Population and Family in the Low Countries* (Dordrecht: Kluwer Academic Publishers), 81–106.

——(1995b). De 'Fertility and Family Survey' in Vlaanderen (Nego V, 1991): De gegevensverzameling (The Fertility and Family Survey in Flanders (Nego V, 1991): Data Collection) (Brussels: CBGS-document 1995/4).

——(1995c). 'Third Births in Flanders: Intensity Regression Results from the 1991 Fertility and Family Survey in Flanders', paper prepared for the Demographic Unit, Stockholm University.

——, W. van Hoorn, and A. de Jong (2000). 'Labour Force Participation of Mothers', in J. de Beer and F. Deven (eds.), *Diversity in Family Formation: The Second Demographic Transition in Belgium and the Netherlands* (European Studies of Population; Dordrecht: Kluwer Academic Publishers).

Commission of the European Communities (1993). *Employment in Europe 1993* (Luxembourg: Office for Official Publications of the European Communities).

Corijn, M. (1996). *Transition into Adulthood: Results from the Fertility and Family Survey 1991–92* (Brussels: NIDI/CBGS Publication, vol. 32).

——A. C. Liefbroer, and J. de Jong Gierveld (1996). 'It Takes Two to Tango, doesn't it? The Influence of Couple Characteristics on the Timing of the Birth of the First Child', *Journal of Marriage and the Family*, 58: 117–26.

Daelemans, I., and M. Callens (1994). De 'Fertility and Family Survey' in Brussel (The Fertility and Family Survey in Brussels) (Brussels: CBGS-document 1994/6).

Eurostat (1992). *Women in the European Community* (Luxembourg: Office for Publications of the European Communities).

Gornick, J. C., M. K. Meyers, and K. E. Ross (1997). 'Supporting the Employment of Mothers: Policy Variation across Fourteen Welfare States', *Journal of European Social Policy*, 7: 45–70.

Henkens, K., J. Siegers, and K. Van Den Bosch (1992). 'Married Women on the Labour Market: A Comparative Study of Belgium and the Netherlands', *Bevolking en Gezin*, 1: 77–99.

Huinink, J. (1995). 'Education, Work and Family Patterns of Men: The Case of West Germany', in H.-P. Blossfeld (ed.), *The New Role of Women: Family Formation in Modern Societies* (Boulder, Colo.: Westview Press), 247–62.

Impens, K. K. (1987). 'De impact van werkloosheid bij vrouwen op de vruchtbaarheid in Vlaanderen' (The Impact of Female Unemployment on their Fertility in Flanders), *Bevolking en Gezin*, 3: 73–98.

Kalmijn, M. (1991). 'Shifting Boundaries: Trends in Religious and Educational Homogamy', *American Sociological Review*, 56: 786–800.

——(1996). 'Effecten van opleidingsniveau, duur en richting op het tijdstip waarop paren hun eerste kind krijgen' (Effects of the Educational Level, Duration and Orientation on the Timing of the First Child among Couples), *Bevolking en Gezin*, 3: 41–71.

Krishnan, V. (1993). 'Religious Homogamy and Voluntary Childlessness in Canada', *Sociological Perspectives*, 36: 83–93.

Liefbroer, A. C., M. Corijn, and J. de Jong Gierveld (1996). *Similarity and Diversity in the Start of the Family Formation Process in the Low Countries* (Brussels: CBGS-document, 3).

Marcum, J. P. (1986). 'Explaining Protestant Fertility: Belief, Commitment, and Homogamy', *Sociological Quarterly*, 27: 547–58.

Mascie-Taylor, C. G. N. (1986). 'Assortative Mating and Differential Fertility', *Biology and Society*, 3: 167–70.

Oppenheimer, V. K., M. Kalmijn, and V. Lew (1993). 'Men's Transition to Work and Marriage Timing", paper presented at the Annual Meeting of the Population Association of America, Cincinnati, Ohio.

Pauwels, K., M. De Wachter, L. Deschamps, and W. Van Dongen (1984). 'Beroepsarbeid van jonge vrouwen met een gezin. Een duurzaam engagement' (Employment of Young Women with a Family: A Long-Term Commitment), *Bevolking en Gezin*, 3: 237–48.

Ramioul, M. (1992). 'Two-Speed Flexibility and the Position of Females on the Labour Market in Flanders', *Bevolking en Gezin*, 1: 169–93.

Ray, J. C. (1997). 'The Role of Demographic and Economic Characteristics of Twelve Member States of the European Union in the Diversity of State Support for Families', *Journal of European Social Policy*, 7: 5–16.

Rogler, L. H., and M. E. Procidano (1989). 'Marital Heterogamy and Marital Quality in Puerto Rican families', *Journal of Marriage and the Family*, 51: 363–72.

Rohwer, G. (1994). *TDA (Transition Data Analysis), version 5.7* (Bremen: Institute for Empirical and Applied Sociology, University of Bremen).

Shehan, C. L., E. W. Bock and G. R. Lee (1990). 'Religious Heterogamy, Religiosity, and Marital Happiness: The Case of Catholics', *Journal of Marriage and the Family*, 52: 73–9.

Smeenk, W., N. D. de Graaf, and W. Ultee (1997). 'The When and Whom of First Household Formation. Socio-Economic Attributes Influencing Timing of First Household Formation and Educational Level of the Partner', paper presented at the NSV Marktdag Sociologie, Utrecht.

Sørenson, A. M. (1989). 'Husbands' and Wives' Characteristics and Fertility Decisions: A Diagonal Mobility Model', *Demography*, 26: 125–35.

Thomson, E. (1990). 'Two into One: Structural Models of Couple Behavior', in C. W. Draper and A. C. Marcos (eds.), *Family Variables: Conceptualisation, Measurement and Use* (Newbury Park, Calif.: Sage), 129–42.

Triest, M. (1993). 'De arbeidsmarktposities van vrouwen in Belgi (en de rol van de verzorgingsstaat' (The Position of Women in the Labour Force in Belgium and the Role of the Welfare State), *Tijdschrift voor Arbeidsvraagstukken*, 9: 63–5.

Tzeng, M. S. (1992). 'The Effects of Socioeconomic Heterogamy and Changes on Marital Dissolution for First Marriages', *Journal of Marriage and the Family*, 54: 609–19.

Van Dongen, W. *et al.* (1995). *De dagelijkse puzzel 'gezin en arbeid'. Feiten, wensen en problemen inzake de combinatie van beroeps- en gezinsarbeid in Vlaanderen* (The Daily Puzzle 'Family and Work': Facts, Wishes and Problems with Regard to the Combination of Work and Family Life) (Brussels: CBGS-Monografie, 2).

Van Hoof, K. (1997). *Tewerkstelling van vrouwen en segregatie* (Female Employment and Segregration) (Brussel: NIS, Monografie 8).

Van Peer, C., and H. Moors (1996). 'Perceived Obstacles to Fertility: Opinions on Family Policies in Flanders and in the Netherlands', in H. Van den Brekel and F. Deven (eds.), *Population and Family in the Low Countries 1995* (Dordrecht: Kluwer Academic Publishers), 41–66.

APPENDIX TO CHAPTER 5: INDEPENDENT VARIABLES

Resources

- The woman's educational level, measured by the legal duration of the educational qualification;
- the woman's social origin, operationalized by the educational level of her father, measured by the legal duration of the educational qualification;
- the partner's educational level, measured by the legal duration of the educational qualification;
- the partner's social origin, operationalized by his father's educational level, measured by the legal duration of the educational qualification;
- the mother's employment, distinguishing no employment at all, employment for less than eight years, employment for eight years or more until the respondent reached age 16;
- the partner's unemployment record, measured by the person-years of unemployment since the completion of education.

Family status

- The woman's premarital employment experience, measured as cumulative duration of her employment (full-time and/or part-time) before marriage;
- the woman's age at marriage;
- the number of children as a time-dependent covariate;
- the presence of a pre-school child as a time-dependent dummy variable, indicating the presence in the family of at least one child under age 3.

Time effects

- the woman's age, included in the models in a linear and quadratic form as a time-dependent covariate;
- the marriage cohort, introduced as three dummy variables: married in 1976–80; married in 1981–85; married after 1985. The reference category is couples married before 1976. For some analyses the two youngest marriage cohorts are taken together to avoid numerical problems.

III

The 'Mediterranean' Welfare State Regime

6

The Employment Behaviour of Married Women in Italy

FABRIZIO BERNARDI

Introduction

THE aim of this study is to analyse the mechanism that accounts for married women's participation in the labour market. More specifically I will be studying the processes that take some women out of the labour market as housewives, as well as the processes taking or keeping other women in it. It has recently been shown that the employment behaviour of married women is strongly dependent on events related to the family life course and, particularly, the partner's parallel career (Bernasco 1994; Bernasco *et al.* 1998). Following this longitudinal approach, in my analysis of the mechanism responsible for female participation in the labour market, I focus on two questions. First, what level of homogamy as regards career resources exists within married couples? This can be considered as a preliminary question and its answer establishes the wives' and husbands' starting conditions in their parallel careers. Secondly, to what extent are women's careers affected by their family situation and in particular by their husbands' resources and careers?

These questions are related to important policy issues. First of all, the well-known increase in the female labour supply is paralleled by an emerging risk of growing differences, or rather, inequalities between women themselves. According to some authors, employment versus non-employment might be the cause of polarization of the female population, with strong consequences in terms of orientations and lifestyles (Gerson 1987; Hakim 1996). Second, it is a widely accepted empirical result that the risk of poverty is higher for single-income families and that the risk is maximum for non-employed mothers who remain in charge of their children after a divorce or death of the partner (Room 1990; Smeeding *et al.* 1990; for Italy, Zanatta 1996). Thus, female employment acts as a protection against the risk of falling into poverty for mothers with children in the case of family break-up or temporary unemployment of the husband. The issue is even more topical since, with the growth of the divorce rate, the number of single-parent families is increasing, while, with a stronger demand for a flexible workforce, interruptions are also becoming more frequent in male careers. Moreover, non-employed women, depending on their husband's income, have less chance to opt for a divorce or end a conjugal relationship that does not satisfy them any more (Barbagli 1990). So these women face a doubly penalizing situation: they have limited autonomy to choose in their conjugal relationship and, should they opt for a divorce, they run a high risk of finding themselves poverty-stricken. Finally, one of the possible solutions suggested to address the current 'welfare state' crisis is, precisely, to promote and support women's participation in the labour market (Esping-Andersen 1999). Therefore, the results of my analysis could give some insights into these problems.

The chapter is organized in the following way. In the next section I shortly review the main theories about women's participation in the labour market. In the third section, in an international comparative perspective, some peculiarities of the Italian labour market and institutional context are reported. Then, in the fourth section, the variables and the data used in the empirical analysis are described; the results are discussed in detail in the fifth section. Finally, I summarize the principal findings of my analysis and try to draw some tentative conclusions.

Theories of Female Labour Supply

I will start by separating the economic from the sociological theories. I have already reviewed the theories on the influences that the husband's resources have on the wife's career in another paper (Bernardi 1999a). Here, I will only recall some important perspectives in the theoretical debate on female employment.

Economic theories

Human capital theory explains the outcome in the labour market by referring to the previous investment made by individuals in their skills and abilities (Becker 1964). This theory has been applied to explain a large range of phenomena including the female labour supply. According to this theory, for women it is less rational to invest in human capital as they will spend a shorter period in the labour market, due to their domestic responsibilities, and so they will have less time to profit from their investment. Female segregation in the labour market and discontinuous employment experiences are then explained on the basis of a smaller investment in human capital made by women.

The New Home Economics (Becker 1991) can be considered an extension of the human capital theory that takes into account the family context to explain female employment behaviour. Becker starts with the assumption that partners in a couple pool their resources and take decisions in order to maximize the joint family utility. A particularly important decision that the couple has to take is how to distribute its time between paid market work and non-paid domestic work. If market and domestic production functions have constant or increasing returns to scale, then it is efficient that a husband and wife should specialize completely in market work or in domestic work. Thus, the crucial point is who specializes in domestic work and who specializes in market work. The couple takes this decision by comparing the husband's and wife's comparative advantage in market work and domestic work. Bernasco (1994: 40) has shown that considering two women with equal market productivity, the likelihood of them specializing in domestic work is higher, the higher the husband's market productivity is. Thus, Becker's comparative advantage theory implies that the husband's resources have a negative effect on the wife's participation in the labour market.

Sociological theories

Labour-market sociology has developed since the second half of the 1970s in opposition to human capital theory and status attainment research which focus almost exclusively on the supply side to explain individual outcomes in the labour market (Kalleberg and Sørensen 1979). In this new approach, defined as neo-structuralism (Sørensen 1986), the analysis shifts to the demand side and, specifically, to the labour market structures: the effects of economic sectors, firms and internal labour markets, occupation, social class, unions, and economic policies become objects of investigation (Kalleberg 1988). In short, it is recognized that the labour market is not actually a market and its workings are ruled by social and institutional factors: among these, one of the most important is the welfare state.

Esping-Andersen's (1990) study offers important indications of the influence that welfare states have for women's employment. More specifically, each of the three welfare state regimes identified by Esping-Andersen is associated with a distinct female career trajectory. In the conservative-corporatist regime, women's participation in the labour market is interrupted (if the woman has ever managed to enter the labour market) at the moment of family formation or events related to the family life course (care of children and the elderly); later on it becomes almost impossible, given the insider–outsider structure of the labour market, for them to succeed in finding a new job. In the social democratic regime, women's employment trajectories tend to be continuous and similar to men's. Finally, in the liberal regime, women's careers are more discontinuous and intermittent: as needs relating to the family life course arise, women temporarily exit from the labour market, to re-enter paid work as soon as the reason for domestic work is over.

Esping-Andersen's analysis has set off a wave of criticism, most of it from a feminist perspective: the criticisms focus on the omission from the study of welfare state regimes of the family and, more generally, of gender relations. So the main task and slogan of a new generation of studies on the welfare state, developed in the last few years, has been 'gendering the welfare state'

(Sainsbury 1994; Orloff 1996). Some authors have argued in favour of considering the support and commitment of the welfare state to female autonomy (O'Connor 1993; Orloff 1993). The indications in Esping-Andersen's study (1990), on the relations between welfare state regimes and female career models, have become the object of an in-depth comparative analysis of public policies supporting mothers' employment: more precisely, it has been studied how maternity leave laws, the availability of public care services for children at different ages, and school schedules affect the employment careers of mothers in different countries (Gornick *et al.* 1997). The results of this research show that there are three prevailing models of policy to support mothers' employment: a model of strong and continuous support that protects mothers' employment throughout the birth and childrearing period (maternity, infant, pre-school, and school age); a model of limited and contradictory support that combines guarantees and support for certain periods of the children's life course with gaps at others (for instance, protection of employment during the maternity period and lack of public care services for children under 3); a model of weak or no support that basically leaves women as solely responsible for handling the roles of mother and worker. These three models of support policy are associated with three distinct career models in the labour market: respectively, a continuous career similar to the male one; a broken career, made up of a single spell in the labour market followed by a definitive interruption; and a fragmented and discontinuous career, made up of many exits and re-entries into the labour market.

Important indications for the analysis of female employment behaviour can also be found in gender studies literature (Lorber and Farrell 1991). The main interest of these studies is investigating the mechanisms that create gender identities: how a division of socially legitimate roles and duties for men and women is constructed. There are various research perspectives in this field (Chodorow 1978; Gilligan 1982; West and Zimmerman 1991). However, the effects that gender identity has on individual employment destinies are more relevant to my research problem than the mechanism by which it is set in motion. In particular, it is important to recognize that female employment behaviour is embedded in a gender system that predefines the division between paid and domestic work for husbands and wives before the couples have a chance to negotiate their roles. To put it differently, the option of becoming a housewife is socially accepted and legitimate for women, but not for men (Milkman and Townsley 1994).

A Tentative Synthesis

Some of the theories reviewed explain female employment behaviour by reference to rational choices: this is the case of the comparative advantage theory proposed by Becker (1991). Other theories, the sociological ones, enlarge the analysis to the opportunity structure that constrains women's decisions relating to labour market participation. Other theories again put the stress on the role played by cultural conditioning. The main contribution made by Gambetta's analysis (1987) of decision mechanisms in education has been to show that a range of mechanisms—rational choice, structural constraints, and cultural conditioning—can be in action at the same time. Gambetta's explicative model can also be adopted to study women's careers in the labour market. The exits and (re-)entries into the labour market can be seen as the outcome of intentional choices, taken in a particular context of opportunities and constraints and conditioned, if not distorted, by the prevailing cultural models that define what is legitimate and acceptable for women and men.[1] Other researchers have already proved the fertility of an approach that integrates individual decisions, structural constraints, and cultural conditioning (England and Farkas 1986; Hakim 1996). In one of the best in-depth studies on this topic, Gerson (1985) has shown that women's careers are the result of complex and often painful decisions and negotiations between individual preferences, cultural orientations, and the set of opportunities and constraints that change over time. Women play an active role re-elaborating preferences and inclinations for paid market work in the light of the constraints and opportunities encountered over the course of their lives. In this process the husband's resources prove decisive because the economic need for the wife to work, at least to a certain extent, depends on these.

Thus, the theories reviewed in this section can be interpreted as being complementary more than alternative. On a theoretical level, women's transitions out of and into the labour market can be seen as the outcome of intentional choices, taken in a context defined by structural and institutional factors and conditioned by the prevailing gender-identity models that define, among the available options, the socially legitimate options for women. Evaluating the relevance of each of these mechanisms becomes an empirical problem.

Women in the Italian Labour Market: A Comparative Perspective

In the last few years Italian women have increasingly offered their labour outside their domestic walls. In spite of overall growth, Italy still has one of the lowest levels of female employment of all developed countries (OECD 2000). At the same time, the incidence of part-time employment is quite low, even if it has increased in the last years (Blossfeld and Hakim 1997). Part-time work is mainly concentrated in low-level unskilled occupations with no training and promotion opportunities (Meulders et al. 1994: 10). Moreover, half of the people working part-time are employed on a temporary basis and involuntary part-time employment is significantly higher than in the other countries: one

---

[1] For a more detailed discussion on the application of Gambetta's explicative model to the study of female employment see Bernardi (1999b).

woman in three working part-time is doing so because she has not been able to find a full-time job (Meulders *et al.* 1994: 30).

Moving to the social policies to support employment of mothers, an ambivalent and contradictory picture appears, made of light and shadow (Saraceno 1994, 1998). Starting with the light Italy has one of the best laws on maternity leave, when the length of the leave and the pay guaranteed are considered (Gornick *et al.* 1997). All working mothers are entitled to a period of five months paid leave (two before and three after childbirth), plus an additional leave period with reduced pay that can alternatively be taken by fathers. Incentives have recently been introduced in order to raise the number of fathers that take this leave. Second, there is a highly developed public system of kindergartens for pre-school children (3–5 years old): more than 95 per cent of children this age are covered by this service.

Coming to the shadow, not all women are equally covered by public policies. It is clear that women employed in the irregular economy do not enjoy any protection or guarantee of maternity leave. Moreover, in spite of the strong formal protection of the maternity period, there is still a risk, particularly strong in the less visible areas of the labour market, for example, in small firms, of an informal regulation of employment relations that penalizes employed women's maternity: in practice, punishments at the time of re-entry after maternity leave, in the form of job downgrading, or the obligation, at the time of hiring, to sign an undated dismissal letter that the employers will use at their discretion in case of maternity, are by no means rare events. On the other hand, some categories of workers enjoy more favourable conditions; such is the case of women employed in the public sector that combines: (*a*) higher employment protection that makes being fired almost impossible, (*b*) more flexible work schedules, (*c*) until 1992 a chance to retire after only sixteen years of work instead of the minimum twenty years required by law in order to gain access to the early retirement programme.

With regard to social services, there is a gap in public day-care for children aged under 2. This service is a non-compulsory local responsibility, is paid for by the users (with growing costs in recent years), and is rationed on the basis of need (there is privileged access for working mothers' children). As a result, only 6 per cent of children aged under 2 have access to this service (ISTAT 1995). The gap in the supply of services for infant children is paralleled by the lack of services for elderly and dependent people. In this case public policy assumes even more explicitly an intergenerational solidarity and entrust the family with primary responsibility for dependent and disabled members. Public care for older people is guaranteed only under two conditions: poverty and lack of family. In other words, the state delegates the care for the elderly to the family and intervenes only when the family fails in this task.

However, there are deep territorial differences, both in the availability of public services and in the labour-market conditions, that make it difficult to portray any single scenario of female employment in Italy. Day-care for children under 3, day-care for older persons, and services for the disabled are less widespread in the South. Moreover, whereas the female unemployment rate is less than 10 per cent in the Northern part of the country, it jumps to 30 per cent in the South (ISTAT 2000). These imbalances make employment conditions for women strongly dependent on the regional context.

To summarize, informal regulation, corporatism, and regional imbalances are indispensable caveats needed in understanding the functioning of the Italian labour market and, in particular, the employment behaviour of married women.

Data and Variables

The analysis is based on data from the Second National Fertility Survey (INF–2), carried out from the end of 1995 until the beginning of 1996 on a nationally representative sample of 4,284 women aged 20–50. By selecting only married couples, I have obtained the sample of 2,958 women used in this analysis. However, the husbands or cohabitants of only a subsample of these women were interviewed: complete data on the parallel careers of both partners of the couple are only available for 579 women.[2]

For the analysis of homogamy I considered the wife's and husband's education, measured by the legal duration of the educational qualifications possessed and social status of their jobs held at the time of marriage (or at the closest time to marriage), measured by the score in the de Lillo-Schizzerotto (1985) stratification scale.[3]

The dataset for the analysis of female employment consists of a series of respondent's employment and non-employment episodes. Following the analytical strategy applied by Bernasco (1994), I have set the starting time of the analysis one year before the date of marriage, defining an 'engagement period'. In this way it is possible to study also the transitions out of the labour market that occur in the months immediately before the marriage. The underlying assumption is that the partners already know each other in this period and decisions regarding labour market participation are possibly taken in view of the marriage.

The dependent variables are the transition rates from (1) employment to housekeeping status and from (2) housekeeping status to employment. Other studies have pointed out the importance of a distinction between full-time and part-time employment when studying female participation in the labour market. It would, thus, be natural, in line with the analysis conducted by Blossfeld *et al.* (Chapter 3 above), to distinguish the transitions from full-time employment to housekeeping status and the transitions from part-time employment to housekeeping status (and the other way round). However, in the Italian case

---

[2] These 579 women tend to be younger, more highly educated, and more frequently employed at the time of the survey when compared with the women of the whole sample. A formal test was made and none of these differences turned out significant with a p-value =0.01.

[3] The scores in the de Lillo-Schizzerotto (1985) scale refer to the social desirability of occupations.

the incidence of part-time employment, as I have mentioned above, is low. For this reason, and also in view of the small size of the sample, I have conducted no separate analysis for women employed full-time or part-time. I have introduced the type of contract—full-time, part-time, and no contract (illicit employment)—as an independent variable in the analysis of the transitions.

There are two kinds of independent variable: time-constant and time-varying variables which change their state over time. To introduce time-varying variables in the transition rate models, I have used the method of episode splitting (Blossfeld and Rowher 1995). A description and some basic statistics of the independent variables are reported in the appendix to this chapter. Some clarification seems to be required for the variables concerning gender identity.[4] First of all, I have considered whether the woman has had an experience of consensual union before marriage; in this way I identified a group of women who displayed a non-traditional or 'culturally deviant' behaviour (Saraceno 1996). In fact, consensual union is still rare in Italy: non-married cohabiting couples made up, in 1991, 1.4 per cent of all couples.[5] My hypothesis is that women who have previously questioned the dominant cultural model, according to which partners start living together at the time of marriage, will also question a traditional role division that relegates them to housekeeping status. Second, I have considered whether the woman's mother has ever worked. In this way it is possible to study whether having grown up in an household with a traditional gender division of labour affects the woman's participation in the labour market.

Results

Table 6.1 summarized information about the transitions out of/into the labour market. I have defined seven different patterns of possible trajectories:

(1) women who, having entered the labour market, have always been employed;
(2) women who have never entered the labour market and have always been housewives;
(3) women who were employed and have become housewives;
(4) women who were employed, became housewives and afterwards have re-entered the labour market;
(5) women with fragmented careers, that is, with more than two exits and re-entries;
(6) women with transitions out of the labour market, different from housekeeping (retirement, student);
(7) women currently unemployed, coming from whatever condition (employment or housekeeping).

---

[4] I have not used women's present attitudes and orientations to explain their previous employment career, for the obvious reason that the direction of causality between orientations and career could not be identified.

[5] The percentage is higher for younger couples, but it still remains very small: in my sample, for women aged 20–49, cohabiting couples made up 3.2 per cent of all couples.

Table 6.1. Patterns of employment trajectories: married women aged 30 to 50 years (*N*=2,450)

Always employed (E)	40.5
Always housewife (H)	21.0
Interruption (E/H)	23.4
Labour market re-entry (E/H/E)	4.3
Fragmented (. . . E/H/E/H . . .)	2.6
Other	3.4
Unemployed (E/U or H/U)	4.8
Total	100.0

E=employed, H=housewife, U=unemployed.

It should be underlined that Table 6.1 offers a snapshot of careers up to the interview date and, hence, refers to an ongoing process. This implies that the final number of transitions is to a certain extent underestimated.[6] Bearing this in mind, Table 6.1 highlights some crucial features of female employment in Italy. First of all, immobility is by large the dominant pattern: who is in, stays in, who is out stays out. Almost two women out of three have either always been employed (40.5 per cent) or always been housewives (21.0 per cent). At the opposite extreme, fragmented careers with many exits and re-entries in the labour market are extremely rare (2.6 per cent).

Second, an indicator for the risk of entrapment in the housekeeping status can be computed, dividing the percentage of women that have re-entered the labour market from an housekeeping status (4.3) by the percentage of women that exited from the labour market towards the housekeeping status (23.4): only one in five women who have left the labour market and have become housewives has managed to re-enter the labour market later on. This means that for married women, once they leave the labour market, the interruption has a high likelihood of being definitive. This result shows that a conservative welfare state, and particularly its Mediterranean variant, such as the Italian one (see Chapter 2 above), is associated with a model of broken careers for women, so that, once the labour market has been left, it is difficult to find a new way in.

But which factors are responsible for the observed differences in the patterns of employment trajectories? In order to answer this question, I started studying the partners' homogamy as regards career resources and then I moved to the micro level of individual and family life courses.

---

[6] Since Table 6.1 refers to an ongoing process, the risk of underestimation of the number of transitions is particularly for the youngest women. For this reason the analysis of the sequences of exit and entry in the labour market has been limited to women aged 30–50.

Homogamy

The homogamy analysis can be considered a preliminary step in my study and it provides a picture of differences between partners in their career resources, at the beginning of their parallel careers in the labour market. Figures 6.1 and 6.2 show the partners' differences as regards education and social status of their jobs at the time of marriage. Two results appear notable. First of all, a high degree of homogamy is found: more than half of the couples have the same level of education and almost 40 per cent of them had a similar occupation at the time of marriage as regards social status (differences in the scores between –5 and +5). This result confirms the high incidence of assortative mating already found for Italy by the National Social Mobility Survey (Cobalti and Schizzerotto 1994), and displays similarities with other cross-national results in this book. Second, the two figures show that there is an ascending and descending mobility through marriage both for men and women. This is particularly true for education: couples with a better educated husband are almost as frequent as couples with a better educated wife. The distribution of social status difference is more irregular due to the occurrence of certain typical situations: the peak at 30 points difference refers to couples where the husband is self-employed and the wife is a low-skilled dependent worker (blue or white collar). There are, however, frequent cases of wives who at the time of marriage

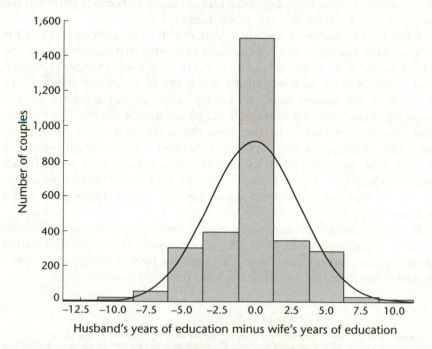

Figure 6.1. Distribution of difference in education: overall sample (N=2958).

had a higher occupational status than their husband: a typical couple situation is that of the wife employed as an executive clerk (with a high education) and the husband employed as a skilled worker (advantage of 15–20 points for the wife).[7]

These results show that the starting conditions of the husbands' and wives' parallel careers are similar: in most of the couples there are no differences and the situations when the wife is at a disadvantage are almost as frequent as the situation when the wife is at an advantage. At a macro level it is not evident that women make any smaller investment in human capital.[8] This result has to be compared with the data of Table 6.1: almost half of the women were housewives at the time of the interview. If the starting conditions for men and women are similar until the time of marriage and the subsequent outcomes are so divergent, that means one has to look *within* the marriage to understand what is going on. One is, thus, forced to move from the final and initial overall pictures of the parallel careers (Table 6.1 and Figures 6.1 and 6.2 respectively) to the dynamic micro story that takes place in the household context: and this is what I shall do in the next section.

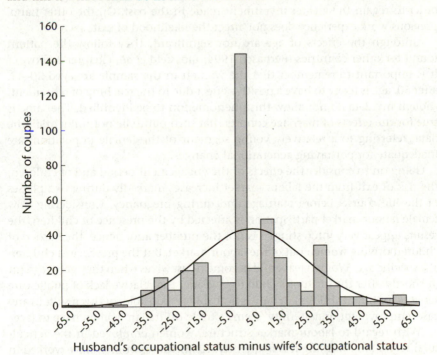

Figure 6.2. Distribution of status score difference: restricted sample (*N*=443).

---

[7] There are also some extreme cases, with the wife being a professional and the husband a manual worker.

[8] This result is consistent with what is known from the analysis on gender educational inequality: in Italy this inequality has fallen in the younger cohorts (Cobalti and Schizzerotto 1994).

Transition from Employment to Housekeeping

Table 6.2 presents the estimated effects on the transition rate of employment exits. In this modelling exercise I apply the following strategy. First, I model the employment exits without taking account of the spouses' resources: in this way I identify a 'baseline model'. Then I assess the 'spouse effect' by adding variables to the baseline model that account for spouses' resources.

Piecewise constant rate models are used to control for the duration dependence in employment. Starting with model 1, while social origin has no significant effect, the higher the educational level and the status of their occupation at the time of marriage, the lower the likelihood of becoming a housewife. That women with a high occupational status remain in the labour market is, to a certain extent, an expected result: the more advantageous an occupation is, the greater the forgone earnings are in leaving it. It is less automatic that education exerts an autonomous influence on female participation in the labour market. According to the human capital theory, given a certain occupation, women with higher education will tend to continue their employment experience in order to regain the greater investment made in the past. On the other hand, previous work experience does not affect the likelihood of exit.

Although the effects of age are not significant, they follow the pattern found for other countries (Bernasco 1994; Blossfeld *et al.*, Chapter 3 above).[9] It is important to remember that the women in the sample are aged 20–49: after 50, age is likely to have a positive effect due to the reaching of retirement, though my data do not allow this phenomenon to be identified. The same is true for the effects of marriage cohorts that turn out to be not influential: the data, referring to a relatively young segment of the female population, are inadequate for portraying generational changes.

Going on to consider the effects of the engagement period and of children, the risk of exit from the labour market increases markedly during two phases of the life course: before marriage and during pregnancy. Considering how female labour-market participation is affected by the presence of children, the results appear very interesting: it is not the number and, hence, the burden of children driving women out of the labour market, but the presence of children at a specific age. Women leave and become housewives when they get pregnant or shortly after the birth of a child (0–3 years): the relative lack of public care services for infant children in Italy is probably responsible for this result. In any case 'employment or maternity' seems a trade-off Italian women have to face.

With regard to labour-market structure, women employed in the agricultural sector stop working less frequently. Historically, women have worked in agriculture, managing to combine this activity with their domestic responsibilities. Employment in this sector is more flexible, requiring the female contribution at strategic moments, and in strict connection with the family

---

[9] I also tried including age in different forms (for instance, five years dummies), but there was no improvement in the fit of models.

context. Generally speaking, employment in agriculture is characterized by a weak separation between the productive and the domestic spheres.

A smaller likelihood of quitting is also found for women employed in the public sector. As I have already mentioned, for these women employment is more safeguarded and labour conditions are, not always but often, more flexible and easier to reconcile with domestic duties. Moreover, in many segments of the public sector there are more opportunities for career advancement than in the private sector: this is true, the more automatic and not discretionary the career mechanisms are (Rella 1990); and other studies have shown that career promotion, through an increase in forgone earnings in case of exit from the labour market or through an increase in job commitment, reduce the likelihood of any subsequent interruption (Gerson 1985). The reverse arguments hold true for women employed with no contract: they have no employment protection, few opportunities to negotiate their work schedules, and almost no chance of career promotion.

The effect of working part-time is not significant: this is quite a surprising result. Part-time work ideally provides more flexibility for women and should facilitate sharing of time between work and family. The logical expectation would be that women employed part-time are less likely to quit the labour market. But part-time employment can also have different implications (Blossfeld and Hakim 1997). For instance, according to the human capital theory, the lower investment in the job (only part-time) should make an interruption less penalizing. Moreover, the wages are lower and so, according to Becker's theory, the comparative advantage for husbands is greater. Thus, there might be opposing mechanisms in action at the same time and this might explain why the effect of part-time work is not significant.

Job seasonality has no significant effect: probably the higher flexibility of this kind of employment is balanced by its temporary nature and by the absence of any career opportunity. Considering the effects of the geographical areas, employment interruptions are more frequent for women in Central and Southern Italy. Thus, the region of residence is, and has been in the recent past, a crucial basis for differentiation among Italian women. The lower availability of social services in certain regions, leaving women with the primary responsibility for family needs, seems to account for this result.

Finally, with regard to the gender-identity variables, women who cohabited before marriage have a lower likelihood of becoming housewives. The result confirms that hypothesis that women who have previously questioned the dominant cultural model, according to which partners start living together at the time of marriage, will also question a traditional division of roles that relegates them to housekeeping status. On the other hand, the hypothesis of an intergenerational transmission of the housekeeping role, through employment interruption, is not confirmed: the effect of having a mother who has never worked on the likelihood of becoming a housewife, although positive, is not significant.

In model 2 all the non-significant effects (apart from woman's age and that of her children) are eliminated and a 'baseline model' is identified. In the next

Table 6.2. Effects on the transition rate from employment to housekeeping

	Model 1	Model 2	Model 3	Model 4	Model 5	Model 6	Model 7
Duration < 6 months	-3.863**	-4.084**	-4.073**	-6.753**	-6.596**	-6.781**	-6.875**
Duration 6–18 months	-2.701**	-2.924**	-2.914**	-5.899**	-5.744**	-5.929**	-6.017**
Duration 1.5—3 years	-3.237**	-3.446**	-3.459**	-7.761**	-7.105**	-7.311**	-7.400**
Duration > 3 years	-3.710**	-3.970**	-3.961**	-7.761**	-7.572**	-7.789**	-7.878**
W's father's education	0.006						
W's education	-0.048**	-0.043**	-0.050**	-0.066**	-0.063**	-0.078**	-0.081**
W's occup. score	-0.016**	-0.017**	-0.017**	-0.019**	-0.018**	-0.019**	-0.011
W's age/10	-0.070	-0.052	-0.055	0.063	0.063	0.062	0.057
(W's age/10) squared	0.001	0.001	0.001	-0.000	-0.000	-0.000	-0.000
Married 1971–80	-0.020						
Married 1981–	0.117						
Engagement	0.648**	0.666**	0.662**	0.873**	0.887**	0.879**	0.878**
No. of children	0.047						
Pregnacy	1.060**	1.059**	1.059**	1.265**	1.261**	1.276**	1.277**
Infant child (0–3)	0.226*	0.286**	0.292**	0.852**	0.843**	0.864**	0.878**
Pre-school (3–6)	-0.213	-0.177	-0.165	0.137	0.111	0.148	0.171

School child (> 6)	-0.081	-0.063	-0.002	-0.015	0.008	0.033
W's full-time exp.	0.001					
W's part-time exp.	-0.001					
W's irregular exp.	0.001					
Agricultural sector	-1.255**	-1.183**	-2.613**	-2.560**	-2.601**	-2.576**
Public sector	-0.820***	-0.850***	-1.286***	-1.261***	-1.295***	-1.329***
No contract	0.493**	0.495***	0.997***	0.971***	0.982***	0.962***
Part-time	0.067					
Seasonal job	0.206					
Centre	0.204**	0.210**	0.378*	0.388*	0.377*	0.397*
South Islands	0.228***	0.272***	0.447***	0.435***	0.454***	0.437***
W's mother never worked	0.120					
Pre-marriage cohabitation	-0.450**	-0.411**	-2.442**	-2.445**	-2.457**	-2.481**
H's education		0.134	0.009*	0.021	0.017	0.019
H's occup. score					0.008	
H's father's education					0.008	0.007
H's comparative advantage in market work						0.407***
N of events	783	783	131	131	131	131

Piecewise constant model. ** significant, $p < 0.05$, * significant, $p < 0.10$.

models, the husband's career resources and social origin are considered. As mentioned above, in the INF–2 survey the information on the husband's occupational status at the time of marriage and social origin are available only for a subsample of 579 women: this explains the lower number of events, starting from model 4. A formal test was performed to check if the results are stable, moving from the large sample to the subsample: the only substantial difference is that the women in the subsample are less likely to quit the labour market.[10] Apart from this important exception (that is captured by the differences in the period effects of the piecewise constant models), the results for the subsample are found to be reliable.

Moving to the interpretation of the results, the spouse's resources have a positive effect on the women's exit from the labour market, as has also been found, for example, in Spain (see Chapter 7 below) or Germany (Chapter 3 above). In particular, the result for the husband's occupational status (model 4) seems to be in accordance with the hypothesis drawn from Becker's theory: the higher the husband's occupational status, the higher the likelihood that the wife will leave the labour market. Given the high level of homogamy, women with high education and high occupational status are likely to be married to a husband with high education and high occupational status. Therefore, these women experience the effects of opposing factors: while their resources make remaining in the labour market possible and convenient, at the same time their husbands' resources drive them into a domestic role.

The effects of the husband's education (model 3) and social origin (model 5), although positive, are not significant. When the husband's resources and social origin are both included in model 6, because of collinearity among variables, the effect of occupational status becomes non-significant.

Finally, in model 7, I introduce a dummy variable that is equal to 1 when the husband has an occupational status higher than his wife's: this dummy can be interpreted as indicating that the husband has a comparative advantage in paid market work. According to Becker's theory, the comparative advantage is the criterion that governs women's choices between paid and domestic work.[11] The positive value of this effect means that, when the husband has a comparative advantage in market work, the wife has a higher likelihood of leaving the labour market.

Transition from Housekeeping to Employment

Table 6.3 presents the estimated effects on the transition rate from housekeeping to employment. First, I identify a 'baseline'model and then I add to it

[10] I performed the formal test in the following way. I started from model 2, on the large sample, and I included a dummy variable, called 'subsample', equal to 1 if the woman is one of the 579 women of the subsample, 0 otherwise. Then I included the interactions between the dummy 'subsample' and all the variables of model 2. The only significant differences (p = 0.01), between the results in the large sample and in the subsample, refer to the baseline rates of the piecewise exponential model (underestimation in the subsample) and to the effect of the variable 'employment with no contract' (overestimation in the subsample).

[11] For a more in-depth test of Becker's comparative advantage theory see Bernardi (1999a).

the variables that account for spouse's resources. Model 1 shows that the exit from a housekeeping status is easier for women with higher career resources: in particular, education is the crucial resource that opens the door to the labour market. For women who have already had work experience, the effect of occupational status at the time of marriage, although positive, is not significant.[12] However, women with longer full-time experience before becoming housewives have a greater likelihood of re-entering the labour market.

While there is no difference according to the marriage cohort, for older women it is more difficult to quit housekeeping status. With regard to the children variables, exit from housekeeping status is more likely when the children have reached school age. At this point of the family life course, the burden of direct childcare becomes lighter and the mothers have a chance to leave the home. Comparing this result with the results of the previous section, the children's presence seems to have contrasting effects on mother's employment: on the one hand, children of a young age (0–3 years) act as a constraint on the mother's employment because of the need to look after them; on the other, once grown up, they might drive the mother into paid work, to meet the increased economic needs of the family.

If one considers the influence of the geographical areas, for women in Central and Southern Italy quitting housekeeping status is more difficult. The disadvantage is particularly strong for women residing in the South of Italy. The transition into employment is constrained by the labour-market conditions or, more simply, by the lack of work: the female unemployment rate in the South of Italy is three times higher than in the North. Moreover, the scant availability of social services can make the fulfilment of domestic needs more costly, so that it becomes less convenient to leave domestic work for paid work.

Finally, women whose mothers have never worked are more likely to remain housewives. This result confirms that there is a transmission, from one generation to the next, of a traditional model of gender role division: this phenomenon has already been identified in other research on Italian women (Bellotti 1993). On the other hand, a non-conformist behaviour, such as cohabitation before marriage, does not lead to a more frequent exit from housewife status: however, the findings of the previous section show that this non-traditional behaviour is associated with not becoming a housewife in the first place.

In model 2 all the non-significant effects are eliminated and a 'baseline model' is identified. In model 3, the husband's social origin and career resources are included. Again, a check was performed to test whether the results are stable, moving from the large sample to the subsample of 579 women: in this case, there were no significant differences and, in spite of the small number of events (N=51), the results for the subsample were found to be stable.[13]

---

[12] The effect of occupational status is evaluated only for housewives with previous work experience, introducing a dummy variable = 1, if the woman has had previous work experience.

[13] I performed the same test on model 2 described in n. 10. In this case, neither the effect of the dummy 'subsample' nor any of the interaction effects turned out to be significant.

Table 6.3. Effects on the transition rate from housekeeping to employment

	Model 1	Model 2	Model 3	Model 4	Model 5	Model 6
Duration < 12 months	-5.086**	-5.155**	-5.092**	-4.905**	-4.957**	-4.874**
Duration 1–3 years	-4.979**	-5.060**	-4.992**	-5.069**	-5.143**	-5.047**
Duration > 3 years	-5.483**	-5.597**	-5.532**	-5.412**	-5.522**	-5.424**
W's father's education	0.002					
W's education	0.083**	0.086*	0.116**	0.088*	0.078*	0.121**
W's occup. score	0.006	0.006	0.006	0.014	0.015	0.015
W's previous work	-0.336	-0.254	-0.267	-0.595	-0.644	-0.653
W's age/10	-0.050**	-0.045**	-0.043**	0.043*	-0.050*	-0.040*
Married 1971–80	-0.230					
Married 1981–	0.146					
No. of children	0.036					
Infant children (0–3)	0.109	0.154	0.138	0.647	0.734	0.652
Pre-school child (3–6)	0.211	0.241	0.215	0.727	0.869	0.741
School child (> 6 years)	0.699**	0.686**	0.646**	0.966**	1.115*	0.973*
W's full-time exp.	0.004**	0.030**	0.003**	0.003*	0.003*	0.003*
W's part-time exp.	0.003					
W's irregular exp.	0.002					
Centre	-0.328**	-0.324**	-0.326**	0.043	0.128	0.048
South Islands	-0.664**	-0.633**	-0.633**	-0.705*	-0.605*	-0.674*
W's mother never worked	-0.340**	-0.354**	-0.327**	-0.810**	-0.780**	-0.756**
Pre-marriage cohabitation	0.097					
H's education		-0.045**	-0.045**			
H's occup. score				-0.014*	-0.049	-0.062
H's father's education						-0.011
N of events	363	363	363	51	51	51

Piecewise constant model. ** significant, $p < 0.05$, * significant, $p < 0.10$.

The husband's education and occupational status (models 3 and 4) constrain exits from housekeeping status: the higher the husband's education and occupational status, the lower the chances of transition to market work. The husband's social origin, however, has no significant effect (model 5). When the husband's education and occupational status are simultaneously included in model 6, due to collinearity, their effects are not significant.

The negative effect of the husband's resources (education and occupational status) on the wife's transition to paid work is in accordance with Becker's theory. And again, two contrasting mechanisms are found to be in action. For a woman with high education the transition into the labour market is: (1) made easier and more profitable by her educational qualifications, (2) constrained, given the high level of homogamy, by her husband's career resources that make her market work less advantageous and necessary. Only if one discounts the effect of husband's resources, does the importance of the wife's resources becomes fully evident.[14]

Conclusions

The aim of this chapter has been to analyse the mechanism underlying female employment behaviour. In particular I have addressed two questions. What is the level of homogamy compared to career resources within married couples? To what extent are women's careers affected by their family situation and particularly by their husbands' resources and careers?

In terms of education and occupational status at the time of marriage, couples show a strong tendency to homogamy. Moreover, heterogamous couples are distributed symmetrically: the couples in which the wife's resources are lower than the husband's are as frequent as couples in which the wife's resources are higher. So, at a macro level, women do not make a smaller investment in human capital before marriage: the starting conditions of husbands' and wives' parallel careers are similar. Later on something happens and the careers diverge more than they run parallel: almost half of the women in the sample were housewives at the time of the survey, while none of the husbands had this status.

Starting with the transition into housekeeping, women's individual resources (education and occupational status at the time of marriage) contribute to keeping them in the labour market, while for older age groups the likelihood of an exit seems to increase: these effects of individual characteristics have also been found by previous studies on female labour supply (Bison *et al.* 1996; Schizzerotto *et al.* 1995).

But the family context and life-course stage also exert a decisive influence on women's careers. My results show that the process of exit has two critical

---

[14] Comparing the results of model 2 and model 3, discounting the negative effect of the husband's education, the size of the effect of the woman's education increases by almost 35% ((0.116–0.086)/0.086).

phases: immediately before marriage and around childbirth. In the first phase, the 'engagement period' following Bernasco's (1994) definition, women tend to become housewives in anticipation of marriage. The second critical moment occurs when women become pregnant or when the child is at the infant stage (0–3 years).

The husband's resources have a negative effect on the wife's career: the decision to quit the labour market and to become a housewife is more frequent the higher the husband's competitive advantage is in paid work. Therefore, this result partly confirms Becker's theory on the division of labour within the couple. Before discussing other factors that make Becker's theory only partially valid, it is important to stress that the traditional omission of family life course and husbands' resources from studies on female employment behaviour leads to an underestimation of the influence of women's individual resources. For a woman with high education and high occupational status, remaining in the labour market is more convenient but, at the same time, made less necessary by the husband's resources which, given the high level of homogamy, are likely to be high as well. So in order to evaluate the effects of women's individual resources correctly, the incentive of husbands' resources towards their playing a domestic role has to be discounted.

But if women appear to decide according to their competitive advantage in market work, with respect to their husbands, my results show that these decisions are constrained by the labour-market structure and shaped by cultural orientations. Women employed in the public sector more frequently keep their jobs, while women employed with no contract have a higher likelihood of becoming housewives. For women resident in the North of Italy, it is more common to have a continuous career and this result can be related to the greater availability of social services in this part of the country. But women's careers also depend on the adhesion to or rejection of a traditional gendered division of labour: women who displayed a non-conformist behaviour before marriage (cohabiting experience), also reject the traditional division of labour within the family and keep their job in the labour market.

Turning to the transitions from housekeeping status to the labour market, for many aspects the process seems to prove complementary to the process of exit from the labour market. In other words, the effects on entry into and exit from the labour market tend to accumulate: the same characteristics and factors that lead women out of the labour market, make (re)entry more difficult. Women with low education become housewives more often and exit more rarely from this condition. The same is true for women in Southern/Central Italy. Again, husbands' resources have this double effect: favouring exit and constraining entry into the labour market. Moreover, an inheritance of the housewife role is found: women whose mothers have never worked are themselves more likely to remain in housekeeping status.

Overall, the housekeeping condition is not a temporary status and the risk of entrapment is high. The indicator, constructed with the data from Table 6.1, shows that only one in five women who become housewives later manages to re-enter the labour market. To this it has to be added that more than 20 per cent of women in the sample have never worked. These results confirm the hypothesis that the type of welfare state and, in particular, the type of support to mothers' employment, give rise to a peculiar female career model: in the Italian case it seems still legitimate to speak of 'never started-interrupted' female careers.

Finally, a few considerations on the policy issues relating to female employment that I briefly touched on in the introduction. Recent Italian studies on the female labour supply, while stressing the growth of women's participation in the labour market, have outlined a trend in the last few years whereby female career trajectories are becoming more similar to those of males: in this way, a homogeneous picture of the female universe is given (Abbate 1995; Oneto 1991). The results of my analysis refer to a relatively young cohort of married women born after 1945 and they are not suitable for evaluating generational changes. However, my results show that the increase in female participation in the labour market implies the possibility of a polarization between women who have never worked (21 per cent) or who interrupted their career due to their domestic responsibilities (23 per cent) and women who remain continuously in the labour market. And it is likely that the lifestyles and needs of these two groups of women will turn out to be radically different. It is by no means so obvious that a new and unique gender-identity model is asserting itself, as some authors seem to take for granted in order to explain the growth in female participation in recent years.[15]

Comprehension of the mechanisms that rule the transitions out of/into the labour market can give important indications for a policy aimed at promoting female employment. An increase in women's participation in market work can come about in three ways: (1) bringing into the labour market women who have never worked (almost one in five married women in Italy), (2) keeping employed women in the labour market (3) facilitating re-entry for women who have interrupted their careers. In particular, the last two options might exclude each other: if a welfare state supports continuous careers then, with fewer interruptions, there is less need of a policy to facilitate re-entries to the labour market. It has already been stressed that a critical phase for women's employment occurs around childbirth: it is at that time that many women exit from the labour market. Thus, in order to support continuous careers for women, a key area of intervention might be developing a public care service for children at the infant stage (0–2 years). In this way women could more easily combine employment and maternity, and get round the trade-off that they face at the moment.

---

[15] On this point see the criticisms made in Hakim (1996).

References

Abbate, C. (1995). 'Cambiamenti generazionali nella famiglia e nel lavoro' (Intergenerational Change in Family and Work), *Economia e Lavoro*, 4: 81–93.

Barbagli, M. (1990). *Provando e Riprovando: Matrimonio, famiglia e divorzio in Italia e in altri paesi occidentali* (Marriage, Family and Divorce in Italy and in other Western Countries) (Bologna: Il Mulino).

Becker, G. (1964). *Human Capital* (New York: Columbia University Press).

——(1991). *A Treatise on the Family* (Enlarged edn. Cambridge, Mass.: Harvard University Press).

Bellotti, V. (1993). 'La partecipazione al lavoro delle donne coniugate' (Female Employment of Married Women), *Polis*, 7/2: 301–20.

Bernardi, F. (1999a). 'Does the Husband Matter? Married Women and Employment in Italy', *European Sociological Review*, 3: 285–300.

——(1999b). *Donne fra carriera e famiglia: Scelte individuali e vincoli sociali* (Women between Career and Family) (Milan: Franco Angeli).

Bernasco, W. (1994). *Coupled Careers: The Effects of Spouse's Resources on Success at Work* (Amsterdam: Thesis Publishers).

——P. de Graaf, and W. Ultee (1998). 'Coupled Careers: Effects of Spouse's Resources on Occupational Attainment in the Netherlands', *European Sociological Review*, 1: 15–31.

Bison, I., M. Pisati, and A. Schizzerotto (1996). 'Disuguaglianze di genere e storie lavorative' (Gender Inequalities and Work Histories), in S. Piccone and C. Saraceno (eds.), *Genere: La costruzione sociale del femminile e maschile* (Bologna: Il Mulino).

Blossfeld, H.-P., and G. Rohwer (1995). *Techniques of Event History Modelling: New Approaches to Causal Analysis* (Mahwah, NJ: Lawrence Erlbaum).

——and C. Hakim (eds.) (1997). *Between Equalization and Marginalization: Part-Time Working Women in Europe and the United States of America* (Oxford: Oxford University Press).

Chodorow, N. (1978). *The Reproduction of Mothering* (Berkeley, Calif.: University of California Press).

Cobalti, A., and A. Schizzerotto (1994). *La mobilità sociale in Italia* (Social Mobility in Italy) (Bologna: Il Mulino).

de Lillo, A., and A. Schizzerotto (1985). *La valutazione sociale delle occupazioni* (Social Evaluation of the Occupations) (Bologna: Il Mulino).

England, P. and G. Farkas (1986). *Households, Employment and Gender: A Social, Economic, and Demographic View* (New York: Aldine Publishing Co.).

Esping-Andersen, G. (1990). *The Three Worlds of Welfare Capitalism* (Cambridge: Polity Press).

——(1999). *Social Foundations of Post-Industrial Economies* (Oxford: Oxford University Press).

Gambetta, D. (1987). *Were they Pushed or did they Jump? Individual Decision Mechanism in Education* (Cambridge: Cambridge University Press).

Gerson, K. (1985). *Hard Choices: How Women Decide about Work, Career and Motherhood* (Berkeley, Calif.: University of California Press).

——(1987). 'Emerging Social Division among Women: Implications for Welfare State Politics', *Politics and Society*, 15/2: 207–12.

Gilligan, C. (1982). *In a Different Voice: Psychological Theory and Woman's Development* (Cambridge, Mass.: Harvard University Press).

Gornick, J. C., M. K. Meyers, and K. E. Ross (1997). 'Supporting the Employment of Mothers: Policy Variation across Fourteen Welfare States', *Journal of European Social Policy*, 7/1: 45–70.

Hakim, C. (1996). *Key Issues in Women's Work: Female Heterogeneity and the Polarisation of Women's Employment* (London: Athlone Press).

ISTAT (1995). *Rapporto annuale. La situazione del paese nel 1994* (Annual report. The Country Situation in 1994) (Rome: Istat).

——(2000). *Rapporto annuale: La situazione del paese nel 1999* (Annual Report. The Country Situation in 1999) (Rome: Istat).

Kalleberg, A. L. (1988). 'Comparative Perspectives on Work Structures and Inequality', *Annual Review of Sociology*, 14: 203–25.

——and A. B. Sørensen (1979). 'The Sociology of Labour Markets', *Annual Review of Sociology*, 5: 351–79.

Lorber, J., and S. A. Farrell (eds.) (1991). *The Social Construction of Gender* (Newbury Park, Calif.: Sage).

Meulders, D., O. Plasman, and R. Plasman, (1994). *Atypical Employment in the EC* (Aldershot: Dartmouth).

Milkman, R., and E. Townsley (1994). 'Gender and the Economy', in N. Smelser, and R. Swedberg (eds.), *The Handbook of Economic Sociology* (Princeton: Princeton University Press).

O'Connor, J. (1993). 'Gender, Class and Citizenship in the Comparative Analysis of Welfare State Regimes: Theoretical and Methodological Issues', *British Journal of Sociology*, 44: 502–18.

OECD (2000). *OECD Employment Outlook* (Paris: OECD).

Oneto, G. (1991). 'Recenti tendenze dell'offerta di lavoro in Italia: Un'analisi della parte-cipazione al mercato del lavoro' (Recent Trends in Labour Supply in Italy), *Economia e Lavoro*, 1: 81–102.

Orloff, A. (1993). 'Gender and the Social Rights of Citizenship: The Comparative Analysis of Gender Relations and Welfare States', *American Sociological Review*, 58: 303–28.

——(1996). 'Gender in the Welfare State', *Annual Review of Sociology*, 22: 51–78.

Rella, P. (1990). 'Le donne nel pubblico impiego' (Women in Public Employment), in A. M. Nassisi (ed.), *Il lavoro femminile in Italia tra produzione e riproduzione* (Rome: Fondazione Istituto Gramsci).

Room, G. (1990). *New Poverty in the European Community* (London: Macmillan).

Sainsbury, D. (ed.) (1994). *Gendering the Welfare State* (London: Sage).

Saraceno, C. (1994). 'The Ambivalent Familism of the Italian Welfare State', *Social Politics*, 1: 60–82.

——(1996). *Sociologia della famiglia* (Sociology of Family) (Bologna: Il Mulino).

——(1998). *Mutamenti della famiglia e politiche sociali in Italia* (Changes in Family and Social Policies in Italy) (Bologna: Il Mulino).

Schizzerotto A., I. Bison, and A. Zoppè (1995), 'Disparità di genere nella partecipazione al mondo del lavoro e nella durata delle carriere' (Gender Inequalities in Labour Market Participation and Duration of Careers), *Polis*, 5/9: 91–112.

Smeeding, T. M., M. O'Higgins, and L. Rainwater (eds.) (1990). *Poverty, Inequality and Income Distribution in Comparative Perspective: The Luxembourg Study (LIS)* (London: Harvester Wheatsheaf).

Sørensen, A. B. (1986). 'Theory and Methodology in Social Stratification', in U. Himmelstrand (ed.), *Sociology from Crisis to Science?* (London: Sage).

West, C., and D. H. Zimmerman (1991). 'Doing Gender', in J. Lorber, and S. A. Farrel (eds.), *The Social Costruction of Gender* (Newbury Park, Calif.: Sage).

Zanatta, A. L. (1996). 'Famiglie con un solo genitore e rischio di povertà' (Lone-Parent Family and the Risk of Poverty, *Polis*, 10/1: 63–79.

APPENDIX TO CHAPTER 6: DESCRIPTIVE STATISTICS FOR THE INDEPENDENT VARIABLES

Time-constant variables

Woman's resources (mean/s.d.)

W's father's education	Legal duration of the father's educational qualifications (5.5/4.0)
W's education	Legal duration of the educational qualifications (9.8/4.0)
W's occup. score	Social status of the job held at the time of marriage (35.9/17.6)

Husband's resources

H's father's education[a]	Legal duration of the husband's father's educational qualifications (5.8/4.1)
H's education	Legal duration of the husband's educational qualification (9.94/4.0)
H's occup. score[a]	Social status of the husband's job at the time of marriage (38.7/19.8)

Gender identity (%)

W's mother never worked	Dummy = 1 if the woman's mother has never worked (56.9)
Pre-marriage cohabitation	Dummy = 1 if the woman has experienced consensual union before marriage (6.1)

Geographical area

Centre	Dummy = 1 if the woman resides in Central Italy (19.5)
South Islands	Dummy = 1 if the woman resides in the South or in the Islands (36.1)

Marriage cohort

Married 1971–80	Dummy = 1 if the woman married between 1971–1980 (35.9)
Married 1981+	Dummy = 1 if the woman married after 1980 (53.5)

Time varying[b] (mean/s.d.)

W's age	Woman's age, increasing by one unit each year (36.9/7.2)
No. of children	Number of children, increasing after each birth or adoption (1.6/0.9)

Previous labour-force experience

W's full-time exp.	Cumulative duration in months of previous FT employment (46.2/67.9)

W's part-time exp.	Cumulative duration in months of previous PT employment (7.1/26.0)
W's irregular exp.	Cumulative duration in months of previous irregular employment (4.6/23.6)

Engagement period — Dummy = 1 in the 12 months before marriage

Children (%)

Pregnant	Dummy = 1 in the 9 months before childbirth
Infant child (0–3)	Dummy = 1 if there is at least one child under 3 years of age in the family (18.2)
Pre-school child (3–6)	Dummy = 1 if no child younger than 3 years but at least one child under 6 years of age is present in the family (15.5)
School-age child (> 6 years)	Dummy = 1 if no child younger than 6 years but at least one older child is present in the family (53.6)

Labour-market structure[c]

Agricultural sector	Dummy = 1 if the job is in the agricultural sector (6.3)
Public sector	Dummy = 1 if the job is in the public sector (32.9)
Part-time contract	Dummy = 1 if the job is part-time (19.0)
No contract	Dummy = 1 if the job is without contract (7.0)
Seasonal job	Dummy = 1 if the job is of a seasonal kind (3.9)

[a] Variables available only for the restricted sample.
[b] The descriptive statistics for the time-varying variables are computed on the basis of the values of the variables at the time of the survey.
[c] The % for the labour-market structure variables refer only to the employed women.

7

Spouses' Employment Careers in Spain

MARÍA JOSÉ GONZÁLEZ-LÓPEZ

Introduction

S PAIN has often been portrayed as a traditional society as far as gender roles are concerned. The legacy of the Catholic Church, the long-lasting authoritarian regime (1939–75), the persistence of cohesive family structures, and the tangibly low presence of women in the labour force, lie at the core of this notion. Legacies of the recent past have unquestionably exerted an immense influence in the professional life chances of many women who were born between the mid-1940s and 1950s, at the height of the dictatorial regime. They suffered the fate of growing up under a state's male-breadwinner ideology which legitimated a rigid sexual division of labour.

The situation for the younger generations of women, who were born in the 1960s, is by no means comparable with the previous ones. They were brought up at the beginning of the newly elected democratic regime, and enjoyed substantially better conditions in terms of accessing education and occupational training. Consequently, they could avoid the traditional homemaker role which was assigned to married women in the previous generations. They, furthermore, also reached working age in a period of high unemployment, which ultimately impelled many of them to fall back on the family and thus postpone their entry into an economically independent adulthood.

In short, modernity and traditionalism have gone forward hand-in-hand in the rapid process of societal transformation since the late 1960s. These changes may be at the roots of some of the demographic patterns which seem to be difficult to interpret today. This is the case, for instance, in regard to the dramatic fall in fertility levels or in the pattern of delayed marriage. Nevertheless, as will be argued in this chapter, these patterns may simply be the result of the transition towards a modern egalitarian society where women's aspirations have changed, while at the same time they have not found parallel institutional support.

The new role of women has had to coexist with the lagging development of institutions, which cannot guarantee that forming a family or having children will not create conflicting interests with their individual career paths. There is a high degree of mismatch between the job requirements of career-oriented women and family demands. These women have a low capacity for individually combining family and career within a traditional gendered division of labour. Of course, this dilemma should not be understood as an individual conflict but as a concern of the couple, if they both aspire to consolidate their position at the workplace while building a family. The aim of this chapter is to investigate the development of the couples' careers since the formation of the union and, more specifically, the effect of assortative mating on women's occupational career. In order to frame the Spanish case-study, a general description of the main societal developments is included in the following sections.

Transformation of Family Life and Gender Relationships

Sociological studies of family change in industrialized societies usually refer both to processes of continuous pluralization of living arrangements and to the social permissiveness to organize intimate relations which have arisen from the advances in women's empowerment (Roussel 1993; Thorne and Yalom 1992). The more these trends are accentuated, the less family life appears to be institutionalized. Spain would be a case in point where the presumed deinstitutionalization of families has not taken place to the same extent as in other northern or central European states (Jurado and Naldini 1996). To understand the present features of family arrangements and the new role of married women, it is necessary to reconstruct the main social transformations that occurred in the period under study (1940–90). No analysis of this period, therefore, can be made without reference to the long-lasting authoritarian regime (1939–75), the take-off of capitalist modernization (around the 1960s), and political democratization (from 1976 onwards).

The Francoist despotic corporatism, which lasted for more than thirty years, very clearly illustrates the role of the state in enforcing the functioning and obligations of family members. In particular, the first years of the dictatorship, during the so-called autarchic period of a closed economy (1939–59), marked a more radical stance in state paternalism, culminating in the implementation of the family wage for male workers. This was a wage-complement which consisted of a series of subsidies (that is, family allowances in 1938, family bonuses in 1945) given to the salaried industrial workers in order to alleviate their burden of dependent relatives. In other countries the family wage was the result of the struggle of working-class men to exclude women competitors from the workplace while reproducing the middle-class housewife model (Fox Harding 1996). In Spain male privileges over married women were imposed by the state. Nevertheless, given that non-salaried workers, who in the 1960s still comprised around 40 per cent of the population, were excluded from this scheme, it did not have the originally desired effect (Meil-Landwerlin 1995).

The end of economic isolation came in 1959 with the implementation of the Stabilization Plan, which gave rise to both the so-called 'economic miracle of the 1960s' and to the urgent reform (1963–73) of the irrational family policy which rewarded workers' family burdens instead of workers' specific skills. The economic growth initiated at that time, which was geographically very concentrated, generated profound internal migrations and the withdrawal of large sectors of the population from agricultural work.

The definitive take-off in female employment, however, did not come until the demise of the authoritarian regime. The democratic regime inaugurated profound social democratic reforms in core issues of women's emancipation. These included the abolition of the reactionary ban on wives' occupation outside the household without the husband's permission in 1975, the legalization of the use of contraceptives, the decriminalization of non-marital unions in 1978, the legalization of divorce, and the full legal recognition of children born outside wedlock in 1981.

Nevertheless, the authoritarian system of social provision provided the context of constraints within which later developments occurred, maintaining the privileges of a social system based on male family headship and women as the main caregivers. They did not enhance individual independence but instead presupposed the individual's (women's and youths') dependence on families. At the same time, the social functions accomplished by cohesive family ties discouraged the state from increasing levels of public provision (Naldini 1999). Other authors argue that there is an indirect gender discrimination deriving from the dual system of contributory and assistance-based benefits, which excludes homemaking married women (entitled to derived benefits as wives) and other workers in irregular working conditions from full citizenship rights. The typical claim is the absolute shortage of publicly funded day-care centres for children under 3. The same applies to elderly care, since almost 90 per cent of home-based assistance is currently provided privately by families (Ditch *et al.* 1996). Part of the explanation for the slow path of social reforms in this field is the fact that other issues, such as the very high unemployment rate (22.2 per cent in 1996), industrial restructuring, or the determination to enhance standards of international competitiveness, have been more important issues.

During the stated period, family life has also experienced an intense transformation. In brief, the 1960s and early 1970s were characterized by the traditional family path of a rapid family formation whereby children would arrive immediately after marriage. By the 1980s women had already adopted an innovative family-formation strategy (Castro 1992) which included the postponement of marriage (on average at age 26.2 for women and 28.7 for men in 1996), postponed arrival of the first child (in 1990 at the average age of 29), a greater period between first and second child, and the having of a rare third child.[1] These combined factors account for the current Spanish 'baby bust' which in 1999 was reflected in a total fertility rate of 1.20 (INE 2000).

---

[1] Figures as quoted in Requena (1997).

The scarce potential for economic autonomy available to women and young people, both facing great obstacles in their initial integration into paid employment, could be one of the causes of this new model of delayed family formation. Generally, young people leave the parental home very late and usually emancipate through marriage rather than constituting one-person households or experiencing pre-marital cohabitation (Delgado and Castro 1998). Equally, the character of protectionism assumed by families which tolerates young people remaining at home for long periods has accordingly altered the cohabiting rules, so that fathers seem to be relatively more tolerant with respect to their children's autonomy (Valero and Lence 1995).

Another aspect of family life liable to change in the recent context of growing women's economic autonomy is the level of marital breakdown. Indeed, the recent figures show an increasing trend, although divorce has a relatively low incidence in comparison with other European states. According to the 1991 Spanish Sociodemographic Survey, in the 1946–1950 marriage cohort only 2 per cent of first marriages ended in divorce and for the younger marriage cohort of 1971–5, 6 per cent had divorced by 1991 (as quoted by Solsona *et al.* 2000). The low rate of divorce should not be attributed to people following the prescriptions of the Catholic Church, but rather to the large number of women with low prospects of economic independence (for example, older marriage cohorts with limited work experience and low educational attainment).

It should be noted, however, that there is not one clear-cut family model but many variations between regions. Culturally cohesive regions have traditionally held different degrees of complexity in the family structure as well as in the marriage markets (Cabré 1999; Reher 1997; Solsona and Treviño 1990). Hence, all analyses conducted at the state level would generally conceal complex geographical patterns.

The Fragility of 'the Marriage Contract' in the Context of the Recent Dynamic of Women's Growing Employment

One of the main features of the gender composition of the labour force is the low presence of women: the total female activity rate (women aged 16 and above) was only 38 per cent as compared with the 63 per cent for men (aged 16 and above) in the second quarter of 1999 (INE 1999). Greater gender differences, however, emerge if the distinction of the working population is made by marital status. Single women display similar behaviour to single men in all the age groups observed, whereas married women over the childbearing interval have significantly lower presence in the labour force.

Despite these differences, the trend in the last years shows rather positive signs. Between 1980 and 1990 women's participation in the labour force grew at a rate of 3.5 per cent, which was the highest rate recorded in Western countries.[2] This cannot just be attributed to the structural effect caused by the limited presence of women in formal paid employment which lasted until almost the mid-1960s, but is also an indicator of the clear emergence of the new role for women committed to their occupational career. In fact, the participation rate of women aged 25–34 in 1998 was 71 per cent, which was not very far from the rates reached by British (74 per cent), German (75 per cent), or Finnish women (77 per cent) in the same age group (OECD 1999). Since the economic recovery of the 1986–1990 period, a high proportion of women have ostensibly become a permanent part of the labour force rather than becoming workers with discontinuous careers (Moltó 1993).

The growing presence of women in the labour force since the mid-1980s, however, has been paralleled by their expansion into unstable and irregular jobs. The reform of the Workers' Statute Law, passed in 1984, aimed at abolishing rigidities in the labour force. However, it actively consolidated the structural marginalization of disadvantaged workers, among whom were the non-qualified, a large proportion of unskilled women, younger first-job-seekers and, recently, newly arrived foreigners. In the second quarter of 1990 as much as 30 per cent of the working population had temporary contracts, one of the highest rates in the European Union (Bel-Adell 1991).

The deregulation of the labour force has reinforced both the segregation of female workers in the service sector, and the fragmentation of the labour market by segments of the working population. In 1996 women had the largest share of part-time employment (68 per cent) as well as the greatest number of temporary contracts (36.7 per cent of women in comparison to 28.3 per cent of men).[3] At the same time, part-time work is not an important tradition. In 1980 only 6.8 per cent of women were working part-time (that is, less than forty hours a week) and 15.9 per cent in 1996.[4] According to Durán (1996) the limited expansion of part-time jobs, which in many other industrialized countries has facilitated the employment of married women, could be ascribed to the fact that trade unions have never been interested in an occupational practice that could jeopardize male-household-head privileges derived from a family wage (that is, full-time, stable, and well-paid jobs to maintain a household economy).

Equally, the growing presence of women in the labour force has gone hand-in-hand with the growth of unemployment. In the second quarter of 1999 23 per cent of women aged 16 and above were unemployed (only 11 per cent of men) and for young people the situation was even more critical as 35 per cent of women aged 20–4 were unemployed (20 per cent of men in the same age group).

---

[2] The figure is taken from Bonke (1995) who relied on the OECD Labour Force Statistics from 1971 to 1991. For the comparison the twelve original members of the European Union together with Norway, USA, and Canada were considered.

[3] Ministerio de Trabajo y Asuntos Sociales (1996).

[4] Data for 1980 was taken from Alcobendas (1984); other recent labour-force statistics are from the Ministerio de Trabajo y Asuntos Sociales.

A question has often risen as to why people have not reacted to the high unemployment rates existing since the mid-1980s in a more politically desta-bilizing way. The answer is that unemployment has not always been perceived as a real social problem because it mainly affects youths, and especially women, rather than male household heads (Torns *et al.* 1995; Carrasco *et al.* 1997). Women and young people are regarded as family dependants without great social stigmatization. Of course, this implies that the family rather than the state would support the unemployed dependants. Indeed, it is common-place that parents sustain their children's educational careers, thus mitigating unemployment's most negative effects, until they have acquired better occu-pational prospects. This welfare function, therefore, places an extra burden on women as caregivers within the family.

In general terms, female paid employment has increased but at the expense of maintaining the double burden of work inside and outside of the house-hold. Although an unequal, gendered division of labour is found in most of the Western industrialized countries, the situation seems particularly critical in Spain. A woman's regular working day (including paid and unpaid work) ends up being almost double that of a man (Durán 1997). As argued by Durán (1997), this result confirms that the present standards of living are essentially maintained thanks to women's enormous contribution of unpaid work. Although not all women are equally overburdened, those who are married and less educated are explicitly bearing the main bulk of domestic work (Ramos 1990).

Assortative Mating in a Context of Growing Education

The current prominent presence of women in the educational system is one of the main achievements of the twentieth century. This can be interpreted as resulting from women's higher aspirations for individual self-fulfilment, which at the same time imply higher bargaining power within their marital relation-ships. Additionally, as postulated by Oppenheimer (1988), better-educated women must be more motivated to secure a good match (marrying a man with a spirit of gender equality) in order not to expose themselves to the high oppor-tunity cost of leaving paid employment after their educational investment.

Female achievement in education is more remarkable if observed in a his-torical perspective. Hence, if at the turn of this century as many as 71 per cent of women were illiterate compared with 56 per cent of men, in the 1930s the proportions changed from 47 per cent to 37 per cent, and by the 1990, from 7.9 per cent to 3.2 per cent respectively.[5] The latter figure, however, mainly concerns the elderly population who were born between 1921 and 1940, that is, those affected by the civil war and the impoverished post-war period. Major

[5] Figures of the illiterate population from 1900 and 1930 are as quoted by Capel (1990) and fig-ures for 1990 are as quoted by Garrido (1992).

changes in the gender balance of pupils came with the economic development of the 1960s and it has continued its upward trend until today.

Overall, there has been a growth of about 54 per cent in the number of registered students between 1975 and 1984 which has been caused to a large extent by the massive presence of women. The number of female students increased by 103 per cent, compared with 26 per cent for men (CIDE 1988). By 1986 the number of women enrolled at university surpassed that of men in all regions, and in 1991 among all graduates aged 25–9 as many as 56 per cent were women. Nevertheless, the pattern of gender segregation by specialities still persists—only 16 per cent of architecture and engineering graduates were female.[6]

The growing presence of women in higher education has been partly explained by the reduced costs of education, the expansion and better geographical distribution of infrastructure, and most importantly by the growing interest of both working-class and middle-class families in providing children with education regardless of their sex, particularly in the current situation of very high levels of youth unemployment (CIDE 1988).

The increase in women's educational attainment would obviously affect the marriage market. In fact, since 1989 the trend of women marrying men with lower educational attainment has timidly emerged among young cohorts (Garrido 1992). In general, the main trait of the marriage market is its occupational endogamy, which is explained by the fact that most of the relationships stem from the spatial proximity of the workplace and other daily activities (Iglesias 1995). As many as one in five marriages were occupationally endogamous in 1980, where 'technicians and professionals' (46 per cent married among themselves) and 'students' (44 per cent) were the categories with a higher degree of endogamy (Iglesia 1995). This high endogamy at marriage raises further doubts on whether these couples may perform a gender roles' flexibilization or, on the contrary, they may simply retain a gendered specialization.

Recent studies have also indicated some association between educational attainment and spinsterhood (Garrido 1992). This would seem to support Becker's theory of marriage whereby the better educated women have less to gain from marriage and, therefore, marry at lower rates. Certainly, better educated women have changed the timing of marriage, but whether they personally perceived remaining single as more attractive is far from evident. Yet, in relative terms, women do not avoid marital or cohabiting unions, rather they postpone them (Miret-Gamundi 1997). Just the same, if the marital or consensual union is perceived as a 'multi-dimensional package of mutual interdependencies' (quoting Oppenheimer 1996) instead of a union of mates with different comparative advantages, it is understandable that efficiency and rewards within marriage might equally benefit the better educated women.

---

[6] Figure for 1986 comes from Garrido (1992) and figures for 1991 are from the Spanish Census of 1991 (INE 1994).

Data

The empirical research is based on the retrospective Socio-Demographic Survey (Encuesta Sociodemográfica, hereafter ESD) collected in the fourth quarter of 1991 by the Spanish National Bureau of Statistics (Instituto Nacional de Estadística, INE). The sample contains around 160,000 individuals aged 10 and above, resident in private households, who provided information about his/her life history, about other members of the household (siblings, children, partners, or any other cohabiting persons), and about his/her parents.

For each woman interviewed who had ever been married or in a stable non-marital union, information on her *male partner* was selected. If a woman had ever had a cohabiting experience but eventually made her union official by a civil or religious marriage, only this last situation was recorded in the survey. Therefore, it is impossible to distinguish between women with previous non-marital experience and women who directly entered into a marital union. Given that these two types of paths into relationships are not discernible in the first place, married women and women in stable non-marital relationships—which may also eventually end up in a marriage—are both considered in the analysis.

As far as the information on male partners is concerned, this is far from ideal for the precise purposes of our research. On the one hand, women were asked about their *current partners* with whom they live. Thus, if a woman has had two or more partners but at the time of the interview (1991) she is divorced or separated, there is not much detailed information on her former partners. Equally, if she is living with her second (third or whatever) partner at the time of the interview, only detailed data on this last partner will be available and, in this case, the analysis on parallel careers would become rather troublesome. On the other hand, the current partner is not asked about his life history retrospectively. His spouse gives information only about his educational attainment and his main position in the labour market in the year of the interview.

To overcome these shortcomings only *women with stable partners* have been selected. In this way, the detailed information available on the current partner will certainly correspond to only the first and current partner. This solution, although far from perfect, is not so problematic given the relatively low incidence of divorce and separation in Spain.

The historical period covered in this analysis goes from the 1940s up to 1991. The population observed are women (and their male partners), who have ever been married or cohabited, born after 1930.

Method and Variables

There are three dependent variables (or hazard rates) to be analysed. They indicate the probability that a married (or cohabiting) woman changes from full-time paid employment to full-time homemaker, from part-time employment to full-time homemaker, and, lastly, from full-time homemaker to full-time paid employment. Characteristics of their male partners as well as family background and contextual information (regions) have also been included in the models.[7] The explanatory variables of the regression model, on which the three above-mentioned dependent hazard rates depend, have been summarized in the appendix to this chapter.

The method for the analysis of the discrete time event-history data is the logit regression *model*. The subject-matter is the probability that an event will occur at a particular time to a particular woman, given that she is at risk at that time. Thus, for the first dependent variable, the hazard rate is the probability of a married woman making a first change in her 'economic status' (that is, becoming a full-time homemaker) within a particular year given that she was at risk (that is, being in a partnership and in full-time employment). The single event is considered as a discrete time because we only know the year in which the transition occurs.

Original ESD data have been transformed into person-year observations to apply this methodology. For each individual known to be at risk a separate observational record has been created. Thus, for example, in our first model a woman who changed from full-time employment to full-time homemaker in the third year would contribute with three person-years. Right censored women will be those who have never experienced this transition during the observed period, so they would contribute with the maximum number of person-years (from their fifteenth birthday until their fiftieth).

The dependent variable is coded 0 for each person-year if a woman was still at risk at that year and 1 otherwise, that is, if she changed her occupational status within this particular year. Women have been observed from their fifteenth to fiftieth birthday. The reason for choosing this age period is that these are the years of family formation in which both spouses achieve their parallel careers.

Results from the Statistical Model

Transition 1: Changes from Full-Time Employment to Homemaking

The main purpose of models introduced here is to identify the net effect of husbands' career resources (that is, the level of education and the social status of their jobs) on wives' occupational behaviour. The analytical strategy, therefore, consists of identifying beforehand the effects of other intervening variables in

---

[7] It is difficult to reconstruct with exactitude women's labour-force biographies from the ESD. Only four cycles of activity/occupation and their corresponding cycles of inactivity were recorded. However, respondents were not required to specify whether they left their last occupation. We only know when they withdraw from the labour force. For the sake of simplicity of the analysis, we assume they left the occupation.

the determination of women's occupational behaviour and then proceeding with the inclusion of the husband's variables.

The first model shows the log-odds of woman leaving full-time employment (to become a homemaker) associated with the employment duration (results presented in Table 7.1). The model shows that the log-odds of exiting employment increase after the first year and decrease from the fifth year onward. The probability of married women leaving full-time employment seem to be, in general, relatively low. Thus, if one imagines a synthetic cohort composed of 1,000 married women in full-time work, by the end of the fifth year 734 of the women would have remained in paid employment (the predicted values using model 8).

Earlier studies support this finding: the low exit of full-timers, which is basically explained by the existence of a very rigid labour market with few women in paid employment. If they exit, the possibility of a future return is not easy, even, if desired, on part-time basis, given its limited availability.

It should be noted that the sample of women in this first model is already a sort of 'favoured group' which belongs to the so-called dual-earner partnerships. It is a favoured group because the proportion of women outside the labour force in Spain is still significant, above all, among mature cohorts. One can hypothesize that employed and married women are less exposed to the risk of becoming homemakers, since they may have taken the decision a priori to participate on a long-term basis in the labour force regardless of their family life. On the other hand, other women may have followed the traditional path whereby marriage or childbearing implies an exit from employment. These two models may largely correspond to the described generational break (or structural change hypothesis), whereby younger cohorts take the chief role of maintaining a permanent economical independence within partnerships before marriage.

Model 2 shows the period effects (marriage cohorts) on the transition into homemaking. Marriage cohorts could also be interpreted as a proxy for the generational change, as it would be generally expected that different births cohorts entered partnerships in the consecutive marriage cohorts. Indeed, the pattern is very distinctive. The reference category (marriage cohort 1955–64) contains women who married during the period of the dictatorship's economic openness in which women started to join the labour force, though they tended to withdraw after marriage. The following marriage cohort (1965–74) corresponds to women who had entered partnerships by the end of the dictatorship and who were also ideologically pushed to reproduce a traditional form of motherhood. This group did not seem to show a significant effect on the transition, which is probably due to their similarity with the reference category. Women forming partnerships from 1975 onwards, however, were less likely to become homemakers. This pattern emerges clearly even after controlling for all the covariates included in model 8.

Women who married at the beginning of the democratic regime, that is after 1975, are within the population that started the trend in the impressive

Table 7.1. Estimates for logit models predicting the probability of a married or cohabiting woman changing from full-time paid employment to full-time homemaker

Variables	Model 1	Model 2	Model 3	Model 4	Model 5	Model 6	Model 7	Model 8
Employment duration								
< 1	—	—	—	—	—	—	—	—
2–3 years	0.6099***	0.5166***	0.5295***	0.5346***	0.1741*	0.2247**	0.2352**	0.2388**
4–5 years	0.7236***	0.639***	0.6475***	0.5888***	0.0874	0.1366	0.1185	0.1097
> 5 years	-0.0693	0.8651***	0.8603***	0.6382***	-0.0185	0.0263	0.0107	0.0202
Women's age		-0.4531***	-0.4469***	-0.3685***	-0.3068***	-0.2191***	-0.2126***	-0.229***
Women's age sq.		0.0048***	0.0047***	0.0036***	0.0027***	0.0021***	0.002***	0.0022***
Marriage Cohorts								
1945–1954		-1.057***	-1.036***	-1.0002***	-0.9428***	-0.8217***	-0.7977***	-0.7734***
1955–1964		—	—	—	—	—	—	—
1965–1974		0.0306	0.0362	0.0952**	0.0747*	0.0697*	0.0610	0.0359
1975–1984		-0.3251***	-0.3224***	-0.201***	-0.2715***	-0.3453***	-0.3689***	-0.4267***
1985 or later		0.0694	0.0798*	0.2366***	0.0836*	-0.1634***	-0.1842***	-0.2515***
Fathers' occupational status			-0.0045***	-0.0017**	-0.0017**	-0.0011	-0.0015*	-0.0012
Mothers' education attainment								
exempted of qualification			—	—	—	—	—	—
primary school			-0.0783**	0.0604*	0.0685*	0.0026	0.0132	-0.0140
secondary school			-0.0793	0.3455**	0.4486***	0.3658**	0.3803**	0.3762**
university degree			-0.5236***	-0.0427	0.0343	-0.0259	-0.0621	-0.1086
Mothers' without work experience			0.4577***	0.4686***	0.3657***	0.3379***	0.3287***	0.2419***
Women's education attainment								
basic education not completed				0.0046	-0.0905***	0.0054	-0.0089	-0.0209
primary school				—	—	—	—	—
secondary school				-0.7292***	-0.4504***	-0.5455***	-0.5327***	-0.5765***
vocational training				-0.4882***	-0.2433***	-0.3128***	-0.2905***	-0.2717***
three years univ. degree				-1.2174***	-0.4865***	-0.623***	-0.6141***	-0.6344***

university degree (5 years)				-1.2741***	-0.448***	-0.6686***	-0.638***	-0.6845***
doctorates and other high. deg.				-1.7527***	-0.8417***	-1.0839***	-1.2178***	-1.2508***
Women's status last job					-0.0201***	-0.0229***	-0.0236***	-0.0229***
Women's type of job contract								
continuous					—	—	—	—
seasonal/temporary					-0.1488***	-0.0704*	-0.0341	-0.0667
occasionally					0.0751	0.1901**	0.2115**	0.1523*
Previous work experience>marriage					0.7638***	0.5546***	0.5816***	0.5567***
Women in public administration					-0.7525***	-0.7588***	-0.7231***	-0.7977***
Number of children						-0.7364***	-0.7322***	-0.7185***
Having a child < 3						0.0964***	0.1068***	-0.454***
Partner's educational attainment								
exempted of qualifications							—	—
primary school							0.079**	0.0624*
secondary school							0.1164**	0.0576
university degree							0.2082***	0.0616
Partner's occupational status							0.0056***	0.0011
North-western								-0.1016*
North-eastern								0.4334***
Madrid and centre								0.6158***
Eastern								—
Southern								0.4394***
Canarias								0.0381
Husband's occup. status*child<3								0.0145***
Constant	-2.428***	5.8197***	5.4986***	4.3647***	4.0768***	2.9414***	2.7773***	3.0236***
-2 log likelihood	76,281	66,620	65,190	64,428	60,714	58,286	53,044	53,044
Subepisodes	132,261	132,261	129,787	129,734	118,231	117,800	106,727	106,727

Source: ESD 1991.
Note: Sample based on person–year observation (time period 1940–1990), women aged 15–50, cohorts born since 1930.
* statistically significant at 0.05 level; ** statistically significant at 0.01 level; *** statistically significant at 0.001 level; — reference category

expansion of women in higher education. Thus, for those women who got married from 1985 onwards, the log-odds of becoming homemaker significantly decreases by −0.2515 when compared to women who married at the height of dictatorship (1955–64).

The log-odds of the older marriage cohort (1945–54) also shows that older women were less likely than the reference category to withdraw from employment, to an even greater extent than younger marriage cohorts. This is simply due to the specific period effect of impoverishment that characterized the post-civil war years, in which married women at work had no other option but to be a family provider. The conception of the traditional marriage in which a woman specialized in caregiving and household chores could not possibly be assumed, above all, for families deriving their living from agriculture, which was a large majority at the time.

The effect of age on the transition appears to operate as if the likelihood of exiting initially declines as a woman's age increases. This pattern continues until women reach a threshold age at which the likelihood slightly increases (around the age 45–50). Therefore, younger women seem to be more at risk but as soon as they reach a certain maturity as workers, say in their thirtieth year and working on a full-time basis, the risk of becoming a homemaker is reduced.

In model 3 the woman's family background has been incorporated. The assumption is that women's occupational behaviour may respond to the values, or social capital, inherited from the family of origin. Indeed, this seems to be the case in model 3. The higher the occupational prestige of the father the less likely women are to withdraw from full-time employment. Equally, the education of the mother describes a neat pattern, whereby the higher the mother is educated the stronger the attachment of the daughter to the labour force. It follows, then, that working-class families (a combination of low occupational prestige and low educational attainment) may transmit rather more traditional gender roles to their daughters than middle-class parents with university degrees.

It should be stressed, however, that the effect of the family background on the daughter's transition into the homemaker role seems to be suppressed (that is, becomes not significant) once we introduced the variable of women's own education. In this case, if women acquire certain human capital they generate further professional expectations regardless of their family background.

An exception to the influence of the family of origin emerges with the variable 'mother's main family role', which is statistically significant even after checking on the women's own educational level. Therefore, having a homemaker mother (out of the labour force) is associated with an increase of 0.2419 in the log-odds of becoming a homemaker (model 8). From this result, it can be stated that mothers seem to play a more significant role than the fathers in transferring values of individual self-fulfilment to their daughters. Furthermore, this pattern is consistent when other variables are included in the consecutive models.

Next, model 4 shows that women's education appears to be a strong and significant predictor of the probability of leaving full-time employment to become a homemaker: the higher the educational attainment the lower the likelihood of quitting employment. The same effect occurs in regard to the occupational prestige at last job (in model 5): the likelihood of leaving employment decreases as the prestige increases. Therefore, highly educated women secure their attachment to the labour force regardless of family life, because even after checking their childbearing biography (in model 6) education still has a significant influence in the transition. This result is illustrated in Figure 7.1, which presents the difference in the predicted probability of becoming homemakers for women of the marriage cohort 1975–84 with both different educational levels and occupational prestige.

It is quite revealing that women in low prestige jobs, such as the labourer in Figure 7.1, are more likely to become homemakers. The differentiated propensity for becoming homemakers by occupational groups can be explained not only by the differentiated rewards obtained from their job—as generally low prestige occupations mean low wages—that may push them to consider caregiving as a 'more attractive' option, but also because low-waged women are more restricted economically in reconciling full-time employment

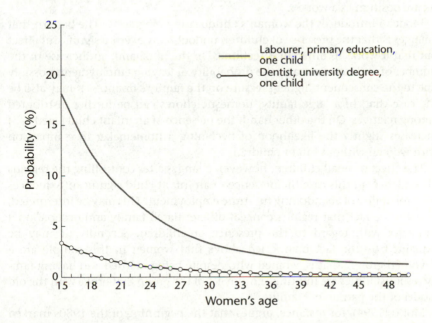

Figure 7.1. Probability of experiencing a transition from full-time employment to homemaking (married or cohabiting women). Predicted values as estimated from the equation of model 7 of the logistic regression (see Table 7.1). Labourer corresponds to unit 19 and dentist to unit 70 of Treiman's (1977) scheme.

and childcare on a private basis. Equally, the fact that less-educated women are given proportionally more occasional work contracts (that is, the most precarious form of work) may further discourage them from remaining in paid employment. Indeed, the likelihood of withdrawing from employment increases if women have occasional contracts in comparison with women with continuous contracts.

Hence, features attributed to the labour supply seem to matter a lot in explaining the transitions of married or cohabiting women from employment to the homemaking role. This is best exemplified by the fact that women working in the public sector systematically, after controlling for all possible covariates, show a significant negative effect. Thus, if women work in public administration, the odds ratio of experiencing a transition to homemaker decreases by 55 per cent.[8] Indeed, the female share of jobs in the public sector has grown in recent years from 29 per cent to 42 per cent between 1983 and 1992, which reflects the general recognition that this sector offers fairly good working conditions and, therefore, largely attracts educated women (Moltó 1992).

Work experience previous to marriage, contrary to the expectations, seems to have a significant positive effect on the log-odds of the transition, which may be attributed to the fact that women with longer working experience hold higher expectations of an easy return than women who only worked after marriage and, therefore, have a shorter professional career and, possibly, a less secure position as a worker.

Model 6 introduces the woman's childbearing biography. The pattern that emerges is that the presence of children undoubtedly exerts a significant effect but that it works in different directions. On the one hand, an increase in the number of children decreases the probability of leaving employment, possibly due to the consequent higher pressure on the family's finances. It may also be the case that, in a large family, domestic chores can be further distributed among relatives. On the other hand, the presence of an infant child (aged 0–3) increases slightly the likelihood of becoming a homemaker in comparison with women without infant children.

The effect of small children, however, changes after controlling the regions of residence, in this case the presence of an infant child significantly reduces the probability of abandoning full-time employment. This may be interpreted, first, by the fact that regions conceal differentiated family and occupational strategies with regard to the presence of children. Secondly, it may be explained by the fact mentioned above that women in this sample are a 'favoured group', that is, women who despite being married and having family responsibilities are full-time employees of the group that broke with the old model of the patriarchal family.

Moltó (1994), for instance, argues that the beginning of the 1980s marked a crucial change in the traditional pattern of employment whereby women made family and working life compatible for the first time. It should be added

---

[8] Since $(\exp(-0.7977)-1) \times 100\% = 54.96\%$.

that compatibility will depend very much on the occupational position of the women or on the availability of family networks to support childcare. Adam (1997) sustains similar arguments in support of the structural change hypothesis, which differentiates between the long-term participating mothers, who do not want to lose human capital investments associated with absences from the labour force, and the a priori inactive mothers.

Now, how do these transitions work when we consider the influence of the husbands? The pattern that emerges is that the spouse's resources have a significant positive effect on the woman's exit from full-time employment. In the case of the husband's education, the estimated odds of becoming homemaker are 14 per cent higher if she marries a man with a university degree than if she married a man who only had primary-school education.[9] The same conclusion arises from the variable for husband's occupational prestige (model 7), in which case the likelihood of becoming a homemaker increases as husband's prestige at work increases.

The result described above seems to be in line with the New Home Economics (Becker 1981), which predicts that individual members of the family take decisions in order to maximize the joint family utility. Then, the person obtaining higher returns from market production would specialize wholly in market work and the other in domestic production. But, in this case, who are the women who—as it was argued above—break with the old model of the family?

Figure 7.2 attempts to summarize the various interactions that take place in the determination of the exits from full-time employment of married women. To simplify the picture slightly, one could say that different groups of women enter partnerships based on different 'gender contracts'.[10] Thus, highly educated women would secure a good quality match by marrying a highly educated men, in which case they would probably reproduce a permanent dual-breadwinner family model. On the other hand, if the husband has higher occupational prestige, this unequal set of conditions drives the wife into caring work within the family as expected in the 'housewife marriage'. Spouses quite possibly hold unequal bargaining power in this type of relationship, although this is only a hypothesis and has yet to be confirmed. However the low-educated woman who marries the low-prestige worker faces a high likelihood of reproducing the 'housewife marriage'. The result obtained reinforces the idea that education stands as a good indicator of non-traditional attitudes towards family models and occupational behaviour. Castro (1992) found similar results

---

[9] The odds ratio associated with the coefficient of husband with university degree is $(\exp(0.2082) - 1) \times 100\% = 23\%$ whereas with primary school education it is $(\exp(0.079) - 1) \times 100\% = 8\%$.

[10] The notion of *gender contract* was developed by Scandinavian feminists who describe it as the unspoken rules, mutual obligations, and rights which define the relations between women and men, between generations, and between the areas of production and reproduction (see Rantalaiho 1994). Other authors have later applied the notion of contract to the concept of a *housewife marriage* (Pfau-Effinger 1994) which denotes the traditional expectation that marriage implies for the husbands, the primacy of market work, and for wives the primacy of care-work in the family. *Contract* denotes rationality and calculation; it refers to a transaction between two (or more) legally competent free parties, their mutual decisions, and the intentional negotiating process (Rantalaiho 1994).

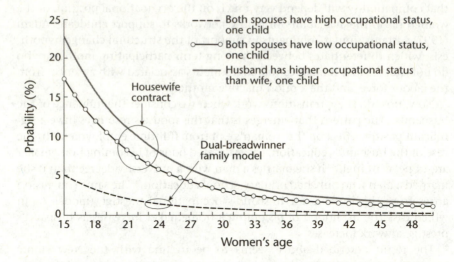

Figure 7.2. Models of gender contracts in partnerships: transitions from full-time employment to homemaking (married or cohabiting women). Predicted values as estimated from the equation of the seventh model of the logistic regression (see Table 7.1). For the couple with both members having a high occupational prestige the unit number 70 of Treiman's (1977) scheme has been used (wife's education= university degree), for the low prestige couple, unit 28 (wife's education= primary school) and for the couple where the husband has higher prestige than wife's unit 70 for him and 24 for her (also with primary school) have been used.

with regard to differences in fertility among educational groups: 80 per cent of women with no education gave birth just after marriage (within two years) as compared with 57 per cent among women with a college degree.

In the last model 8 an interaction term has been introduced between the husband's occupational status and the presence of an infant child. This interaction turns out to be positive and statistically significant, which means that having both a husband in an upwardly mobile career trajectory and a small child increases the likelihood that the wife may abandon full-time employment. In other words, wives support their husbands' careers while facilitating them, or allowing them, to 'enjoy fatherhood'.

Lastly, regional effects are shown as well in model 8. It should be stressed that almost all regions exert a significant effect. The influence of living in the north-western region, however, is particularly different—in this case it is more likely that women will not leave employment than in a similar situation in the eastern region. This pattern can be explained by the large share of female employment in small family agricultural holdings as found in Galicia, Asturias, or Cantabria. Regions may also conceal cultural differences in the approach to work and the family, while there are also economic constraints associated with labour supply and the availability of infrastructures such as day-care centres.

Transition 2: Changes from Part-Time Employment to Homemaking

The proportion of women employed in part-time jobs is relatively small. As mentioned before, it embraces only 6.8 per cent of the working female population in 1980 and 15.9 per cent in 1996. Our data can only capture those transitions that took place prior to 1991. Yet, a similar analytical strategy has been followed for a subsample of married or cohabiting women who woked part-time.

For this group of women (see Table 7.2) it emerges that the older and younger marriage cohorts were significantly less likely to withdraw from part-time jobs to become homemakers in comparison with the marriage cohort 1955–64 (reference category). However, once we check the husband's education and the regions of residence, marriage cohorts lose statistical significance. It seems that the elements that encourage part-timers to remain at work are having a high education (five years university degree), having had a working mother, and having a large family (number of children).

The fact that women in part-time work are given temporary contracts also significantly increases the likelihood of becoming homemakers by almost 38 per cent. Of course, part-time contracts on an occasional or temporary basis are certainly most precarious of possible working conditions. By contrast, women in public administration are less prone to abandon part-time work.

As far as the effect of the male partners is concerned, whether married or cohabiting, it seems to reflect the pattern previously described: a woman working part-time who marries a man with a university degree is 30 per cent more likely to withdraw from the labour force than if the man only had primary education (as estimated by the log-odds of model 1).

Table 7.2. Estimates for logit models: change from part-time employment to full-time homemaker

Variables	Model 1	Model 2	Model 3
Employment duration			
< 1	—	—	—
2–3 years	0.2045	0.2465	0.2437
4–5 years	−0.2544	−0.2554	−0.2643
> 5 years	−0.1257	−0.1621	−0.1651
Women's age	−0.3627***	−0.3559***	−0.3577***
Women's age sq.	0.0045***	0.0044***	0.0044***
Marriage cohorts			
1945–1954	−0.5887***	−0.5074**	−0.4397*
1955–1964	—	—	—
1965–1974	0.0851	0.0802	0.0629
1975–1984	−0.0462	−0.0375	−0.1188
1985 or later	0.2891*	0.2779*	0.1576

Table 7.2. *cont.*

Variables	Model 1	Model 2	Model 3
Fathers' occupational status	0.0018	0.0028	0.0029
Mothers' education attainment			
exempted of qualifications	—	—	—
primary school	0.0173	0.0253	–0.0285
secondary school	–0.1013	–0.0138	–0.1175
university degree	–0.1654	–0.0843	–0.1357
Mothers' without work experience	0.2404**	0.2348**	0.1892*
Women's education attainment			
basic education not completed	–0.0291	–0.0906	–0.0806
primary school	—	—	—
secondary school	–0.2011	–0.1337	–0.1435
vocational training	–0.1632	–0.1000	–0.1085
three years univ. degree	–0.3713	–0.3141	–0.3931
university degree (5 years)	–1.1557***	–1.0343***	–1.1024***
doctorates and other high. deg.	–1.7366*	–1.6025*	–1.8341*
Women's status last job	0.0016	–0.0005	–0.0016
Women's type of job contract:			
continuous	—	—	—
seasonal/temporary	0.2964***	0.2762**	0.3244***
occasionally	0.1299	0.1233	0.1120
Previous work experience>marriage	0.8783***	0.8425***	0.8924***
Women in public administration	–0.3379*	–0.3395	–0.3801*
Number of children	–0.516***	–0.5136***	–0.5233***
Having a child < 3	–0.221*	–0.1739	–0.5196*
Partner's educational attainment			
exempted of qualifications	—		—
primary school	0.1911*		0.2498**
secondary school	0.1644		0.2008
university degree	0.4115*		0.4372*
Partner's occupational status		0.0043	–0.0002
North-western			0.2524*
North-eastern			0.4024***
Madrid and centre			0.6249***
Eastern			—
Southern			0.5322***
Canarias			0.3986*
Husband's occup. status*child<3			0.0091
Constant	3.5785***	3.5247***	3.2921***
–2 log likelihood	7,287	8,070	6,570
Subepisodes	16,197	14,417	14,387

Source: ESD 1991.
* statistically significant at 0.05 level;** statistically significant at 0.01 level; *** statistically significant at 0.001 level;
— reference category.

Transition 3: Changes from Homemaking to Full-Time Employment

As it was hypothesized before, there is a distinct division between those female workers with a permanent attachment to the labour force (mostly analysed in the first transition) and those with truncated labour-force biographies.[11] The latter may largely fall into the sample analysed here.

The first model (see Table 7.3) provides information about the influence of the time women spent as homemakers in their transition to employment. The pattern that emerges is very clear: the longer they stayed as homemakers the more difficult it was to realize a transition to full-time employment. It should be stressed, however, that the probability of entering (or of returning for some women) into full-time employment is relatively low, although it has grown significantly for the younger marriage cohorts. Moltó (1995), for instance, states that the exclusion of housewives from the economically active population in Spain is almost structural.

In our sample, the pattern of entry into employment after homemaking is as follows. Supposing a synthetic cohort (married between 1965–74) consisting of 100 homemaker women, by the end of the fifth year only thirteen women would have entered (or returned) into full-time employment. For the following marriage cohort (1975–84) the proportion would have grown to twenty and for the youngest cohort (married from 1985 onwards) as many as thirty-three women would have entered.[12] This is not a large proportion, yet the traditional model of not returning at all seems to be gradually changing.

Therefore, who are the women most likely to experience a transition from homemaking to full-time employment? Again, educational attainment seems to be a strong and significant predictor of the future integration of women in the labour force. As happened in the case of women who exited from full-time employment (first transition analysed), mother's education has a significant positive effect, in the sense that having a highly educated mother increases the log-odds of women entering the labour force, but as soon as we check the effect of women's own education it turns out to be not significant. This reveals that it is the woman's own education which most determines her labour-force biography, regardless of the presumed social capital inherited from the family of origin. Interestingly, however, if the mother performed a traditional homemaker role this seems to increase the likelihood of the daughter reproducing this family model. This effect comes out even after checking women's family characteristics or other labour-market features.

---

[11] According to the data drawn from ESD (1991), among all women in the birth cohort 1956–60 only 15% returned to the labour force after the first interruption. In the younger cohort 1961–5 the proportion slightly increased, with 24% returning. In the case of men from the same birth cohorts, who usually exit the labour force for the completion of compulsory military service, by the age of 24 as many as 90% had returned.

[12] Probabilities estimated from coefficients in model 2 (see Table 7.3) and interpreted with the logic of a life table.

Table 7.3. Estimates for logit models: change from homemaking to full-time employment

Variables	Model 1	Model 2
Time in full-time homemaking		
< 1	—	—
2–3 years	0.5974***	0.5872***
4–5 years	0.3678***	0.353***
> 5 years	0.195*	0.1759*
Women's age	–0.037	–0.0296
Women's age sq.	0.0002	0.0001
Marriage cohorts		
1945–1954	–0.0796	–0.0963
1955–1964	—	—
1965–1974	0.4675***	0.4591***
1975–1984	0.9149***	0.9198***
1985 or later	1.4735***	1.4835***
Fathers' occupational status	0.0009	0.0003
Mothers' education attainment		
exempted of qualifications	—	—
primary school	0.0132	0.0156
secondary school	–0.0117	0.0162
university degree	–0.1379	–0.0999
Mothers' without work experience	–0.3579***	–0.2911***
Women's education attainment		
basic education not completed	–0.2164***	–0.1769**
primary school	—	—
secondary school	0.4253***	0.4327***
vocational training	0.692***	0.6698***
three years univ. degree	1.2797***	1.3263***
university degree (5 years)	1.2897***	1.3311***
doctorates and other high. deg.	1.679***	1.7298***
Previous work experience	0.0848	0.0544
Number of children	0.1393***	0.1445***
Having a child < 3	–0.4923***	–0.7154***
Partner's educational attainment		
exempted of qualifications	—	
primary school	0.153**	
secondary school	0.1364	
university degree	0.1004	
Partner's occupational status	–0.0039*	–0.0073**
North-western	–0.2226**	
North-eastern	–0.55***	
Madrid and centre	–0.6019***	
Eastern	—	
Southern	–0.4056***	
Canarias	–0.259*	
Husband occup. status * child<3	0.006	

Table 7.3. *cont.*

Variables	Model 1	Model 2
Constant	−4.3551***	−4.1806***
−2 Log likelihood	25,871	25,871
Sub-episodes	305,254	305,254

Source: ESD 1991.
* statistically significant at 0.05 level;** statistically significant at 0.01 level; *** statistically significant at 0.001 level; — reference category.

Furthermore, if women had previous work experience, this increases the likelihood of entering full-time employment. However, again, when we check for the presence of children and their husband's occupational status, previous work experience turns out to be not significant.

The influence of childbearing on homemaker women is twofold. On the one hand, an increase in the number of children increases the likelihood of a woman entering full-time employment. However, the probability grows very slowly as the number of children increases, and large families are not common anyway, given the current low Spanish fertility level.[13] On the other hand, the presence of an infant child seems to discourage women from entering employment even after checking the geographical context in model 2. Therefore, the presence of small children clearly prevents women who are already out of the labour force from entering into paid employment.

To sum up: what is the influence of husbands' or cohabiting partners' on the wives' transition into full-time employment? In this case, partner's education turns out to be not significant in almost all educational categories, except for primary school. So, being married to a man with only primary-school education significantly increases the log-odds of entry into full-time employment in comparison with women who are married to husbands with a Ph.D. Furthermore, an increase in the occupational prestige of the husband significantly decreases the wife's likelihood of abandoning homemaking. For instance, if a homemaker woman is married to a sanitary officer her likelihood to enter full-time employment decreases by 30 per cent, but if her husband is promoted to an official dentist later on, the likelihood will have decreased by almost 40 per cent.

Discussion and Last Remarks

This chapter has dealt with the question of whether assortative mating has a positive effect on women's occupational career and enhances wives' chances

---

[13] The predicted probability of a woman for the younger marriage cohort (1985 onwards) entering full-time employment while having from one to three children only changes from 7 to 9% as estimated from the equation in model 2 holding constant all covariates (see Table 7.3).

of performing parallel careers. The results show that marrying a highly educated man does not necessarily guarantee the spouses' parallel careers or
greater role compatibility. I summarize the main findings as follows.

If the husband has much higher labour-market resources than the wife (that
is, educational attainment or occupational status), the couple tends to perform
a gender role complementary in which the wife carries the main bulk of
domestic work and childbearing, while supporting their husbands' careers. In
the case of these partnerships Becker's rationale of comparative advantage
seems to work. This comparative advantage presumably explains gender roles
within heterogeneous partnerships. However, this research has also shown
that even working-class homogamous partnerships (that is, both spouses have
identically low labour-market resources) tend to perform a gender role specialization. In these partnerships wives have a higher probability of withdrawing from the labour force than wives in middle-class homogamous
partnerships. Here the term of class is taken as the proxy of spouses' occupational prestige. These differences were illustrated in Figure 7.2.

The gender specialization among partners with similarly low earning potentials cannot be easily explained by the economic theory of the marriage. In
principle, there should not be a rational calculation that justifies woman's
specialization in home production. The only explanation has to be found in
the same characteristics of the labour market and the fact, not acknowledged
by Becker, that in equal conditions women will always face some degree of discrimination in the labour market (that is, segmented labour force, higher job
temporality, and so on). Women's limited opportunities are, moreover, accentuated within the category of workers with low occupational prestige. In this
case, gender specialization has to be understood as the result of wives' constrained choices rather than the formation of an efficient division of labour
within the family.

It was also hypothesized that highly educated women could avoid gender
asymmetrical relationships by searching for a good quality match, namely individuals with the same earning potentials. In this way, they would not be
exposed to the high opportunity costs of having to leave paid employment after
high investments in human capital. For this specific category of highly educated
women the likelihood of abandoning full-time employment is relatively low,
and in case of an early exit from the labour force the return tends to be invari-
ably high, regardless of the husbands' educational attainment. Male partners do
not exert a negative effect on their occupational career. This means that the rise
in wives' earnings potential does not reduce their gains from marriage, as specified by Becker, because by no means can they be required to disregard their
career for the family. Therefore, they can secure a satisfactory marital match—
using Oppenheimer's (1988) terminology—through an assortative partnership.

In this research the significant negative effect that precarious forms of
employment, for example, working with temporary-fixed and low-paying
jobs, have on the decision of women to abandon paid-employment is
also manifest. Labour-market rigidity has an additional negative effect. This

rigidity refers to the impossibility of women's continuous entries and exits from the labour force. These flows are common for married women in many other northern European states. In Spain, however, relatively few women enter or return to employment after homemaking. Large proportions of homemaker women have become structural outsiders to the labour force, above all among the oldest marriage cohorts. Only women with high labour-market resources enjoy a high probability of remaining at work.

The probability of women living with a partner and remaining in full-time employment, regardless of the husband's characteristics, varies markedly according to the occupational prestige they have. These differences indicate the presence of an enormous polarization in mothers' employment, whereby only a favoured group, for example, those with high human capital investment, seem to be able to minimize the effect of motherhood on their employment patterns and seem to acquire a greater ability to return to work in case of interruptions.

References

Adam, P. (1997). 'Labour Force Transitions of Married Women in Spain'. Ph.D. thesis, Department of Economics, European University Institute, Florence.

Alcobendas, M. P. (1984). *The Employment of Women in Spain* (Luxembourg: Commission of the European Communities).

Becker, G. (1981). *A Treatise on the Family* (Cambridge, Mass.: Harvard University Press).

Bel-Adell, C. (1991). 'Generación de empleo en los últimos años: El empleo precario' (Job Creation in the Last Years: Precarious Jobs), *III Jornadas de la Población española* (Third Spanish Congress on Population) (Torremolinos and Malaga: Departamento de Geografía, Universidad de Málaga), 221–30.

Bonke, J. (1995). 'Education, Work and Gender: An International Comparison', *IUE Working Paper EUF*, 95/4 (European University Institute, Florence).

Cabré, A. (1999). *El Sistema català de reproducció* (The Catalan System of Reproduction), (Barcelona: Proa).

Capel, R. M. (1990). 'Debate, conquistas y espectativas de la enseñanza de la mujer española durante la Edad de Plata' (Debate, Gains and Expectations of Education amongst Spanish Women during the Silver Age), in Sociedad Española de Historia de la Educación (ed.), *Mujer y Educación en España, 1868–1975* (Conference proceedings; Santiago de Compostela: Universidad de Santiago).

Carrasco, C., A. Alabart, M. Mayordomo, and T. Montagut (1997). *Mujeres, trabajos y políticas sociales: Una aproximación al caso español* (Women, Work, and Social Policies: An Approach to the Spanish Case) (Serie Estudios, 51; Madrid: Instituto de la Mujer).

Castro, T. (1992). 'Delayed Childbearing in Contemporary Spain: Trends and Differentials', *European Journal of Population*, 8: 217–46.

CIDE Instituto de la Mujer (1988). *La presencia de las mujeres en el sistema educativo.* (Women's Access to the Educational System) (Madrid: Ministerio de Cultura, Instituto de la Mujer).

Delgado, M., and T. Castro (1998) 'Encuesta de Fecundidad y Familia 1995' (Fertility and Family Survey), *Opiniones y Actitudes*, 20 (Madrid: Centro de Investigaciones Sociales).

Ditch, J., J. Bradshaw, and T. Eardley (1996). 'Developments in National Family Policies in 1994', *European Observatory on National Family Policies* (York: University of York, Social Policy Research Unit).

Durán, M. A. (1996). 'El trabajo invisible en España: Aspectos económicos y normativos' (Invisible Work in Spain: Normative and Economic Aspects), *Revista de estudios sociales y de sociología aplicada*, 105: 137–57.

——(1997). 'El papel de mujeres y hombres en la economía española' (The Role of Women and Men in the Spanish Economy), *Revista Información Comercial Española*, 760: 9–29.

European Commission Network on Childcare (1996). *A Review of Services for Young Children in the European Union 1990–1995* (Brussels: Equal Opportunities Unit).

Fox Harding, L. (1996). *Family, State and Social Policy* (London: Macmillan).

Garrido, L. J. (1992). *Las dos biografías de la mujer en España* (The Two Biographies of Women) (Madrid: Instituto de la Mujer, Ministerio de Asuntos Sociales).

Iglesias, J. (1995). 'Trabajo y Familia en España' (Work and Family in Spain), *Revista Internacional de Sociología, Tercera Epoca*, 11: 171–98.

INE (1999). *Encuesta de Población Activa* (Spanish Labour Force Survey) (Madrid: INE).

——(1994). *Censo de Población y Viviendas 1991* (Population and Dwelling Census), i *Resultados Nacionales* (Madrid: INE).

——(2000). *Datos avance del Movimiento Natural de la Población 1999* (First Release of Data on the Natural Increase of the Population) (Madrid: INE).

Jurado, T., and M. Naldini (1996). 'Is the South so Different? Italian and Spanish Families in Comparative Perspective', *South European Society and Politics*, 3/1: 42–66.

Meil-Landwerlin, G. (1995). 'La política familiar española durante el franquismo' (Spanish Family Policy in the Francoist Period), *Revista Internacional de Sociología, Tercera Epoca*, 11: 47–88.

Ministerio de Trabajo y Asuntos Sociales (1996) *Anuario de Estadísticas Laborales y de Asuntos Sociales* (Statistical Yearbook on Labour and Social Affairs) (Madrid: Ministerio de Trabajo, A.S., S.G. de Estadística).

Miret-Gamundi, P. (1997). 'Nuptiality Patterns in Spain in the Eighties', *GENUS*, 53/3–4: 183–98.

Moltó, M. L. (1992). 'Occupational Segregation in Spain', *European Commission Network of Experts on the Situation of Women in the Labour Market: Final Report.*

——(1993). 'Las mujeres en el proceso de modernización de la economía española' (Women in the Modernization Process of the Spanish Economy), in J. Rubery (ed.), *Las mujeres y la recesión* (Women and Recession) (Col. Economía y Sociología del Trabajo; Madrid: Ministerio de Trabajo y Seguridad Social), 183–210.

——(1994). 'Changing Patterns of Work and Working-Time for Men and Women in Spain: Towards the Integration or the Segmentation of the Labour Market', *European Commission Network of Experts on the Situation of Women in the Labour Market: Final Report.*

——(1995). 'Women and the Employment Rate in Spain: The Causes and Consequences of Variations in Female Activity and Employment Patterns', *European Commission Network of Experts on the Situation of Women in the Labour Market: Final Report.*

Naldini, M. (1999). 'Evolution of Social Policy and the Institutional Definition of Family Models: The Italian and Spanish Cases in Historical and Comparative Perspective', Ph.D. thesis, Department of Social and Political Sciences. European University Institute, Florence.

OECD (1999). *Labour Force Statistics 1978–1998* (Paris: OECD).

Oppenheimer, V. K. (1988). 'A Theory of Marriage Timing', *Americal Journal of Sociology*, 94/3: 563–91.

——(1996). 'The Role of Women's Economic Independence in Marriage Formation: A Skeptic's Response to Annemette Sørensen's Remarks', in H.-P. Blossfeld, (ed.), *The New Role of Women* (Oxford: Westview Press), 236–43.

Pfau-Effinger, B. (1994). 'The Gender Contract and Part-Time Work by Women: Finland and Germany Compared', *Environment and Planning*, 26/9: 1355–76.

Ramos, R. (1990). *Cronos dividido: Usos del tiempo y desigualdad entre mujeres y hombres en España* (Divided Timing: Use of Time and Inequalities between Women and Men in Spain) (Madrid: Instituto de la Mujer).

Rantalaiho, L. (1994). *The Gender Contract* (Working Paper, University of Tampere, Finland; Tampere: Department of Public Health).

Reher, D. S. (1997). *Perspectives on the Family in Spain, Past and Present* (Oxford: Clarendon Press).

Requena, M. (1997). 'Sobre el calendario reproductivo de las mujeres españolas' (Some Notes on the Timing at Fertility of Spanish Women), *Revista Internacional de Sociología*, *Tercera Epoca*, 79: 43–79.

Roussel, L. (1993). 'Fertility and Family', in United Nations Economic Commission for Europe (ed.), *European Population Conference* (Conference proceedings, Geneva; New York: United Nations), 37–110.

Solsona, M., and R. Treviño (1990). *Estructuras familiares en España* (Family Structures in Spain) (Madrid: Ministerio de Asuntos Sociales, Instituto de la Mujer).

——R. Houle, and C. Simó (2000). 'Separation and Divorce in Spain', in M. J. González, T. Jurado, and M. Naldini (eds.), *Gender Inequalities in Southern Europe: Women, Work and Welfare in the 1990s* (London: Frank Cass), 195–222.

Thorne, B., and M. Yalom (1992). *Rethinking the Family: Some Feminist Questions* (Boston, Mass.: Northeastern University Press).

Torns, T., P. Carrasquer, and A. Romero (1995). *El perfil socio-laboral femenino en España* (Labour and Social Profile of Women in Spain) (Madrid: Instituto de la Mujer, Ministerio de Asuntos Sociales).

Treiman, D. J. (1977). *Occupational Prestige in Comparative Perspective: Quantitative Studies in Social Relations* (New York: Academic Press).

Valero, A., and C. Lence (1995). 'Nupcialidad, fecundidad y familia: La paradoja del comportamiento de la nupcialidad y la fecundidad en España' (Nuptiality, Fertility, and Family: The Paradox of the Nuptiality and Fertility Behaviour in Spain), *Revista Internacional de Sociología, Tercera Epoca*, 11: 89–114.

APPENDIX TO CHAPTER 7: TIME-CONSTANT AND TIME-VARYING COVARIATES, DEFINITIONS AND BRIEF DESCRIPTION

Duration   Time-dependent variable that measures the time spent in employment or in homemaking (cumulative number of years) prior to the transition.

The woman's family
background:

father's occupational status[a]   Ordinal variable (time constant) representing the
occupational status of the father when women were aged
16. The ESD classification of occupations has been
adapted to the *Standard International Occupational Prestige
Scale* (SIOPS) of Treiman (1977) which provides a
hierarchical ordering of occupations with respect to their
social prestige.

mother's educational   Time-constant dummy variable that measures the highest
attainment   educational level attained by mothers when women were
16.

mother's main family role   Time-constant dummy variable where 1 = mothers who
had labour-market experience (reference category), 0 =
mothers who were mainly full-time homemakers when
women were 16.

Woman's educational   Time-varying dummy variable that measures the highest
attainment   educational level attained in a given particular year of
observation.

Woman's occupational   Time-constant variable that indicates the highest
status at her last job (or   occupational status attained at the time when she
current job if she did not   decided to quit paid employment and become a full-time
drop out)   homemaker. Coded according to the SIOPS.

Woman's type of job   Time-constant dummy variable.
contract

Woman's occupational   Dummy variable where 1= worked before marriage
experience before marriage   (reference category), 0 otherwise. For the analysis of entry
into full-time employment the variable measures work
experience prior to being a homemaker.

Woman in public   Time-constant dummy variable (1 = works in public
administration   administration, 0 = otherwise).

Woman's age   Time-varying variable. It has been included in the model
both in a linear and in a quadratic form to test for the
baseline rate over the life course.

Marriage cohorts   Dummy variable that measures the woman's year of
marriage.

Childrearing history:
Number of children   Time-varying variable (number of children accumulated).
Presence of an infant child   Time-varying dummy variable (coded 1 = child aged 0–3,
(aged 0–3)[b]   or 0 otherwise).
Partner's characteristics:
Partner's educational   Time-constant dummy variable that measures the highest
attainment   educational level achieved by the partner.
Partner's occupational status Time-constant variable coded according to the SIOPS.

Region of residence (NUT I) Residence at the time of the interview (dummy variable).
Autonomous Communities included in north-western
region = Galícia, Asturias and Cantabria), north-eastern =
País Vasco, Navarra, la Rioja, and Aragón, Madrid and
centre = Castilla-León, Castilla La Mancha, and
Extremadura, eastern = Cataluña, Comunidad
Valenciana, and Baleares, southern = Andalucía, Murcia,
Ceuta and Melilla, and Canarias.

[a] Mother's occupational status was not included because it turned out to be highly correlated with
the variable 'mother's main family role'.

[b] The relevance of this age category is related to the availability of publicly managed day-care
facilities. The coverage of publicly funded services is only 2% of children under 3 and almost 84%
for children aged 3–5 (European Commission Network on Childcare 1996). Compulsory schooling
starts at the age of 6.

IV

The 'Liberal' Welfare State Regime

8

Married Women's Employment Patterns in Britain

ANDREW MCCULLOCH AND SHIRLEY DEX

Introduction

As married women's employment participation has grown, a parallel interest in couples' employment patterns has been voiced. However, the consideration of interactions between two individuals' employment decisions has proved conceptually and operationally difficult. It is important to have more understanding of the interaction between husbands' and wives' employment as more dual-earner and dual-career couples emerge. In the past, it would have been assumed that the male partner was the breadwinner and his decision-making would take priority, partly because his potential earnings would be considerably greater than those of the female partner. There are a number of reasons why this position has been changing. Whilst earnings comparisons within many households still favour men, more couples are emerging where there is either approximate equality of earnings or even where women have larger earnings than their partners. There is also evidence of attitude changes in men and women about whether the male partner should automatically be viewed as the breadwinner.

Much of the research on women's employment participation has been carried out from within a conventional economics framework where individual decision-making is the common unit of analysis. The econometric estimations of female labour-force participation have usually been based on the assumption of separate decision-making. Husbands or partners have been built into the largely cross-sectional analyses in a number of ways: either their employment status has been added as an additional variable or set of variables; or their earnings have been included as unearned income to their wife. In the case of husbands' earnings, the expectation is that higher earnings will have a negative effect on a wife's participation, as a conventional (unearned) income

We wish to thank the Data Archive at Essex University for permission to use the British Household Panel Study (BHPS) data and the Economic and Social Research Council in Britain for funding the collection of these BHPS data. Thanks are also due to Heather Joshi and other authors in this volume for comments on an earlier draft.

effect on the wife; individuals are expected to choose more leisure (less work) as their income rises. In the case of a husband's employment status, the most common expectation has been that this is linked to the social security benefit regime; in cases where husbands who are not employed have their benefit entitlement affected by their wife being employed, there is likely to be a negative effect on the woman's participation. Other studies have gone as far as extending the cross-sectional relationships over a longitudinal period divided up into discrete time periods. However, the framework then has still been to consider husbands' and wives' decisions to be separate, and for resources within households to be entirely shared. The attempts to consider the joint nature of husbands' and wives' participation decisions have been limited.

This chapter reviews the changes which have been occurring in married women's and couples' employment patterns in Britain. In the light of this we present some analyses of married women's employment participation which extend the way husbands' status and employment is taken into consideration. The remainder of the chapter is organized as follows. In the next section we review the changes in married women's and couples' employment in Britain. We then describe the data and method used to estimate a number of models of women's labour-force transitions which extend the incorporation of husband's status from earlier models. We describe the results from our estimations before drawing our conclusions.

Married Women's Employment Trends in Britain

The labour-force participation rate of married women aged 16–59 in Britain increased from 25 per cent in 1951 to 35 per cent in 1961, and to 49 per cent in 1971 and 1981 (Dex *et al.* 1993). In 1996, the same participation rate was 67 per cent (Sly *et al.* 1997). This growth in married women's participation rates has increased the overall women's participation rate. In 1951, 38 per cent of the women's workforce were married women. In 1971, this percentage was 63 per cent and in 1996 it was 68 per cent. Hakim (1996) cautions against interpreting this increase in participation as an increase in labour supply, since total hours of work for women remained largely unchanged over much of the post-Second-World-War period and women's rate of full-time employment remained stable up to the mid-1980s. Much of the early growth in participation in Britain over the 1950s to 1970s was a growth in married women's part-time employment. In 1971, when statistics on part-time employment became reliably available, 33 per cent of women employees were in part-time work; in 1981, this percentage had risen to 42 per cent; it rose further, to 44 per cent in the 1980s where it has remained since (Dex *et al.* 1993). In the 1980s, there was a growth of married women's full-time participation rates. Also, women with young children were more likely to participate than previously. Between 1986 and 1996 the economic activity rate for women with children under 5 rose from 40 to 54 per cent (Sly *et al.* 1997).

Behind these aggregate statistics, changes in women's life-cycle patterns of employment were occurring in Britain. Many women went from stopping work when they first got married in the 1940s and earlier, to stopping work when they had their first child. A trend to return to work part-time after child-birth started to grow in the 1950s and 1960s, although in these early years the gap out of employment was large and lasted many years. This gap got pro-gressively shorter as women made faster returns to work, and women started returning between childbirth (Dex 1984; McRae 1991). Cohort comparisons provide measures of the changes which occurred. The median gap between the first birth and the next job was seventy months for a cohort of mothers born in a certain week in 1946; the same gap had a median length of twenty-nine months for a similar cohort of mothers born in 1958 (Macran *et al.* 1996).

Amongst British mothers in the 1980s, a pattern of continuous employment has become more common, along with a polarization at the upper and lower ends of the occupational scale. McRae (1993) found that the polarization has revolved around taking maternity leave to have a child. In 1991 in Britain only 50 per cent of economically active women were entitled to take maternity leave and these would be likely to be at the top end of the occupational hier-archy. A division has emerged, therefore, between those who take maternity leave, have relatively short breaks from employment, and return to full-time jobs, thus maintaining their occupational status, and those who do not. The latter have longer breaks from employment, and they may lose occupational status and earning power when they return to low-paid part-time work. Hakim (1996) characterizes this polarization in terms of whether or not women work part- or full-time. Modelling mothers' choice between working either full- or part-time has confirmed that there are some different determinants and also that different weight is attached to the presence of young children by those choosing to work full-time compared with part-time (Joshi *et al.* 1996).

The British econometric studies of female participation have found evi-dence of other changes, some of which support the picture described above. The early cross-sectional studies revealed that the age of the youngest child was the single most important determinant of women's participation rates (Joshi, 1984). Studies using longitudinal data have found that the importance of the age of the youngest child has declined and that of the woman's own wage or earnings potential has grown in importance (Dex *et al.* 1998). Previously, it was thought that delaying childbirth was also a feature of the new polarized group of women at the top end of the hierarchy. Delayed child-birth is highly correlated with continuous employment in the highly educated group. However, Dex *et al.* (1998) found that, after controlling for education, earning power, and the other common determinants of female labour-force participation, having a first child in one's thirties did not add anything sig-nificant to the explanatory power of models after controlling for the other known determinants of participation.

Another change which has been noted in cohort comparisons is that the neg-ative effect on a wife's participation of her husbands' earnings (or household income) has declined (Joshi and Hinde 1993). This has been regarded as evidence of an attitude change having occurred such that married women are entering paid employment increasingly out of choice rather than out of necessity. Ginn and Arber (1995) noted that household characteristics were important determinants of women in their forties, but that by their fifties, women's own characteristics were the most important determinants of their participation.

Couples' Employment

Descriptions of the interactions between couples' cross-sectional employment status have been produced (Dex *et al.* 1995*a*). These matrices have quantified the extent to which different types of sole- and dual-earner statuses are combined in British households in the 1990s. Table 8.1 is reproduced from Dex *et al.* (1995*a*) for couples in British households in 1991: 28 per cent of couples were both employed full-time and a further 21 per cent contained a husband who was employed full-time and wife employed part-time. Couples with a husband employed full-time and a wife who was economically inactive (17 per cent), or couples where both spouses were inactive (17 per cent) were the next largest groups. Other relationships between couples' employment status which are suggested by this table are as follows: that a husband is employed full-time will get progressively less likely as wives move to being less economically active; for women employed full-time, 87 per cent of husbands were in full-time jobs, whereas, for inactive wives, 43 per cent of husbands had full-time jobs. The percentage of wives working full-time and the percentage working part-time declines as men's economic activity weakens through part-time work and unemployment to inactivity. To some extent these results are replicating well-known relationships where unemployed men are far less likely to have employed wives than employed men (Cooke 1987) and the effect of the means-tested unemployment benefit system on this relationship (Dex *et al.* 1995*b*). Attempts to go beyond treating household factors as exogenous in models of female labour-force participation have been few. Wales and Woodland (1976) and Ashworth and Ulph (1981) are some of the few who have tried to model decision-making at the household level using British data.

Changes in the relationships between husbands' and wives' hours of work were documented by Dex *et al.* (1995*a*: Table 4.8, p. 19). Whereas in 1968 in Britain, 82 per cent of husbands in couples with dependent children worked more hours than their wives, in 1991 this figure was 75 per cent. In the case of husbands in couples without dependent children the decline was more dramatic; 64 per cent of husbands worked more hours than their wives in 1968 compared with 46 per cent in 1991.

A further analysis carried out for this chapter compares the occupational status in 1992 of dual-earner husbands and wives using the Hope–Goldthorpe rankings. The plot of the difference in Hope–Goldthorpe score of the husband

Table 8.1. BHPS 1991: husband's and wife's employment status (%)

Husband/wife	Full-time			Part-time			Unemployed			Inactive			N
	(1)	(2)	(3)	(1)	(2)	(3)	(1)	(2)	(3)	(1)	(2)	(3)	
Full-time	28.4	86.9	41.8	20.9	82.9	30.8	1.2	62.7	1.8	17.3	43.2	25.5	2,024
Part-time	0.0	1.9	20.9	0.0	3.2	27.9	0.0	1.7	1.2	1.4	3.6	50.5	86
Unemployed	1.5	4.5	21.4	0.0	3.7	13.6	0.0	22.0	6.3	4.1	10.1	58.7	206
Inactive	2.2	6.7	9.7	2.6	10.2	11.5	0.0	13.6	1.2	17.3	43.2	77.5	667
N		973			753			59			1,198		2,983

Source: Dex *et al.* (1995*a*).
(1) % of all couple households; (2) % of husbands in given employment status; (3) % of wives in given employment status.

minus that of the employed wife (Figure 8.1) shows that there are more men with higher occupational status than their wives than there are wives with higher occupational status than their husbands. However, overall there is enormous variety; 67 per cent of 1,109 dual-earner couples had a husband who had a higher Hope–Goldthorpe occupational score than his wife; in 33 per cent of cases, the ranking was the other way round. An alternative view would be to take bands of scores rather than the precise rankings; in which case, approximately one-quarter of dual-earner couples had similar occupational rankings, one-quarter had a wife with a higher score than the husband,

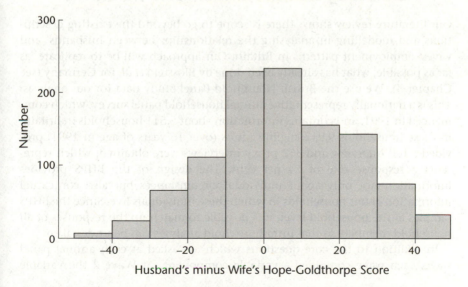

Figure 8.1. Husband's Hope-Goldthorpe score minus wife's Hope Goldthorpe score for not previously married couples where both partners were employed at BHPS Wave 1 in 1991.

and in one-half of couples the husband had a higher occupational status than the wife.

Gershuny (1996) has done some longitudinal analyses of the Hope-Goldthorpe occupational scores of husbands and wives. He found that, whereas at marriage the average gap between these scores is quite narrow, only four points on the Hope-Goldthorpe scale,[1] as time from marriage elapses, the average gap in the husbands' and wives' scores widened as the husbands' mean score gradually increased and the wives' mean scores rose initially and then fell. Gershuny noted, however, that women who took only a short domestic break (presumably to have children) kept up their mean score, which rose over their lifetime alongside that of the husband. The widening gap, therefore, was one which characterized couples where the wife had a sizeable domestic break. Figure 8.2 presents data on these profiles of couples' Hope–Goldthorpe occupational scores from the time of marriage until the interview for two marriage cohorts. Women's occupational scores clearly suffer from the long break whereas a short break retains the woman's occupational status. Men, on the other hand, do not suffer from a long break from employment, although relatively few are in this group. One implication of this finding is that assortative mating may be more pronounced than cross-sectional comparisons might imply, since it is after marriage that more of the gaps emerge. The occupational downgrading of women's status which is evident in these results has been found in other sources (Dex 1987).

Estimating Women's Labour-Force Transitions

Our literature review shows there is scope to go beyond the existing descriptions and modelling in analysing the relationships between husbands' and wives' employment patterns in Britain. Our approach will be to replicate, as far as possible, what has already been done by Blossfeld *et al.* for Germany (see Chapter 3). We use the British Household Panel Study data for our analysis. This is a nationally representative annual household panel survey, which commenced in 1991, and contains information about 5,511 households in Britain; in these households 9,912 eligible adults (over 16 years of age in 1991) provided a full interview and 352 proxy interviews were obtained, which represents a response rate of 74 per cent. The design of the BHPS provides information not only about individual circumstances but also contextual information about households in which these individuals live. Since the BHPS samples at the household level, it is possible to match up the responses of all household members so that intra-household analyses can be undertaken.

In addition to the core questions which are asked at each annual panel wave, each wave contained a variable component. At Wave 2 the variable

---

[1] The Hope–Goldthorpe scale used in the BHPS data is the reduced 12-point social class classification. The scale is based on the job characteristics in the three-digit Standard Occupational Classification and employment status as outlined in Goldthorpe and Hope (1974).

Marriage 1965–74

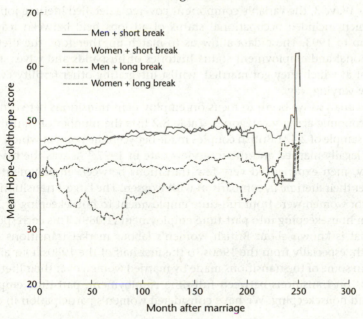

Marriage 1975–84

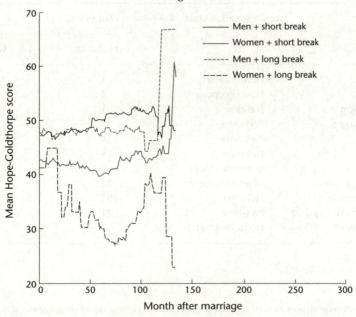

Figure 8.2, a, b. Mean Hope–Goldthorpe score plotted against month after marriage for men and women with long and short career breaks for marriage cohorts 1965–74 and 1975–84.

component covered individuals' employment status, marital and fertility histories. At Wave 3, the variable component covered a detailed lifetime job history, which included occupational status of all jobs held between leaving school up to 1993. These data allow us to match up, therefore, the lifetime occupational and employment status histories of husbands and wives, from the point at which they got married, whilst integrating other fertility events in a time-varying way.

In this analysis we begin to focus on employment transitions between different economic activity categories. Table 8.2 lists the number of transitions which a sample of 2,421 British couples made between the point at which they first got legally married and the interview date in 1992.[2] As was the case for Germany, men experienced very few transitions between employment statuses over their lifetime in comparison with women. The largest transition categories for women were from full-time employment to housekeeping (1,258) and from housekeeping into part-time employment (1,089). This corresponds with what is known about British women's labour market transitions over childbirth, especially from the 1960s to the first half of the 1980s. Our aim is to explain some of the transitions made by married women over their lifetime. We focus on transitions between full-time employment, part-time employment, and housekeeping. We have considered women's participation in each

Table 8.2. Employment transitions for couples, from marriage to interview in 1992

Origin state	Destination state	N of events	
		husbands	wives
Full-time	Housekeeping	1	1,258
Part-time	Housekeeping	0	534
Housekeeping	Full-time	1	317
Housekeeping	Part-time	0	1,089
Full-time	Part-time	34	196
Part-time	Full-time	14	207
Full-time	Unemployment	609	185
Part-time	Unemployment	12	61
Unemployment	Full-time	293	98
Unemployment	Part-time	21	66
Unemployment	Housekeeping	2	24

Source: BHPS Wave 2.
Total couples in sample: 2,421.

[2] The BHPS employment history at Wave 2 collected individuals' dated employment status histories in twelve categories. These have been aggregated into five categories: full-time employment, part-time employment, unemployment, housekeeping, and other; the latter includes BHPS categories of maternity leave, long-term sick, on government training scheme, in the war, full-time student, and something else.

month since they got married as a dichotomous state and use a logistic model to estimate the effects of a set of time-constant and time-varying covariates.

Blossfeld and Rohwer (1995) advocate a causal approach to studying wives' and husbands' careers which tackles the simultaneity problem of these inter-dependent processes, builds in the temporal nature of the effects, and holds the possibility of identifying lags between causes and effects. They call this approach the principle of conditional independence.

Given two parallel employment careers of a husband (Y_t^A) and his wife (Y_t^B), a change in Y_t^B at any specific point in time t' may be considered as being dependent on the history of both processes up to but not including t'. If we take a transition rate model for the joint careers,

$$Y_t = (Y_t^A, Y_t^B)$$

and assuming the principle of conditional dependence, the likelihood for this model can be factorized into a product of the likelihoods for two separate careers; a transition rate model for Y_t^B which is dependent on Y_t^A as a time-dependent covariate, and a transition rate model for Y_t^A which is dependent on Y_t^B as a time-dependent covariate. We use a full discrete time model for estimating this process for wives. Wives were the only group with a sufficient number of transitions. The model incorporates time-constant and time-dependent covariates and starts at the point at which the women first got legally married.

The range of covariates included a set of time-constant variables representing the woman's own status (father's occupation and woman's first job); time-constant variables reflecting women's age and human capital when they got married (highest education, full-time, and part-time work experience before marriage); time-varying age; a set of time-varying variables capturing the woman's childrearing history; a set of time-constant variables reflecting the partner's resources (father's occupation, partner's education, and partner's first job); and a time-varying partner's employment status. In addition, a set of marriage cohort dummy variables were included to capture period changes over time. A list of these variables with their definitions are presented in the appendix to this chapter. Whilst these independent variables were included to cover the known determinants of women's labour-force participation, the particular measures used were chosen to match, as far as possible, variables which Blossfeld *et al.* included in the analysis of German couples in Chapter 3.

The Transition from Full-Time Employment to Housekeeping

As we noted earlier, it has been common in Britain since the 1960s for women to work full-time after leaving full-time education until their first childbirth. Table 8.3 shows the initial status of wives across consecutive marriage cohorts.

The proportion of housewives at the time of marriage declined with successive marriage cohorts, from 36 per cent of those marrying before 1954 to 17 per cent of those marrying after 1985. The difference was mainly taken up in a rising percentage of women in full-time employment at marriage: 55 per cent of the cohort marrying before 1954 and approximately two-thirds in cohorts marrying after 1965. As in Germany, unemployment increases in the 1980s were another feature of the figures, reducing women's full-time employment status at marriage and increasing their unemployment status (classified as 'other' in Table 8.3).

Table 8.4 presents the estimated effects on the hazard rate of employment exits from full-time jobs. The duration dependence effect on the hazard was included as a set of dummy variables, with less than six months being the omitted base category. The general pattern in the duration dependence in full-time work was as follows; compared with individuals who had been in full-time employment for up to six months, those who stayed full-time up to three years had a reduced likelihood of exiting to housework. From three to five years the likelihood rose but fell again after five years. However, compared with the duration of less than six months, the likelihoods of exiting to housekeeping was not significantly different for longer duration of full-time employment.

We then followed the German example of including sets of variables in a stepwise fashion.[3] As women got older their probability of exit from full-time employment to housekeeping fell, although the positive quadratic term meant that the probability started to increase towards the end of the working life, as we would expect. Women's age at marriage was systematically significant, with higher marriage ages increasing the likelihood that women would make this transition to housework. Here the effect is likely to be capturing the pressure to start childbearing earlier after marriage, the older the woman is when marriage

Table 8.3. British women's employment status at the time of marriage for various marriage cohorts (%)

	Married 1954 or before	Married 1955–64	Married 1965–74	Married 1975–84	Married 1985–
Full-time employment	55	60	69	66	63
Self-employment	1	1	2	2	2
Part-time employment	3	7	4	7	10
Housewife	36	30	21	21	17
Other	5	2	3	5	8
N	43	394	544	571	551

Source: BHPS Wave 2.

[3] Interaction terms were also included between husbands' occupation and children of different ages, following Blossfeld *et al.* (Ch. 3). Since none of these effects were significant we dropped this model 8 from the presentation of the results.

Table 8.4. Effects on the transition rate from full-time work to housekeeping

Variables	Model 1	Model 2	Model 3	Model 4	Model 5	Model 6	Model 7
Duration							
6–12 months	-0.163	-0.199	-0.150	-0.149	-0.156	0.020	0.021
1–3 years	-0.049	-0.068	-0.081	-0.078	0.020	0.009	0.021
3–5 years	-0.004	-0.037	-0.143	-0.138	-0.004	-0.008	0.011
> 5 years	-0.146	-0.160	-0.209	-0.204	-0.108	-0.066	-0.045
W social origin	-0.009	-0.005	0.004	0.004	0.007	0.031	0.028
W education	-0.002	-0.024	-0.025	-0.032	-0.021	-0.024	
W 1st occ.		0.0002	0.0004	-0.025	-0.027	-0.022	
W FT < marr.				-0.048**	-0.075	0.222	0.240
W PT < marr.				0.036**	0.225	0.179	0.156
W age			-0.110**	-0.110**	-0.030	-0.034	-0.036
W age sq.			0.086**	0.086**	0.035	0.042	0.049
W age at marr.			0.054**	0.054**	0.023**	0.031**	0.026**
No. of children					0.341**	0.345**	0.353**
Pre-school child					0.301**	0.251	0.267**
School age					-0.147	-0.038	-0.017
Child 7–16					-0.236	-0.390	-0.408
H social origin						0.012	0.013
H education						-0.035	-0.031
H 1st occ.						-0.006	-0.008
Marriage cohort							
1955–64							0.062
1965–74							0.018
1975–84							0.044
1985–							0.560**
Intercept	-3.237**	-3.220**	-1.898**	-1.849**	-3.495**	-3.678**	-3.677**

BHPS discrete time model. ** $p < 0.01$, * $p < 0.05$.

takes place. The (time-varying) existence of a pre-school child and more than one child increased the likelihood of leaving full-time work for housework, compared with the months where children were not present. This is perhaps not surprising. This result could be reflecting either a pattern of childbirth where mothers returned to work between births or a pressure to stop work, even after deciding to return full-time, because of the stress of combining full-time work with young children. The group who are in full-time employment with young children are likely to be those who took maternity leave and returned to full-time employment whilst their children were young. They are a group more committed to continuous employment, compared with all women. None the less, the pressures of combining employment and young children are such that they still have an increased likelihood of leaving their full-time jobs.

Human capital up to marriage was not significant when first entered (model 4) in the direction we might expect. However, in the final model (model 7), after cohort effects were controlled, part-time employment experience before marriage had a positive effect on the likelihood of exiting to housekeeping. It was relatively unusual in Britain to have had part-time work experience before marriage until recently. The recent increase has been largely related to increasing unemployment and more pressures on students to work part-time as a way of funding their higher and further education. This group will not be represented in these data to any great extent. The positive coefficient of part-time employment probably represents a fairly untypical group of older women who started to work part-time before they got married, a group who have largely disappeared now.

The effects of husbands, as captured by these variables, support earlier British findings: that husbands' status has relatively little effect on wives' participation after controlling for other variables. 'Husbands with degrees' was the only significant husband's status variable; a degree-educated husband made the transition to housekeeping less likely. This is some evidence of assortative mating. However, husbands' employment status was not significant.

Marriage cohort effects were relatively insignificant in these transitions from full-time employment to housekeeping, with the exception of the most recent cohort married after 1985; the cohort frequencies of full-time employment per month led us to expect that cohort effects would be minimal (Figure 8.3). Most women who became mothers across the cohorts have made this transition. Cohort differences have been more pronounced on the duration of the gap spent in housekeeping and on the status and hours of the first return.

The Transition from Part-Time Employment to Housekeeping

Transitions from part-time work to housekeeping will usually occur after British women have had a child and later return to work part-time. These women may subsequently stop being employed to have further children.

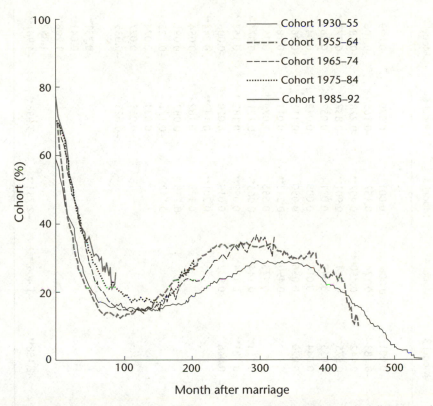

Figure 8.3. Percentage of women in five marriage cohorts who were in full-time work, plotted against month after marriage. Couples remained married in 1992 and had not been previously married.

These transitions are associated with certain patterns around childbirth; those of returning to work after completing childbirth or returning between births. But women who make these transitions to part-time from housekeeping are a selective sample of women. They have usually opted not to take maternity leave or return quickly, but to have a longer break and then return to a part-time job, and face a relatively high risk of downward occupational mobility in the process. They do not include, therefore, many of the group of highly edu-cated women who have been delaying childbirth, taking short maternity breaks, and returning to a full-time job. The results in Table 8.5 in many ways reflect the sample selection effect we have implicitly built into this model.

The duration dependence effects are more significant in this transition. The likelihood of exiting from part-time work to housework appears to decline as the duration of time in part-time employment increased. This trend may be visible in these results because women who do not fit it have been excluded from the model by not being in part-time work in the first place. We see in the final model (7) that the main determinants of this transition are the marriage cohort effects; these suggest that more recently married couples had higher

Table 8.5. Effects on the transition rate from part-time work to housekeeping

Variables	Model 1	Model 2	Model 3	Model 4	Model 5	Model 6	Model 7
Duration							
6–12 months	-0.018	-0.016	0.001	0.006	0.001	0.070	0.099
1–3 years	-0.265**	-0.281**	-0.183	-0.174	-0.157	-0.165	-0.106
3–5 years	-0.625***	-0.609***	-0.442**	-0.450**	-0.407***	-0.278	-0.187
> 5 years	-1.147***	-1.136***	-0.875***	-0.924***	-0.901***	-0.837***	-0.777***
W social origin	0.009**	0.069**	0.055	0.047	0.031	0.057	0.063
W education		0.060**	0.044	0.016	0.008	0.048	0.047
W 1st occ.			0.020	0.056	0.050	0.111*	0.066
W FT < marr.				-0.490*	-0.543***	0.011	0.184
W PT < marr.				0.473	0.555	1.079***	0.352
W age			-0.154**	-0.144**	-0.065*	-0.121**	-0.074
W age sq.			0.181**	0.174**	0.099**	0.182**	0.153**
W age at marr.			0.046**	0.032**	0.019	0.020	-0.006
No. of children					0.201**	0.149**	0.244**
Pre-school child					0.123	0.162	-0.054
School age					-0.138	-0.082	-0.091
Child 7–16					-0.142	-0.171	-0.123
H social origin						0.034	0.024
H education						0.051	0.027
H 1st occ.						-0.025	-0.035
Marriage cohort							
1955–64							0.331*
1965–74							0.841**
1975–84							1.208**
1985–							1.852**
Intercept	-3.553***	-4.165**	-2.158**	-1.406**	-2.733***	-3.958**	-4.961**

BHPS discrete time model. ** $p < 0.01$, * $p < 0.05$

probabilities of making these transitions. This is a trend described in the literature, of returning to work between births instead of after all births were completed. The woman's own human capital in the form of educational qualifications was significant in reducing the likelihood of moving to housekeeping when she had either O level or A level qualifications compared with no qualifications. The higher the number of children, the more likely this transition is. Larger numbers of children create a pressure for more income but also create more work in the home.

Before cohort effects were controlled, husbands' education was significant in increasing the likelihood of the transition in three cases. Compared with husbands who had no education, those with degrees, those with O level or GCSE, and those with vocational qualifications were more likely to have wives who moved from part-time work to housekeeping. This may be some evidence of an income effect, although it is not measured precisely; nor is it consistent across all levels of education. Demographic effects tended to dominate in this model over human capital, social origin, and husbands' status effects, possibly, again, because of the sample selection effects having reduced the variation in these other variables.

The Transition from Housekeeping to Full-Time Employment

The effects of covariates on the transitions from housekeeping to full-time employment are set out in Table 8.6. Here the duration dependence effect was significant. From a low starting-point for duration of time in housework up to six months, there was a large increase in the six- to twelve-month period, followed by a gradual decline. The large increase in exit rates from housework in the six- to twelve-month period is probably due to maternity leave entitlement ending. Statutory maternity leave in Britain since 1974 has given employees the right to return to their job up to twenty-nine weeks after the birth. Since most of those taking maternity leave will have been in full-time employment and be expected to return to the same hours of work, this is being reflected in these duration effects. Where women did not take maternity leave, a significant duration dependence effect was visible whereby the probability of returning to full-time employment declined the longer the time spent housekeeping. The coefficients of the marriage cohorts show a very strong and dominating effect, with the probabilities of moving from housekeeping to full-time employment increasing dramatically in the more recently married groups. However, women who married at older ages experienced a slight dampening effect on this trend, as did those with a pre-school child. These strong cohort and duration dependence effects were also visible in the cohort frequencies of women in housework in any particular month (Figure 8.4).

Women's social origins, when first entered, did make the transition from housework to full-time employment more likely. However, these effects were not

Table 8.6. Effects on the transition rate from housekeeping to full-time work

Variables	Model 1	Model 2	Model 3	Model 4	Model 5	Model 6	Model 7
Duration							
6–12 months	0.183	0.198	0.236	0.237	0.422*	0.241	0.280
1–3 years	-0.684**	-0.662**	-0.638**	-0.634**	-0.340	-0.612**	-0.518**
3–5 years	-0.906**	-0.919**	-0.946**	-0.935**	-0.571**	-0.729**	-0.556*
>5 years	-0.665**	-0.636**	-0.916**	-0.915**	-0.856**	-1.086**	-0.805**
W social origin	0.071**	0.667	0.071	0.074	0.063	0.090	0.079
W education		0.072**	0.061*	0.053	0.044	0.030	0.039
W 1st occ.			-0.027	-0.036	0.006	0.059	0.051
W FT < marr.				-0.659**	-0.605**	-0.807**	-0.498
W PT < marr.				-0.459	-0.622	-1.138	-1.393**
W age			0.040**	0.043	-0.015	0.000	0.040
W age sq.			0.010	0.008	0.015	0.010	-0.000
W age at marr.			-0.033*	-0.034*	0.000	-0.038	-0.051**
No. of children					-0.222**	-0.135	-0.007
Pre-school child					-0.589**	-0.453**	-0.475**
School age					0.298	0.403	0.357
Child 7–16					0.618**	0.635**	0.471
H social origin						-0.037	-0.089
H education						-0.023	-0.020
H 1st occ.						-0.044	-0.078
Marriage cohort							
1955–64							0.574**
1965–74							0.914**
1975–84							1.420**
1985–							2.137**
Intercept	-3.894**	-4.742**	-5.019**	-4.340**	-3.238**	-2.241**	-3.784**

BHPS discrete time model. ** $p < 0.01$, * $p < 0.05$.

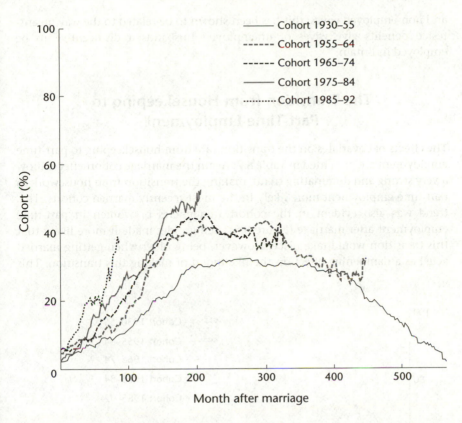

Figure 8.4. Percentage of women in five marriage cohorts who were in housework, plotted against month after marriage.

sustained after introducing human capital measures of education. The effect of having a degree or higher education made this transition to full-time employment more likely, as did having a vocational qualification or an O level compared to having no qualifications. The effect of increasing age at marriage was to reduce the likelihood of this transition occurring from housekeeping to full-time employment. Having a pre-school child made it less likely that women would take up full-time employment, whereas having an older child made it more likely that they would do so. Marriage cohort effects were significant and made the transition increasingly more likely for the more recent cohorts. This trend is evident in the cohort plots of the frequency of full-time employment (Figure 8.3).

Husbands' education was also significant. Where the woman had a husband who had either higher qualifications or A/O evels she was less likely to make this transition to full-time employment compared with women whose husbands had no qualifications. Having a husband who was employed also made it less likely she would make this transition. We have here some evidence of an income effect, as far as our variables capture this. In the case of employed husbands we may also be reflecting the association between unemployed husbands and non-employed wives; this has been shown to be related to the way means-tested benefits give wives of unemployed husbands a disincentive to be employed in Britain.

The Transition from Housekeeping to Part-Time Employment

The effects of covariates on the transition rate from housekeeping to part-time employment are presented in Table 8.7. Again the marriage cohort effects show a very strong and dominating trend, making the transition from housework to part-time employment more likely in the most recently married cohorts. This trend was also evident in the cohort frequencies of women in part-time employment after marriage (Figure 8.5). Being older made it more likely that this transition would take place. However, being older when getting married acted as a dampening effect on the likelihood of making this transition. This

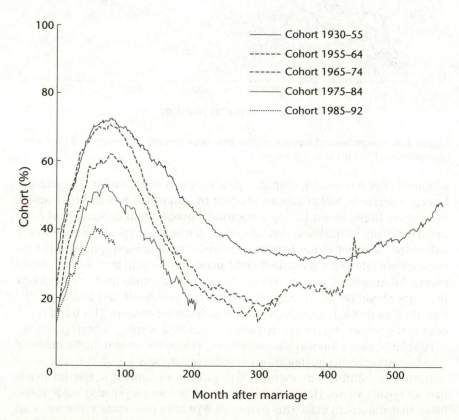

Figure 8.5. Percentage of women in five marriage cohorts who were in part-time work, plotted against month after marriage.

latter group may be the more recent highly educated cohort of those who have been delaying childbearing and returning to full-time employment after childbirth.

Increasing numbers of children made the transition to part-time employment less likely; having a child of school age made the transition more likely. Higher human capital in the form of a degree or higher education qualification served to increase the likelihood of this transition compared with those who did not have any educational qualifications.

It is difficult to find evidence of any effects from husbands on this transition. The one significant effect is that husbands with higher social status reduce the likelihood of women returning to part-time employment. There are two possible reasons for this effect. Either this could be a conventional economic income effect which reduces the financial pressure for women to return to work after having children; or under assortative mating, the higher social origin husbands may be married to women who are making transitions back to full-time employment. The fact that husbands' status was significant in the transitions to full-time employment considered earlier (Table 8.6) points to assortative mating as the explanation of this result. However, it should be borne in mind that women who make this transition to part-time employment after childbirth are again a selected sample of those whose earnings capacity is relatively low, and who place more importance on carrying out their own childcare, and having work which is convenient and close to home (Dex 1988). They have more traditional attitudes and have accepted a more traditional role within the family. It is also possible, although largely uninvestigated, that these women are also characterized by allowing themselves to be more influenced by their husbands than other women.

Conclusions

In this study we have taken a life-cycle and longitudinal view of women's employment histories. A number of trends have been confirmed in our results. We found evidence of the increase in the pattern of returning to work between childbirth and of the increasing trend to return to part-time work in the post-Second-World-War period. The results as a whole support the view that polarization has been occurring more recently between British married women in the workforce. The group of highly educated, short-break maternity leavers returning to full-time jobs was apparent; and the more traditional returnees to part-time work, after a longer break, were also evident.

One aim of this cross-national study of couples' employment patterns has been to investigate the extent to which spouses marry assortatively and how this affects their subsequent employment patterns over the family life cycle. Our preliminary comparisons of husbands' and wives' occupational statuses at marriage, and other studies, revealed that mating is assortative in Britain and characterizes at least one-quarter of couples. The effects of highly educated

Table 8.7. Effects on the transition rate from housekeeping to part-time work

Variables	Model 1	Model 2	Model 3	Model 4	Model 5	Model 6	Model 7
Duration							
6–12 months	0.593*	0.606**	0.622**	0.628**	0.621**	0.964**	1.015**
1–3 years	−0.239**	−0.262**	−0.282**	−0.265*	−0.268**	0.039	0.154
3–5 years	−0.246**	−0.259**	−0.390**	−0.360**	−0.428**	−0.072	0.128
> 5 years	−0.052	−0.037	−0.551**	−0.518**	−0.732**	−0.436**	−0.186
W social origin	0.058**	0.031	0.022	0.015	0.017	0.025	0.015
W education		0.084**	0.062**	0.048**	0.051**	0.053*	0.020
W 1st occ.			0.057*	0.080**	0.094**	0.144**	0.103*
W FT < marr.				−0.200	−0.113	0.211	0.273
W PT < marr.				1.399**	1.309**	1.655**	0.253
W age			0.206**	0.212**	0.042	0.043	0.103*
W age sq.			−0.205**	−0.211**	−0.011	−0.007	−0.048
W age at marr.			−0.056**	−0.064**	−0.043**	−0.052**	−0.076**
No. of children					−0.473**	−0.436**	−0.309**
Pre-school child					−0.100	−0.101	−0.157
School age					0.472**	0.549**	0.500**
Child 7–16					−0.253*	−0.306*	−0.301*
H social origin						−0.063*	−0.082*
H education						0.034	0.029
H 1st occ.						−0.018	−0.031
Marriage cohort							
1955–64							0.459**
1965–74							0.722**
1975–84							1.496**
1985–							2.422**
Intercept	−4.449**	−5.310**	−8.073**	−7.794**	−4.884**	−5.710**	−6.806**

BHPS discrete time model. ** $p < 0.01$, * $p < 0.05$.

husbands were seen most clearly in reducing the likelihood of the wife's transition from full-time employment to housekeeping. There was some evidence of the reverse transition also being less likely for women with qualified husbands. However, at the same time transitions from full-time to housekeeping, from part-time to housekeeping, or from housekeeping to full-time employment, showed that women's own status and cohort changes over time probably dominate the explanations of women's life-cycle behaviour patterns; the effects of husbands were of less importance.

Before leaving this issue we need to consider whether this is a true representation of British women's behaviour. There is the possibility that our measures of husbands' status, chosen to correspond with German analyses, do not reflect British husbands' influence effectively. We suspect that there is some truth in this and that, were it available, a time-varying measure of husbands' income would reveal more influence than the effect of his first occupation. None the less, the fact that husbands' education is not significant in some of the models suggests that husbands' economic position does have a weaker effect than that seen in the German results. In addition, there are very strong and often dominating marriage cohort effects to consider. Are these effects picking up the influence of variables which are not well measured in our analyses and thus overstating cohort change effects at the expense of other effects? In general we think not, since strong cohort effects have been noted in other studies (Macran *et al.* 1996).

A husband's social status in Britain was found to have an effect on only one set of transitions, and because of the conditional nature of these transitions, on one group of women: those engaging in the most traditional patterns of combining employment and family responsibilities. Women who returned to work part-time after having a child did so taking their husband's status (or possibly his income) into account. Over the post-war period this was an increasing trend, with as many as two-thirds of mothers returning to a part-time job at the height of this behaviour pattern. In this respect, therefore, this has been and probably still is a majority pattern amongst British couples, albeit a declining majority. Also, even here, the strength of this effect in Britain appears to be much weaker than the same effect in Germany.

Why should Britain be different in the amount of influence women allow their husbands to have on their behaviour? These results suggest that individualistic thinking is much stronger in Britain than in Germany. The results also suggest that commitments to more traditional family organization and sexual division of labour are now weaker in Britain than in Germany. Changes in economic and social policy regimes in Britain support this suggestion. For example, the British tax system, unlike the German tax system, moved to be based on individual assessment in 1991 and the tax allowance for being married or having children has been significantly reduced or removed over time. Similarly, Britain's tax and social security benefit systems have, over time, successively reduced the burden of direct taxation on single people relative to married couples.

Of course, in principle, other models of combining employment and family are possible than the one where women take most of the caring responsibilities at the expense of their employment careers. It is possible to think of men taking career breaks to look after children, and Scandinavian and more recently German policies allow for this model. Again Britain, to date, has not considered this to be a desirable policy option, and has even resisted the introduction of statutory rights to short periods of paternity leave at childbirth. Combining the low priority given to men's participation in childrearing with the relatively short periods of maternity leave offered to women, it is perhaps not surprising to see growing polarization between British women (and possibly couples) in the way they plan their family responsibilities and employment participation, although it is not necessarily desirable.

References

Ashworth, J. S., and D. T. Ulph (1981). 'Household Models', in C. V. Brown, *Taxation and Labour Supply* (London: Allen & Unwin).

Blossfeld, H.-P., and G. Rohwer (1995). *Techniques of Event History Modeling: New Approaches to Causal Analysis* (Mahwah, NJ: Erlbaum).

Cooke, K. (1987). 'The Withdrawal from Paid Work of Wives of Unemployed Men: A Review of Research', *Journal of Social Policy*, 16: 371–82.

Dex, S. (1984). *Women's Work Histories. An Analysis of the Women and Employment Survey* (ResearchPaper, 46; London: Department of Employment).

——(1987). *Women's Occupational Mobility* (Basingstoke: Macmillan).

——(1988). *Women's Attitudes Towards Work* (Basingstoke: Macmillan).

——P. Walters, and E. Alden (1993). *French and British Mothers at Work* (Basingstoke: Macmillan).

——M. Taylor, and A. Clark (1995a). *Household Labour Supply* (London: Employment Department Research Series, 43).

——S. Gustafsson, N. Smith, and T. Callan (1995b). 'Cross-National Comparisons of the Labour Force Participation of Women Married to Unemployed Men', *Oxford Economic Papers*, 47: 611–35.

——H. Joshi, S. Macran, and A. McCulloch (1998). 'Women's Employment Transitions around Childbearing', *Oxford Bulletin of Economics and Statistics*, 60: 79–100.

Gershuny, J. (1996). 'From Gemstone to Millstone', *The Times Higher Education Supplement* (2 Aug.).

Ginn, J., and S. Arber (1995). 'Exploring Mid-Life Women's Employment', *Sociology*, 29: 73–94.

Goldthorpe, J., and K. Hope (1974). *The Social Grading of Occupations: A New Approach and Scale* (Oxford: Clarendon Press).

Hakim, C. (1996). *Key Issues in Women's Work: Female Heterogeneity and the Polarisation of Women's Employment* (London and Atlantic Highlands, NJ: Athlone Press).

Joshi, H. (1984). *Women's Participation in Paid Work: Further Analysis of the Women and Employment Survey* (Research Paper, 45; London: Department of Employment).

——and P. R. Hinde (1993). 'Employment after Childbearing in Post-War Britain: Cohort Study Evidence on Contrasts and across Generations', *European Sociological Review*, 9: 203–27.

——S. Macran, and S. Dex (1996). 'Employment after Childbearing and Women's Subsequent Labour Force Participation', *Journal of Population Economics*, 9/3: 325–48.

McRae, S. (1991). *Maternity Rights in Britain* (London: Policy Studies Institute).

——(1993). 'Returning to Work after Childbirth: Opportunities and Inequalities', *European Sociological Review*, 9/2: 125–37.

Macran, S., H. Joshi, and S. Dex (1996). 'Employment after Childbearing: A Survival Analysis', *Work, Employment and Society*, 10/2: 273–96.

Sly, F., A. Price, and A. Risdon (1997). 'Women in the Labour Market: Results from the Spring 1996 Labour Force Survey', *Labour Market Trends*, 105/3: 99–120.

Wales, T. J., and A. D. Woodland (1976). 'Estimation of Household Utility Functions and Labour Supply Responses', *International Economic Review*, 17: 397–410.

APPENDIX TO CHAPTER 8: DESCRIPTION OF VARIABLES USED IN DISCRETE TIME MODELS

Time-varying = tv, time-constant = tc.

6–12 months	Duration in origin state from 6 to 12 months (tv)
1–3 years	Duration in origin state over 1 to 3 years (tv)
3–5 years	Duration in origin state over 3 to 5 years (tv)
> 5 years	Duration in origin state over 5 years (tv)
W social origin	Wife's father's Hope–Goldthorpe scale (tc)
W education 1	Wife has degree as highest qualification (tc)
W ed. 2	Wife has higher education as highest (tc)
W ed. 3	Wife has A-level or equivalent as highest (tc)
W ed. 4	Wife has O-level or equivalent as highest (tc)
W ed. 5	Wife has vocational qualification (tc)
W 1st occ.	Wife's Hope–Goldthorpe scale of first job (tc)
W FT < marr.	Wife's full-time work experience before marriage as % of working time before marriage (tc)
W PT < marr.	Wife's part-time work experience before marriage as % of working time before marriage (tc)
W-age	Wife's age in years (tv)
W age sq.	Wife's age squared/100 (tv)
W age at marr.	Wife's age in years at marriage (tc)
N children	Number of children (tv)
Pre-school child	Has child under 5 (tv)
School age	Has child aged 5–15 (tv)
Child 7–16	Has child aged 16 or more (tv)
H social origin	Husband's father's Hope–Goldthorpe scale (tc)
H education 1	Husband has degree as highest qualification (tc)
H ed. 2	Husband has higher education as highest (tc)
H ed. 3	Husband has A-level or equivalent as highest (tc)
H ed. 4	Husband has O-level or equivalent as highest (tc)
H ed. 5	Husband has vocational qualification (tc)

| H 1st occ. | Husband's Hope–Goldthorpe scale of first job (tc) |
| H employed | Husband employed (tv) |

Marriage cohort

1955–64	Woman got married between 1955–1964 (tc)
1965–74	Woman got married between 1965–1974 (tc)
1975–84	Woman got married between 1975–1984 (tc)
1985-	Woman got married since 1985 (tc)

9

Coupled Careers: Pathways Through Work and Marriage in the United States

SHIN-KAP HAN AND PHYLLIS MOEN

Work and Family in the USA Today

BOTH the family and workplace in the United States have been radically altered by events of the last four decades, and are still in flux. One of the most significant changes that directly bears on the occupational as well as family 'careers' of Americans is the large increase in the labour-force participation of women, especially married women, including mothers with young children. For instance, the labour-force participation rate of married women with children under age 6 increased rapidly in the United States in the latter half of the twentieth century, from 12 per cent in 1950 to 64 per cent in 1995 (US Bureau of the Census 1977: 392; 1996: 400). As of 1995, 70 per cent of US mothers with children under age 18 were in the labour force, and the corresponding figure was 61 per cent for mothers of children under age 3 (US Bureau of Labor Statistics 1996: 400). This parallels the historical trends in women's employment described in the chapters on European countries.

While these changes have transformed the life course and work experience of women, they have also altered the composition of the workforce, with radical consequences for both employers and families, and increasingly for men. Specifically, nearly half (48 per cent) of all workers in the US now come from 'dual-earner couples' (US Bureau of Labor Statistics 1994). Only 9.4 per cent of workers come from so-called 'traditional families', with a male breadwinner and a full-time female homemaker. By the year 2000, the estimates are that dual-earner couples will rise to the majority (51 per cent) of all families. This would be up from 41 per cent in 1980.

These statistical highlights provide a quantitative perspective on the magnitude of change, underscoring that the traditional breadwinner/homemaker

The research was funded by the Alfred P. Sloan Foundation (Sloan FDN #96–6–9) and by the National Institute on Aging (#IT50-AG11711). We would like to thank Marin Clarkberg for her helpful comments on earlier draft.

model no longer adequately describes the way the family and workplace interact with each other in the United States. In fact, this model is rapidly becoming a cultural relic, producing what Riley and Riley (1994) characterize as
structural lag.

How do dual-earner couples (or single parents) manage in a world predicated on the male breadwinner/female homemaker model? One strategy
involves a modification of this traditional gendered division of labour, producing a neo-traditional family arrangement. In some cases, the state plays a
role, as the discussions in prior chapters on the European context describe in
their analysis of the role of the welfare state. Traditional welfare states, such as
Germany and the Netherlands, have facilitated the part-time employment of
wives and mothers, thereby enabling women to sustain an attachment to
employment without fundamentally altering the conventional (male) breadwinner career model.

The United States, by contrast, lacks the institutional support for combining work and family roles and responsibilities characteristic of the welfare
states in Europe (Moen 1989). In fact, it was only in 1992 that any federal
parental leave policy was instituted. Private-sector policies present a patch-
work of family supports, contingent on one's employer, manager, and particular occupation. Moreover, 'part-time' employment in the US is typically
low-wage work, with little security and seldom any benefits. None the less, the
neo-traditional pattern is evident in the US as well. And, as in much of Europe,
wives and mothers in the US have been perceived typically as secondary earners, pursuing 'jobs', not 'careers'. The cultural discourse in the US has defined
the work–family nexus as women's problem, reflecting their private troubles
rather than a public issue that needs to be joined by government and/or
employers (Moen 1992).

As we turn the century, however, this neo-traditional model—which retains
the male as the principal breadwinner—is increasingly being challenged by
the reality of increasing numbers of dual-earner couples where both spouses
pursue careers and/or where wives (or single-parent women) earn the major
share of the household income. The fact that the majority of American men
now have wives who are employed and the majority of workers, male or
female, typically confront family constraints is slowly, yet steadily, redefining
the work–family interface. Increasingly, it is seen as no longer just a women's
issue but a challenge confronting workers, managers, and employers, if not the
nation (see e.g. Barnett and Rivers 1996; Hochschild 1997).

These changes are embedded in and affected by four related trends: (1) the
globalization of the economy (raising issues of productivity, competitiveness,
and consumption), (2) innovations in technology (decoupling work and the
workers from the workplace, blurring work/non-work boundaries, and realign-
ing communities), (3) the restructuring of employment relations in the United
States ('downsizing' and relying more on 'contingent' workers, producing a
decline in benefits and job security), and (4) the changing composition of the
American workforce (fewer younger workers, more women, more workers with

either dependent children or ageing parents). These trends are also reshaping the implicit, if not explicit, contracts between husbands and wives regarding work and family roles. These fundamental shifts provide the underlying rationale for a reappraisal of the traditional paradigm of careers as well as the organization of the life course in terms of the work–family interface so as to address the changed, and changing, social reality.

In this chapter, we shift the frame of reference from occupational status or mobility at particular points in time to trajectories over the life course. These trajectories encompass not only men's (and especially husbands') work careers, but also those of women (and especially wives). We also recognize that these work careers are embedded in yet another trajectory: that of the family. Our theoretical perspective is further elaborated in the following section, presenting a conceptual model. The methodology section follows, where we also describe our data. Given our analytical focus on trajectories, our method and data are rather distinct from the ones employed by other chapter authors in this volume. We then present our findings in three parts: work career, family experience, and work–family interface. Finally, we discuss the findings and their implications in broader contexts and suggest directions for future research.

The Model

Couples: Interlocking Dimensions

Figure 9.1 illustrates the conceptual model of the traditional interface between work and family that has permeated American culture since the industrial revolution. The two spheres, work and family, were separated from each other along the gender line. In this model, the notion of single breadwinner, family wage, and male provider ideology were packaged together along with the image of women as the family caretakers of husbands, children, infirm relatives, and responsible for the domestic work of the household (Moen 1992, 1994).

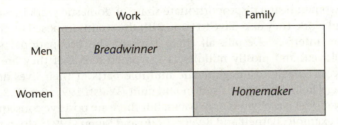

Figure 9.1. Breadwinner–homemaker

This gendered model remains pervasive in individual identities and expectations as well as in the structure of work, despite changes in the labour-force involvement of women, wives, and mothers. 'I lost my job, I failed my family,' says James E. Sharlow, a former manufacturing executive, who recently lost his job (Bragg 1996). One defines the other. For men, it is paid work that is primary: he was successful as a husband and father precisely because of a great job. He says, 'Kodak' (the firm from which he was 'downsized') 'was everything. [. . .] I worked late nights, weekends, holidays. [. . .] I remember going to a dance recital and saying to Gayle [his wife], "That girl on the end is really good." And she said, "Jim, that's your daughter." ' For women, at least for some, the model has also held sway. Gayle says, 'Everyone should know. He has always been a very good provider for his family. I want to make sure everyone understands that.'

In a sense, this traditional model was one of the ways to effectively deal with the tension between the two 'greedy institutions' (Coser 1974). Men developed comparative advantage on the job, while their wives became adept at homemaking, reproducing a gendered division of labour that frequently 'made sense' given the constraints of managing responsibilities at work and at home (Becker 1991 [1981]). But this model reflects what Riley and Riley (1994) describe as structural lag, with the institutions of both work and family yet to come to terms with the changing realities of dual-earner and single-parent families.

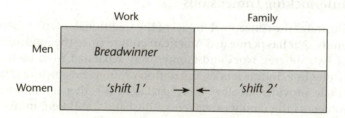

Figure 9.2. The second shift

Figure 9.2 shows the dilemma most married employed women face today, what Hochschild (1989) has termed as 'The Second Shift'. Not only do American women bear a disproportionate share of domestic work in addition to their paid work, they also have to cope with the strains imposed by the new work–family interface. Despite all their gains in the occupational sphere, many employed, and mostly middle-class, women feel as if they are living 'divided lives', unable to integrate the multiple parts of their lives and frequently overwhelmed with frustration and guilt (Walsh 1995: 24–5).

This new model has obvious drawbacks. But there are positive consequences as well. For example, Barnett and Rivers (1996) and Moen (1992; Moen and Yu 1997) report that:

- Paid work is positively related to both women's and men's health and emotional well-being.
- Because working wives bring money into the household, their work helps equalize the balance of power in their marriages.
- Feeling successful at work is typically related to feeling successful at home, for both husbands and wives.

These are positive in the sense that they show dual-earner couples successfully negotiating the work–family interface. Overall, however, the findings are rather mixed, offering no clear and simple pattern. They also report that:

- Women and men are increasingly experiencing overload and strain in managing work and family responsibilities.
- Wives continue to bear a disproportionate burden of housework, while husbands continue to put in more hours at work.

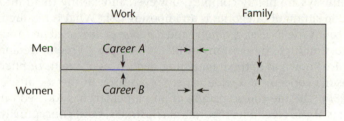

Figure 9.3. Two-career couple

What Figure 9.3 describes might be an ideal situation, where both men and women are equally involved in both spheres. One of the respondents in Hood's (1983) study of two-job families puts it aptly, 'It's more of a 50/50 deal. We're both providers and we're both homemakers and we're both parents.' However, as indicated by the arrows, there are more boundaries to be negotiated, and thus, more potential tensions and strains. And as occupational careers and domestic arrangements are currently structured, husbands and wives may find it problematic to be simultaneously successful in both their work and their private lives (Moen and Yu 1997; Schor 1991; Hochschild 1997).

We start, therefore, by explicitly recognizing the multiple and interlocking dimensions built into the structure of work–family interface (as depicted by the arrows in the figures). In so doing, we conceptualize couples as our basic unit of analysis, taking into account the two-sidedness of this unit (Chapter 3 above; Bernasco 1994).

Careers: A Life-Course Perspective

Scholars are only beginning to consider the work–family interface as it unfolds over time. And yet a central tenet of the life-course perspective is that to understand behaviour at any one life stage requires knowledge of prior transitions and trajectories (Elder 1995; Elder *et al.* 1996; Moen *et al.* 1995). While both concepts—transitions and trajectories—provide important information, the analysis of transitions has been far more developed than that of trajectories (Pavalko 1995). Much of the reason for this appears to be methodological, with the increased attention to transitions fuelled by growing interest and availability of event-history analysis techniques (Pavalko 1995; see Tuma and Hannan 1984; Blossfeld *et al.* 1989). However, the two are dual concepts; transitions are always embedded in the trajectories that give them distinctive forms and meanings (Elder 1995), and trajectories are shaped by prior, and prospective, transitions. Such a perspective points to the connections between widely separated events and experiences (O'Rand and Henretta 1982). It is thus of both theoretical and methodological importance to be able to sort out empirically the diverse 'career pathways'.

Career pathways are highly complex, however, and sorting them into discernible and meaningful categories is an imposing task. What is required is to take into account the *incidence, timing,* and *duration of diverse events,* and *their sequence* across multiple dimensions of life. We propose a sequence analysis technique, also known as optimal matching. Sequences of events or phenomena have been a concern of a wide variety of research in the social sciences (Abbott 1995*b*). The life-course paradigm, in particular, has focused on this issue, which is at the core of its theoretical constructs, both conceptually and methodologically. The notion of careers, for instance, represents one of the few conceptual languages that depicts a *temporal dimension* or *process* (Barley 1989). However, the methods developed and used thus far have not been able to capture entire trajectories (Pavalko 1995). In the approach we take here, as discussed below, we do consider whole sequences. In other words, the overall patterning of career pathways is both the conceptual and analytical unit. We first delineate a set of equivalent pathways. These are, in turn, used to explain the career side of the interface.

Coupled Careers: Work and Marriage, Men and Women

Figure 9.4 illustrates our analytical framework, which puts both work careers and family (or marital) careers together over the life-course progression. The framework underscores the multiple, interlocking interfaces between men and women and work and family over time. We call this 'coupled careers', emphasizing the interlocking, and interweaving, nature of trajectories and transitions, within and across life stages between both men and women and work and family (Bernasco 1994).

For instance, the life-course paradigm also posits a process of cumulating of advantage (Merton 1968; Elder *et al.* 1996; Moen and Shore 1997); those who are better off in terms of status and other resources accrue still greater advantage as they progress through the life course. Similar arguments can be made within the human capital theory paradigm of the New Home Economists (see e.g. Becker 1991, 1993), where those with higher human capital are expected to be at comparative advantage. From this perspective, given statistical and normative discrimination in the opportunity structure, employed men should have the more optimal career paths, as should those with the greater education. Working women and those without higher education, by contrast, should have more disorderly career paths (Wilensky 1961). But this is looking at the career pathways as distinct and separable from the context of family. How does the marital trajectory interface with occupational mobility? And does one's spouse's occupational experience influence an individual's own career experience? We suspect that both these processes are heavily gendered, with marriage more significantly (and negatively) related to the orderliness of women's career pathways and spouse's employment more significantly (and negatively) related to the orderliness of men's.

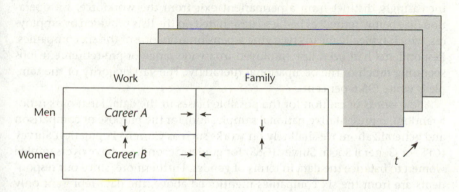

Figure 9.4. Coupled careers: double interface over the life course

Using life-history data on the labour-force experiences of men and women, we first identify and describe the various pathways traversed by men and women across their working years, taking into consideration the overall pattern of work as well as important work transitions within that pattern. A set of typical pathways will be empirically delineated. These occupational pathways will be considered in tandem with the marital trajectory as well as with the spouse's career pathway.

Data and Methods

Data

We analyse data collected in the first wave of the Cornell Retirement and Well-Being Study (CRWB). The respondents are 458 retirees from six large manufacturing and service companies in four cities of upstate New York who were aged 50 to 72 at the time they were interviewed in 1995. They were randomly selected from lists provided by their employers and initially contacted by letter and telephone to request their participation and arrange for an interview. The interviews, ranging from one to two and a half hours, were conducted face to face, save for those who had relocated to new communities, which were conducted by telephone.

The principal survey instruments include a structured interview schedule and a booklet of self-administered questions drawn from a number of sources, including the *Health and Retirement Survey* (Juster 1992) and the *Quality of Employment Survey* (Quinn and Staines 1979). These instruments were extensively pre-tested prior to administration. Of special interest to us is the respondents' employment history, which we draw from the collection of detailed life-history data.

The total sample was composed of 212 women (46 per cent) and 246 men (54 per cent) with an average age of 63 years, who have spent anywhere from one month to more than nineteen years in retirement. Because retirement is increasingly distinct from a permanent exit from the workforce, we operationalize being 'retired' as being so designated on the lists provided by employers, which typically means receiving a pension from one of the six companies. Respondents had been last employed in a wide range of pre-retirement jobs spanning much of the occupational hierarchy. The vast majority of the sample is white (95.6 per cent).

A few words of caution for the possible biases in the data. First, ours is not a random, representative national sample, and, for the purpose of comparison and generalization, we shall rely on works such as Current Population Survey (CPS) or General Social Survey (GSS) for guides. Second, we have oversampled women to balance the data in terms of gender. Furthermore, since our respondents are from the six companies mentioned above, the data represent only the experiences of men and women who have been employed. Thus, what our findings show might be closer to the national average picture for men, but might be rather skewed for women in the general population (in that those women who have been exclusively full-time homemakers, for instance, are not included in the sample). Third, the sample is limited with respect to the cohorts represented, for we rely on data on retirees aged 50 to 72 in 1995. Born between 1923 and 1943, the respondents lived through the last half-century of changes in gender roles and in the economy. Yet their careers during their thirties and forties were relatively unaffected by the drastic changes (for example, corporate restructuring) that occurred in the 1980s and 1990s. Some of the findings we report below, thus, should be interpreted as conservative estimates. Finally, note also that the six companies from which we collected our data do not represent the broad spectrum of all the companies in the United States. Rather, they belong to the upper tier of the spectrum, several being blue-chip companies with better jobs. Our respondents are, consequently, typically representative of those who have been under the best of the circumstances in their careers. One might suspect that the problems and conflicts of managing work and family careers might be even more severe for those employed in less favourable settings.

Sequence Analysis Method

This is a new method for old ideas (Abbott 1995*b*). Recall that the notion of careers represents one of the few conceptual languages that depicts a temporal dimension or process (Barley 1989; Hughes 1937; Goffman 1961). However, the methods developed and used thus far have been mostly stepwise, Markovian, approaches. Event-history analysis is typical of these, where individual spells are employed as the unit of analysis, and transitions between spells are primarily of interest (Tuma and Hannan 1984; Blossfeld *et al.* 1989). In other words, despite the apparent power of event-history analytic techniques to model causal relationships, these methods focus on individual events, not the sequence as a whole, that is, sequence qua sequence.[1] The approach that we adopt here takes the whole sequence as its unit of analysis.

Through an examination of the life-history data detailing various dimensions of career transitions and trajectories over the life course, we chart a set of typical career pathways for men and women. The differences and similarities between career pathways in terms of timing, sequence, and turning-points are measured. This approach builds on, and extends, previous efforts to capture temporal patterns; see Abbott and Hrycak (1990) for an extended introduction to this technique, and Abbott and DeViney (1992), Abbott (1991), Chan (1995), Blair-Loy (1996), Stovel *et al.* (1996), and Han and Moen (1999*b*) for its application in substantive areas. Other works focusing on the temporal aspects of the life course and informing this research include studies by Wilensky (1961), Hogan (1978), O'Rand and Henretta (1982), Henretta and O'Rand (1983), Moen (1985), Rindfuss *et al.* (1987), Henretta (1992), George (1993), and Pavalko *et al.* (1993).

The data on employment histories of retirees provide information on transitions and trajectories over the life course in occupation, work status, and organization from age 30 until retirement. Among the retirees, reconstruction of complete employment histories was possible for 401 cases (87.6 per cent). Using yearly interval as unit-time, the data were transformed into sequence data format, that is, strings of codes. Figure 9.5 shows an example of a typical female retiree, say, Katie. Having been out of the labour force for a long time (work status = 5, occupation = 64, organization = 0), Katie started working full-time at age 37, preparing and serving food (work status = 1, occupation = 42, organization = 1). After three years, at age 40, she moved to another company to work, again full-time, as a machine operator (work status = 1, occupation = 60, organization = 2), from which she retired after nineteen years of continuous employment. This serves as an illustration of the strings that contain information on incidence, timing, duration, and sequence for each of the three dimensions of employment history.

The optimal matching algorithm produces measures of similarity and dissimilarity between these sequences, as defined above, which are then used as

[1] We think the two can be complementary though (see Halpin and Chan 1995; Pavalko 1995).

Age :	30	31	32	33	34	35	36	37	38	39	40	41	42	43	44	45
Occupation :	64	64	64	64	64	64	64	42	42	42	60	60	60	60	60	60
Organization :	0	0	0	0	0	0	0	1	1	1	2	2	2	2	2	2
Work status :	5	5	5	5	5	5	5	1	1	1	1	1	1	1	1	1

Age :	46	47	48	49	50	51	52	53	54	55	56	57	58	59	60	...
Occupation :	60	60	60	60	60	60	60	60	60	60	60	60	60	.	.	...
Organization :	2	2	2	2	2	2	2	2	2	2	2	2	2	.	.	...
Work status :	1	1	1	1	1	1	1	1	1	1	1	1	1	.	.	...

Figure 9.5. Sequence data: an example

inputs for subsequent analyses.[2] Hierarchical clustering is performed on all three of the dimensions simultaneously to detect typical pathways. We were able to discern in the data five distinct clusters, based on the criteria of F-ratios and other *post-hoc* tests.[3] We call these 'occupational career pathway types', or 'pathway types' for short. They are labelled as 'delayed entry pathway' (cluster 1), 'orderly pathway' (cluster 2), 'high-geared pathway' (cluster 3), 'steady part-time pathway' (cluster 4), and 'intermittent pathway' (cluster 5), respectively, for easy identification and reference. The labels describe major characteristics observed in each type (Han and Moen 1999a; Moen 1985; O'Rand and Henretta 1982).

Analysis and Findings

Charting the Career Pathways

Baseline characteristics: The five pathway types differ from one another with respect to the baseline characteristics of the sequences clustered together. On the one hand, in terms of sequence length (that is, the average number of years from age 30 to retirement), orderly career type (27.7 years) is significantly shorter than delayed-entry (29.9 years), high-geared (30.2 years), and intermittent types (30.4 years).[4] In other words, those whose careers are characterized by—or, those who followed the path of—orderly career have retired

---

[2] For optimal matching of sequences for this analysis, we used an adapted version of DISTANCE by Stovel (1996) written in SAS/IML. For datasets with smaller N, see OPTIMIZE (v. 2.12) by Abbott (1995a).

[3] The solution is based on a 7-cluster solution. Two of the clusters are dropped from the analyses reported below due to the small N, leaving five clusters. The cases we leave out are a small number of rather atypical careers. One cluster (N = 7), for example, includes a mechanic who retired at age 40 from a utility company. The other cluster consists of three women retired from a hospital. Although they are highly skilled technical specialists, they have either mostly worked on a part-time basis or interrupted their career quite extensively.

[4] $F_{(4,386)} = 8.447$, $p = .000$.

earlier than those followed types 1, 3, and 5. (We will discuss this issue in detail shortly.) Yet, note that the difference between the longest and shortest pathways is only about 2.5 years. In other words, length in and of itself is not the defining factor in discerning the pathway types. On the other hand, the number of transitions they have experienced during that period, indicating how stable or unstable their career had been, varies as well. High-geared (4.2 transitions) and intermittent types (5.3 transitions) have a significantly higher number of transitions than do delayed-entry (2.6 transitions), orderly (2.7 transitions), and steady part-time types (2.5 transitions).[5]

Recall that the differences between the five pathway types are based on three parallel sequences: occupations, organizations (companies or employers worked for), and work status (employed full-time, part-time, or not employed). In what follows, we examine the trajectories of the five pathway types in terms of each of the three dimensions in turn. The first column in Figure 9.6 illustrates how respondents have experienced their careers in terms of occupational status and mobility. The vertical coordinate indicates occupational prestige in SEI score (Nakao and Treas 1994). The line represents the average SEI score across age (30 to 70) for each of the five pathway types.[6] The dashed vertical line indicates the age where half of the respondents in each pathway type have retired (that is, median retirement age). One may, thus, focus more on the left-hand side of each figure to see the occupational trajectory in the prime, 'career-building' years. For SEI scores, on average, high-geared pathway type is the highest, while delayed-entry and intermittent types are the lowest.[7] High-geared pathway consists mostly of those in executive and managerial positions, while delayed-entry and intermittent types are primarily made up of those in clerical positions. (See Table 9.1 for details.) However, in terms of change and status mobility, the contrast is between orderly and high-geared types and those of delayed-entry, steady part-time, and intermittent pathway types. While the former show a steady and continuous upward mobility, the latter reflect quite a bit of fluctuation. Steady part-time type seems to show a slightly upward trend despite the dip around age 50. Delayed-entry and intermittent types show peaks in occupational status around age 40, which subsequently subside.

The second column in Figure 9.6 shows how the respondents have moved between companies (employers). The vertical coordinate indicates the number of companies or employers they have worked for up to that age. Again, the dashed vertical lines denote the median retirement age. With respect to interorganizational mobility, the basic contrast is between high-geared and intermittent pathway types and those of delayed-entry, orderly, and steady part-time types.[8] The former seem to consist of active 'movers' (2.8 and 3.7 organizations, on average, respectively), whereas the latter are 'stayers' (1.5,

[5] $F_{(4,386)} = 12.159$, $p = .000$.
[6] The averages SEI scores are calculated only for those who are employed at the time.
[7] $F_{(4,386)} = 13.897$, $p = .000$.
[8] $F_{(4,386)} = 57.006$, $p = .000$.

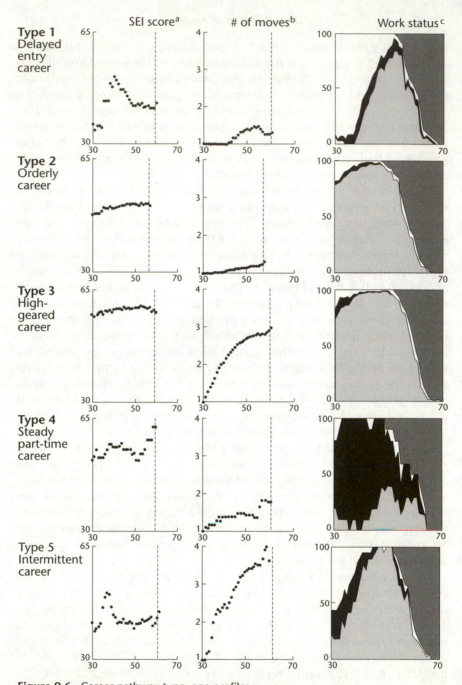

Figure 9.6. Career pathway type: age profiles.
[a]Average assigned SEI score. Dashed vertical line indicates age where half of respondents in each pathway type have retired (i.e. median retirement age). [b]Average no. of companies or employers worked for up to that age. [c]White area represents proportion of respondents unemployed or out of labour force, light-grey area those employed full-time, black area those employed part-time, and dark-grey area those retired.

1.2, and 1.7, respectively). There is a subtle, yet important, difference among the movers, however. For the high-geared type, the level of mobility continues to be high until the mid-forties, yet tapers off afterwards. In contrast, for intermittent pathway type, mobility remains high until retirement.

Finally, we examine respondents' trajectories over time with respect to their work status. The last column in Figure 9.6 shows the work-status profile for each pathway type across age. (See Table 9.1 for the average amount of time spent in each status over the entire period.) We see three distinct groups based on work status over the life course. First, orderly and high-geared pathway types are typical full-time careers. Second, steady part-time pathway seems to primarily consist of part-time careers. Lastly, delayed-entry and intermittent pathway types typically have an extended period of being out of the labour force, particularly in the early stages, suggesting that they start their work careers late. Delayed-entry and intermittent pathways also show a significant presence of part-timers.[9]

Taking all of these findings into account, we can elaborate on some of the findings discussed earlier. First, the high levels of interorganizational mobility found in high-geared and intermittent types turn out to be based on two entirely different dynamics. For the former, changing jobs across organizations seems to be a way of achieving upward mobility, while for the latter, job shifts across organizations are merely an indication of instability, reflecting frequent exits and re-entries. Second, high-geared pathway also provides an interesting contrast to orderly type. Both experience upward mobility, but that of orderly type is likely to be based on ladder climbing in the same firm, that is, moving up through the internal labour market. This is more or less what the ideal type of employment history, as constructed in the USA in the 1950s, 1960s, and 1970s, would look like, that is, continuous employment in a single organization for entire span of career. By contrast, mobility captured in high-geared pathway type is based on 'ladder hopping' (Kanter 1989; Kotter 1995).

The five pathway types obtained from the sequence analysis of the life-history data can be summarized as in Table 9.1 with respect to the basic sequence characteristics, three aspects of employment history, and the other background variables we examine below.

Background characteristics: In this section, we examine three background characteristics of the respondents sorted into the five pathway types described above. First, gender is a crucial dimension which we expect to shape many aspects of career pathways. Second, age and cohort are also of importance, providing the basic setting for, and shape of, career pathways (Burkhauser and Quinn 1989, 1990; DeViney and O'Rand 1988; Palmore et al. 1985). Third, as expected from the human capital perspective, educational attainment should have a substantial impact on career pathways (Becker 1993 [1964]; Mincer 1974).

---

[9] Full-time (per cent): $F_{(4,386)} = 237.179$, $p = .000$; Part-time (per cent): $F_{(4,386)} = 158.922$, $p = .000$; Unemployed/OLF (per cent): $F_{(4,386)} = 203.340$, $p = .000$.

Table 9.1. Five pathway types and their characteristics

Pathway type	1 Delayed-entry	2 Orderly	3 High-geared	4 Steady part-time	5 Intermittent
N	46	154	160	10	21
Sequence length** [a] (mean)	(29.9)	Shortest (27.7)	(30.2)	(29.0)	Longest (30.4)
No. of transitions** [a] (mean)	Infrequent (2.6)	Infrequent (2.7)	Frequent (4.2)	Infrequent (2.5)	Most frequen (5.3)
Gender composition** [b] (% men:women)	Exclusively women (0:100)	Men and women (64.9:35.1)	Men and women (61.9:38.1)	Mostly women (30:70)	Exclusively women (0:100)
Year born** [a] (mean)	Earliest (1928)	Latest (1932)	(1929)	(1929)	(1929)
Education** [a] (mean)	Lowest (12.64)	Lowest (13.25)	Highest (14.61)	(13.40)	(12.86)
Men's education	—	Lowest (13.45)	Highest (15.27)	(14.67)	—
Women's education	(12.64)	(12.89)	Highest (13.54)	(12.86)	(12.86)
SEI** [a] (mean)	Low (42.8)	3rd highest (50.3)	Highest (58.5)	2nd highest (54.6)	Lowest (42.5)

Direction in SEI over age		Upward	Upward	Upward	
The most common occupation	Secretaries	Managers	Managers	Health ass't & treating	Secretaries
(%)c	(22.6)	(14.0)	(16.9)	(21.6)	(70.9)
The 2nd most common occupation	Admin. support	Technicians	Executives	Construction, supervisors	Teachers
(%)c	(11.3)	(9.3)	(11.8)	(12.6)	(6.3)
The 3rd most common occupation	Technicians	Secretaries	Admin., supervisors	Science & planning	Librarians
(%)c	(7.4)	(8.9)	(5.6)	(11.9)	(2.8)
No. of organizations** [a] (mean)	Low (1.5)	Lowest (1.2)	High (2.8)	Low (1.7)	Highest (3.7)
Work status, full-time (%)** [a, c]	Full-time (47.4)	Full-time (94.6)	Full-time (94.4)	(26.2)	(73.7)
Work status, part-time (%)** [a, c]	(9.3)	(1.5)	(2.3)	Primarily part-time (69.6)	Primarily part-time (10.6)
Work status, unemployed/OLF (%)** [a, c]	Started late (43.4)	(3.9)	(3.3)	(4.2)	(15.7)

* $p < .01$, *** $p < .001$.
[a] Where F-test is conducted.
[b] Likelihood ratio (L^2) test
[c] Where the figure is calculated on the basis of total person-years.

First, with respect to gender composition, there is a clear distinction between occupational career paths (see Table 9.1). Almost all the men are found either in orderly or high-geared pathway types. But while these two are predominantly male, there is a significant presence of women as well (35.1 and 38.1 per cent, respectively). Delayed-entry and intermittent types consist exclusively of women, while steady part-time pathway is predominantly composed of women. In general, pathway type is significantly related to, or determined by, gender, as shown by the likelihood ratio chi-square statistics ($L^2_{(4)}$ = 117.159, p = .000). In other words, there seem to be highly distinct and separate career pathways for men and women. Furthermore, men's career paths tend to be much more standardized, following only a couple of career pathways, whereas working women seem to have travelled quite diverse paths.

The sizeable presence of women in orderly and high-geared pathway types, on the one hand, suggests the gap between men and women has been closing. Women's work patterns—which have been characterized historically by more tangential and transient ties to the labour force (Brinton 1988; Moen 1992; Tomaskovic-Devey 1993; Wolf and Fligstein 1979)—have increasingly taken on the appearance of men's, that is, full-time permanent attachment (Masnick and Bane 1980; Kreps and Clark 1975; Waite 1981; Moen 1985). On the other hand, there is also some evidence that men—some, at least—have been experiencing changes in the social organization of work and family over the last several decades by taking on the patterns that used to be associated with women's careers, as shown in steady part-time type. Both illustrate that the issue of gendered careers cannot be addressed simply by contrasting stylized career paths of men with those of women. Rather, one needs to have a more refined perspective on the differentiation between as well as among men and women within particular historical contexts.

Second, career paths tend to differ in terms of cohort, defined by year born (see Table 9.1).[10] Orderly type is the latest (1932), whereas delayed-entry type is the earliest (1928). The difference between the two, though, is only four years, which is not so substantial.[11] The other three pathways seem to be rather close to one another in terms of cohort, which is approximately 1929. Men are on average born later than women, and the differences among the pathway types generally hold across gender. The exception is steady part-time pathway, where one finds men of earlier cohorts and women of later cohorts clustered together. Overall, despite these statistically significant differences, the span covered by the sample is too narrow to provide much substantive leverage.

Third, level of schooling seems highly related to the manner in which respondents are sorted into various career pathways (see Table 9.1).[12] Partly, this is due to the confounding of gender and education effects. Men are, on the

---

[10] $F_{(4,386)}$ = 10.575, p = .000.
[11] This could be expected, given the narrow span of cohorts in the data, which is one of the limitations.
[12] $F_{(4,386)}$ = 8.026, p = .000.

whole, more educated than women in this sample, as in the general population of this age group. Yet, even after controlling for gender, the five types show substantial differences in average level of education.[13] High-geared type is the most highly educated, followed by orderly and steady part-time types. Delayed-entry and intermittent types seem to be the occupational career pathways typical of those with the least schooling. Delayed-entry and intermittent pathways are travelled mostly by high-school graduates, whereas high-geared type is a path common to college graduates. Among women, high-geared type stands alone as consisting of the more educated, while the other four are close to one another. In orderly type, the difference between men and women is the smallest.

These background variables can shed light on one of the puzzling issues raised earlier. On the one hand, the peak in SEI score for delayed-entry pathway type occurs around age 40, when only a small proportion of the respondents in that pathway type are in the labour force full-time. On the other hand, a massive influx into the labour force takes place in the mid-forties, which is accompanied by a rapid decline in SEI score. Intermittent pathway shows a similar pattern, but the timing is a bit different. The peak in SEI score for intermittent type is just before age 40, when a substantial proportion of the respondents are in the labour force, either on a full-time or part-time basis (about 20 per cent each). The rate of entry into the labour force is a lot higher for intermittent type, quickly reaching a very high level of employment. The common thread between these two pathway types is their gender composition, that is, they both consist exclusively of women. Most women in delayed-entry and intermittent pathway types are not in the labour force in their thirties, having and raising their children full-time; but they return to paid work in their forties. Yet the fact is that they return to jobs with little prospect of upward mobility.

Orderly pathway type seems to represent the ideal-typical career path, that is, stable, continuous, and upwardly mobile. Delayed-entry pathway type starts working late, with an extended period of being out of the labour force early on. It consists exclusively of women entering the labour force after their childbearing years. Although they work typically at low SEI jobs, these jobs are relatively stable. High-geared type is for those on the fast track. They are highly educated and upwardly mobile. They start off high on the occupational ladder, and move about quite a bit. Steady part-time pathway consists of a small group of people working mostly part-time. Yet they show a low level of interorganizational mobility, and are relatively successful in terms of SEI score and upward mobility. Intermittent pathway type is another type consisting exclusively of women and the least stable of all. Although it shares many of the characteristics of delayed-entry type, it distinguishes itself from delayed-entry type by a trajectory of higher mobility across organizations, mostly due to the frequent exits and re-entries.

[13] Two-way (pathway type, gender) F-tests—pathway type: $F_{(4,383)} = 5.960$, $p = .000$; gender: $F_{(1,383)} = 25.082$, $p = .000$; pathway type * gender: $F_{(2,383)} = 12.752$, $p = .156$.

Family Experience

The preceding section described the ways in which men and women respondents have experienced their work lives over their adult life course. In this section, we provide a picture of their pathways through family life, focusing specifically on marriage.

Table 9.2 shows the respondents' marital history by gender, with both observed frequency and the expected frequency from the independence model. Bold letters are used where the observed frequency is larger than the expected frequency. The relationship between the two is statistically significant. Men tend to be better off by a large margin. In particular, they are far more likely to be currently married. The results are in agreement with the US population in general, as can be seen in the data from the General Social Survey (1996). Recall, however, that the women in this sample are all retirees who have worked for some significant portion of their prime adulthood. For these women, the likelihood of both getting married and staying married is far lower than that of their male co-workers. For instance, among the sixteen people in this sample who have never married, fourteen of them are women. A marital stability score, constructed from the detailed marital history, produces the same significant result favouring men (3.68 versus 3.41, $p < .001$).[14]

Table 9.2. Marital history by gender

Marital history	Men		Women		Total (%)
	Obs.	Exp.	Obs.	Exp.	
Never married	2	8.2	14	7.8	16 (4.0)
Married once, currently div./separated	8	17.5	26	16.5	34 (8.5)
Married twice, currently div./separated	6	5.7	5	5.3	11 (2.8)
Married once, currently widowed	6	16.5	26	15.5	32 (8.0)
Married twice, currently widowed	0	3.6	7	3.4	7 (1.8)
Married once, currently married	149	124.1	92	116.9	241 (60.3)
Married more than once, currently married	35	30.4	24	28.6	59 (14.8)
Total	206	(51.5%)	194	(48.5%)	400

Interfaces: Men and Women, Work and Marriage

Work and family: How, then, do these various dimensions—men's and women's careers in both work and marriage—interact with one another? How, for instance, does gender influence careers of men and women at work? How do family experiences enter into that relationship? Using a log-linear model,

[14] Marital stability score is obtained on the basis of number of marital spells and current marital status as follows: 1 = (never married), 2 = (married twice, currently divorced/separated) or (married more than twice, currently married), 3 = (married once, currently divorced/separated) or (married twice, currently married or widowed), and 4 = (married once, currently married or widowed).

Table 9.3. Gender, career pathway, and marital history

No.	Fitted Marginals	G²	df	p	Nos.	ΔG²	Δdf	p
1	{G}	1032.805	68	0.000				
2	{P}	742.014	65	0.000				
3	{M}	525.822	63	0.000				
4	{G}{P}	741.511	64	0.000	1	291.293	4	0.000
					2	0.503	1	0.478
5	{G}{M}	525.319	62	0.000	1	507.486	6	0.000
					3	0.503	1	0.478
6	{P}{M}	234.528	59	0.000	2	507.486	6	0.000
					3	291.293	4	0.000
7	{G}{P}{M}	234.026	58	0.000	1	798.779	10	0.000
					2	507.988	7	0.000
					3	291.796	5	0.000
					4	507.486	6	0.000
					5	291.293	4	0.000
					6	0.503	1	0.478
8	{GP}{M}	116.218	54	0.000	7	117.808	4	0.000
9	{GM}{P}	178.011	52	0.000	7	56.014	6	0.000
10	{PM}{G}	175.881	34	0.000	7	58.145	24	0.000
11	{GP}{GM}	60.201	48	0.111	8	56.017	6	0.000
					9	117.811	4	0.000
12	{GP}{PM}	58.068	30	0.002	8	58.149	24	0.000
					10	117.813	4	0.000
13	{GM}{PM}	119.867	28	0.000	9	58.144	24	0.000
					10	56.014	6	0.000
*14	{GP}{GM}{PM}	7.556	24	0.999	11	52.645	24	0.001
					12	50.512	6	0.000
					13	112.311	4	0.000
15	{GPM}	0.000	0	1.000	14	7.556	24	0.999

G = gender, P = pathway type, M = marital history. * Indicates the preferred model.

we first examine the relationship between gender, career pathway, and marital history.

Table 9.3 shows various models that are estimated and their goodness-of-fit. The last four columns, in particular, report the relative improvement in fit. For example, model 4 significantly improves upon model 1 by $G^2 = 291.293$ with four more degrees of freedom. Model 14 in Table 9.3 is the preferred, 'best-fitting' model. This model posits no three-way interaction, but allows all three of the two-way interactions. Those three two-way interactions are (1) gender–pathway {GP}, (2) gender–marital history {GM}, and (3) pathway–marital history {PM}. Since both (1) and (2) have been discussed above, we turn to (3), the two-way interaction between pathway type and marital history.

Table 9.4 shows the joint frequency distribution between the two variables. Again, bold letters are used where the observed frequency is larger than the expected frequency. Although the overall relationship between the two is significant ($L^2_{(24)} = 58.149$, $p = .000$), the pattern, if any, is not easy to find. When the table is divided by gender, however, a clear picture of the interface between work and family and men and women emerges. Table 9.5 shows that the bivariate relationship is, in fact, not significant among men ($L^2_{(10)} = 11.987$, $p = .286$). However, among women the relationship between occupational and marital careers holds strongly ($L^2_{(24)} = 48.212$, $p = .002$). Those women who experienced orderly or high-geared occupational pathway types, the relatively smooth, orderly, and upwardly mobile career tracks, are very likely to have also experienced marital instability. As a case in point, all the fourteen women who never married are found in either of the two career pathway types, typical 'male' patterns! The opposite is true for women in delayed-entry or steady part-time types. In both cases, marital stability appears to come at the expense of success in career, or vice versa. Women in these pre-baby-boom cohorts apparently could not have it both ways. The only exception is the women in intermittent type, who seemed to have suffered on both fronts.

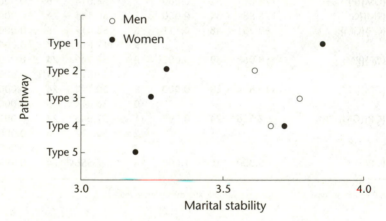

Figure 9.7. Marital stability by pathway type and gender

Figure 9.7 depicts the relationship between occupational career pathway type and marital stability by gender, corroborating the result discussed above. This explains why so many women who are highly successful in their careers are so often without the families and/or children that seem to be taken for granted for upwardly mobile men. What Bernard (1982) observed in *The Future of Marriage*, that (1) for most American couples being married is a much better 'deal' for the husband than for the wife, and (2) married men are healthier, happier, and saner than the unmarried, while just the opposite is true for wives, seems to hold true for the men and women in our sample. The asymmetry between the sexes operates in such a way that forces a zero-sum game—

Table 9.4. Marital history by pathway type

Marital history	Pathway type						%
	1	2	3	4	5	Total	
Never married	0	7	9	0	0	16	4.1
Married once, currently div./separated	3	8	14	1	5	31	7.9
Married twice, currently div./separated	0	3	5	0	3	11	2.8
Married once, currently widowed	12	7	11	1	1	32	8.2
Married twice, currently widowed	0	2	2	1	2	7	1.8
Married once, currently married	27	92	104	6	7	236	60.5
Married more than once, currently married	4	34	15	1	3	57	14.6
Total	46	153	160	10	21	390	
%	11.8	39.2	41.0	2.6	5.4		

Pathway: type 1, delayed-entry; type 2, orderly; type 3, high-geared; type 4, steady part-time; type 5, intermittent.

Table 9.5. Marital history by pathway type by gender

Marital history	Pathway type					%	
	1	2	3	4	5	Total	
Men's marital history							
Never married	0	1	1	0	0	2	1.0
Married once, currently div./separated	0	3	5	0	0	8	4.0
Married twice, currently div./separated	0	3	3	0	0	6	3.0
Married once, currently widowed	0	1	5	0	0	6	3.0
Married twice, currently widowed	0	0	0	0	0	0	0.0
Married once, currently married	0	68	76	2	0	146	72.3
Married more than once, currently married	0	24	9	1	0	34	16.8
Subtotal	0	100	99	3	0	202	
%	0.0	49.5	49.0	1.5	0.0		
Women's marital history							
Never married	0	6	8	0	0	14	7.4
Married once, currently div./separated	3	5	9	1	5	23	12.2
Married twice, currently div./separated	0	0	2	0	3	5	2.7
Married once, currently widowed	12	6	6	1	1	26	13.8
Married twice, currently widowed	0	2	2	1	2	7	3.7
Married once, currently married	27	24	28	4	7	90	47.9
Married more than once, currently married	4	10	6	0	3	23	12.2
Subtotal	46	53	61	7	21	188	
%	24.5	28.2	32.4	3.7	11.2		

Pathway: type 1, delayed-entry; type 2, orderly; type 3, high-geared; type 4, steady part-time; type 5, intermittent.

that is, a trade-off between their occupational careers and their family careers—on women. That, in turn, leads to the development and persistence of unequal comparative advantages and life chances between men and women at work, at home, and in the links between the two.

The findings of the log-linear analysis in Tables 9.3, 9.4, and 9.5 can be summarized as follows. First, men and women tend to be sorted into different career pathways, with men faring far better in terms of staying on orderly and upwardly mobile tracks. To put it more succinctly, career pathways tend to be gendered (G→P: Arrow 1 in Figure 9.8). Second, working women (that is, the women in our sample) tend to suffer higher degrees of marital instability than do men (G→M: Arrow 2). Finally, type of career pathway and marital history are strongly related for women. Amongst women, those on the better career tracks suffer more in terms of marital stability, or vice versa (P→M and/or M→P: Arrow 3).

The second point (G→M) requires a bit of further elaboration. Given that 'it takes two to tango', that is, we cannot have a man experience a divorce, for instance, without a woman (his wife) also experiencing the event at the same time, it is difficult to make sense of this. But instead of seeing gender as related directly to marital history (G→M), we can think of gender as shaping marital history indirectly through career pathway type (G→P→M). The asymmetry in (G→M), therefore, reflects the combination of relationships between gender and career pathways (G→P) and pathway and marital history (P→M).

His and her careers: We now turn to the situation where two careers, husband's and wife's, have to be negotiated. Since we do not have full data on spouse's work history, our analyses are limited, yet the goal here is to show the potential interdependence between the couples' two careers.

Table 9.6 shows the result of a log-linear analysis of the relationships between gender, pathway type, and spouse's work history. The estimated models are specified by the fitted marginals, and their goodness-of-fit is reported in the table. Model 8 is our preferred model, which posits only one two-way interaction, between gender and pathway type. The top panel in Table 9.7 shows the relationship between respondents' occupational career path and their spouse's work history. The latter is a rough estimate of work history for the current spouse only, and thus, we limit our analysis for those who are currently married. As earlier, bold letters are used where the observed frequency is larger than the expected frequency obtained from the model of independence, that is, null association. The overall relationship between the two is not statistically significant ($L^2_{(12)} = 13.297$, $p = .348$). When the table is divided by gender, however, the bivariate relationship is significant among men (the middle panel, $L^2_{(6)} = 13.041$, $p = .042$), while it is not so among women (the bottom panel, $L^2_{(12)} = 10.564$, $p = .567$).

In other words, for the wives of the men in this sample, their work patterns are tightly coupled with, and highly contingent upon, their husbands' career.

Table 9.6. Gender, career pathway, and spouse's work history

No.	Fitted marginals	G^2	df	p	Nos.	ΔG^2	Δdf	p
1	{G}	321.608	38	0.000				
2	{P}	190.245	35	0.000				
3	{S}	232.018	36	0.000				
4	{G}{P}	183.399	34	0.000	1	138.208	4	0.000
					2	6.846	1	0.009
5	{G}{S}	225.172	35	0.000	1	96.436	3	0.000
					3	6.846	1	0.009
6	{P}{S}	93.810	32	0.000	2	96.436	3	0.000
					3	138.208	4	0.000
7	{G}{P}{S}	86.964	31	0.000	1	234.644	7	0.000
					2	103.282	4	0.000
					3	145.054	5	0.000
					4	96.436	3	0.000
					5	138.208	4	0.000
					6	6.846	1	0.009
*8	{GP}{S}	26.814	27	0.474	7	60.149	4	0.000
9	{GS}{P}	83.758	28	0.000	7	3.206	3	0.361
10	{PS}{G}	73.671	19	0.000	7	13.293	12	0.348
11	{GP}{GS}	23.608	24	0.484	8	3.206	3	0.361
					9	60.149	4	0.000
12	{GP}{PS}	13.516	15	0.563	8	13.298	12	0.348
					10	60.155	4	0.000
13	{GS}{PS}	70.464	16	0.000	9	13.293	12	0.348
					10	3.206	3	0.361
14	{GP}{GS}{PS}	11.519	12	0.485	11	12.089	12	0.439
					12	1.997	3	0.573
					13	58.945	4	0.000
15	{GPS}	0.000	0	1.000	14	11.519	12	0.485

G = gender, P = pathway type, S = spouse's work history. * Indicates the prefered model.

This is not the case for the women in the sample; that is, their husbands' work histories are not constrained by how the women themselves have worked in any patterned way. This finding, once again, documents the heavily skewed relationship between the experiences of men and women (Bernasco *et al.* 1998).

The way in which husband's and wife's careers are coupled is quite distinct. As shown in the middle panel, for instance, the wives of the men in orderly career path are more likely not to have worked at all, whereas the opposite seems to be true for the wives of the men in high-geared career path. The bottom panel illustrates that men are more likely to have worked continuously, regardless of their wives' career pathway type. A rather conspicuous exception

Table 9.7. Spouse's work history by pathway type

	Respondent's career pathway						%
	Type 1	Type 2	Type 3	Type 4	Type 5	Total	
Spouse's work history							
Continuously worked	13	40	30	1	5	89	52.4
Intermittently worked	4	24	22	2	1	53	31.2
Started working late	3	2	4	0	0	9	5.3
Never worked	1	12	4	1	1	19	11.2
Total	21	78	60	4	7	170	
%	12.4	45.9	35.3	2.4	4.1		
For men's wives							
Continuously worked	0	27	22	0	0	49	48.0
Intermittently worked	0	20	15	2	0	37	36.3
Started working late	0	1	4	0	0	5	4.9
Never worked	0	9	1	1	0	11	10.8
Subtotal	0	57	42	3	0	102	
For women's husbands							
Continuously worked	13	13	8	1	5	40	58.8
Intermittently worked	4	4	7	0	1	16	23.5
Started working late	3	1	0	0	0	4	5.9
Never worked	1	3	3	0	1	8	11.8
Subtotal	21	21	18	1	7	68	

Pathway: type 1, delayed-entry; type 2, orderly; type 3, high-geared; type 4, steady part-time; type 5, intermittent.

is that the women following orderly and high-geared career paths are more likely to have been with a husband who never worked.[15]

To combine the two models analysed above into a more comprehensive model—one with four factors: gender, career pathway, marital history, and spouse's work history—would have been a natural next step to take, yet the data at hand are too limited to allow that.[16] Based on what we have seen so far, however, we speculate that the picture linking all the dimensions of the work and marriage interface might be a highly complex one.

[15] Recall that our sample represents only the experiences of men and women who have been employed long enough to be eligible for a pension. For men in this age group, this sampling scheme does not pose much trouble. For women, however, it produces a rather skewed picture, as can be expected, compared to the population in general. These men, the husbands of working women in our sample, who have never worked, are such a case. Although we lack the data to probe into the cause of this, we can consider the following possibilities: (1) disabled (can't work), (2) independently wealthy (don't have to work), (3) loafing (don't want to work), or (4) male homemaker (need to take care of home), or any combination thereof.

[16] We have about 170 cases with valid values, while the model with all four factors will create a matrix of 280 cells with a lot of zero cells.

Discussion

How to understand the careers of American men and women who find themselves having to negotiate the two spheres of life, work and family, and also with each other over the life course is the research question that motivated this chapter. The question arises, on the one hand, in the context of the changes in the last few decades that radically altered the ways in which we structure two most fundamental institutions, work and family, and the interface between them. On the other hand, the question presents itself as a challenge to old ways of understanding these issues, necessitating a new approach to address the phenomena at hand.

In this chapter, we proposed a model that addresses the multiple interfaces between work and family and between men and women as they unfold over time. What we have examined in this chapter bears on the two interfaces, (1) and (2) in Figure 9.8, with (1) reflecting the facilitation of work and marital careers of men and (2) reflecting the strains between work and marital careers of women. Interface (3) has also been the topic of extensive study by many scholars of the household division of labour, which is often discussed in conjunction with interface (4) (see e.g. Hood 1983; Sørensen and McLanahan 1987; Becker 1991; Bielby and Bielby 1992). We touched on interface (4) as well, in an attempt to consider the dynamic interface between couples' careers.

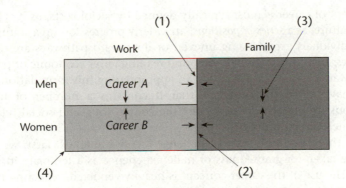

Figure 9.8. Multiple interfaces in two-career couples

We found the notion of coupled careers and its proper and direct formulation critical to understanding the dynamics of the work–family interface over the life course. The asymmetry between the husbands and wives in their distinctive work–family interfaces—as in interface (1) *vis-à-vis* (2), and also in interface (4)—was the most consistent finding.

A more definitive study, which we are currently in the process of launching, should be able to track all the information necessary to complete the picture.

In addition, ideally, we need a longer time span to examine historically situated changes in the interface. For example, we know that cohort succession is an important source of attitude change, with female labour-force participation both a cause and consequence of such change (Bielby and Bielby 1992; Moen 1992). This is critical, given that the USA is in the midst of fundamental transformations in the larger opportunity structure, and in the implicit as well as explicit contracts between employers and employees. During the past fifteen years, in particular, many companies have sought to move away from the traditional model of employment where most employees—typically males—were connected to their employers on a full-time, relatively permanent basis. They are dismantling this internalized system of mutual obligations, the 'implicit contract', between employees and the firm, which emerged in the post-Second-World-War era of rising productivity and US economic dominance (Kalleberg *et al.* 1995). Leading these efforts are such blue-chip companies as IBM, AT&T, GM, and Kodak. The key elements of their elaborate employment systems—job security and loyalty, orderly pay schedules, extensive internal labour markets, and structured promotion opportunities (Osterman 1984)—are being disassembled, profoundly affecting the lives of individual workers (see also Kanter 1989, 1993; Kotter 1995). These, in turn, are affecting the family as well (Hochschild 1997).

Conclusion

The concept of career is most typically defined by sociologists, as it is in the broader culture, as a *series of positions*, an orderly progression up a status hierarchy. Individuals experiencing uneven or downward pathways are seen as deviant, less committed to their jobs, and reaping fewer economic or psychological rewards (Wilensky 1961). But in appropriating this formulation, sociologists have failed to point out that it contains a number of hidden assumptions—about the nature of the life course, jobs, and social relations within which careers unfold.

Two of those assumptions we challenged in our analysis. First, we questioned the taken-for-grantedness of male experience as a template in career research. The use of the career concept is heavily gendered, reflecting men's, not women's, experiences (Bem, 1994). Thus, 'career' commonly refers to moving through a series of (related) jobs over the life course, the typical experience of men. Such stylized typification is valid to the extent that it was, in fact, the empirical reality when most of the labour force was male and many followed a standard career template. But as both the composition of the labour force and the nature of work attachments are being transformed, the concept of career needs to be reformulated to better reflect current, and emerging, realities. By documenting the mechanisms underlying the divide between the genders, we provide a new way to explore the changing reality.

Second, and closely related to the point just made, we argued for an alternative to the individual as the unit of analysis. Most researchers focus on individuals, oftentimes men, effectively removing them from the family context. Careers are similarly defined as typically reflecting men's occupational mobility patterns, without the spouse's job or other family exigencies factored in. When women's careers are considered, family factors are rendered easily visible. With the increasing commonality of the dual-career couples we would expect that family considerations will increasingly impose themselves upon the career paths of *both* men and women. This suggests the importance of couples, families, or households as the appropriate unit of analysis in modelling career paths (Bernasco 1994; Chapter 3 above; Goldthorpe 1983). What is required is a perspective that addresses the duality of couples' careers both in their work lives and their family lives.

Elder's (1994) notion of 'linked lives' becomes key to adequately understanding this new reality, to which we also explicitly incorporate possible inequality and asymmetry by gender (see e.g. Sørensen and McLanahan 1987; Bielby and Bielby 1992; also see the other chapters in this volume). The approach we have taken in this chapter also allows us to consider the *counterfactuals* (Tilly 1999), in terms of what did *not* occur. In our analysis of a particular generation of American workers in upstate New York, for instance, we find that women often did not prevail in managing both family and work careers as men did. What are missing are women in stable marriages with successful work careers. In addition to tracing antecedents or consequences of paths taken, we have also inquired as to why other alternative paths are missing.

As Heinz (1996: 58–9) points out, status passages 'link institutions and actors by defining time-tables and entry as well as exit markers for transitions', constructed by 'biographical actors, but also involving "institutional guidelines"'. The employer/employee contract has been predicated on a concept of career, most likely that of type 2 in this chapter, which has served as the time frame for most aspects of life, from marriage to residential mobility. A number of life-course scholars (see e.g. Chudacoff and Hareven 1979; Kohli 1986; Mayer and Müller 1986; Riley and Riley 1994) have pointed to occupational careers as providing the organizational blueprint for the life course.

But these organizational blueprints do change as well, as Stovel *et al.* (1996) illustrate in their analysis of career systems at Lloyds Bank from 1890 to 1970. We are witnessing such a transformation in the USA as we move to the twenty-first century, in tandem with changing gender roles and institutional arrangements at work as well as at home. In describing the construction of typologies based on empirical regularities in career lines, Spilerman (1977) points out the discrepancy between career characterizations and accounts on the one hand, and actual patterns of job sequences on the other. In the context of the remarkable changes occurring in the US, the gap between the two widens rapidly; the need for empirically grounded accounts of contemporary careers becomes increasingly obvious. We believe that such a research agenda is likely to provide important insights into the factors that shape how American men and women reconcile the inherent dual tensions—work versus family and wife versus husband—built into coupled careers. That is one of the tasks we have begun in this chapter.

References

Abbott, A. (1991). 'The Order of Professionalization: An Empirical Analysis', *Work and Occupations*, 18: 355–84.

——(1995*a*). *OPTIMIZE*, v.2.12 (Chicago: Department of Sociology, University of Chicago).

——(1995*b*). 'Sequence Analysis: New Methods for Old Ideas', *Annual Review of Sociology*, 21: 93–113.

——and A. M. Hrycak (1990). 'Measuring Resemblance in Sequence Data: An Optimal Matching Analysis of Musicians' Careers', *American Journal of Sociology* 96: 144–85.

——and S. DeViney (1992). 'The Welfare State as Transnational Event: Evidence from Sequence of Policy Adoption', *Social Science History*, 16: 245–74.

Barley, S. R. (1989). 'Careers, Identities, and Institutions: The Legacy of the Chicago School of Sociology', in M. B. Arthur, D. T. Hall, and B. S. Lawrence (eds.), *Handbook of Career Theory* (New York: Cambridge University Press), 41–65.

Barnett, R., and C. Rivers (1996). *She Works/He Works: How Two-Income Families are Happier, Healthier, and Better-Off* (San Francisco, Calif.: Harper).

Becker, G. S. (1991 [1981]). *A Treatise on the Family* (Cambridge, Mass.: Harvard University Press).

——(1993 [1964]). *Human Capital: A Theoretical and Empirical Analysis with Special Reference to Education* (Chicago: University of Chicago Press).

Bem, S. L. (1994). *The Lenses of Gender: Transforming the Debate on Sexual Inequality* (New Haven, Conn.: Yale University Press).

Bernard, J. S. (1982 [1972]). *The Future of Marriage* (New Haven, Conn.: Yale University Press).

Bernasco, W. (1994). *Coupled Careers: The Effects of Spouse's Resources on Success at Work* (Amsterdam: Thesis Publishers).

——P. M. de Graaf, and W. C. Ultee (1998). 'Coupled Careers: Effects of Spouse's Resources on Occupational Attainment in the Netherlands', *European Sociological Review*, 14: 15–31.

Bielby, W. T. and D. D. Bielby (1992). 'I will Follow him: Family Ties, Gender-Role Benefits, and Reluctance to Relocate for a Better Job', *American Journal of Sociology*, 97: 1241–67.

Blair-Loy, M. (1996). 'Career Patterns of Executive Women in Finance', paper presented at the 91st annual meeting of the American Sociological Association, New York.

Blossfeld, H.-P., A. Hamerle, and K. U. Mayer (1989). *Event History Analysis: Statistical Theory and Application in the Social Sciences* (Hillsdale, NJ: L. Erlbaum).

Bragg, R. (1996). 'The Downsizing of America: Big Holes Where the Dignity Used to Be', *The New York Times* (5 March).

Brinton, M. (1988). 'The Social-Institutional Bases of Gender Stratification: Japan as an Illustrative Case', *American Journal of Sociology*, 94: 300–34.

Burkhauser, R. V. and J. F. Quinn (1989). 'American Patterns of Work and Retirement', in W. Schmähl (ed.), *Redefining the Process of Retirement: An International Perspective* (Berlin: Springer-Verlag), 91–114.

——and ——(1990). 'Economic Incentives and the Labor Force Participation of Older Workers', in L. Bassi and D. Crawford (eds.), *Research in Labor Economics*, ix (New York: JAI), 159–79.

Chan, T. W. (1995). 'Optimal Matching Analysis: A Methodological Note on Studying Career Mobility', *Work and Occupations*, 22: 467–90.

Chudacoff, H. P. and T. K. Hareven (1979) 'From the Empty Nest to Family Dissolution: Life Course Transitions into Old Age', *Journal of Family History*, 4: 69–83.

Coser, L. A. (1974). *Greedy Institutions: Patterns of Undivided Commitment* (New York: Free Press).

DeViney, S., and A. M. O'Rand (1988). 'Age, Gender, Cohort Succession and Labor Force Participation of Older Workers, 1951–1984', *Sociological Quarterly*, 29: 525–40.

Elder, G. H., Jr. (1994). 'Time, Human Agency, and Social Change: Perspectives on the Life Course', *Social Psychology Quarterly*, 57: 4–15.

——(1995). 'The Life Course Paradigm: Social Change and Individual Development', in P. Moen, G. H. Elder, Jr., and K. Lüscher (eds.), *Examining Lives in Context: Perspectives on the Ecology of Human Development* (Washington, DC: American Psychological Association), 101–39.

——L. K. George, and M. J. Shanahan (1996). 'Psychological Stress over the Life Course', in H. B. Kaplan (ed.), *Psychological Stress: Perspectives on Structure, Theory, Life Course, and Methods* (Orlando, Fla.: Academic Press), 247–91.

George, L. K. (1993). 'Sociological Perspectives on Life Transitions', *Annual Review of Sociology*, 19: 353–73.

Goffman, E. (1961). 'The Moral Careers of the Mental Patient', in E. Goffman, *Asylum* (New York: Anchor), 125–70.

Goldthorpe, J. (1983). 'Women and Class Analysis', *Sociology*, 17: 465–88.

Halpin, B., and T. W. Chan (1995). 'Optimal Matching of Moderately Many Class Careers', paper presented at the 90th annual meeting of the American Sociological Association, Washington, DC.

Han, S.-K., and P. Moen (1999*a*). 'Work and Family over Time: A Life Course Approach', *The ANNALS of the American Academy of Political and Social Science*, 562: 98–110.

——and ——(1999*b*). 'Clocking Out: Temporal Patterning of Retirement', *American Journal of Sociology*, 105: 191–236.

Heinz, W. R. (1996). 'Status Passages as Micro-Macro Linkages in Life Course Research', in A. Weymann and W. R. Heinz (eds.), *Society and Biography: Interrelationships between Social Structure, Institutions, and the Life Course* (Weinheim: Deutscher Studien Verlag), 67–81.

Henretta, J. C. (1992). 'Uniformity and Diversity: Life Course Institutionalization and Late-Life Work Exit', *Sociological Quarterly*, 33: 265–79.

——and A. O'Rand (1983). 'Joint Retirement in the Dual Worker Family', *Social Forces*, 62: 504–19.

Hochschild, A. R. (1989). *The Second Shift* (New York: Viking).

——(1997). *The Time Bind: When Work Becomes Home and Home Becomes Work* (New York: Metropolitan Books).

Hogan, D. P. (1978). 'The Variable Order of Events in the Life Course', *American Sociological Review*, 43: 573–86.

Hood, J. C. (1983). *Becoming a Two-Job Family* (New York: Praeger).

Hughes, E. C. (1937). 'Institutional Office and the Person', *American Journal of Sociology*, 43: 404–13.

Juster, F. T. (1992). *Health and Retirement Survey* (Ann Arbor, Mich.: Survey Research Center, Institute for Social Research, University of Michigan).

Kalleberg, A. L., D. Knoke, and P. V. Marsden (1995). 'Interorganizational Networks and the Changing Employment Contract', *Connections*, 18: 32–49.

Kanter, R. M. (1989). *When Giants Learn to Dance* (New York: Simon & Schuster).

——(1993). *Men and Women of the Corporation* (New York: Basic Books).

Kohli, M. (1986). 'The World we Forget: A Historical Review of the Life Course', in V. W. Marshall (ed.), *Later Life: The Social Psychology of Aging* (Beverly Hills, Calif.: Sage), 271–303.

Kotter, J. P. (1995). *The New Rules: How to Succeed in Today's Post-Corporate World* (New York: Free Press).

Kreps, J. M., and R. Clark (1975). *Sex, Age, and Work: The Changing Composition of the Labor Force* (Baltimore, Md.: Johns Hopkins University Press).

Masnick, G., and M. J. Bane (1980). *The Nation's Families: 1960–1990* (Boston, Mass.: Auburn House).

Mayer, K. U. and W. Müller (1986). 'The State and the Structure of the Life Course', in A. B. Sørensen, F. E. Weinert, and L. R. Sherrod (eds.), *Human Development and the Life Course: Multidisciplinary Perspectives* (Hillsdale, NJ: L. Erlbaum), 212–45.

Merton, R. K. (1968). 'The Matthew Effect in Science', *Science*, 159: 56–63.

Mincer, J. (1974). *Schooling, Experience, and Earnings* (New York: National Bureau of Economic Research/Columbia University Press).

Moen, P. (1985). 'Continuities and Discontinuities in Women's Labor Force Activity', in G. H. Elder, Jr. (ed.), *Life Course Dynamics: Trajectories and Transitions, 1968–1980* (Ithaca, NY: Cornell University Press), 113–55.

——(1989). *Working Parents: Transformations in Gender Roles and Public Policies in Sweden* (Madison, Wis.: University of Wisconsin Press).

——(1992). *Women's Two Roles: A Contemporary Dilemma* (Westport, Conn.: Auburn House).

——(1994). 'Women, Work, and Family: A Sociological Perspective on Changing Roles', in M. W. Riley, R. L. Kahn, and A. Foner (eds.), *Age and Structural Lag: The Mismatch between People's Lives and Opportunities in Work, Family, and Leisure* (New York: John Wiley & Sons), 151–70.

—— and R. P. Shore (1997). 'Status Transitions and the Cumulation of Advantage: The Case of Retirement, Downsizing, and Depression', unpublished manuscript, Cornell University.

——and Y. Yu (1997). *Does Success at Work Compete with Success at Home?* (Bronfenbrenner Life Course Center Working Paper, 97–06; New York: Cornell University).

——G. H. Elder, Jr., and K. Lüscher (eds.) (1995). *Examining Lives in Context: Perspectives on the Ecology of Human Development* (Washington, DC: American Psychological Association).

Nakao, K., and J. Treas (1994). 'Updating Occupational Prestige and Socioeconomic Scores: How the New Measures Measure Up', *Sociological Methodology*, 24: 1–72.

O'Rand, A. M. and J. C. Henretta (1982). 'Delayed Career Entry, Industrial Pension Structure, and Early Retirement in a Cohort of Unmarried Women', *American Sociological Review*, 47: 365–73.

Osterman, P. (ed.) (1984). *Internal Labor Markets* (Cambridge, Mass.: MIT Press).

Palmore, E. B., B. M. Burchett, G. G. Filenbaum, L. K. George, and L. M. Wallman (1985). *Retirement: Causes and Consequences* (New York: Springer).

Pavalko, E. K. (1995). 'Transitions and Trajectories as Concepts for Understanding Social Change and Individual Lives', paper presented at the 90th annual meeting of the American Sociological Association, Washington, DC.

——G. H. Elder, Jr., and E. C. Clipp (1993). 'Work Lives and Longevity: Insights from a Life Course Perspective', *Journal of Health and Social Behavior*, 34: 363–80.

Quinn, R. P. and G. L. Staines (1979). *The 1977 Quality of Employment Survey* (Ann Arbor, Mich.: Survey Research Center, Institute for Social Research, University of Michigan).

Riley, M. W., and J. W. Riley, Jr. (1994). 'Structural Lag: Past and Future', in M. W. Riley, R. L. Kahn, and A. Foner (eds.), *Age and Structural Lag* (New York: J. Wiley), 15–36.

Rindfuss, R. R., G. Swicegood and R. A. Rosenfeld (1987). 'Disorder in the Life Course: How Common and does it Matter?', *American Sociological Review*, 52: 785–801.

Schor, J. (1991). *The Overworked American: The Unexpected Decline of Leisure* (New York: Basic Books).

Sørensen, A., and S. McLanahan (1987). 'Married Women's Economic Dependency, 1940–1980', *American Journal of Sociology*, 93: 659–87.

Spilerman, S. (1977). 'Careers, Labor Market Structure, and Socioeconomic Achievement', *American Journal of Sociology*, 83: 551–93.

Stovel, K. (1996). *DISTANCE* (Chapel Hill, NC: Department of Sociology, University of North Carolina at Chapel Hill).

——M. Savage, and P. Bearman (1996). 'Ascription to Achievement: Models of Career Systems at Lloyds Bank, 1890–1970', *American Journal of Sociology*, 102: 358–99.

Tilly, C. (1999). 'Durable Inequality', in P. Moen, D. Dempster-McClain, and H. Walker (eds.), *A Nation Divided: Diversity, Inequality, and Community in American Society* (Ithaca, NY: Cornell University Press), 15–33.

Tomaskovic-Devey, D. (1993). 'Labor-Process Inequality and the Gender and Race Composition of Jobs', *Research in Social Stratification and Mobility*, 12: 215–72.

Tuma, N. B. and M. T. Hannan (1984). *Social Dynamics: Models and Methods* (Orlando, Fla.: Academic Press).

US Bureau of the Census (1977/1996). *Current Population Survey* (Washington, DC: US Department of Commerce).

US Bureau of Labor Statistics (1994/1996). *Employment and Earnings Characteristics of Families* (Washington, DC: US Department of Labor).

Waite, L. J. (1981). *US Women at Work* (Washington, DC: Population Reference Bureau).

Walsh, E (1995). *Divided Lives: The Public and Private Struggles of Three Accomplished Women* (New York: Simon & Schuster).

Wilensky, H. L. (1961). 'Orderly Careers and Social Participation: The Impact of Work History on Social Integration in the Middle-Class', *American Sociological Review*, 26: 521–39.

Wolf, W., and N. Fligstein (1979). 'Sex and Authority in the Workplace: The Causes of Inequality', *Annual Review of Sociology*, 44: 235–52.

V

The 'Social Democratic' Welfare State Regime

10

Earnings as a Force of Attraction and Specialization in Sweden

URSULA HENZ AND MARIANNE SUNDSTRÖM

Introduction

THE growth in female labour-force participation in industrialized countries during the 1960s and 1970s gave rise to a large body of research about factors influencing female labour supply. A common finding of these studies was that the woman's own wage tended to increase her labour-market activity, while the income of the husband tended to reduce it, and that the former effect exceeded the latter (see e.g. Killingsworth and Heckman 1986 for a review). For the last two decades participation rates in the USA have, however, been observed to rise disproportionately among women married to men with higher earnings, at the same time as household inequality has grown and the correlation of spouses' earnings has increased (Karoly and Burtless 1995). These trends have spurred research interest in assortative mating, since one possible explanation for the rise in participation of wives of higher earning men is that these wives have higher market-earning capacity, that is, that there is positive assortative mating based on labour-market characteristics (homogamy). An alternative explanation is, of course, that the impact of husbands' earnings on wives' labour supply has declined over time.

This chapter studies the degree of specialization in market work and non-market work between spouses within marital and consensual unions and its changes over time. With this purpose we analyse how labour-market transitions of married and cohabiting women are influenced by their own earnings as well as by their spouses' earnings and other characteristics. Any specialization (or change) we would observe could, however, be the result, in part, of pre-union specialization and, in part, of potential spouses being attracted to each other on the basis of such characteristics (or changes in either of these). Therefore, we also review our previous results on the degree of earnings homogamy among married and cohabiting couples, its changes with duration of marriage or cohabitation, and its changes over calendar time.

We use data from the 1992 Swedish Family Survey supplemented by earnings information from the national taxation register. A unique aspect of this dataset is that it has information on both married and cohabiting couples as well as completed life histories from age 17 and longitudinal information on earnings for the respondent/woman and her spouse, including former spouses, if they were married or had children together. A limitation is that there is no information on former spouses other than their age and earnings. Pre-union earnings data are available only for respondents.

The plan of the chapter is as follows. In the next section we review the literature on assortative mating and specialization within the family on market work and household work, in particular with regard to the impact of the spouse's earnings. The following sections describe our dataset, sample, and variables. After that we give an overview of trends in cohabitation and marriage in Sweden and of previous findings on earnings homogamy in Sweden. Next, we discuss the method, hazard regression, used in the analysis of women's labour-market transitions. We report our findings in the following section and end with a concluding discussion.

Related Literature

According to the well-known theory of Becker (1991), the major economic gains to marriage arise from specialization and exchange based on the relative comparative advantages of spouses. The male spouse is said to have a comparative advantage in market work if the ratio of his wage rate in the market to his marginal product in the household is higher than the same ratio for his spouse. A man with such a comparative advantage will supply more time to market work and less time to household work than his spouse. (Complete specialization does not follow.) These time allocations will be less different when the time of the two is more complementary and less substitutable (Becker 1991: 39). In modern times, complementarities are likely to have become more important since women have become less specialized in household work and men are spending more time in household activities. In particular, the emphasis in rich countries on the 'quality' of children, rather than quantity, has made the incentives of men and women to invest in human capital more equal. Becker further argues that positive assortative mating on most traits will dominate, that is, 'high-quality' men and women will tend to marry each other rather than selecting 'lower-quality' mates when these qualities are complements (Becker 1991: 114). He also cites empirical evidence in support of this proposition. The simple correlations between intelligence, education, age, race, non-human wealth, religion, ethnic origin, height, place of origin, and many other traits of spouses are positive and strong. He goes on to argue that a negative sorting by wage rates should be optimal, but has difficulties finding comforting evidence on that.

This is not surprising, since a positive correlation is not inconsistent with a gender-based specialization within the household if women either have lower wage rates than their spouses or higher household productivity. Also, positive sorting on wage rates (or potential wage rates for non-participating women) does not preclude wives of higher earning men from working fewer market hours than wives of lower earning men, everything else being equal. In fact, Davies *et al.* (1998) argue that considerations of search costs, too, might lead us to expect positive sorting based on wages because if the educational and work environments also function as partnership brokerages, men and women with similar wage rates are more likely to encounter each other than those with very different wage rates. They suggest that the importance of this consideration has grown over time due to the increased participation of women in higher education, decreased occupational segregation, and the declining importance of other social institutions such as churches.

Another reason why spouses' traits may be positively correlated is that there may be other economic gains to marriage than those from specialization. Blau and Ferber (1986) and Weiss (1997) emphasize gains such as the sharing of collective goods, risk-sharing, and positive externalities from the consumption of the other spouse. These gains will be greater if the spouses are positively correlated in traits.

A critical issue is, however, at which point in time correlations are measured. To make inferences about whether there is positive (or negative) sorting in a trait that might change over time, such as wage rates, we need information on the mates prior to union formation. This is because, for example, the wages we observe during partnership are the result, in part, of the pre-partnership characteristics of the spouses and, in part, of the changes in the division of labour that take place during marriage or cohabitation, given these characteristics.

Studies analysing assortative mating using post-partnership-formation data have generally focused on traits that do not change over time, such as race, or traits that are not likely to change much over time, such as educational level. Addressing the latter topic using data on newlyweds, Mare (1991) finds an increasing association between spouses' schooling from the 1930s to the 1970s, but a stable or decreasing one for the 1980s. He attributes this trend to the shortened time between school-leaving and marriage from the 1930s to the 1960s, due to increases in schooling and lowered age at marriage; this time gap grew in the 1970s and 1980s as a result of rising age at marriage. The time gap is crucial because marriages between persons with similar amounts of schooling are more likely among those who marry shortly after leaving school.[1] Evidence of increased homogamy over time remains, however, after adjustment for time between school and marriage has been made. Mare (1991) suggests that this is due to increased competition in the marriage market for wives with good labour-market prospects.

[1] For Sweden this pattern only seems to hold for the highly educated, however. The low educated are more likely to find a more educated partner shortly after leaving school and more likely to form a homogamous union the longer the time after leaving school (Henz and Jonsson forthcoming).

Another critical issue is the extent to which studies of assortative mating take into account the changes in the availability of potential spouses. Qian and Preston (1993) distinguish between changes in the availability of eligible partners and changes in the forces of attraction between men and women of particular characteristics. Their results show that neither age nor educational homogamy increased in the 1970s, but educational homogamy increased in the 1980s and age homogamy increased when measured over the whole period 1972–87. Further, in 1972–87 the force of attraction for women age 25 and over who had completed high school or attended college rose sharply, as compared to that for younger women, especially when the declining avail-ability of eligible partners for such women was taken into account. They asso-ciate these changes with the diverging trends in real earnings for full-time and full-year employed women aged 25–44 years, as compared to those younger than 25 in the same period; for the older group real earnings grew, for the younger they declined. For us the study for Finland by Cancian and Jäntti (1997) is of particular interest since few studies of assortative mating are avail-able for Sweden and since it is one of the few studies which uses information on earnings of spouses, both before and after marriage. They find spouses' pre-marriage and post-marriage earnings to be positively correlated and to have become increasingly so over the four marriage cohorts (1970/75–1985/90) analysed. Further, for all marriage cohorts, the correlations of pre-marriage earnings are higher than those of post-marriage earnings, which in turn do not change much during five years of marriage. A decomposition reveals that the rising correlation over marriage cohorts is not due to changes in the distribu-tion of earnings among eligible men and women, but rather to a stronger pos-itive sorting based on earnings.

Davies *et al.* (1998) use pre- and post-union-formation data on spouses' earnings to analyse assortative mating and specialization among British mar-ried and cohabiting couples. They find a strong tendency towards positive assortative mating by earnings power. The correlation between the estimated potential earnings of partners at the time of union formation is about half, while the correlation of current earnings is lower. Their results further show that the initial spousal wage gap had a significant effect on the patterns of spe-cialization, after controlling for correlates of domestic productivity. For exam-ple, the initial wage gap had a significantly negative effect on the woman's full-time experience after partnership formation and so had union duration. Interestingly, these two relationships held for married couples but not for cohabitants. The results on the labour-supply effects of own earnings and spouse's earnings are as expected, but as to why effects would differ between married and cohabiting couples, research has not yet come up with an answer and it is interesting to see what we find for Sweden.

What has happened to labour-supply effects of women's own earnings ver-sus those of their spouses over time? Unfortunately, it is difficult to draw any conclusions from the recent studies that have used advanced methods to take account of taxes and transfers, since the range of estimates is wide (see e.g.

Aronsson and Walker 1997). The findings of Leibowitz and Klerman (1995) on the employment of US married mothers suggests, however, that the positive effect of female earnings intensified over the period 1971–90 and that the effect of men's earnings became less negative. Consistent with these results, Sundström found positive effects of Swedish women's wages on annual hours worked for the years 1967, 1973, and 1980, and smaller, as well as declining, negative effects of husbands' annual earnings net of taxes; the effect for 1980 was not even significant (1987: 132).

Data

Our empirical analyses of correlations between spouses' earnings and of women's labour-market transitions are based on the 1992 Swedish Family Survey (SFS) conducted by Statistics Sweden. The survey contains retrospective histories of respondents' partnerships, childbirths, educational activities, employment, and other activities, as well as information on family background. The SFS consists of samples from five birth cohorts, namely 1949, 1954, 1959, 1964, and 1969, but information on men is restricted to birth cohorts 1949, 1959, and 1969. In total, 4,984 persons have been interviewed, of whom 3,317 were women. The survey information has been combined with data on annual earnings for respondents and their partners from the national taxation register. Information about partners' earnings is available for all years for married couples but for cohabiting couples only in the years after they had a child together. Therefore, the following analyses are restricted to the 2,321 women in the SFS who had at least one child and, consequently, women's labour-market transitions before first birth are not analysed. With this restriction we are, however, able to compare labour-market transitions for married and cohabiting women.

The SFS life histories are, further, not complete for episodes shorter than three months. This is because respondents were asked to report only episodes of three months or longer. If shorter episodes were reported they have been retained for the sake of greater precision, but most periods shorter than three months are not recorded and, therefore, the following analyses do not take short episodes fully into account.

The correlation analysis includes all mothers with available earnings data for themselves and their spouses. For the analysis of transitions, the sample has been further restricted by the exclusion of women for whom no partner could be identified after first childbirth (186)[2], those for whom there is no information about own earnings before or at the first birth (132), those for whom no information about partner's earnings is available (405), women who did not report any parental leave after childbirth (48), women who were never employed (19), and, finally, women who were self-employed before the birth

---

[2] The numbers refer to the size of the group defined by the previous selection.

of the first child (22). This leaves us with a sample of 1,509 women. We follow their labour-market activities from January of the year in which they turned 17 or from the birth of their first child, whichever occurred later.[3] The observation period ends either at separation from the partner or at interview, whichever occurred first. Altogether our sample covers the calendar period from 1968 until 1993. For the observation period, all episodes of full-time employment, part-time employment,[4] full-time education, and parental leave are identified. Remaining gaps are classified as non-employment and are only taken into account if they were longer than three months. The episodes analysed start either at the beginning of the observation period or immediately after the transition to the state of interest and, consequently, episodes end at the transition to another state or at the end of the observation period, except for parental leave episodes. The latter are censored if, and when, a new birth occurs more than ten months after the beginning of the leave. A new leave episode starts at the time of the new birth. We do so because since 1980 closely spaced births have allowed Swedish women to retain entitlement to parental leave benefits (see Hoem 1993) and longer parental leave spells due to another birth, therefore, do not necessarily imply a weaker labour-market attachment.

Table 10.1 reports the resulting number of labour-market transitions for women and, for comparative purposes, for men. Shifts between, on the one hand, part-time or full-time work and, on the other hand, parental leave are the most frequent transitions women make. Part-time work is often taken up after non-employment. During the period studied, the entitlement period of maternity leave was stepwise extended from six months (since 1962) to fifteen months (since 1989) (for further details see Rønsen and Sundström 1996). Since women's employment, and thereby the proportion of women entitled to maternal/parental leave, has grown during the period studied, the duration of time spent outside the labour force following childbirth has decreased across cohorts, accompanied by only a minor increase in the duration of parental leave. Thus, while the average duration of periods of non-employment dropped from forty-seven months in cohort 1949 to about fifteen months in each of the two youngest cohorts, average duration of parental leave rose only from 11.4 months for cohort 1949 to 14.9 months for cohort 1969. A factor contributing importantly to this trend was no doubt the expansion of highly subsidized childcare (see Rønsen and Sundström 1996). The number of transitions by men reflects their strong attachment to full-time work. Men experienced far fewer transitions than women. However, the shifts between full-time work and full-time education and those from full-time work to non-employment reach levels comparable to those of women. The frequencies shown underestimate the extent to which fathers participated in the parental-leave programme since episodes shorter than three months are under-reported.

---

[3] For immigrant women, the earliest start of observation period is the date of immigration to Sweden.

[4] Part-time employment refers to 16–34 weekly working hours. Employment for less than 16 hours per week has not been recorded.

Table 10.1. Numbers of selected labour-market transitions for women and men

Origin	Destination	Women	Men
Part-time work	Full-time work	301	17
	Parental leave	564	5
	Non-employment	139	1
	Full-time education	103	0
Full-time work	Part-time work	179	16
	Parental leave	319	39
	Non-employment	113	97
	Full-time education	74	72
Parental leave	Part-time work	1,080	6
	Full-time work	487	36
	Non-employment	191	0
	Full-time education	52	2
Non-employment	Part-time work	318	4
	Full-time work	183	97
	Parental leave	33	0
	Full-time education	98	16
Full-time education	Part-time work	98	2
	Full-time work	93	76
	Parental leave	11	1
	Non-employment	58	22

Variables

The earnings data refer to earnings from employment and also comprise income-related transfers, such as parental-leave benefits and sick pay, and benefits in kind, such as company cars. To adjust for inflation, earnings are expressed in 1992 Swedish crowns (in thousands).[5] For the respondents, the complete earnings history until interview is available. Earnings of the partner are linked to the respondent when the tax authorities register the marriage or the birth of a common child, which they generally do in the following year. The variable *spouse's earnings* is the partner's annual earnings at the earliest time available after marriage or childbirth but no later than two calendar years after childbirth. Since men have been employed full-time most of the time, we use this variable as a proxy for spouse's earnings potential in the early stages of partnership.

Women's earnings exhibit a larger variation than men's, mainly because of the greater variation between women in hours worked. Figure 10.1 shows the distribution of earnings for married and cohabiting women in the year of their

[5] Two changes in taxation laws create discontinuities in the time series. The first took place in 1970, when joint taxation of married couples was abolished. The second took place in 1974 from which year transfers were made taxable.

first birth. We see that the spread of earnings is broader among married than among cohabiting women. In particular, the share of women with extremely low earnings or no earnings at all in the year of first birth is higher among married women. For high earnings, the fractions are about the same for married and for cohabiting women. Why do the two distributions differ? First, as the older cohorts constitute a larger share of the married than of the cohabiting women and as female real earnings have risen over cohorts,[6] cohabiting women tend to have higher earnings than married women at first birth. Second, labour-market behaviour may differ according to marital status; for example, the following analysis shows that married women have a higher propensity than cohabiting women to leave the labour-market.

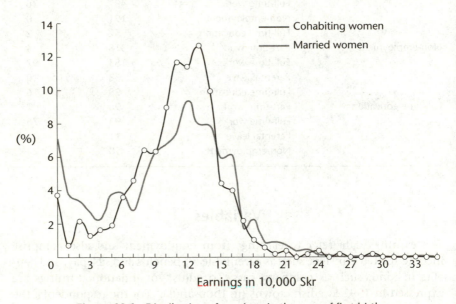

Figure 10.1. Distribution of earnings in the year of first birth

To obtain a measure of women's earnings potential that is less affected by transitions surrounding childbirth, we instead use the *woman's maximal annual earnings* before or in the year of first birth. Figure 10.2 shows the development of average maximal annual earnings for women and the annual earnings for their spouses by calendar year of first birth. We see that during the late 1960s and the 1970s the earnings gap decreased and virtually disappeared in the early the 1980s, presumably because women's earnings increased much more rapidly than men's. But in the course of the 1980s and early 1990s, the

---

[6] This is because female wages have increased and because first births have gradually been postponed until higher ages when earnings are higher. Also, parental-leave benefits are included in earnings from 1974 but not before that.

earnings gap widened again, as women's earnings flattened and men's increased. Figure 10.3 displays the frequency distribution of the difference between women's highest earnings before or at childbirth and the annual earnings of the spouse around childbirth. Interestingly, for almost 30 per cent of the couples the woman's highest earnings exceed the actual earnings of her spouse.

To assess the effect of own and spouse's earnings on women's labour-market transitions we control for other characteristics of the woman and her family. A first group of covariates relates to her accumulated human capital. Her *age* is

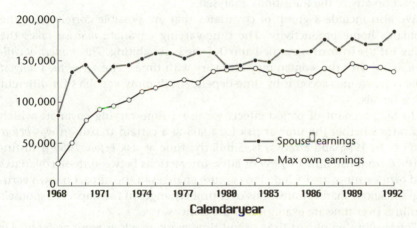

Figure 10.2. Average earnings by year of first birth

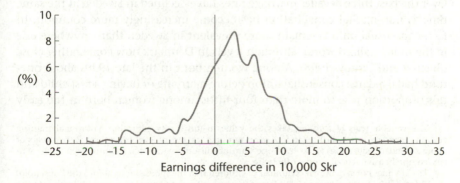

Figure 10.3. Earnings differences within couples (male minus female earnings)

measured in years since age 17 and varies with time. To capture non-linear age effects, *age squared* is also used. Another age-related covariate, which is used in some models, is *age at first birth*. Women's education is measured in approximate *years of schooling*[7] and may change over time. The variables *full-time experience* and *part-time experience* measure months of work experience of the two types before first birth.

Social background may influence the woman's labour-market transitions by shaping her preferences and values. If the woman's mother was gainfully employed any time prior to the respondent's sixteenth birthday, the dummy variable *mother worked* takes the value 1, and 0 otherwise. Indicators of parents' religiosity and father's occupational status were tested, but had no significant impact on any of the transitions analysed.

We also include a group of covariates that are possible correlates of the woman's home productivity. The time-varying covariate *married* takes the value 1 if the woman is married and 0 if she is cohabiting. The *number of children* living with the woman may also vary with time.[8] The *age of the youngest child* is taken into account by time-dependent dummy variables for different age intervals.

To take account of period effects we use a time-varying covariate which indicates whether the time at risk for making a certain transition was *before 1985* or in 1985 and afterwards. Similarly, time at risk *before 1989* is distinguished from risk time in 1989 or later. Interactions between these covariates and own earnings are included to capture changes in the impact of own earnings on labour-market transitions over time; changes in the impact of spouse's earnings over time are examined in the same way.

For resumption of part-time or full-time work, previous work preference is taken into account. The covariate *last job full-time* takes a value of 1 if the last employment was full-time, and 0 otherwise.

Trends in Union Formation in Sweden

Over the past three decades marriage rates have declined in Sweden at the same time as non-marital cohabitation has become increasingly more common. In fact, consensual unions remain more prevalent in Sweden than anywhere else in the industrialized world, although levels in Denmark now come rather close (Bracher and Santow 1998). Among women born in the late 1930s about one-third had lived in a consensual union before marrying or having a first child and this proportion rose to more than four-fifths among women born in the early

---

[7] The variable *years of schooling* takes the values 6 (university education, vocational training beyond secondary level), 3 (three to four years at upper secondary level education), 2 (two years of upper secondary education), 1 (at least one term of full-time vocational training beyond elementary/comprehensive school), and 0 otherwise.

[8] The SFS does not give the exact number of children that the spouse brought into the household. We add one child to the number of children if the spouse brought any of their own children into the household.

1950s (Hoem and Rennermalm 1985). Marrying without prior cohabitation has thus become more and more rare; the rate dropped from about 20 per cent among women born in 1949 to 8 per cent among those born in 1964 (Hoem 1995). Another reason why marriage rates have gone down is that the duration of cohabitation has increased considerably; among women born in 1949 almost two-thirds had married their partner within five years of cohabitation, but this was true only for about one-third of women born in 1964 (Bracher and Santow 1998). The propensity to enter into a union has thus not declined; four-fifths of women and two-thirds of men born between 1949 and 1964 had been in a union (marital or consensual) at least once by age 25 (Hoem 1995).

Marriage rates have not decreased uniformly, however, among all groups in the Swedish population. As shown by Bracher and Santow (1998), some groups have not experienced any decline at all; this is true, for example, for men and women with at least one religious parent and for those brought up in a non-Nordic country. Also, some groups have much higher rates of entry into marriage from cohabitation than others, including women who (and men whose partners) were pregnant or parturient, women whose fathers were not blue-collar workers, women with higher education, and men with co-resident children. For these reasons marriage has become increasingly selective and the groups of cohabiting and married couples have become increasingly different in basic respects. One aspect of this selection process is that over time the married have come to consist mainly of couples with children.

Henz and Sundström (forthcoming) found that, already at the time of first birth, the starting-point of this analysis, the composition of the married and cohabiting couples was very different and the differences increased over the study period, 1968–92. Being married tended to be associated with variables indicating higher social status compared to being in a consensual union, and this tendency became stronger over time. Among the married, more women had a university degree, fewer had only compulsory education, fewer had a father who was a blue-collar worker, and their earnings were higher and so were those of their spouse. Also, married women were older on average than cohabiting women at the time of first birth, had longer experience of full-time work, and had lived with their partner longer before first birth. Further, among the married, the proportion with at least one religious parent was double that among the cohabiting women and the proportion born outside Sweden was also more than double. Clearly, there are many differences between married and cohabiting women already at first birth, at the same time as there seems to be greater heterogeneity among the married. But what about the women and men in the couple—are they more similar if they are married than if they are cohabiting?

Homogamy among Married and Cohabiting Couples

As mentioned above, evidence of increased homogamy (or positive assortative mating) based on pre-marriage characteristics over time among married couples has been found for Finland, Britain, and the USA. For Sweden Björklund (1992) found a strong positive correlation in educational level among married couples in 1981. However, when it comes to trends Henz and Jonsson (forthcoming) report a decrease in educational homogamy in first partnerships of married and cohabiting Swedes born in 1915–29 and 1945–59. They found the same pattern for parents of Swedes born in 1898–1973.

In Henz and Sundström (forthcoming) we computed the correlations in spouses' annual earnings for married and cohabiting couples in the first and fifth year after first birth over the years 1968–92. This was because for cohabiting women we only had information about the earnings of the spouse if they had any children together. We found that the earnings of spouses were positively correlated for both married and cohabiting couples, but lower and less significant among cohabitants. Possibly, the latter reflects the fact that earnings of cohabitants at first birth diverge more from their potential earnings since they are younger on average than the married. Interestingly, we also found that the correlation in earnings increased over calendar periods of first birth for married couples, which suggests that the degree of specialization has decreased among the married. Among cohabiting couples we found no change over time. Looking at *all* Swedish couples it is thus possible that earnings homogamy has not increased, although it has for married couples, since cohabitation has become widespread and earnings correlations are lower among cohabitants. In fact, it is even possible that earnings homogamy has decreased among all couples, in line with the results on educational homogamy of Henz and Jonsson (forthcoming), who in part study an earlier period than Henz and Sundström (forthcoming), however.

Methods

We analyse selected labour-market transitions for women using piecewise constant exponential hazard rate models (Blossfeld and Rohwer 1995). The dependent variable is the hazard rate

$$r\left(t\,|\,X(t)\right) = \lim_{\Delta t \downarrow 0} \frac{P\left(t, t + \Delta t \,|\, T \ge t, X(t)\right)}{\Delta t}$$

where T is the time of the event of interest, t is any fixed point in time under risk and $P(t, t + \Delta t)$ is the probability that the event occurs in the interval $(t, t + \Delta t)$. $X(t)$ represents the vector of explanatory variables, which may, or may not, vary with duration t. In piecewise constant models, the time axis is divided into intervals and the hazard rate is assumed to be constant in each interval. The effects of the covariates on the hazard rate are assumed to be constant over the observation period. As duration intervals we chose multiples of six months, the choice of which varies between transitions analysed depending on the transition rates observed.

Our units of observation are women's spells in the different labour-market states, not the individual women, so some women may have more than one spell of the same type. If the recurrent spells are influenced by unobserved characteristics, the model assumption of independence between episodes will be violated. As a consequence there is a possibility that the estimated standard errors of the model parameters will be too low and that the estimated parameters will be biased.

To check for dependence among observations, we follow a procedure suggested in Allison (1995) and estimate models for second episodes with the duration of the first episode of that type included as a covariate.[9] If the duration of the first episode has no significant impact on the duration of the second episode, possible dependence between episodes can be ignored. This is indeed the case for the analyses where full-time employment, part-time employment, and non-employment are origin states. For these origins, we therefore analyse first spells jointly with spells of second or higher order.

By contrast, when parental leave is the origin state, duration of first and second episodes turns out to be strongly correlated and the correlation is not accounted for by other explanatory variables in the model. Such heterogeneity could perhaps reflect differences between women in preferences ('tastes') for care of own children versus paid work, or differences across municipalities in the availability of public childcare. To remove dependence between a woman's episodes we estimate separate models for first and second spells of parental leave. This procedure requires no assumptions about the form of dependence. If the process is essentially the same, however, the procedure will be statistically inefficient. In fact, the process may be the same although the resulting estimates differ significantly, because of, for example, selectivity of women at risk.

The survivor functions of the transitions, presented for a similar sample in Henz and Sundström (forthcoming), showed that shifts between full-time and part-time work as well as exits from the labour market occurred at a lower rate than re-entries into employment from parental leave or from non-employment. The latter transitions took place within a shorter time but comprised larger proportions of women at risk. Swedish women were found to have close ties to the job market; the transition that they were least likely to make was the one of leaving the labour market for more than three months. After ten years of either full-time or part-time work, only about 18 per cent of the spells had resulted in an exit from the labour market.

Shifts between full-time and part-time work took place at a rather constant rate over the ten-year period described. After ten years of continuous part-time employment about half of the episodes had ended with a transition to full-time. Thus, the relatively high mobility between part-time and full-time work in Sweden does not square with part-time jobs being 'dead-end jobs' as has sometimes been suggested for other countries (see e.g. Beechey and Perkins 1987).

[9] Duration of the first episode is measured in months minus 12, that is, if the first episode lasted for 12 months it takes the value zero.

Consequently, spells of non-employment were relatively short. Both in the first and in the second year at risk 20 per cent of episodes resulted in re-entry. But the fact that we did not observe any re-entries after five years of absence suggests that, for a non-negligible fraction of women, the decision to leave the labour market is final. For transitions from parental leave, two survivor functions were estimated, one for returns to full-time work and another for returns to part-time work. The rather steep downward sloping curves indicated that exits from leave take place at a relatively high rate, exits to part-time work occurring sooner (Henz and Sundström forthcoming).

Findings

Our main finding is that women's labour-market transitions are more influenced by own earnings than by spouse's earnings; own earnings have a significant impact on three of the transitions analysed (columns 1–3, Table 10.2) (and a small impact on a fourth transition, column 6), while spouse's earnings only affect one transition (column 1) (and weakly, a second transition, column 5). (The parameter estimates of a series of nested models for all transitions analysed are reported in Tables 10.3–10.10). Also, the effect of spouse's earnings on shifts from part-time to full-time is only present in the period before 1985, as is the effect of own earnings (column 1 and Table 10.3). Further, while the negative effect of own earnings on exits from the labour force is as expected (column 3 and Table 10.5), the negative effect on shifts from part-time to full-time (though present only before 1985) is unexpected (column 1 and Table 10.3) and so is the positive, but non-linear, effect on shifts in the opposite direction. These results suggest that mothers who continue to work part-time or shift to part-time from full-time are those who are more able to afford to do so. Possibly, the effect is intensified by positive assortative mating based on earnings. Moreover, to the extent that spouses' earnings have any impact independent of women's own earnings, it seems to be that of increasing women's labour-market activity. For example, high earnings for the spouse reduce the woman's risk of leaving the labour market (column 3) and increase her risk of shifting to full-time work before 1985 (column 1).

Another interesting result is that marriage appears to be associated with a more gender-based specialization in the family than consensual unions; married women have a higher risk of interrupting work (column 3 and Table 10.5) and a lower risk of re-entry (column 4 and Table 10.6) than cohabiting women. (For the transitions where the estimates are insignificant, the signs are all negative.) One possible explanation is that married couples have more traditional values than cohabiting couples and that this is also reflected in their division of labour. It is possible also that couples that prefer such a specialization also prefer to get married, since marriage gives the woman stronger legal protection and greater (income) security.

Table 10.2. Effects of own and spouse's earnings on women's labour-market transitions

	PT→FT	FT→PT	PT/FT→NE	NE→PT/FT	Leave1→PT	Leave1→FT
Own earnings	-0.154	0.095	-0.065	n.s.	n.s.	n.s.
Own earn. sq.	n.s.	-0.005		n.s.	n.s.	0.003
Spouse's earnings	0.189	n.s.	-0.043	n.s.	n.s.	n.s.
Spouse's earnings squared	n.s.	n.s.	0.001	n.s.	n.s.	n.s.
Own earn.* after 1985	0.184			n.s.	n.s.	n.s.
Own sq.* after 1985	n.s.			n.s.	n.s.	n.s.
Spouse earn.* after 1985	-0.191			n.s.	n.s.	n.s.
Spouse sq.* after 1985	0.007			n.s.	-0.002	n.s.
After 1985	n.s.		+	+	—	—
Controls:						
Married	n.s.		+	+	n.s.	n.s.
Age			—	—	n.s.	n.s.
Age squared			+	+	n.s.	n.s.
Age at 1st birth				—		
Schooling	n.s.		—	+	+	n.s.
Mother worked		n.s.			—	
FT experience			n.s.	n.s.	n.s.	—
PT experience	+			n.s.	n.s.	n.s.
Child ≥ 6 years						
1 child*< 2yrs		+				
Child < 2yrs		n.s.		—		
One child		n.s.	—	—		
No. of children					n.s.	n.s.
Last job FT	+				—	+
After 1989			+			
No. of transitions	301	179	248	517	576	308
No. of parameters	17	12	14	23	23	21
Likelihood ratio	53.2	32.0	169.6	240.6	851.9	218.2

Summary of effects in final models; significant effects only. FT = full-time, PT = part-time, NE = non-employment, n.s. = not significant. Effects of duration and reference groups are excluded. For control variables only signs of significant effects are reported. Blank means that the covariate was not used in the model. Results on exits from second spells of parental leave are not shown, but parameter estimates of the nested models for all transitions are presented in Tables 10.3–10.10. The single * in the left-hand column is exclusively used by so-called interaction-variables

Table 10.3. Parameter estimates for women's transitions from part-time to full-time work

	(1)	(2)	(3)	(4)	(5)
Duration					
0–11 months	−5.653***	−5.588***	−5.690***	−5.880***	−6.434***
12–23 months	−5.438***	−5.371***	−5.475***	−5.659***	−6.221***
24–35 months	−5.141***	−5.085***	−5.190***	−5.359***	−5.926***
36+ months	−5.200***	−5.359***	−5.467***	−5.608***	−6.193***
Years of schooling^t	0.0212	0.0266	0.031	0.034	0.034
Own max. earnings	−0.017	−0.016	−0.023	−0.025	−0.154*
Own max. earnings squared	0.000	0.000	0.000	0.001	0.006
Married^t		−0.272*	−0.265*	−0.239*	−0.182
Cohabiting^t		0	0	0	0
Youngest child ≥ 6 years^t		0.505***	0.505***	0.463***	0.362***
Youngest child < 6 years^t			0	0	0
Spouse's earnings			0.020	0.020	0.189**
Spouse earnings squared			−0.001	−0.001	−0.007
Last job full-time^t				0.320***	0.387**
Last job part-time/no job^t				0	0
At risk in 1985 or later^t					0.456
At risk before 1985^t					0
Own earn.* after 1985					0.184*
Own earn. sq.* after 1985					−0.007
Spouse's earn.* after 1985					−0.191**
Spouse's earn. sq.* after 1985					0.007**
No. of transitions	301	301	301	301	301
No. of parameters	7	9	11	12	17
Likelihood ratio	13.8	27.2	28.4	35.8	53.2

^{t} stands for a time-varying covariate. *** p ″ .01, ** p ″ .05, * p ″ .10.

Table 10.4. Parameter estimates for women's transitions from full-time to part-time work

	(1)	(2)	(3)	(4)
Duration:				
0–11 months	−5.325***	−5.762***	−5.752***	−5.721***
12–23 months	−5.587***	−6.022***	−5.977***	−5.946***
24–35 months	−5.304***	−5.735***	−5.677***	−5.645***
36+ months	−6.208***	−6.644***	−6.591***	−6.554***
Years of schooling[t]	0.033	0.051	0.052	0.051
Own max. earnings		0.097*	0.093*	0.095*
Own max. earn. sq.		−0.005*	−0.005*	−0.005*
Only one child			−0.100	−0.099
Two or more children			0	0
Youngest child < 2 years[t]			−0.243	−0.240
Youngest child ≥ 2 years			0	0
One child * < 2 years			0.588*	0.586*
Spouse's earnings				−0.007
Spouse earn. sq.				0.000
No. of transitions	179	179	179	179
No. of parameters	5	7	9	12
Likelihood ratio	23.2	28.6	31.8	32.0

[t] stands for a time-varying covariate. *** p " .01, ** p " .05, * p " .10.

We, furthermore, tested several control variables for each of the transitions and ended up using those that most improved the fit of each model. Accumulated human capital, as measured by years of schooling, is seen to have expected and significant effects on three transitions: it reduces exit risks (column 3), raises re-entry risks (column 4), and speeds up return to part-time work from parental leave (column 5). Also, the risk of exiting and re-entering the labour market varies significantly with age. Level of home productivity, as measured by age and number of children, influences four of our transitions in an expected and significant way. For example, women are more likely to shift from part-time to full-time work when their children reach school age (column 1) and number of children increases time spent non-employed (column 4). In addition, women's preferred hours of work, as expressed by whether their last job was full-time, exert a strong influence on their transitions; women whose previous job was full-time are more inclined to take up full-time work again (columns 1 and 6) and less inclined to take up part-time work (columns 4 and 5). We further find that most transitions are significantly affected by calendar period at risk. Thus, re-entry rates were higher during the economic upturn of the late 1980s (column 4) and exit rates increased with the recession in the early 1990s (column 3). Lastly, we see that there is a considerable variation in the explanatory power of our final models; it is rather

Table 10.5. Parameter estimates for women's transitions from full-time and part-time work work to non-employment.

	(1)	(2)	(3)	(4)	(5)
Duration					
0–11 months	−3.939***	−3.550***	−3.307***	−2.991***	−3.045***
12–23 months	−3.848***	−3.464***	−3.401***	−3.076***	−3.114***
24–35 months	−3.917***	−3.530***	−3.505***	−3.178***	−3.209***
36+ months	−4.704***	−4.317***	−4.259***	−3.924***	−3.943***
Age^t	−0.169***	−0.161***	−0.205***	−0.205***	−0.201***
Age squared	0.004**	0.004**	0.005***	0.005***	0.004**
Years of schooling^t	−0.105***	−0.054	−0.050	−0.058**	−0.059*
FT work experience^t	−0.124***	−0.053*	−0.047	−0.046	−0.038
Own max. earnings		−0.071***	−0.066***	−0.060***	−0.065***
Married^t			0.313*	0.295*	0.322**
Cohabiting^t			0	0	0
Youngest child < 2 years^t			−0.428**	−0.419**	−0.405**
Youngest child ≥ 2 years^t			0	0	0
Spouse's earnings				−0.042**	−0.043**
Spouse's earn. sq.				0.001*	0.001*
At risk in 1989 or later^t					0.345**
At risk before 1989^t					0
No. of transitions	248	248	248	248	248
No. of parameters	8	9	11	13	14
Likelihood ratio	133.2	152.2	161.0	164.6	169.6

^{t} stands for a time-varying covariate. *** p ″ .01, ** p ″ .05, * p ″ .10.

Table 10.6. Parameter estimates for women's re-entry into the labour market

	(1)	(2)	(3)	(4)	(5)	(6)
Duration						
0–5 months	-6.271***	-4.724***	-3.629***	-3.653***	-3.571***	-3.559***
6–17 months	-4.528***	-2.978***	-1.855***	-1.877***	-1.785***	-1.771***
18–35 months	-5.038***	-3.506***	-2.332***	-2.351***	-2.226***	-2.212***
36–59 months	-5.517***	-4.014***	-2.823***	-2.838***	-2.650***	-2.634***
60+ months	-5.656***	-4.254***	-3.127***	-3.139***	-2.922***	-2.910***
Age^t	0.132***	0.170***	0.260***	0.257***	0.242***	0.242***
Age squared^t	-0.004**	-0.004***	-0.006***	-0.006***	-0.006***	-0.006***
Years of schooling^t	0.030	0.070***	0.075***	0.078***	0.073***	0.073***
Own max. earnings	0.053	0.028	0.025	0.029	0.028	0.062
Own max. earn. sq.	-0.002	-0.000	0.002	0.000	0.000	-0.002
FT experience	-0.055**	-0.012	-0.019	-0.019	0.001	-0.001
PT experience	-0.072*	-0.011	-0.018	-0.020	-0.045	-0.044
Age at 1st birth	-0.088***	-0.088***	-0.132***	-0.130***	-0.131***	-0.131***
Married^t			-0.377***	-0.374***	-0.297***	-0.303***
Cohabiting^t			0	0	0	0
Number of children^t			-0.277***	-0.278***	-0.300***	-0.297***
Spouse's earnings				-0.000	-0.000	-0.015
Spouse's earn. sq.				-0.000	-0.000	0.000
Last job full-time					-0.173*	-0.174*
Last job part-time/no job^t					0	0
At risk in 1985 or later^t					0.333***	0.332***
At risk before 1985^t					0	0
Own earn.* after 1985^t						-0.056
Own earn. sq.* after 1985^t						0.003
Spouse's earn.* after 1985^t						0.026
Spouse's earn. sq* after 1985^t						-0.001
No. of transitions	517	517	517	517	517	517
No. of parameters	12	13	15	17	19	23
Likelihood ratio	183.5	198.8	225.1	226.6	239.2	240.6

^{t} stands for a time-varying covariate. *** p ″ .01, ** p ″ .05, * p ″ .10.

low for the transitions between full-time and part-time work but quite high for the exits from first spells of parental leave to part-time work.

As already discussed, we estimate separate models for the first and second spells of parental leave episodes because we expect them to differ. Comparing the estimates for the transition to part-time work from the first and second leave spell we see that this is indeed the case (Tables 10.7 and 10.8). Level of education has a positive and significant impact on exits from the first spell, but none on exits from second spells. If the woman's mother worked for pay it reduces her exit rate from first spell, but not that from the second spell, the first of which is a puzzling finding. (A possible, though slightly far-fetched, explanation is that mothers who did not work for pay when their daughters grew up were also less likely to do so when their grandchildren were born and thus were more able to help with childcare so that their daughters could return to work sooner.) Further, the length of full-time work experience and the number of children both have negative and significant effects only on exits from the second spell. On the other hand, last job being full-time and calendar period at risk being after 1985 have similar effects on first and second spells.

Turning to transitions from parental leave to full-time work, we again see that the first and second leave episodes differ (Tables 10.9 and 10.10). Second spells are more influenced by age, length of (full-time and part-time) work experience, and spouse's earnings than first spells. The impact of own earnings, working hours in the last job, and calendar period is similar, however.

Concluding Discussion

In this chapter we ask the following questions. Is there positive assortative mating based on earnings in Sweden and, if so, how has it changed over time? What impact do women's own earnings and those of their spouses have on women's allocation of time between the home and labour-market activity and how have these effects changed? To that end we report previous results on correlations between spouses' earnings for married and cohabiting couples in Sweden, and analyse the effects of the two partners' earnings on women's labour-market transitions. Earnings were positively correlated both among married and cohabiting couples, but correlations were higher among the married. Among the latter the degree of earnings homogamy had increased over time, which suggests a decreasing degree of specialization. It is however unlikely that earnings homogamy has increased among all Swedish couples, since the fraction of cohabiting couples has risen and earnings correlations were lower among them.

The analysis of women's labour-market transitions shows own earnings to affect more transitions and to have greater impact on them than spouse's earnings. Higher earning women are less likely to interrupt work than lower earners, but more likely to shift to part-time if they work full-time and to continue

Table 10.7. Parameter estimates for women's transitions from leave to part-time work, only first leave episodes

	(1)	(2)	(3)	(4)	(5)
Duration					
0–5 months	-6.366***	-6.373***	-6.449***	-6.081***	-6.192***
6–11 months	-3.399***	-3.407***	-3.486***	-3.090***	-3.198***
12–17 months	-2.308***	-2.319***	-2.399***	-1.949***	-2.052**
18–23 months	-1.592***	-1.607***	-1.688***	-1.218***	-1.306**
24+ months	-2.344***	-2.384***	-2.472***	-2.059***	-2.131***
Age^t	-0.001	-0.002	0.004	0.002	-0.004
Age squared^t	-0.003	-0.002	-0.002	-0.002	-0.002
Mother worked	-0.219***	-0.215**	-0.212**	-0.155*	-0.147*
Years of schooling^t	0.045*	0.041*	0.042*	0.055**	0.057**
Own max. earnings	-0.007	-0.004	-0.006	0.023	0.041
Own max. earn. sq.	0.000	0.000	0.000	-0.000	-0.001
FT experience	0.015	0.014	0.008	0.028	0.034
PT experience	0.090***	0.092***	0.084**	0.030	0.023
Married^t		0.116	0.113	0.033	0.031
Cohabiting^t		0	0	0	0
Number of children^t		-0.048	-0.072	-0.109	-0.119
Spouse's earnings			0.019	0.015	-0.005
Spouse earn. squared			-0.001	-0.001	0.001
Last job FT				-0.644***	-0.644***
Last job PT/no job^t				0	0
At risk in 1985 or later^t				-0.513***	-0.512***
At risk before 1985^t				0	0
Own earn.* after 1985^t					-0.070
Own earn. sq.* after 1985^t					0.002
Spouse's earn.* after 1985^t					0.041
Spouse's earn. sq *after 1985^t					-0.002**
No. of transitions	576	576	576	576	576
No. of parameters	13	15	17	19	23
Likelihood Ratio	790.2	792.0	794.5	842.6	851.9

^{t} stands for a time-varying covariate. *** p ″ .01, ** p ″ .05, * p ″ .10.

Table 10.8. Parameter estimates for women's transitions from leave to part-time work, only second leave episodes

	(1)	(2)	(3)	(4)	(5)
Duration					
0–5 months	−7.844***	−6.046***	−6.075***	−5.719***	−5.490***
6–11 months	−5.394***	−3.480***	−3.510***	−3.136***	−2.904**
12–17 months	−3.938***	−2.028***	−2.057***	−1.588**	−1.348
18–23 months	−3.180***	−1.282*	−1.310*	−0.776	−0.519
24+ months	−3.860***	−1.955**	−1.987**	−1.085	−0.820
Age^t	0.110	0.157***	0.157***	0.098	0.091
Age squared^t	−0.003	−0.004	−0.004	−0.002	−0.002
Mother worked	−0.074	−0.064	−0.069	−0.006	−0.012
Years of schooling^t	−0.035	−0.048*	−0.047	−0.044	−0.046
Own max. earnings	0.146***	0.098*	0.090*	0.053	0.007
Own max. earn. sq.	−0.004**	−0.003*	−0.002	−0.001	0.001
FT experience	−0.078***	−0.094***	−0.100***	−0.053*	−0.053*
PT experience	−0.074*	−0.095**	−0.096**	−0.062	−0.061
Married^t		−0.158	−0.148	−0.100	−0.101
Cohabiting^t		0	0	0	0
No. of children^t		−0.822***	−0.821***	−0.720***	−0.728***
Spouse's earnings			0.014	0.013	0.004
Spouse earn. sq.			−0.001	−0.001	0.000
Last job FT				−0.670***	−0.665***
Last job PT/no job^t				0	0
At risk in 1985 or later^t				−0.222*	−0.257**
At risk before 1985^t				0	0
Duration 1st leave episode				−0.070***	−0.070***
Own earn.* after 1985^t					0.058
Own earn. sq.* after 1985^t					−0.002
Spouse's earn.* after 1985^t					0.010
Spouse's earn. sq.* after 1985^t					−0.001
No. of transitions	411	411	411	411	411
No. of parameters	13	15	17	20	24
Likelihood ratio	624.4	639.1	641.6	745.5	749.7

^{t} stands for a time-varying covariate. *** p ≤ .01, ** p ≤ .05, * p ≤ .10

Table 10.9. Parameter estimates for women's transitions from leave to full-time work, only first leave episodes

	(1)	(2)	(3)	(4)	(5)
Duration					
0–11 months	-3.758***	-3.944***	-3.883***	-5.278***	-5.535***
12–17 months	-2.505***	-2.689***	-2.628***	-3.977***	-4.229***
18–23 months	-1.985***	-2.168***	-2.109***	-3.490**	-3.730***
24+ months	-2.147***	-2.342***	-2.274***	-3.741***	-3.966***
Age^t	-0.044	-0.062	-0.061	-0.052	-0.053
Age squared^t	0.001	0.001	0.001	0.003	0.002
Years of schooling^t	-0.003	0.002	0.003	0.001	0.006
Own max. earnings	-0.048	-0.040	-0.037	-0.058	-0.061
Own max. earn. sq.	0.003**	0.002**	0.002**	0.003**	0.003**
FT experience	-0.047	-0.038	-0.039	-0.072**	-0.066**
PT experience	-0.214***	-0.200***	-0.199***	0.006	0.021
Married^t		0.115	0.120	0.055	0.064
Cohabiting^t		0	0	0	0
No. of children^t		0.101	0.098	0.216	0.210
Spouse's earnings			-0.007	-0.005	0.025
Spouse's earn. sq.			0.000	0.000	-0.001
Last job FT				1.693***	1.729***
Last job PT/no job^t				0	0
At risk in 1985 or later^t				-0.394***	-0.367***
At risk before 1985^t				0	0
Own earn.* after 1985^t					-0.021
Own earn. sq.* after 1985^t					-0.000
Spouse's earn.* after 1985^t					-0.040
Spouse's earn. sq.*after 1985^t					0.002
No. of transitions	308	308	308	308	308
No. of parameters	11	13	15	17	21
Likelihood ratio	161.4	162.6	163.1	215.2	218.2

^{t} stands for a time-varying covariate. *** p".01, ** p".05, * p".10.

Table 10.10. Parameter estimates for women's transitions from leave to full-time work: only second leave episodes

	(1)	(2)	(3)	(4)	(5)
Duration					
0–11 months	−4.565***	−4.554***	−4.823***	−7.222***	−8.219***
12–17 months	−2.566***	−2.556***	−2.822**	−4.952***	−5.924***
18+ months	−2.760***	−2.750***	−3.022**	−5.034***	−6.019***
Age^t	0.103	0.100	0.096	0.262**	0.275**
Age squared^t	−0.004	−0.004	−0.003	−0.008*	−0.009*
Years of schooling^t	0.022	0.019	0.019	−0.007	0.011
Own max. earnings	−0.135***	−0.134***	−0.133***	−0.059	−0.074
Own max. earn. sq.	0.005***	0.005***	0.005***	0.003***	0.003***
FT experience	−0.104**	−0.105**	−0.114**	−0.120***	−0.117***
PT experience	−0.287***	−0.282***	−0.281***	−0.187*	−0.182*
Married^t	0	0	0.120	−0.057	−0.043
Cohabiting^t	−0.043		0	0	0
No. of children^t	−0.234	−0.035	−0.230*	−0.234*	
Spouse's earnings			0.038	0.065	0.179**
Spouse's earn. squared			−0.001	−0.002	−0.005*
Last job FT			1.896***	1.905***	1.905***
Last job PT/no job^t					0
At risk in 1985 or later^t				−0.403**	−0.360*
At risk before 1985^t				0	0
Duration 1st leave episode				−0.095***	−0.095***
Own earn.* after 1985^t					−0.003
Own earn. sq.* after 1985^t					−0.000
Spouse's earn.* after 1985^t					−0.177**
Spouse's earn. sq.*after 1985^t					0.005
No. of transitions	148	148	148	148	148
No. of parameters	10	12	14	17	21
Likelihood ratio	159.7	160.1	161.9	294.1	299.1

^{t} stands for a time-varying covariate. *** $p \leq .01$, ** $p \leq .05$, * $p \leq .10$.

working part-time rather than shifting to full-time (though the effect is only present before 1985). These results suggest that a large fraction of Swedish women prefer to work part-time during the childrearing years if they can afford to. Possibly, the effects of own earnings are intensified by the positive sorting based on earnings. High earnings for the spouse reduce the woman's risk of leaving the job market and raise her risk of shifting to full-time if she works part-time, but the impact is small in magnitude and the latter effect is only present before 1985. On the whole, Swedish women are found to have strong and close ties with the job market; the transition that they are least likely to make is the one of interrupting work. Women with high earnings or a higher earning partner are more likely to be in the job market, so being full-time housewives is not what they choose if they can afford it, rather they choose part-time work. This strong preference for work and the relatively limited impact of own and spouse's earnings on women's labour-market choices is perhaps best understood in light of the incentives created by the Swedish social security and tax system. This system is completely individualized, so that each individual pays his/her own taxes and works up eligibility for social benefits. To become entitled to social benefits (above a low minimum level), such as sick pay, parental benefits, and pensions, one has to be employed and the benefit level depends on prior earnings.

References

Allison, P. D. (1995). *Survival Analysis Using the SAS System: A Practical Guide* (Gary, NC: SAS Institute Inc.).

Aronsson, T., and J. R. Walker (1997). 'The Effects of Sweden's Welfare State on Labor Supply Incentives', in R. B. Freeman, R. Topel, and B. Swedenborg (eds.), *The Welfare State in Transition* (Chicago: University of Chicago Press).

Becker, G. S. (1991). *A Treatise on the Family* (Enlarged edn. Cambridge, Mass.: Harvard University Press).

Beechey, V., and T. Perkins (1987). *A Matter of Hours* (Cambridge: Polity Press).

Björklund, A. (1992). 'Rising Female Labour Force Participation and the Distribution of Family Income: The Swedish Experience', *Acta Sociologica*, 35: 299–309.

Blau, F. D., and M. A. Ferber (1986). *The Economics of Women, Men and Work* (Englewood Cliffs, NJ: Prentice-Hall).

Blossfeld, H.-P., and G. Rohwer (1995). *Techniques of Event History Modeling* (Matwah, NJ: Lawrence Erlbaum).

Bracher, M., and G. Santow (1998). 'Economic Independence and Union Formation in Sweden', *Population Studies*, 52/3: 275–94.

Cancian, M., and M. Jäntti (1997). *Assortative Mating on Labor Market Characteristics* (Working Paper, Åbo: Åbo Akademi University).

Davies, H., R. Peronaci, and H. Joshi (1998). *The Gender Wage Gap and Partnership* (Discussion Paper in Economics, 6; London: Birkbeck College, University of London).

Henz, U., and J. Jonsson (forthcoming). 'Who Marries Whom in Sweden?', in H.-P. Blossfeld and A. Timm (eds.), *Who Marries Whom: Educational Systems as Marriage Markets in Modern Societies*.

Henz, U., J. Jonsson and M. Sundström (forthcoming). 'Partner Choice and Women's Paid Work in Sweden: The Role of Earnings', *European Sociological Review*, 17/3.

Hoem, B. (1995). *Kvinnor och mäns liv. Del 2: Parbildning och separationer* (Women's and Men's Lives. Part 2: Partnership Formation and Separation) (Stockholm: Statistics Sweden).

Hoem, J. M. (1993). 'Public Policy as the Fuel of Fertility', *Acta Sociologica*, 36: 19–31.

——and B. Rennermalm (1985). 'Modern Family Initiation in Sweden: Experience of Women Born between 1936 and 1960', *European Journal of Population*, 1: 81–112.

Karoly, L. A., and G. Burtless (1995). 'Demographic Change, Rising Earnings Inequality, and the Distribution of Personal Well-Being, 1959–1989', *Demography*, 32: 379–405.

Killingsworth, M., and J. Heckman (1986). 'Female Labor Supply: A Survey', in O. Ashenfelter and R. Layard (eds.), *Handbook of Labor Economics*, i (Amsterdam: North-Holland).

Leibowitz, A., and J. A. Klerman (1995). 'Explaining Changes in Married Mothers' Employment over Time', *Demography*, 32: 365–78.

Mare, R. D. (1991). 'Five Decades of Educational Assortative Mating', *American Sociological Review*, 56: 15–32.

Qian, Z., and S. H. Preston (1993). 'Changes in American Marriage, 1972 to 1987: Availability and Forces of Attraction by Age and Education', *American Sociological Review*, 58: 482–95.

Rønsen, M., and M. Sundström (1996). 'Maternal Employment in Scandinavia: A Comparison of the After-Birth Employment Activity of Norwegian and Swedish Women', *Journal of Population Economics*, 9: 267–85.

Sundström, M. (1987). *A Study in the Growth of Part-Time Work in Sweden* (Stockholm: Almqvist & Wiksell International).

Weiss, Y. (1997). 'The Formation and Dissolution of Families: Why Marry? Who Marries Whom? And What Happens upon Divorce', in M. R. Rosenzweig and O. Stark (eds.), *Handbook of Population and Family Economics*, iA (Amsterdam: North-Holland).

11

Work Careers of Married Women in Denmark

SØREN LETH-SØRENSEN AND GÖTZ ROHWER

Introduction

THE purpose of this analysis is to evaluate some of the factors which might influence changes in married women's labour-market status. In particular, the focus is on the effects of husbands' characteristics and the social position of the fathers of the spouses. It is interesting to consider the effects of the husband in Denmark, a country where women have a very high participation rate. Denmark is also considered one of the leading countries with respect to gender equality.

First, a brief account of conditions in Denmark which are of importance to women's labour-market status and selected institutional factors is given. Secondly, the data used in the subsequent empirical analysis are described. The analysis begins with a description of the women's situation the year before they marry for the first time. Furthermore, some results showing the extent of homogamy in Denmark are presented. Finally, the importance of selected conditions for married women's transitions in the labour market are discussed.

Female Labour Supply

Over the past decades there has been a convergence of male and female labour-market participation rates. The participation rate for women has increased, but the rate for men has fallen slightly (Bonke 1997). Changes in the distribution of adult women's status in relation to the labour market have been monitored in surveys. In 1974, for instance, 34 per cent of women aged 16 or older were not economically active. These women were either unemployed, had retired, or were housewives. In 1991 too, 34 per cent of women were inactive, but the proportion of housewives changed from 14 per cent to a negligible 3 per cent. At the same time, the proportion of women who were unemployed or retired increased correspondingly (Christoffersen 1993).

A sample from the IDA-database (Leth-Sørensen 1997) can be used to describe changes in women's status in relation to the labour market by age. The information describes the situation in the last week of November of each year and can be categorized as follows:

- full-time participation
- part-time participation (under 30 hours a week; 27 hours from 1988)
- unemployed
- out of labour force (housewives and students)
- retired (pension, early retirement scheme)

Figure 11.1 shows the distribution by age for a random sample of all women in 1980 and 1994, that is, the first and last year of our analysis. Therefore, the distribution for 1980 is the point of departure for analysing transitions in the following years.

One major development during this period was an increase in the proportion of full-time working women aged 25–9 or older. A general decline in the proportion of women working part-time has taken place since the end of the 1970s. For women aged 35 or over, there was a dramatic decrease in numbers of those not in the labour force, see Figure 11.2. The proportion of retired women has risen, and two-thirds of women aged 60–6 were retired in 1994. Also the proportion of unemployed elderly women has increased, resulting in a U-distribution of unemployment by age.

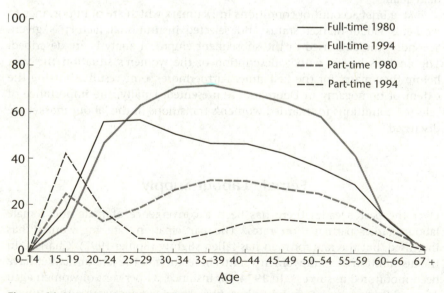

Figure 11.1. Women 1980 and 1994 by participation in the labour market
Source: 2.5% sample of IDA database.

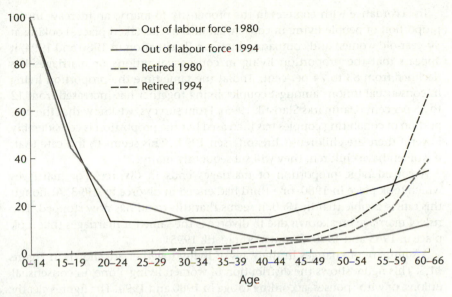

Figure 11.2. Women 1980 and 1994 retired/out of labour force
Source: 2.5% sample of IDA database.

Family Formation and Fertility

Since the beginning of the 1960s there has been a major change in the propensity to marry. This development naturally reflects the acceptance of cohabitation as a modern way of life. The diminishing rate of marriage can be shown by a few figures. In 1960 the highest number of women marrying for the first time was amongst 21-year-olds. The number of married women per 1,000 at this age was 143; this number declined to 21 in 1991. A decline to one-seventh is a remarkable change. For women over 25, the first-marriage rate has been rising. As an example for women aged 30, the rate increased from 10 to 33 per 1,000 in the same period. Thus, the mean age at first marriage increased from 22.9 years in 1960 to 27.9 years in 1991. With respect to birth cohorts, the proportion of married women aged 25 years for the cohort born 1937–8 was 80 per cent, whereas the corresponding figure for the 1966–7 birth cohort was only 21 per cent (Danmarks Statistik 1993). Though there has also been a continued postponement of marriage since 1980, the development has been less pronounced in recent years.

Because rates of marriage have risen for older women, a kind of 'catching up' occurred. However, from a cohort perspective, it still does not seem likely that the total proportion of ever-married women among the younger generation will be as high as it was before. This process means that information on a person's legal marital status no longer suffices in monitoring a person's family situation. Therefore, the actual way in which the person has arranged his/her family situation should also be included.

In accordance with changes in the propensity to marry, an increase in the proportion of people living in consensual unions has taken place. Looking at 30-year-old women and comparing their family situation in 1980 and 1994, it appears that the proportion living in consensual unions or marriages has declined from 83 to 74 per cent. And at the same time the proportion living in consensual unions amongst couples living together has increased from 12 to 35 per cent (Danmarks Statistik 1995). From surveys, we know that the proportion of cohabiting couples has increased but the proportion is considerably lower if there are children (Christoffersen 1993). This seems to indicate that, if women have children, they will subsequently marry.

A considerable proportion of marriages ends in divorce. For marriages which took place in 1980, one-third had ended in divorce by 1993. Although this rate is double that in 1960, it seems that this trend has now stopped. The risk of marriage breakdown due to divorce is the same for marriages that took place in 1985 and 1990 (Danmarks Statistik 1995).

A summary of changes in the ways of living together are shown in Figure 11.3. This figure shows the distribution of women living alone, in consensual unions, or with spouses, according to age in 1980 and 1994. The figures clearly show the trend from living in marriages to living in consensual unions to a greater extent, especially for the younger generations. Furthermore, it should be noted that there has been a slight increase in persons living alone.

Since the beginning of the 1960s, the net reproduction rate has been declining in Denmark. After 1969 the rate fell to under 1,000 daughters born per

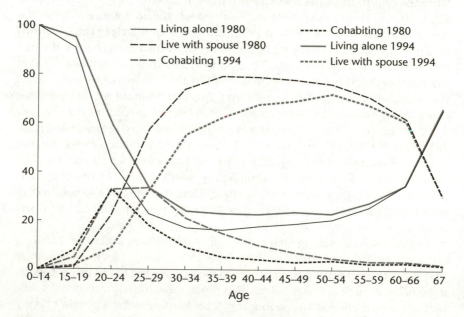

Figure 11.3. Women 1980 and 1994 by status in family
Source: 2.5% sample of IDA database.

1,000 women during their reproductive period, which is the required number if the population is not to decline in the long run. The net reproduction rate was at its lowest in 1983 (662) and afterwards it rose. In 1995, the rate was 867, still far too low to maintain the population at the present level (Danmarks Statistik 1997*b*). Because the proportion of married couples has declined among the younger generation, non-married women now account for almost half of all births (Danmarks Statistik 1995).

The mean age of women at first birth has been increasing since 1960 and has risen from around 22 to 27 years. Also, the corresponding figure for men has gone up from 27 to 29 years (Christoffersen 1997). The low rate of fertility in Denmark has occurred at the same time as the proportion of women in the labour force has been rising. It has been shown that women in higher occupations account for the highest proportion of women at age 44 who have never had a child (Knudsen 1993). These figures also illuminate the difficulties that women have in combining a career with childcare. It is interesting to note that the proportion for men who have not become a father increases the further that one goes down the social ladder. As many as 50 per cent of men on an early retirement pension have never been a father.

Institutional Characteristics of the Danish Labour Market

A well-known characteristic of the Nordic Welfare Model has been the expansion of the public sector. In Denmark the proportion employed in the public sector increased from 10 per cent in 1960 to 30 per cent in 1990 (Blossfeld and Hakim 1997). Many of the new jobs in the public sector were occupied by women, particularly in the following areas: health, social institutions, and education. Close to 45 per cent of employed women are now working in the public sector.

A prerequisite for this development was the provision of day-care facilities for infants. In concurrence with married women entering the labour market at the beginning of the 1960s, there was an expansion of day-care facilities for children in municipal day-care institutions and in other day-care types. In 1996, 13 per cent of all infants under one year were enrolled in such day-care facilities and for children aged 5 years, the figure was as high as 86 per cent (Danmarks Statistik 1997*b*). In addition, some parents let their children be looked after by means of private arrangements.

At the beginning of the 1980s, maternity leave was fourteen weeks, but in 1985 it was extended to twenty-four weeks. At the same time, it also became possible for couples to share maternity leave. The father had the possibility of taking two weeks off immediately after the birth. As far as economic compensation is concerned, public employees are entitled to full pay during maternity leave; salaried employees receive half their pay for five months or they may be entitled to full pay in accordance with their collective agreements. Other persons are entitled to a compensation of up to 100 per cent of their previous pay, but not higher than a given amount corresponding to the rates for normal sickness benefits.

It is quite easy to become a member of an unemployment insurance fund. Ten weeks' employment entitles a person to membership, and newly trained persons can become members immediately after completing their training. During the years covered in this analysis, one had to have been working for at least half a year during the previous three years to receive unemployment benefits. Furthermore, the period in which a person is entitled to unemployment benefits is relatively long. To avoid persons with a long unemployment period from being no longer entitled to unemployment benefits, measures were implemented to provide jobs for those who would otherwise have forfeited their right to claim unemployment benefits.

One explanation for the relatively liberal rules for membership of an unemployment insurance fund is that there are relatively few and limited rules concerning dismissals. These rules are usually agreed upon by both sides of the labour market and therefore depend on the area in question. For example, salaried employees are entitled to a maximum of six months notice, and the rules for giving notice of dismissal can for some groups be only weeks. However, large-scale dismissals require that notice be given.

In Denmark 67 per cent of all couples are owners of their one-family house and 4 per cent live in owner-occupied apartments (Bonke 1997). Furthermore, about one-third of all domestic total consumption is spent on housing, fuel, and electricity (Danmarks Statistik 1992). Gross interest payment thus account for a relatively large proportion of the family's total consumption. For families with a high proportion of fixed expenditures there is little scope for a reduction in income, for example, due to one of the spouses leaving the labour market.

Denmark has had an almost independent income taxation system for married couples for a long time so there is no tax incentive to marry, which is very different than, for example, in Germany (see Chapter 3 above). Previously, families with children were entitled to a taxable allowance, but this has been replaced by the payment of family allowances to all families regardless of their income. The amount is highest for children aged 0–2 years, while it is slightly lower for older children.

Data and Variables

IDA Database

The data used here consist of a random sample of persons from the IDA database which has been established by Statistics Denmark (Danmarks Statistik 1991). The IDA database is constructed as a panel, and includes the whole population as well as all enterprises with employees. The collection of data started in 1980; data used in our analysis are from the period 1980–95. The database was constructed by using data from public registers and linking these data. Thus, it has been possible to give information on the status of the total population in relation to the labour market at the end of November each year. The basic sample used here is a 2.5 per cent random sample of the total population.

The operational definitions for the Danish statistics about families are also adapted from registry data. The definition of family units is not only based on the legal relationship between the persons. To belong to the same family unit, persons have to live at the same address. This means that if a married couple is for some reason not living at the same dwelling unit, two families will be counted. Cohabiting couples are also defined using the information from the population registers. Similarly, the number of children in the family indicates the number of children living at the same address as their parents. The family status for a person is his/her situation at the end of each year.

Because our analysis is mainly based on adults we distinguish between three different situations with regard to a person's status in a family:

- living without a partner (also child in family)
- cohabiting (not married to partner)
- married, living with spouse

Our main unit of interest is women. From our basic sample, we selected all women who were unmarried and living alone in the first year for which we had an observation, and who experienced at least one of the following transitions during 1980–1994: (*a*) from living without a partner to living with a spouse (getting married), or (*b*) from cohabiting (with a later spouse or other person) to living with a spouse. Based on information on the legal status of the woman before marriage, we selected only women who married for the first time. For the selected women, information was available for the years in which they were present in the 1980–94 population statistics. If they were not present, they did not appear in the data for the relevant years.

One important item of information for women related to the male partner if the woman was not living alone. Information on the identification number of the woman's partner was extracted from the population registers. By using this as a key, we derived data for this group of men for the years between 1980 and 1994 in which they were present in the population records.

In the population registers, data are also available on a person's father (and the mother) for the cohorts born after 1960; for birth cohorts 1950–60, these data are incomplete. For example, for women who were 20–4 years in 1980, information was available for 74 per cent of the fathers, and for women 25–9 years of age, data were available for 34 per cent only. Naturally, the problem concerning lack of information on the father for women born before 1950 also applies to the partner.

Since one of the objectives of this analysis is to assess the significance of parental social position on women's behaviour following marriage, we have only included married couples if information was available for the fathers of both spouses. Due to the lack of information on fathers for both women and men, our final sample covers fewer couples from the beginning of the 1980s. This means that the number of couples increased between 1981 and 1994. Another consequence is that in the sample the mean marrying age for women increased over the years. In 1981, the mean age was nearly 22 years and in 1994 the mean age was just over 27 years. It should therefore be borne in mind that in our sample persons marrying at the beginning of the period will be characterized by being relatively young. Our final sample consists of 3,124 women over the period 1980 to 1994.

Besides information on women's status in the labour market, we have a number of variables for women and men and for their fathers. The variables used are background variables (age, education, family status, children), unemployment, and income. All variables are based on registry data. A complete list is given in the appendix to this chapter.

Situation for Women before Marriage

Before the analysis of the transitions in the labour supply of married women, we briefly describe the women's situation before they married. The year before marriage, more than three-quarters lived in a consensual union. Women under 20 years of age account for the lowest proportion (47 per cent) while older women account for the highest proportion (85 per cent of women over 30 years). Of course, this also reflects the problems that young people have in establishing their own household. For example, it may be difficult for a young couple to rent or buy a flat or house.

Before marrying more than one-quarter of the women had a child between 0 and 6 years of age, but only 3 per cent had a child between 7 and 17 years old. One-sixth of the women were still in the educational system. Of these, only a small proportion (9 per cent) had a child from 0 to 6 years old. Therefore, being in the educational system seems to delay having a first child (see Blossfeld and Huinink 1991 for comparable results for Germany).

The year before marrying, 74 per cent of the women worked full-time and 8 per cent worked part-time. The proportion of those unemployed is 10 per cent, while women out of the labour market only account for 8 per cent. This means that as many as 92 per cent of the women were in the labour force the year before they married. This forms the point of departure for investigating the labour supply of married women Among the older women, almost all had more than two years of labour-market experience one year before getting married. Since labour-force experience and age are so closely related in Denmark, the proportion of women having more than two years of work experience is smaller among the young women. But still one-quarter of the women under 20 years of age had more than two years work experience at the time of marriage.

Looking at the women just before first marriage we get the impression that they lived in a situation rather similar to that of a married couple. A majority of the women lived in consensual unions and more than one-quarter had a child before getting married. At the same time, almost all women had some kind of attachment to the labour market and had had this for several years, except for the quite young women. This gives the impression of a rather mature and independent group of women when they marry.

Homogamy: Woman's Father—Husband's Father

For the fathers of the women and their partners, information is available on their level of education and gross income in 1980. It appears that there is a positive correlation between the educational level of the two fathers and also with respect to their income in 1980.

Another source for studying the relationship between the characteristics of husband and wife results from a survey conducted by the Danish Institute of Social Research on social conditions for newly-born children. The survey is based on interviews with 6,000 new mothers. The fathers were also asked to fill out a questionnaire which was sent to the Institute. One result from this survey is that the occupational position of the grandfathers, more frequently than expected, is the same (Christoffersen 1997).

Homogamy: Woman—Husband

Age: In our final sample of married couples, it should be expected that the difference in age will be less than in the official statistics. The reason is, as previously mentioned, that information on parents is only available for persons born since 1950. Married couples with a relatively large difference in age are therefore less likely to be included in the sample used. In most cases, the husband is older than the wife. The most common difference in age is that the man is one year older than the woman. This applies in almost three-quarters of all cases. It also appears that, for almost three-quarters of the cases, the difference in age is under five years. For 23 per cent of the married couples, the husband is more than five years older than the woman, while there are only a few cases where the woman is more than five years older than the man.

Information from the previously mentioned study of parents of new-born children shows that the distribution of difference in age between the parents is similar to the above mentioned distribution. This implies that, despite the problems in selecting our data, it does not seem to have any significant influence on the distribution with respect to difference in age between the two spouses (Christoffersen 1997).

It is difficult to make a direct comparison with the published official statistics. These statistics use five-year age intervals for women as well as men. But it appears that for first marriages (for both partners), about two-thirds of the women aged 25 to 29 are married to a man who is also classified in this age group (Danmarks Statistik 1997*b*).

Education: There is a relatively close relationship between the educational level of the woman and the husband when marrying. For example, men with over thirteen years of education marry, more frequently than expected from an equal distribution, a woman with a corresponding level of education. The proportion of women at this educational level is double what would be expected. Other Danish surveys have provided similar results (Hansen 1995; Christoffersen 1997). Furthermore, there are just as many cases where the man has a longer education than the woman (measured in months) as the reverse. For nearly one-sixth of the couples, the two partners have precisely the same length of education. In the previously mentioned study conducted by the Danish National Institute of Social Research, it appears that men have, generally speaking, a longer vocational education than women. It should be noted that in this analysis we use the total length of education, including schooling, which may explain the different results.

Socio-economic status: A classification of women and their husbands according to their socio-economic status in the first year of their marriage provides a more diverse picture than the classification by education. But here too the patterns are quite distinct. For example, there is a greater propensity for a man who is a salaried employee to be married to a woman who is also a salaried employee. Similarly, the propensity is more than twice as great for a man who is unemployed at the end of November to be married to a woman who is also unemployed at that time.

Unemployment: Looking at the overall unemployment rate over the year in which the couple is married, there is also in this case a positive correlation between unemployment among the woman and the husband.

Income: In the year in which the couple married there is a positive correlation between gross income for the woman and the man. However, it is more common that the man has a higher income than the woman. This applies to 80 per cent of the couples.

There is, generally speaking, a relatively high degree of homogamy between Danish spouses and their fathers. This can in part be explained by the fact that many young people meet each other in the course of education and training.

Models for Married Women's Labour Supply

Women's status in relation to the labour market describes the situation in the last week of November each year. It has been categorized as follows:[1]

---

[1] To establish this classification, several types of registry data have been used. Information from tax registers is used to find those who are employed at this time. The distinction between full-time and part-time participation is mainly based on information regarding the kind of insurance category in the unemployment system. If the person is not insured against unemployment, then the categorization is made by using information on the amount of payments into the supplementary pension scheme. The payments depend on the number of hours worked per week. Persons who are self-employed or assisting spouses are categorized as working full-time. The unemployed women are found by using information from a register on unemployment on a weekly basis. If a person is to be classified as 'unemployed', this person has to be unemployed during the relevant week in November.

- full-time participation
- part-time participation (under 30 hours (27 hours from 1988) and not in educational system)
- unemployed
- in educational system (students)
- outside the labour force (housewives, early retirement scheme, pensioners)

This classification differs from the one usually used because people who work part-time and are in full-time education are considered to be students.

Our main interest is to evaluate the influence of different covariates on transitions between these states. To this end, we use transition rate models, but the analysis will be based on two simplifications. First, since we only have data for a specific point in time in each year, we proceed on a discrete time basis. Second, since we only have observations for a short period, we will not take duration dependence into account. Based on these simplifications, we use a discrete time logistic transition rate model (Allison 1982).

Table 11.1 shows the baseline transition rates without any covariates. It can be seen from the table that several transitions have a relatively high probability. However, for some of the transitions, the number of cases are so few that it is not possible to conduct a reasonable analysis.

Table 11.1. Characteristics of various transitions for married women

Origin state	Destination state	Episodes	Coefficient	Rate
Full-time employment	Part-time employment	123	−4.4593	0.011
	Unemployed	609	−2.8128	0.057
	Student	43	−5.5177	0.004
	Out of labour force	177	−4.0902	0.016
Part-time employment	Full-time employment	127	−1.5359	0.177
	Unemployed	26	−3.2800	0.036
	Student	8	−4.4844	0.011
	Out of labour force	34	−3.0001	0.047
Unemployed	Full-time employment	552	−0.5366	0.369
	Part-time employment	29	−3.9237	0.019
	Student	14	−4.6621	0.009
	Out of labour force	238	−1.6650	0.159
Student	Full-time employment	128	−1.1141	0.247
	Part-time employment	13	−3.6596	0.025
	Unemployed	18	−3.3242	0.035
	Out of labour force	19	−3.2682	0.037
Out of labour force	Full-time	181	−1.4256	0.194
	Part-time	35	−3.2459	0.037
	Unemployed	91	−2.2261	0.097
	Student	15	−4.1152	0.016

Transitions from Full-Time Employment

Full-Time to Part-Time Employment

In the first model in Table 11.2, information on the educational level of the woman's father and of the women herself are used. The educational level of the father appears to be of no significance but the women's own education is of significance for transitions to working part-time in that better educated women work part-time, to a lesser degree. However, if information on the woman's own income is used as in model 2, the woman's education is of no significance, and women with a higher income are less likely to switch from full-time to part-time employment. However, it is of no importance in itself whether the woman is a white-collar worker or a blue-collar worker. As far as the importance of the woman's age is concerned, it appears that with increasing age the propensity to change to part-time work diminishes. The lower propensity for slightly older women to shift from working full-time to part-time is a general feature that also applies to the transition into unemployment and out of the labour force.

It is surprising that children in the family are of no major importance. This could be explained by the fact that a large proportion of children are looked after in kindergartens, where it is common for children to spend most of the day. The economic conditions in families with infants can also imply that it is difficult for women to work part-time and thereby see a reduction in the family's income.

In the last model, information is also included on husbands and their fathers. It appears that neither the husband's educational level nor income have an impact on the propensity for women to work part-time. It is interesting to note that the husband's income has no impact, and there are other Danish survey results which show similar tendencies. From an analysis conducted by the Ministry of Economic Affairs of the labour supply of women, it

Table 11.2. Transitions for married women working full-time

	Model 1	Model 2	Model 3	Model 4
From full-time employment to part-time employment				
Constant	−4.3586*	−3.8476*	−3.8430*	−3.7654*
Education of woman's father: long	0.3592	0.3848*	0.3813*	0.3564
Woman's education: 12–13 years	−0.3971	−0.2957	−0.2869	−0.3300
Woman's education: 13+ years	−0.5861*	−0.3581	−0.2390	−0.3520
White-collar worker		0.0225	0.0570	0.0122
Gross income: middle		−0.8700*	−0.7545*	−0.7626*
Gross income: high		−1.4413*	−1.1640	−1.2543
Age: 25–9 years			−0.2851	−0.3600
Age: 30+ years			−0.7255*	−0.8477*
Children 0–6 years			0.2813	0.2881

	Model 1	Model 2	Model 3	Model 4
Children 7–17 years			0.0358	0.0515
Husband's education: 12–13 years				0.2197
Husband's education: 13+ years				0.3175
Husband's gross income: middle				−0.2267
Husband's gross income: high				0.1220
Husband unemployed				−0.6244*
Education of husband's father: long				0.0666
From full-time employment to unemployed				
Constant	−2.2019*	−1.5859*	−1.6215*	−1.4907*
Education of woman's father: long	−0.1952*	−0.1405	−0.1510	−0.1285
Woman's education: 12–13 years	−0.5971*	−0.3853*	−0.3727*	−0.3374*
Woman's education: 13+ years	−1.3479*	−0.9582*	−0.7582*	−0.6300*
White-collar worker		−0.4247*	−0.3644*	−0.2921*
Gross income: middle		−0.7154*	−0.5215*	−0.4797*
Gross income: high		−1.7100*	−1.2029*	−1.1318*
Age: 25–9 years			−0.4976*	−0.4470*
Age: 30+ years			−1.3161*	−1.2357*
Children 0–6 years			0.5458*	0.5790*
Children 7–17 years			−0.0387	−0.0594
Husband's education: 12–13 years				−0.2186*
Husband's education: 13+ years				−0.5623*
Husband's gross income: middle				−0.2383*
Husband's gross income: high				−0.0640
Husband unemployed				0.2150*
Education of husband's father: long				−0.0823
From full-time employment to out of labour force				
Constant	−3.5188*	−2.6844*	−2.9231*	−2.7730*
Education of woman's father: long	−0.2011	−0.1252	−0.1240	−0.1016
Woman's education: 12–13 years	−0.6450*	−0.2479	−0.2249	−0.1772
Woman's education: 13+ years	−0.9363*	−0.2454	−0.1164	−0.0020
White-collar worker		−0.9251*	−0.8763*	−0.8123*
Gross income: middle		−0.9096*	−0.7715*	−0.7426*
Gross income: high		−1.6026*	−1.2457	−1.2179
Age: 25–9 years			−0.4038*	−0.3674
Age: 30+ years			−0.8661*	−0.8230*
Children 0–6 years			0.6867*	0.7168*
Children 7–17 years			−0.0571	−0.0761
Husband's education: 12–13 years				−0.2647
Husband's education: 13+ years				−0.5014*
Husband's gross income: middle				−0.1708
Husband's gross income: high				0.0924
Husband unemployed				0.1884
Education of husband's father: long				−0.1571

* significant at 5% level.

appears that women in the higher income brackets are not inclined to work part-time. Furthermore, it also appears that the husband's income has no impact on whether the woman works part-time or not (Ministry of Economic Affairs 1991). In a panel study of labour supply and taxes in Denmark, married couples were monitored over the 1980–6 period. It appears that the number of hours which the spouses worked were positively correlated (Smith 1995). In other words, three different surveys conducted in Denmark all show that women who are married to a man with a relatively high income do not work fewer hours than other women.

Model 4 also includes information on whether the husband has experienced unemployment during the year. This diminishes the propensity for the transition from full-time to part-time work. This means that women whose husbands have been unemployed for a shorter or longer period do not decide to work part-time. Based on the assumption that the family's income has to be secured, this seems to be a reasonable result. The previously mentioned analysis of the labour supply among married couples from 1980 to 1986 shows a similar trend. Women with a husband who has been unemployed work more than other women (Smith 1995).

Information on the level of education for the husband's father seems to have no impact on the married women's transition to working part-time.

Full-Time to Unemployment

The first model analyses the impact of education of the woman's father (Table 11.2). This appears to be of statistical significance, implying that women whose fathers have more education have a smaller risk of becoming unemployed. There is a positive correlation between educational level of the woman and her father, and it appears in the following model that the woman's own education is also of importance for the risk of becoming unemployed. Women with more education run the lowest risk of becoming unemployed. Also women's occupational status and own income are related to the unemployment risk. Women who are blue-collar workers have a greater risk of becoming unemployed, and this risk is higher if the woman has had a lower income.

If there are infants 0–6 years old in the family, the woman runs a greater risk of becoming unemployed, but there is no effect from children aged 7–17 years. The fact that women with small children run a greater risk of becoming unemployed is not a new result for Denmark (Christoffersen 1997; Smith 1995). Other results from Denmark show that among the younger age groups without children, women and men have almost the same risk of being unemployed. However, looking at unemployment among women with children it is slightly higher than for women without children. The opposite applies to men, as men with children account for the lowest unemployment rate (Ministry of Economic Affairs 1994). There may be several explanations for this. A survey has shown that nearly 10 per cent of the women were dismissed in connection with giving birth (Christoffersen 1990). This is surprising since it is illegal for an employer to fire a woman because she is pregnant or has recently given birth. It might partly be explained by difficulties in finding day-care facilities for the child.

Model 4 includes information on the husband and the woman's father, and it appears that women who are married to a husband with longer education have a lower risk of becoming unemployed. In this instance the man's income is not of any significance. Finally, it appears that the woman's risk of becoming unemployed also depends on whether the husband was unemployed during the year. By contrast, the educational level of the husband's father is not related to the risk of becoming unemployed.

Full-Time to Out of Labour Force

This transition concerns women who shift from full-time work to out of the labour force (Table 11.2). This is not related to the educational level of the woman's father; however, the woman's own education is of importance, as women who have spent longer in education are less likely to leave the labour force.

It appears that, if information on woman's occupation and income, as in model 2, is included, then the effect of the woman's educational level disappears. It can be seen that women who are employed in what must be assumed to be good jobs—salaried employees and women with jobs in the higher income brackets—have a lower propensity to leave the labour force. Having children in the family aged 0–6 years is also related to the propensity for this transition, as women who have children at that age are also more likely to leave the labour force. However, this does not apply to those with children aged 7–17 years.

The characteristics of the husband appear to have an impact, implying that for men who have spent longer time in education the propensity for the wives to leave the labour market is lower than for other wives. The other items of information on the husband concern unemployment during the year, and income and information on the educational level of the husband's father is not related to the propensity to leave the labour force. This implies that there are no indications that husband's income is related to the propensity to leave the labour market. It is rather the cultural aspect which is of significance, as the educational level of the husband is related to this transition.

The Transition from Part-Time Employment

Part-Time to Full-Time Employment

For women who are working part-time, we concentrate on transitions to full-time work since the number of transitions to the other destinations are low. In this transition, neither the educational level of the woman's father nor of the woman's educational level have any significant influence (Table 11.3). In model 3 one sees that age has the effect of making the probability of a transition to full-time work less likely. In model 4 it can be seen that having children has a negative effect in going from part-time to full-time work. At the same time, the effect of age is somewhat smaller. Having children might be a confounding influence here, since it is so closely related to age. The introduction of variables for the husband does not improve the results and these are therefore not presented.

Table 11.3. Transitions for married women working part-time to full-time employment

	Model 1	Model 2	Model 3	Model 4
Constant	−1.6094*	−1.4971*	−1.0474*	−0.6831*
Education of woman's father: long	0.1260	0.1346	0.1362	0.0515
Woman's education: 12–13 years		−0.1885	−0.0122	−0.0214
Woman's education: 13+ years		−0.2632	0.1209	0.1017
Age: 25–9 years			−0.6218*	−0.4281
Age: 30+ years			−1.0448*	−0.5712
Children 0–6 years				−0.5691*
Children 7–17 years				−0.6413

* significant at 5% level.

Transitions from Out of the Labour Market

Out of the Labour Market to Full-Time Employment

For women who are out of the labour market we will concentrate on transitions to full-time employment. The other transitions are either few, or for transitions to unemployment specific rules have to be followed. In Table 11.4,

Table 11.4. Transitions for married women out of the labour market to full-time employment

	Model 1	Model 2	Model 3	Model 4
Constant	−1.4911*	−1.6985*	−1.4695*	−1.6489*
Education of woman's father: long	0.1434	0.1130	0.1370	0.1012
Woman's education: 12–13 years		0.3090	0.3233	0.2389
Woman's education: 13+ years		0.8004*	0.9941*	0.8323*
Age: 25–9 years			−0.2262	−0.1390
Age: 30+ years			−0.8109*	−0.4611
Children 0–6 years				0.2931
Children 7–17 years				−1.1236*

* significant at 5% level.

model 2, one can see that women who have a higher level of education have a higher probability of getting a full-time job. Once again, with higher age the likelihood of starting full-time employment decreases. Having a child aged 7–17 years also decreases the probability of going into full-time work.

Conclusions

This analysis of married women's status in the labour market shows that women are quite independent of their own family when they marry. A considerable proportion have lived in a consensual union and some have even had their first child before getting married. Moreover, most women were already in the labour market and the majority were working full-time.

With respect to homogamy, it can be noted that there is a positive correlation between education and income of the fathers of the spouses. Also, information on the spouses points to homogamy in age, education, socio-economic status, and income.

In the detailed transition models, social origin of the couples is not related to the propensity to shift. Nor does the employment situation of the husband have a great influence on the labour supply of women. It is only for women working full-time that husband's unemployment experience decreases the rate of women's shifts to part-time work, and increases the risk of becoming unemployed. Furthermore, the husband's educational level has an impact. Women married to better educated husbands have a lower risk of becoming unemployed and leaving the labour force. It turns out that the husband's income is not related to any of the transitions which we have analysed.

The educational level is of significance in connection with the woman's transition from full-time work to unemployment. Also, women who are either unemployed or out of the labour force have a higher probability of going into full-time work if they have a higher educational level. Concerning their own income, women in higher paying jobs do not shift from full-time to part-time work, and they have a lower probability of becoming unemployed or leaving the labour market.

If there are infants in the family, this has an impact on the women's risk of becoming unemployed and leaving the labour market, but not on the propensity to shift to working part-time. Women working part-time with small children are less likely to return to full-time work. Also, women who are unemployed have a higher probability of returning to full-time work.

It seems reasonable to conclude that, for married women in Denmark, the situation of the husband has a relatively low significance in explaining the transitions of women in the labour market. We see a sharing of roles and a corresponding low degree of dependence between the spouses. When there is an effect, it points to the direction also observed in Sweden (Chapter 10) or Hungary (Chapter 13): husband's occupational resources reduce the risk of leaving full-time employment.

The characteristics of the women themselves, however, have a greater explanatory power concerning employment transitions: Among the significant variables, one could mention the educational level and income of the women. Women who have better jobs do not stop working full-time.

References

Allison, P. D. (1982). 'Discrete-Time Methods for the Analysis of Event Histories', in S. Leinhardt (ed.), *Sociological Methodology* (San Fransisco: Jossy-Bass).

Blossfeld, H.-P., and C. Hakim (eds.) (1997). *Between Equalization and Marginalization: Part-Time Working Women in Europe and the United States* (Oxford: Oxford University Press).

——and J. Huinink (1991). 'Human Capital Investment or Norms of Role Transition? How Women's Schooling and Career Affect the Process of Family Formation', *American Journal of Sociology*, 97: 143–68.

Bonke, J. (ed.) (1997). *Levevilkår i Danmark: Statistisk oversigt 1997* (Life Conditions in Denmark. Statistical Overview 1997) (Copenhagen: Danmarks Statistik).

Christoffersen, M. Nygaard (1990). *Barselsorlov: Mænd og kvinders erhvervsmæssige baggrund for at tage orlov* (Parental Leave: The Employment Background of Men and Women Taking Leave) (Rapport 90/18; Copenhagen: Socialforskningsinstituttet).

——(1993). *Familiens ændring* (Changes to the Family) (Rapport 93/2; Copenhagen: Socialforskningsinstituttet).

——(1997). *Spædbørnsfamilien* (Families with Small Children) (Rapport 97/25; Copenhagen: Socialforskningsinstituttet).

Danmarks Statistik (1991). *IDA—en integreret database for arbejdsmarkedsforskning, Hovedrapport* (An Integrated Database for Labour Market Research) (Copenhagen: Danmarks Statistik).

——(1992). *Levevilkår i Danmark: Statistisk oversigt 1992* (Life Conditions in Denmark: Statistical Overview 1992) (Copenhagen: Danmarks Statistik).

——(1993). *Befolkningens bevægelser 1991* (Population Development 1991) (Copenhagen: Danmarks Statistik).

——(1995). *Befolkningens bevægelser 1993* (Population Development 1993) (Copenhagen: Danmarks Statistik).

——(1997a). *Befolkningens bevægelser 1995* (Population Development 1995) (Danmarks Statistik.

——(1997b). 'Den sociale ressourceundersøgelser januar 1996' (The Social Resources Audit, January 1996), *Social sikring og retsvæsen*, 1997/5.

Hansen, E. J. (1995). *En generation blev voksen: Den første velfærdsgeneration* (A Generation has Grown Up: The First Welfare-State Generation) (Rapport 95/8; (Copenhagen: Socialforskningsinstituttet).

Knudsen, L. B. (1993). *Fertility Trends in Denmark in the 1980s* (Statistiske Undersøgelser, 44; (Copenhagen: Danmarks Statistik).

Leth-Sørensen, S. (1997). 'IDA-databasen—en forskningsdatabase i Danmarks Statistik' (A Research Database in Danmarks Statistik), *Samfundsøkonomen*, 1997/4.

Ministry of Economic Affairs (1991). *Lovmodel* (The Law Model).

——(1994). *Kvinder i økonomien* (Women in the Economy).

Smith, N. (1995). 'A Panel Study of Labour Supply and Taxes in Denmark', *Applied Economics*, 27: 419–29.

APPENDIX TO CHAPTER 11: LIST OF VARIABLES USED
FROM THE IDA DATABASE

Legal status of women (at the end of the year):
  Unmarried
  Married
  Divorced
  Widowed
  Other
Status in family (at the end of the year):
  Alone (not with partner)
  Cohabiting
  Living with spouse
  Other

Covariates

Completed education

Length of education measured in months.

From the Educational Classification Module at Statistics Denmark, information is available on the highest level of education attained or completed, vocational training, and education in progress. For those who have not completed vocational training, the level of general education is used. According to the level of attained education, information is available concerning the time duration normally require to complete this education. We have classified this information into the following categories:

Woman's and husband's education (%)

	Woman	Husband
up to 12 years of education (including general education)	32	28
12–13 years	46	48
13+ years	22	24

Socio-economic status of woman

  self-employed
  assisting spouse
  white-collar worker
  skilled blue-collar worker
  unskilled blue-collar worker
  other employed
  unemployed
  out of the labour force

two categories: white-collar worker (58 per cent), reference: other categories (42 per cent).

Gross income

Women's incomes in Danish kroner. The amount is deflated.

Low income: < 74999	34 per cent
Middle income: 75000–149999	63 per cent
High income: > 150000	3 per cent

Husbands' incomes:

Low income: <109999	37 per cent
Middle income: 110000–149999	39 per cent
High income: > 150000	24 per cent

Reference: low gross income.

Age of woman

up to 24 years	21 per cent
25–29 years	48 per cent
30+ years	31 per cent

Reference: young (up to 24 years).

Degree of unemployment in year

0–1000, 1000 indicates unemployed during the whole year. For persons 16–66 years.

Husband unemployed:

Husband has experienced unemployment during the year	(20 per cent)
Reference: husband not unemployed	(80 per cent)

For women: number of children

Children in the family 0–6 years:

No children	(30 per cent)
Children 0–6 years	(70 per cent)

Children in the family 7–17 years:

No children	(88 per cent)
Children 7–17 years	(12 per cent)

Reference: no children in age group.

Completed education (fathers)

Length of education measured in months. Information on the educational level of the fathers of the women and their husbands is also available. We used the level for the fathers in 1980, and for this group we treat the information as being independent of time.

Completed education	Woman's father	Husband's father
Short: up to 12 years	46 per cent	50 per cent
Long: 12 years or more	54 per cent	50 per cent

VI

The (Former) 'State-Socialist' Regime

12

Employment Patterns of Married Women in Poland

SONJA DROBNIČ AND EWA FRĄTCZAK

Introduction

NEW household economics (Becker 1993; Cigno 1991) draws attention to the fact that an individual's allocation of time to the market and unpaid work in the home can be best understood within the context of the family, taking the interdependence of family members into account. A core feature of this model is that spouses tend to specialize within the marriage because specialization is the most efficient productive strategy and maximizes the utility for the household as a whole. The economic theory of the family predicts that specialization of a husband and a wife towards either market or unpaid household work will follow the principle of comparative or relative efficiency. It does not *per se* assign the housework to women since differences in efficiency are not determined by biological differences. The person who has more marketable skills, higher productivity, and higher earnings capacity will specialize in paid work; the other partner's main responsibility will be the maintenance of the home and childrearing.

The economic approach to the family is based on assumptions of utility maximization, stable preferences, and equilibrium in the markets. Markets can be implicit, as in the case of marriage markets, or explicit, such as product and labour markets in the so-called market economies. However, former socialist economies that were based on a central planning system denied market regulations in the sphere of labour. Employment in former socialist countries was defined as a state-guaranteed social right and not as an outcome of market forces. Therefore, a question emerges: To what extent can the basic assumptions of the economic theories of the family be applied to economies under non-market regulations? Poland had a centrally planned economy for over forty years and is a good example for testing these assumptions in a non-market system. The objective of this chapter is to examine how the employment behaviour of married women in Poland was affected by the characteristics of their households, such as the number and ages of children, and education and social origin of their husbands. Also, the question concerning the degree of marriage homogamy and changes in women's employment patterns across marriage cohorts will be addressed.

The empirical analysis is based on the Polish Family and Fertility Survey 1991 (PFFS).[1] These data were collected during the initial phases of the transformation to a market economy. Since the PFFS is a retrospective survey, data refer to the pre-transition period to a large extent. Since not much is usually known about the family and employment regulations in former socialist countries, we will briefly address some of the issues that were specific in these countries—and in Poland in particular—before proceeding with our analysis.

Labour-Force Participation in Non-Market Economies

Full employment was one the essential concepts and objectives of state socialism and an important factor of legitimization (Ferge 1992; Drobnič 1997). Under the conditions of central planning, the state was a major employer; the demand for labour was high and a chronic shortage of workers was a permanent concern. Demand as a rule exceeded the labour supply, and open unemployment was negligible.[2]

The aggregate level of prime-age labour-force participation in Central and East European countries was much higher than that in Western Europe. The difference in participation rates mainly resulted from a high female labour-force participation, with women accounting for on average 45–51 per cent of the total labour force at the end of the 1980s (Einhorn 1993). Also, women typically worked full-time; part-time employment was not usually considered a means of reconciling employment and household responsibilities (Drobnič 1997). In general, two full-time work wages were necessary to fulfil basic household needs.

When comparing former socialist countries with Western Europe, the differences in female participation rates were particularly evident in childbearing and childrearing stages of women's lives. Employment of married women and mothers with young children was much more common in Central and East European countries (Jackman and Rutkowski 1994). Women were generally encouraged—and even obligated—to work in labour-intensive and low-productivity economies. Incentives for female employment were present on both the supply and demand sides of the labour market. Due to a low wage level and the official ideology which emphasized the role of work in gender equality and emancipation, there was a strong financial and ideological pressure on women to enter paid employment. Legal and institutional regulations

---

[1] The Polish Family and Fertility Survey was conducted in 1991 under the project undertaken by the Population Activities Unit of the United Nations Economic Commission for Europe (UN/ECE) (Holzer and Kowalska 1997).

[2] For illustration, there were 86 registered vacancies for every job seeker in Poland in 1988 (Socha and Sztanderska 1991).

facilitated female labour-force participation through generous maternity and childcare benefits. The state as well as large work organizations provided various services and benefits, such as subsidized childcare facilities. Non-participation in formal paid employment could lead not only to economic hardship but also to social deprivation and marginalization.

Siemieńska (1997: 65) distinguishes two routes of women's integration into the labour force after the Second World War: through 'outwardly controlled' mechanisms, characteristic of the countries in Eastern and Central Europe, and 'inwardly controlled' ones, which are more descriptive of the situation in Western European countries. Although neither of them appeared in a pure form, their importance differs for former socialist and capitalist countries. The West European model more often reflected changes in the professional consciousness of women, which gave them an incentive to search for jobs outside their families and households. The characteristic shift of women in Central and East European countries towards paid employment was to a large extent a result of an outside pressure on women and their families from authorities who controlled the distribution of economic goods. In centrally planned economies with their extensive production, low productivity, and low wages, the breadwinner model, with the male as a sole provider for the family, was not economically feasible (Kotowska 1997: 85).

Under such circumstances, are the assumptions of the economic theory of the family viable? To be able to better understand the context within which couples' employment patterns in Poland are analysed, we give a short overview of the Polish labour market, household characteristics, and family policies.

The Labour Market in Poland

Under the central planning system, post-war Poland went through rapid reconstruction and industrialization processes. These resulted in high labour-force participation rates for both men and women. Female labour-force participation in post-war Poland was about 15 percentage points above the average of Western countries, yet slightly below the average of the states in the former communist bloc (Puhani 1995). Women typically worked full-time. Part-time employment, which is in many West European countries closely associated with women's employment and the family life cycle, was not widespread among Polish women. Rather, it was popular among men who held a second job or amongst pensioners who took a part-time job after early retirement (Drobnič 1995, 1997).

It has been argued that Poland is quite traditional with respect to normative expectations about male and female roles. Since a great majority of women see family life as the most important sphere of their lives, and the prestige assigned to women is based largely on an evaluation of their traditional roles, it is mainly an economic motivation that pushes many women to work. Low male wages coupled with a high (by Western standards) number of children in the household produced the high labour-force participation rate of Polish women (Mach *et al.* 1994: 8).

However, there have been important variations in employment levels over historical periods and across individuals' life cycles. Figure 12.1 shows cross-sectional employment rates for women in different age groups in the 1960–95 period.[3] In the first two decades after the Second World War, the pattern of labour-market participation can be illustrated by an M-shaped curve, with a dip in labour-force participation at ages 25–34. Such a shape across the life course is commonly attributed to the responsibility of childrearing (Teachman *et al.* 1987). However, already in the 1960s, a rapid growth in the prime-age female employment rate was observed; this generated a new profile of employment across the life course, with increasing participation up to the age group 40–4.

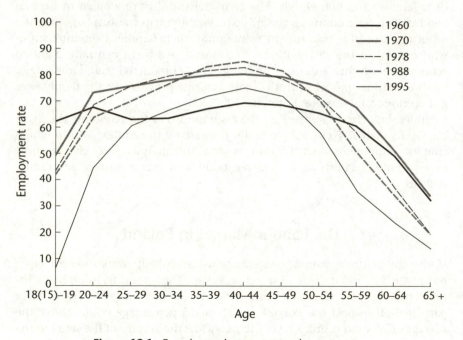

Figure 12.1. Female employment rates, by age groups

Source: 1960–1988 National Census (economic activity rate), youngest age group 18–19: Micro Census (employment rate), youngest age group 15–19.

During the post-Second-World-War decades, only the youngest (women under age 20) and the oldest age groups (over 50) experienced a decline in their employment level (Figure 12.1). For young women, this decline was associated

---

[3] In the past, the term 'economically active population' was used in Polish employment statistics. Since unemployment was non-existent, the economically active population basically corresponded to the 'labour-force participation' rate. Since 1990, with the eruption of unemployment, the labour-force participation rate and employment rate have been diverging.

with extended schooling and was partly due to the introduction of maternity leave and family allowances. A decrease in the economic activity of women aged 50 and over was attributed to a deterioration of health (increased number of disabled persons) and to the introduction of new legal regulations for early retirement.

In the 1980s, the employment rate started to decline. This tendency accelerated in the 1990s at the onset of economic transition. Male employment also declined considerably (Figure 12.2). As a result of the collapse of communism

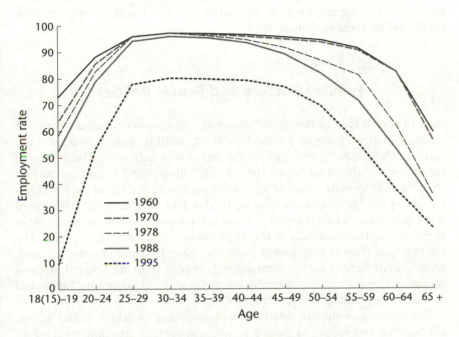

Figure 12.2. Male employment rates, by age groups

Source: 1960–1988 National Census (economic activity rate), youngest age group 18–19: Micro Census (employment rate), youngest age group 15–19.

and the reforms associated with the transition to a market economy, Poland has been experiencing a large-scale social and economic upheaval. Starting in 1990 and 1991, the first round of economic reforms took place, resulting in the deterioration of living conditions of large parts of the population. The most serious problem in Polish labour-market transition is unemployment.

In the past, full employment did not imply full and efficient allocation and use of human resources. Firms used manpower inefficiently and maintained too many and often overqualified workers. Labour hoarding was a common phenomenon while open unemployment was non-existent. In the first officially published statistics on unemployment in January 1990, the unemployment rate was 0.3 per cent. After that, unemployment grew dramatically and reached its peak in mid-1994; at this time, about three million people were unemployed and the unemployment rate amounted to 16 per cent. In the following years, unemployment declined and levelled off at about 10 per cent.

Besides large geographical variations, one of the characteristics of unemployment in Poland, gender differences are significant. Labour shedding has been widespread in administrative units of large state-owned enterprises and in semi- or unskilled occupations in light industry, both marked by a high concentration of female workers. This contributed to an increasing share of women among the total registered unemployed. Moreover, once unemployed, chances of finding employment are particularly low for the young, less educated, and for females (Puhani 1995).

Family Structure and Family Policies

Over the last three decades, most European countries experienced significant changes in the sphere of family formation, fertility, family structure and divorce. This applies to Poland to a limited extent only. At the beginning of the 1990s, family formation in Poland still followed the traditional pattern characterized by early marriage and childbearing. At the age of 24, for example, seven out of ten women born in 1962–6 had married and two-thirds of them had born a child. Consensual unions are rare and few women remain single. The attitudinal data of the PFFS confirm that marriage remains the fundamental form of partnership and is the basis for family formation. Also, single-parent families are less common in Poland than in most other European countries, due both to the relatively low frequency of extramarital births and to less divorce (Holzer and Kowalska 1997).

The Polish government has had no population or family policy *per se*, although various social and economic policies may have had important implications for women's participation in paid employment and family life. According to Holzer and Kowalska (1997), Polish women typically interrupted economic activity and devoted themselves to their families when they had their first child. If they decided to resume work later, it usually occurred when their youngest child started kindergarten.

Policies with respect to maternity leave have not changed radically in recent decades. Maternity leave was first introduced in 1924 in a rudimentary form. In 1948, its duration was set at twelve weeks. In the 1970s, it was extended to sixteen weeks with full pay at the time of the first birth, and eighteen weeks at second and subsequent births. This was supplemented by an unpaid childcare leave, introduced in 1968. Since 1981, childcare leave has been paid, dependent on family income and the number of children. However, the value of this child allowance has decreased considerably. It reached about 35 per cent of the average wage in 1981, but only 6 per cent in 1989. Also, the number of families receiving childcare allowances decreased during the transition period. At the same time, the number of families dependent on the welfare system increased considerably, from 0.8 million in 1989 to three million families in 1993. Currently, social policy is mainly oriented to poor, large-size families and the system is being continuously reformed to adjust to rapidly changing living conditions (Wiśniewska and Frątczak 1997).

The Household Division of Labour and Gender Gap in Earnings

When examining the allocation of time to market and household activities, time budget studies are helpful in describing the division of work on the aggregate level. Surveys of time budgets were conducted in Poland in 1984 and 1995, and summarized results of these studies are presented in Table 12.1. In 1984, women's time spent on *household activities* was 2.4 times longer than that of men; in 1996, the ratio decreased to 1.9. This means that men contribute about one-third of the total housework. When only time devoted to childcare is taken into account, discrepancies between men and women are relatively small. Among those who performed the given activities, the differences amounted to five hours per week in 1984 and two hours in 1996 to the disadvantage of women.

Over the period under study, changes which occurred in the time devoted to *market work* activities show that the average values changed slightly over time: they decreased somewhat for women and increased for men. Nevertheless, the total number of daily working hours in the market and household remains longer for women than men. Men's contribution to total family housework has increased over time; however, this is mostly the effect of a decline in women's time spent on household tasks rather than a substantial increase in men's involvement in household activities.

Despite some of the earliest equal pay legislation, the state socialist economies were characterized by a gender gap in incomes which was not very different from that in Western Europe. Women earned on average 66–75 per cent of men's salary across all branches of economic activity (Einhorn 1993). Although women were well represented in industry overall, they remained clustered in female-dominated light industrial production and in the clerical and administrative branches of both light and heavy industry.

Skilled workers in heavy industry and mining comprised the élite of these economies in terms of earning power. Due to occupational segregation, even women employed in the prioritized sectors of the economy earned a fraction of male wages. But most women were concentrated in lower status jobs within low-paid sectors of the economy. In Poland, women were over-represented in selected branches, such as education, services, and trade. These were typical areas with low wages as compared to male-dominated branches of the economy. Analyses by Kotowska (1996) show that the gender gap was higher for blue-collar than for white-collar workers in the 1980s; however, since 1991 this relation has

Table 12.1. Time use of women and men in selected activities

	Paid work		Unpaid household work				Physiological needs		Other activities	
			Total		Childcare					
	F	M	F	M	F	M	F	M	F	M
1984	6.21	7.12	5.09	7.12	2.06	2.10	10.18	10.15	2.52	4.63
1996	6.01	7.28	4.50	7.28	1.47	2.36	11.02	10.59	2.47	3.77

Source: Surveys of Time Budget, Central Statistical Office.

Notes: Hours per day, average time per person performing given activities.
In 1984, sample consisted of 21,600 households. In 1996, 1,000 households were interviewed, survey was conducted in co-operation with Eurostat. F - females, M = males.

been reversed for the highest wages. Gender differences for low-paid workers diminished over time, particularly for very low wages, but increased considerably for highly paid white-collar workers. During the first years of the transition, the following main changes in the wage distribution occurred in Poland: the rise in wage dispersion and inequality (particularly for white-collar workers), increasing returns to education, and the flattening of age-earnings profiles (Rutkowski 1995, 1997; Kotowska 1996). In light of the disadvantageous employment conditions for women in the transition period, it comes as no surprise that women experience barriers in pursuing professional careers; therefore, the gender gap in earnings is increasing for this group of women.

Hypotheses

Married women's employment patterns over the life course evolved within the economic and social context that we briefly presented above. It should be emphasized that we included some details on recent developments primarily for information purposes. The PFFS survey was conducted in 1991, at the initial stages of the transition period. Therefore, the retrospective data used in the analysis cover for the most part the period under the planned socialist economy.

The main aim of our analysis is to examine how the dynamics of women's employment behaviour over the life course varied with women's own characteristics and the characteristics of their households, such as the number and ages of children, and the education and social origin of their husbands. Also, we will examine whether there were additional discernible changes over historical time, as depicted by various marriage cohorts of Polish couples.

The increase in *educational attainment* of post-Second-World-War generations in Poland has been striking, particularly for women. The proportions of persons having a secondary- and especially tertiary-level education have sharply risen. Over the period 1960–95, the number of people who completed university or another type of programme at that level multiplied nearly four-fold for men and nearly eightfold for women (Holzer and Kowalska 1997). Higher education and qualifications raise employment aspirations, opportunities, and earning power. Due to specific rules of wage determination, it is indisputable that education in centrally planned economies was less of a straightforward indicator of the income level than in Western countries. Nevertheless, educational attainment did indicate a rough earnings hierarchy, as well as increased opportunities for a second job, particularly for highly qualified experts. The educational level also indicated a general 'cultural' capital and the social status of the family. We therefore expect that in Poland too the educational level of women will have an effect on women's participation in paid employment, with higher educated women having a higher probability of entering and remaining in the labour market.

Woman's *social origin* may have the opposite effect. It was the explicit policy in Poland to improve educational opportunities particularly for children in lower social strata. A large majority of people who themselves reached higher levels of education had parents with much lower educational attainment. Those whose fathers had higher levels of education were thus more likely to come from families which were better off already in the pre-Second-World-War period. Such families were more likely to transfer traditional 'bourgeois' values to their daughters, among them the legitimizing of the homemaking status for women.

Age will be included in our models to capture various life-course effects which have an influence on employment participation beyond the effects of schooling and family life cycle. Since such effects have often been found to have an inverse U-shape, this variable will be included in non-linear form. Also, *age at marriage* has proved to be an important determinant of subsequent employment patterns after controlling for other factors. Both in Germany (Blossfeld *et al.* 1998; see Chapter 3 above) and in the USA (Sørensen 1983), women who married late were more likely to follow the traditional pattern, leaving the labour force at the time of increased family responsibilities. The explanation for this would be that a woman who marries late is more likely to be in a situation where her family can afford her non-employment.

However, as argued by Sørensen (1983), the family-economy argument is only plausible if traditional sex roles dominate women's labour-force decisions. If career prospects, labour-force experience, and the quality of jobs also influence women's employment decisions after marriage, women who marry late should be least likely to leave the labour force. It is not immediately apparent which argument is more in tune with the Polish situation. On the one hand, the family-economy argument is supported by a general pressure on female employment due to economic necessity, and also due to the prevalence of traditional female role attitudes (Mach *et al.* 1994). But on the other hand, an early increase in employment participation of Polish women in the post-Second-World-War decades and their catching-up with men in terms of educational attainment might have 'modernized' women's attitudes towards pursuing careers and reversed the effect of the age at marriage.

Next, the duration of *work experience before marriage* will be included in the analysis. It is hypothesized that longer work experience leads to stronger attachment to the labour market and increases employment participation after marriage. To include an indicator of structural opportunities in the labour market, the *place of residence* will be included in the models. There are important differences between urban and rural areas in terms of labour-market conditions. However, towns are also more secularized than the rural countryside. To prevent religious values intermingling with the place of residence, *religion* will be explicitly included in our model estimations. Poland is a monolithically Catholic country with strong religious values and Church influence. We assume that more religious women, with regular church attendance, have more traditional family values and lower participation in paid employment.

The *age of the youngest child* is hypothesized to have a strong effect on women's employment patterns. The younger the children, the higher the demands on their mother's time and other resources, which influence the timing of labour-force participation and the number of hours that women can spend in paid work. We predict that pre-school children in particular will have a negative effect on women's employment. A higher *number of children* indicates the greater financial needs of large families on the one hand, also implying a greater need for the woman's income and higher employment participation. On the other hand, several children—particularly when all of them are young—require more time input and make the organization of family life more strenuous if both parents are employed. These two effects point in disparate directions and it is not clear which effect will prevail.

To test the propositions of the economic theory of the family that interpret the differences in the allocation of time between market and household production on the basis of comparative advantages between spouses, husbands' characteristics will be included in the analysis. *Husband's educational attainment* is an indicator of the level of his investment in marketable human capital and an indicator of family economy. It is then predicted to have a significant effect on the household's time allocation decisions. Husband's higher education will decrease wife's participation in paid employment. *Husband's social origin* is assumed to have the same effect as wife's social origin. The higher the husband's social origin, the lower the wife's labour-force participation.

Next, to assess the impact of social change over historical time, information on *marriage cohorts* will be included in the analysis. In most Western and Northern European countries there has been a gradual increase in women's employment participation over the last decades. In Central and East European countries, however, women were massively integrated into the labour market soon after the Second World War. Also, in Poland, the need for country-wide post-war reconstruction and an accelerated process of industrialization led to a high labour demand. The dominance of labour-intensive technologies, low productivity, and widespread overstaffing produced a general shortage of labour (Drobnič 1992, 1997; Mach *et al.* 1994). Under such economic conditions, coupled with the official ideology equating women's emancipation with employment, women were integrated into paid employment earlier and on a more massive scale than in Western countries. However, since couples in our sample are relatively young, the period of intensive integration of women into the labour force is not captured with our data.[4] Therefore, we do not expect an increase in employment participation over the cohorts. Rather, the opposite may be the case. After controlling for women's education and the characteristics of their households, the improved family standard of living and the easing of ideological pressure over time could lead to lower employment participation.

Finally, information on the type of employment will be included in the models. Since *part-time* employment was truly a marginal phenomenon, we expect it to have a more volatile character than the usual full-time employment. Therefore, we predict more movements into and out of part-time jobs. There is

---

[4] Only 3% of couples were married before 1965.

also information on other forms of work, consisting mostly of workers in agriculture, which was not collectivized by the communist regime. A large proportion of the Polish population is still rural and lives from small-scale agricultural production. We assume that this type of employment is very stable; women who are self-employed or helping family members on a family farm will have a high level of employment participation throughout their life course.

Data, Variables, Methods

The empirical analysis is based on data from the Polish Family and Fertility Survey (Frątczak *et al.* 1996). The PFFS was a retrospective longitudinal survey carried out in 1991 by the Institute of Statistics and Demography, Warsaw School of Economics (SGH), and the Central Statistical Office. The sample consisted of 4,313 households and 8,544 individuals living in selected dwelling units. Two separate instruments were used in the survey: a household questionnaire which supplied information on the family structure and household characteristics, and individual questionnaires covering all members of a household aged 18–49. This restricted age range reflected the main focus of the survey—namely, fertility issues. However, if in the case of couples one person was older than 49 years, this person was interviewed, too. This research design enabled us to identify and match married couples; 2,888 couples with valid information were identified in the dataset. Women served as a basis for matching.

For all individuals included in the study, information on a number of characteristics and processes in the life course was available, such as schooling history, educational level, parents' education, employment episodes, residential mobility, dwelling history, partnerships, and children. This allowed us to reconstruct employment and childbearing histories for the individuals. Event histories were collected on a monthly basis.

For the analyses presented here, we first reconstructed women's employment episodes, for which explicit information on starting and ending times was available. Employment episodes consisted of regular full-time work, part-time employment, and other forms of work. In the category 'other forms of work', agricultural workers prevailed (probably on their own farms), but also included were the self-employed and other minor categories of workers. Since full-time employment was the dominant form of employment, and part-time and other forms of work represented only a small share of employment spells, all three types of employment were combined and joined in a single 'employment' state. Information on type of employment arrangement was then coded as a dummy and used in the analysis to control potential differences in entry and exit rates.[5]

Next, inactivity episodes were created if gaps between employment episodes existed, if there was a gap between schooling and first employment, or if a per-

---

[5] From 1,521 exits out of employment, less than 4% pertain to part-time work or other forms of work. Out of 1,337 transitions into employment, 3% are into part-time employment and 7% into other forms of work.

son who completed her education had no employment spells (yet). Based on additional information, it was possible to identify three specific statuses: schooling, unemployment, and retirement. These spells were excluded from the analysis. The remaining residual spells were labelled 'non-employment'. Although no specific information on the status of 'housewife' is available in the data, the non-employment status is in our opinion a good proxy for a homemaking status. A large majority of women in this status primarily depend on their partners for support, and the reasons for inactivity most often given were childcare leave, care of family members, or own health problems.

Dependent variables in our analysis are thus transition rates between employment and non-employment statuses. The observation window 'opened' at the time of marriage. Independent variables are of two types: time-constant and time-varying variables which can change over the duration of marriage. To introduce time-varying covariates into the rate equation, we used the episode-splitting method (Blossfeld, *et al*. 1989). This means that for time-varying covariates, the values are not fixed at the beginning of the spell but can change within the duration of an employment/non-employment episode. An episode was split every time when a time-varying covariate changed its value. We also split each episode into yearly subspells to be able to include relevant information on age. We distinguish between different sets of independent variables: a woman's own characteristics and resources accumulated before she got married, characteristics of her husband, and the family characteristics that evolve within the course of marriage:

Wife's characteristics and resources which she brings into marriage:
- wife's social origin, measured by the educational level of her father
- wife's education
- wife's age in a linear and quadratic form, measured as a time-varying covariate
- wife's age at marriage
- wife's cumulative employment experience before marriage
- wife's place of residence, time-varying dummy variable (1 = town; 0 = village)
- wife's religiousness (1=religious or very religious and regular practising; 0=otherwise)

Childbearing history:
- number of children, time-dependent covariate
- age of the youngest child: pre-school, school or grown-up child, time-varying covariate

Partner's characteristics:
- husband's social origin, measured by the educational level of his father
- husband's education

Marriage cohorts, dummy variables:
- couples married before 1971
- married 1971–5
- married 1976–80

- married 1981–5
- married 1986–91.

Event-history analysis was used to analyse transition rates. This type of analysis is described in detail elsewhere (Blossfeld and Rohwer 1995; Blossfeld *et al.* 1989; Tuma and Hannan 1984; Allison 1984; Kalbfleisch and Prentice 1980; Yamaguchi 1991). The dependent variable is the instantaneous rate of change from one state, j, to another state k. It is defined as:

$$r_{jk}(t) = \left(\lim_{\Delta t \to 0} \frac{1}{\Delta t} P_{jk} \right) \left(t \leq T < t + \Delta t \,|\, t \leq T \right), j \neq k$$

where r_{jk} is the instantaneous probability of having an event in a certain time interval [t, t + Δt], conditional on having had no event until t. Parameters in the models are estimated by using a maximum likelihood estimation which permits censored events to be included in the analysis. To estimate the transition rates, we used a piecewise constant model, a modification of a standard exponential model which can take into account the time-dependence in the process under consideration (Blossfeld and Rohwer 1995; Rohwer and Pötter 1998). This type of modelling is very flexible, allowing the baseline hazard rate to vary within the duration of a spell without having to specify the exact hazard rate path. The basic idea of the model is to split the time axis into time intervals and to assume that the transition rate is constant within the intervals but can change between them.

Results

Educational Marriage Homogamy

Before we present the estimation results, we briefly examine the level of educational homogamy among Polish spouses. According to the economic theory of the family, educational attainment as an indicator of the level of individual's investment into marketable human capital affects the household's time allocation decisions. Educational levels considered in the analysis are: (1) incomplete primary education, (2) primary education, (3) basic vocational, (4) secondary general, (5) secondary professional, (6) post-secondary, (7) university or other higher education, (8) postgraduate level. Information refers to the highest completed educational level at the time of interview.

Figure 12.3 shows the difference between husbands' and wives' educational levels. There is a strong prevalence of homogamous marriages with no or small differences in educational levels. In almost half of all couples, both partners have exactly the same level of education. Marriages in which partners differ considerably in their educational attainment—where, for example, one partner surpasses the other by three or more educational levels—are not common. However, when they do occur, such constellations exist for both men and women. In effect, there are somewhat more cases where women have considerably higher educational resources than their husbands.

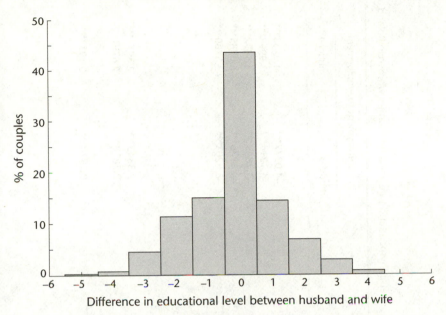

Figure 12.3. Educational homogamy among married couples

Transition from Employment to Non-Employment

Table 12.2 shows the 'initial' status of wives at the time of marriage across cohorts. In the oldest marriage cohort, every fifth woman was non-employed at the time of marriage. As explained earlier, there are strong indications that this corresponds to the housekeeping status. Since the 1970s, the proportion of women in this status has declined and the proportion of employed women has increased to over 80 per cent. This makes employment a natural starting-point for the analysis of transitions in employment states of married women.

Table 12.3 presents the estimated effects on the hazard rate of employment exits. In model 1, employment duration, type of employment, and women's own characteristics are included in the analysis. Piecewise constant rate models

Table 12.2. Women's employment status at the time of marriage, for various marriage cohorts (%)

	Married before 1971	Married 1971–5	Married 1976–80	Married 1981–5	Married 1986–91
Employed	74.1	80.0	83.6	85.1	82.3
Non-empl.	20.5	13.4	10.6	9.2	12.5
Other[a]	5.4	6.6	5.8	5.7	5.2
N	425	425	482	424	552

[a] Other statuses: in school, unemployed, retired.

Table 12.3. Parameter estimates for rate models of transitions from employment to non- employment and vice versa for married women in Poland

	Employment to non-employment		Non-employment to employment	
	model 1	model 2	model 3	model 4
Episode duration				
< 6 months	-2.8907***	-2.7402***	-4.0277***	-4.0733***
6–12 months	-2.0316***	-1.9307***	-4.1214***	-3.9998***
1–3 years	-2.0570***	-2.0158***	-3.7849***	-3.5892***
3–5 years	-2.6204***	-2.5668***	-3.3176***	-3.0885***
> 5 years	-2.6469***	-2.5026***	-3.8201***	-3.5780***
Leaving:				
part-time empl.	-0.1009	-0.1803		
Other forms of work	-2.1886***	-2.1846***		
(ref.= full-time empl.)				
Entering				
part-time empl.			2.3343***	2.3977***
other forms of work			2.7818***	2.6791***
(ref.= full-time empl.)				
W's education	-0.1112***	-0.1316***	0.1978***	0.1913***

W's father's educ.	0.0913***	−0.0291	−0.0311
Age	−0.2789***	−0.0683*	0.0099
Age sq.	0.0021***	0.0011*	0.0004
Age at marriage	0.1651***	−0.0192	−0.0510***
Work experience before marriage	−0.0047***	−0.0017	−0.0014
Town	0.0861	0.2268***	0.2120***
Religious	−0.0239	−0.1510***	−0.1485***
Number of children			−0.1953***
The youngest child is:			
pre-school	0.4367***		−0.7335***
school age	0.0741		−1.1532***
18 or older	0.8778**		−1.3836***
(ref.= no children)			
H's father's educ.	0.0326		−0.0086
H's education	0.0547**		−0.0024
Married			
1971–5	−0.0246		0.0675
1976–80	0.2900***		−0.1021
1981–5	0.5533***		0.0201
1986–	0.9067***		0.0463
(ref.= before 1971)			
Number of Events	1,521		1,337

Piecewise constant model. *** $p < .01$, ** $p < .05$, * $p < .1$.

have been used to control for the duration dependence in a particular state. The exit rate is low in the initial period, increases when the person is in employment for six to twelve months, and falls again over the time spent in employment.

There are no significant differences in the exit rates between full-time and part-time jobs; however, women are very unlikely to leave other forms of employment, such as self-employment or work as a helping family member. Also, education has a predicted negative effect on the exit rate. With each higher level of education, the exit rate decreases by 11 per cent. Women's social origin, however, has the opposite effect. The higher their fathers' educational level, the higher the likelihood that women will exit employment. Age has been included in this model in linear and quadratic form to assess the baseline rate over the life course. The shape of the hazard rate has a decreasing tendency and only starts increasing late in life. Also, age at marriage has a significant positive effect on the transition rate, as predicted by our hypotheses. The older the women are when they marry, the more rapidly they leave employment. However, those who had accumulated longer work experience before marriage are less likely to exit employment. With each year of employment before marriage, the transition rate declines by about 5 per cent.[6] Contrary to what we expected, neither religion nor place of residence has a statistically significant effect on transitions out of employment.

In model 2, information on children, husband, and marriage cohort is added to the individual characteristics of women. All factors that were important in model 1 qualitatively keep the same effect and remain statistically significant. The only important quantitative change is a considerably smaller effect of women's social origin. Although fathers' higher educational level still has a dampening effect on daughters' employment, the size of the effect diminished noticeably. Wives' social origin correlates with the characteristics of their own families and with the social origin of their husbands. Therefore, part of the effect that was attributed to the wife's social origin in model 1 translates to these other factors in model 2.

The number of children has no significant effect on the exit rate; however, the age of the youngest child is important. If a woman has a pre-school child, her transition rate to non-employment is 55 per cent higher than that of a married woman without children. If the youngest child reaches school age and the mother is employed, the child has no effect on the hazard rate. But when children grow up, the exit rate increases again. Women whose youngest child is over 18 have a high probability of leaving employment. When other factors are controlled, their hazard rate is 141 per cent higher than the hazard rate of childless women. This is a much stronger effect than the effect of pre-school children and an unexpected one. The exit out of employment at this stage of the family cycle can hardly be attributed to increased family responsibilities and household demands. On the contrary, family-related responsibilities

---

[6] Work experience is measured in months. Therefore, the effect of this variable is estimated by the following calculation: $\Delta r = (\exp(-0.0047*12)-1)*100\% = -5.48$ per cent.

diminish at that time, and it is generally assumed that women will increase their participation in the labour market.

This is not the case in Poland. The effect of grown-up children is strong and robust. Since we excluded from the analysis exits into early retirement, this effect is not a confounded effect of retirement transitions. Also, due to the upper age limit in the survey, our sample is relatively young; we tested the possibility that a very small number of cases produced this unexpected result. However, as noted earlier, in Poland women marry and have their children early. At the time of interview, 293 women or 10 per cent of the sample had children that were already 18 or older. Therefore, the estimate does not seem to be an artefact due to a small number of cases. We will discuss this point below.

Next, husband's education has a significant effect on wife's exit rate. With each higher level of husband's education her exit rate increases by about 6 per cent. Husbands' educational resources thus have an opposite effect on women's employment to their own resources, which supports the predictions of the economic theory of the family. Interestingly, this result is opposite to the effect of husbands' education on wives' exit rate in Hungary (see Chapter 13 below).

Finally, marriage cohorts are considered in the analysis. They capture the structural and historical conditions that women encounter (and which influence women) in a distinctive stage of the life course, decidedly shaping their lifelong labour-market attachment. Marriage cohorts show a strong consistent trend across time: starting in the mid–1970s, the exit rate of married women began to increase. Women who married in the second part of the 1980s are 2.5 times more likely to leave employment than women who married in the previous two decades. In light of the specific developments in former socialist economies, this is an expected outcome.

Transition from Non-Employment to Employment

Since a large majority of women are employed at the time of marriage, transition from non-employment to employment mostly refers to a re-entry after an employment interruption and not to first employment spell after schooling. Model 3 in Table 12.3 presents estimates of the transition rate when only women's own characteristics are taken into account. The usage of the piecewise constant exponential model reveals that the estimates of the baseline hazard rate vary across duration in the origin state. Although the differences are not dramatic, it is evident that women have the highest propensity to start a job after spending three to five years in a non-employment status. Also, the type of job is important in determining the likelihood of employment entry. The hazard of entering part-time or other forms of work is much higher than entering full-time employment.

Women's social origin does not play any role in employment decisions after being non-employed; however, their own educational level is very important. Each higher educational level increases the likelihood of employment entry by

22 per cent. Age in this model specification has a non-linear effect, with the hazard rate first decreasing until the age of 31 and increasing afterwards. Age at marriage and duration of work experience before marriage are not statistically significant. However, religion and the place of residence are important determinants of employment behaviour. As predicted, more religious women with a presumably strong family-orientation have a lower rate of employment entry. Women living in towns and cities have more opportunities for employment and show a higher tendency to enter the labour market.

At the next stage, family-related factors are added to the models to assess their effects on the likelihood of a transition to employment (model 4, Table 12.3). The type of job remains important, with part-time and other forms of work having a higher entry rate. Wife's education fosters her employment. Her father's education tends to lower the entry rate but the effect is not statistically significant. The inclusion of family variables modifies the non-linear effect of age. Coefficients are not significant anymore. When age in a linear form is estimated, the tendency to enter employment increases over the life course (not shown). The age at marriage has a negative effect on the hazard rate; the later a woman marries, the less likely she is to (re-)enter employment.

Women with large families have a lower likelihood of starting paid employment. Each additional child in the family decreases the risk by 18 per cent. The ages of children play an important role but the outcomes challenge the theoretical predictions (Becker 1993). The presence of a pre-school child lowers the probability of the mother starting employment by 52 per cent as compared to married childless women. However, the older the youngest child is, the stronger his/her inhibiting effect on mother's employment entry, provided she is not employed in the first place. This contradicts the prevailing view on employment–family compatibility. It is generally assumed that women's family responsibilities ease and the tendency to seek employment increases when children grow older. It is not immediately apparent why this is not the case in Poland. We will address this question again in the discussion.

We proceed by examining the effects of spouses and marriage cohorts. Husband's education and social origin have no effect on the wife's likelihood of transition into employment. The estimated parameters are statistically and substantively insignificant. Also, the time of marriage has no effect on entering employment; there is no discernible trend across marriage cohorts.

Discussion

High female labour-force participation has been one of major labour-market characteristics in former socialist countries. There has generally been less variation in women's employment over the life course than in Western European countries. It has been argued that economic necessity along with ideological justification played an important role in this early and massive integration of women into the work sphere. We can nevertheless find discernible patterns over the life course when we examine the employment of Polish women. Not only women's own attributes but also family characteristics play a distinctive role in shaping their entry into and exit from the labour market.

Taking women's own resources into consideration, education plays the most important role in their employment level. Higher education in general reflects the job reward potential of a woman. Within the economic approach to the family, higher education indicates an increased affinity to invest in market-specific human capital, which changes the opportunity costs of working or withdrawing from the labour force. Our analysis confirms these patterns also for married Polish women: the higher the educational level, the higher the participation rate. The effect of education is strong and consistent; it decreases the propensity to leave employment and increases the likelihood of (re-)entering employment after a period of inactivity.

Also, family-related factors have a significant impact on married women's employment patterns. Husband's higher education increases a wife's risk of exiting employment, which has also been found in Germany (Chapter 3 above), Italy (Chapter 6 above), or Spain (Chapter 7 above). Husbands' educational resources thus have an opposite effect on women's employment to women's own resources. When the transition from non-employment into employment is observed, husband's education has no effect on wife's employment entry hazard rate. Overall, we conclude that husbands' characteristics do to some extent determine wives' employment behaviour, and the effects are in line with the arguments of the economic theory of the family and human capital theory. Husband's higher investment into marketable resources encourages the specialization of work within the couple and promotes his wife's leaving of employment. However, since the wife's own educational resources have a strong dampening effect on the exit rate, only a very large difference in education would 'neutralize' her own resources: for example, if a man with a university degree marries a woman with primary-level education.

The effects of children are strong, consistent, and partly unexpected. We anticipated finding the effects of pre-school children on their mothers' moves into and out of employment. Indeed, the presence of young children increases the likelihood of employment exit and lowers the (re-)entry rate. However, in addition to the influence of young children, we also found strong effects of older children on both the entry and exit rate. Concerning the (re-)entry rate into employment, various explanations for strong inhibiting effects of older children are plausible. One might speculate that these women stayed out of the labour market for extensive periods of time and could encounter difficulties if they wished to (re-)enter. Also, the result could be partly explained by the composition effect. In a country where female employment is common in all stages of the family cycle, women who are non-employed when children reach school age and even later may be a highly selected group with specific unmeasured characteristics, such as traditional sex-role attitudes. When the transition rate is calculated on the basis of such a pre-selected risk set and relevant attributes are not included in the analysis, the age of children appears to have a causal effect on the hazard rate. This is a plausible explanation; however, since the exit rate out of employment is particularly high for women with grown-up children, it seems that this explanation does not suffice.

We hypothesize that there are several possible substantive explanations for the effect of grown-up children on their mothers' employment participation in addition to the more technical considerations concerning the effect of the risk-set composition. First, the financial pressure on the family eases when children become independent. This enables women who have been working for economic reasons only to quit employment. To explore this line of argument, we further examined employment transitions by including the interaction effect of husband's educational level and the age of the youngest child in model estimations (not shown). The results indicate that particularly women with highly educated husbands interrupt their employment when children grow up and have low entry rates at that stage of the family cycle. This implies that women whose husbands have high career resources are more able to afford to not be employed. An additional explanation for non-employment in the post-childrearing period of the life course would be a need to assist younger generations in childrearing. Due to the pattern of early family formation and housing shortage, three-generation households are fairly common in Poland. One possible arrangement is that the grandmother takes care of the grandchildren when the young couple works. Third, a deteriorating health situation may induce women to stop working if they can afford to. Health problems may be serious enough to make employment a strain, yet not serious enough for women to qualify for disability and early retirement.

Finally, trends across marriage cohorts in Poland show a distinctive pattern which differs from developments in Western European countries. Since the mid–1970s, moves out of employment have become more and more common among married Polish women, holding individual and household characteristics constant. At the same time, the (re-)entry rate has not increased. This implies that over the last two decades before the economic transition, married women's employment propensity was actually declining.

References

Allison, P. D. (1984). *Event History Analysis: Regression for Longitudinal Event Data* (Newbury Park, Calif.: Sage).

Becker, G. S. (1993). *A Treatise on the Family* (Enlarged edn. Cambridge, Mass.: Harvard University Press).

Blossfeld, H.-P., and G. Rohwer (1995). *Techniques of Event History Modeling: New Approaches to Causal Analysis* (Mahwah, NJ: L. Erlbaum).

——S. Drobnič, and G. Rohwer (1998). 'Les trajectoires professionnelles des couples mariés en Allemagne: Une étude longitudinale de long terme de carrières des époux en Allemagne de l'Ouest' (Occupational Trajectories of Married Couples in Germany: A Long-term Longitudinal Analysis of Spouses' Careers in West Germany), *Revue française de sociologie*, 39/2: 305–51.

——A. Hamerle, and K. U. Mayer (1989). *Event History Analysis: Statistical Theory and Application in the Social Sciences* (Hillsdale, NJ: L. Erlbaum).

Cigno, A. (1991). *Economics of the Family* (Oxford: Oxford University Press).

Drobnič, S. (1992). 'Rigidities in the Labour Markets of Transition Economies and New Organizational Forms', *LICEES Working Paper 7/1992* (Leuven: Leuven Institute for Central and East European Studies).

——(1995). 'Nestandardne oblike zaposlovanja v Srednji in Vzhodni Evropi' (Non-Standard Forms of Employment in Central and Eastern Europe), *Teorija in praksa*, 32/9–10: 796–811.

——(1997). 'Part-Time Work in Central and East European Countries', in H.-P. Blossfeld and C. Hakim (eds.), *Between Equalization and Marginalization: Women Working Part-Time in Europe and the United States* (Oxford: Oxford University Press), 71–89.

Einhorn, B. (1993). *Cinderella Goes to Market: Citizenship, Gender and Women's Movements in East Central Europe* (London and New York: Verso).

Ferge, Z. (1992). 'Unemployment in Hungary: The Need for a New Ideology', in B. Deacon (ed.), *Social Policy, Social Justice and Citizenship in Eastern Europe* (Aldershot: Avebury), 158–75.

Frątczak E., I. Kowalska, G. Rohwer, S. Drobnič, and H.-P. Blossfeld (1996). *Polish Family and Fertility Survey: A User's Guide* (Warsaw and Bremen: University of Bremen and Warsaw School of Economics—SGH).

Holzer, J. Z., and I. Kowalska (1997). *Fertility and Family Surveys in Countries of the ECE Region. Standard Country Report—Poland* (New York and Geneva: United Nations).

Jackman, R., and M. Rutkowski (1994). 'Labor Markets: Wages and Employment', in N. Barr (ed.), *Labor Markets and Social Policy in Central and Eastern Europe: The Transition and Beyond* (Oxford: Oxford University Press), 121–59.

Kalbfleisch, J. D., and R. L. Prentice (1980). *The Statistical Analysis of Failure Time Data* (New York: John Wiley & Sons).

Kotowska, I. E. (1996). 'Women's Position in the Labour Market in Poland: Do they Benefit From Economic Recovery?' paper presented at the 8th Annual Conference of EALE, Mediterranean Agronomic Institute of Chaina, Crete, 19–22 Sept.

——(1997). 'Równość kobiet i mężczyzn na rynku pracy' (Equality of Women and Men in the Labour Market), in R. Siemieńska, (ed.). *Wokół problemów zawodowego równouprawnienia mężczyzn i kobiet: Fundacja Promocji Prawa Europejskiego* (Warsaw: Wydawnictwo Naukowe Scholar), 85–106.

Mach, B. W., K .U. Mayer, and M. Pohoski (1994). 'Job Changes in the Federal Republic of Germany and Poland: A Longitudinal Assessment of the Impact of Welfare-Capitalist and State-Socialist Labour-Market Segmentation', *European Sociological Review*, 10/1: 1–28.

Puhani, P. (1995). 'Labour Supply of Married Women in Poland: A Microeconometric Study Based on the Polish Labour Force Survey', *ZEW Discussion Paper*, 95/12.

Rohwer, G., and U. Pötter (1998). *TDA User's Manual. Version 1* (Bochum: Ruhr-Universität Bochum).

Rutkowski, J. (1995). 'Changes in the Wage Structure During Economic Transition in Central and Eastern Europe', *World Bank, Data Series*, 1 (May).

——(1997). *The New Rich and New Poor: Distributional Consequences of the Economic Transition* (Warsaw: The World Bank Poland Resident Mission).

Siemieńska R. (1997). 'Wartości i postawy warunkujące obecność kobiet na rynku pracy' (Values and Attitudes Influencing Women's Position in the Labour Market), in R. Siemieńska (ed.). *Wokół problemów zawodowego równouprawnienia mężczyzn i kobiet: Fundacja Promocji Prawa Europejskiego* (Warsaw: Wydawnictwo Naukowe Scholar).

Socha, M. W., and U. Sztanderska (1991). *Labour Market in the Transition to the Market Economy in Poland* (PPRG Discussion Papers, 2; Warsaw: Polish Policy Research Group, Warsaw University).

Sørensen, A. (1983). 'Women's Employment Patterns after Marriage', *Journal of Marriage and the Family*, 45: 311–21.

Teachman, J. D., K. A. Polonko, and J. Scanzoni (1987). 'Demography of the Family', in M. B. Sussman and S. K. Steinmetz (eds.), *Handbook of Marriage and the Family* (New York and London: Plenum Press), 3–36.

Tuma, N. B. and M. T. Hannan (1984). *Social Dynamics: Models and Methods* (New York: Academic Press).

Wiśniewska, A., and E. Frątczak (1997). 'Monitoring of the Social Welfare System in Poland—Basic Information', *Polish Population Review*, 11 (Warsaw: Polish Demographic Society).

Yamaguchi, K. (1991). *Event History Analysis* (London and New Delhi: Sage).

13

Employment Patterns in Hungarian Couples

PÉTER RÓBERT, ERZSÉBET BUKODI, AND RUUD LUIJKX

Introduction

ALTHOUGH researchers tend to agree that the family is the proper unit of stratification, most studies have been based on individuals rather than families. Class position, measured either by the EGP classification (Erikson *et al.* 1979; Erikson and Goldthorpe 1992) or by Wright's class scheme (1979, 1985, 1997), is based on individual characteristics. Most of the status attainment analyses are based on the classic model by Blau and Duncan (1967) where social origin is taken into account, but how present family or events of family formation contribute to the process of stratification is investigated less.[1]

Since employment and occupation have always been the main characteristics used for grouping people (see the so-called ISA paradigm or Glass 1954), most classic studies focused on men only, not even sampling women who were not gainfully employed. As females' employment started to increase in modern societies after the Second World War, the gap between the educational level of genders also declined, women's educational level even surpassed that of men in some countries (Shavit and Blossfeld 1993). Moreover, in recent decades women no longer completely gave up their gainful work activities after marriage or childbirth, even if they interrupted their participation in the labour force for shorter or longer periods.

Analysing both men and women provides a better and more reliable view on social inequalities and status attainment in modern societies, but this picture

The original analysis for this chapter was carried out at the Netherlands Institute for Advanced Study (NIAS) when the first and the last author were visiting fellow there in 1996/1997 and a member of the NIAS-nucleus group 'Stratification in Eastern and Western Europe in the 1990s'. We are grateful for the comments and advice from Sonja Drobnič and Paul M. de Graaf.

[1] In fact, Blau and Duncan include a chapter in their monograph on assortative mating and estimate the impact of wife's education and wife's father's occupational status on respondent's (husband's) occupational status and conclude that although these effects are modest they cannot be neglected (Blau and Duncan 1967: 341–5).

is still far from a complete understanding of the process of stratification. It was the research on status homogamy of husbands and wives—a rediscovery of a topic suggested a long time ago by Lipset and Zetterberg (1970 [1956])—which truly increased the value of inclusion of women in stratification research. The investigation of homogamy between husbands and wives was considered either as an alternative to the association between father's and offspring's status for analysing 'social openness' (Hout 1982), or was regarded as a multidimensional approach to assortative mating in respect of ascription and achievement as well as of cultural or economic occupational status (Kalmijn 1991, 1994).

The growing interest in dynamics of social processes and the reproduction of inequalities led to datasets of increasing quality from large-scale longitudinal or panel surveys. Pooled data files based on series of cross-sectional data are the other important sources for dynamic analyses in the field of stratification research. Studies—also partly applying a life-course perspective—cover topics such as demographic change, family formation, labour-force participation, class career processes (see e.g. Cramer 1980; Bernhardt 1993; Blossfeld 1986, 1995; Blossfeld and Mayer 1988; Mayer *et al.* 1989, etc.). The next—and quite recent—step in this direction was the inclusion of further dynamic determinants in the analysis of status attainment and career developments: changes in family formation and impact of spouse's resources (see e.g. Bernasco 1994; Chapter 3 above).

In the following sections, we are going to present an analysis of females' employment transitions in Hungarian couples during their marriages. The research focuses on four moves: (1) employment exit to maternity leave after childbirth; (2) employment exit to housewife status in the family; (3) (re-)entry into employment from maternity leave; (4) (re-)entry into employment from housewife status. All transitions are investigated as functions of the wife's social characteristics, such as social background, educational investments, occupation, and labour-force experience, family cycle (number and age of children present in the family), and husband's social characteristics.

In the next section we provide a general description of family formation and females' employment in Hungary in the decades after the Second World War. Then we present hypotheses based on theoretical considerations. After describing the data and variables, the analyses and the results are shown. In the final section of this chapter we discuss the findings.

Family Formation and Females' Labour-Force Participation in Hungary after 1945

In Hungary, legal marriage is the typical form for couples living together in the same household. Cohabitation is rare, the proportion of cohabiting partners was below 5 per cent in the 1990 census. Nevertheless, cohabitation started to increase among young couples after 1990. In fact, the 'inclination to marriage' started to decline in Hungary from the beginning of the 1970s (Klinger and Monigl 1981) and this trend continued in the 1980s (Csernák 1992).

The age at entry into marriage is traditionally lower in Hungary compared to Western Europe and the country belongs to the so-called 'non-European type' of marriage customs and fertility rates (Hajnal 1965). However, there is a growing tendency to postpone marriage until higher ages, partly due to the increase in females' educational attainment and—consequently—the longer time women spend in education causing a delay in the transition to adulthood (Róbert and Blossfeld 1995). The same holds for the age at entry into motherhood, which is also relatively low in Hungary, and the timing of childbirth and marriage are close to each other. But growing participation in education as well as higher levels of educational attainment result in an increase in age at entry into motherhood as well (Róbert and Blossfeld 1995).

As in most industrialized societies, fertility rates in Hungary are in decline and this trend has been present since the beginning of the twentieth century. There is some relative fluctuation in fertility due to formal policy measures in respect of childbirth and childcare. Abortion was practically prohibited between 1953–6, so-called 'childcare leave' or 'maternity leave' was introduced in 1967, and these events generated peaks within the general decreasing tendency. When daughters of the '1953-generation' entered the childbearing age, live birth rates increased again, but the trend has declined since then. Approaching women's age at childbirth from the viewpoint of live birth, Kamarás (1997) shows that live births declined in Hungary and the most frequent age at which women give birth to a child increased from 21 to 25 within the last fifteen years.

Labour-force participation of women was part of the official ideology and politics in the communist societies, and full employment guaranteed by the state was one of the major ideological concepts in the communist countries. Full employment referred to both men and women, thus married couples in Hungary typically consisted of two earners. As in other areas of the state economy, central regulations were applied to wages as well, in order to keep them low and to force all members of the family to be employed. In addition to low wages, other policy measures were also applied to influence the supply side of the labour-force and ensure the required labour power. Employment was a necessary condition for, for example, the use of childcare facilities, applying for an apartment for a young couple, having a vacation in a holiday resort owned by the trade union, or—at first—even for getting health treatment in case of sickness.

As a consequence of the labour-force policy in Hungary described above, females' labour-market participation was high. The female labour force started to increase formally after 1949, the communist take-over.[2] Employment

---

[2] Hakim (1993) argues that the historically low level of female employment is due to measurements in official statistics where unpaid family workers (mostly women) have been excluded from the labour force. If they had been counted then the rise in female employment would no longer be so dramatic. This holds for Hungary as well, where the majority of women worked as unpaid family members, mostly in agriculture, before 1949.

among females is still high although it dropped strongly after 1990—partly due to unemployment, partly due to the early exit from the labour force into retirement. In line with increasing labour-force participation, women's enrolment into secondary and tertiary education has also grown in the last decades and educational inequalities declined between men and women (Simkus and Andorka 1982; Róbert 1991).

The Hungarian labour market—despite the claim of gender equality—was segmented and gender-segregated; gender differences contributed to the segmentation (Galasi and Sziráczki 1985). In respect of income position, earning scales of occupations and proportion of women in occupations seem to be correlated. Earnings of women lag behind those of men, and in terms of job selection, women are over-represented in the worst paid and less prestigious jobs. This fact influenced both educational selection and occupational choices; gender-specific educational strategies as well as gender segregation in the labour market continue to exist.

Females' employment, like males' employment, was almost solely full-time in Hungary. Part-time employment was not reconcilable either with the labour-force demand of the economy or with the financial needs of the families. Although there have been slight changes in this respect since 1990, not more than 2 per cent, a very small minority, of female employees work part-time (Drobnič 1997). Part-time work is more typical among pensioners: a survey in the early 1990s found that every second women in part-time employment was retired (Frey and Gere 1994). After finishing their education and entering the labour market, Hungarian women spent most of their working life in full-time employment. Therefore, research on transitions between full-time and part-time work cannot be applied to this population. The most frequent interruption in labour-force participation occurs when women give birth to children and take maternity leave. This option became available—as mentioned before—after 1967. Before this time, an exit into housekeeping was the only possibility for women if they wanted to leave the labour market. The period women could spend at home on maternity leave with the new-born child varied over time, but its maximum has never exceeded three years.[3] Only women with a certain period of previous employment were eligible for maternity leave. Financial compensation for maternity leave was also subject to changes: it was a fixed amount in 1967 and it was changed to 75 per cent of the mother's last salary before pregnancy from 1985. It is important to note that maternity leave does not mean a legal interruption of employment. Mothers staying at home with their children remain 'in status' (that is, employed) and are counted as 'inactive earners' in official statistics.

---

[3] If the mother gave birth to a second child before her first child turned 3, she could stay at home for more than three years altogether.

Theories and Hypotheses

Following Becker (1981), the economic approach to the family states that human capital investments are gender-specific; men's and women's investments differ because they have different ambitions and expectations with respect to their family roles and labour-force participation. Human capital theory argues that women accumulate less human capital because they have the task of childcare and related family obligations in addition to gainful employment (Polachek 1981). Even if women are in the labour force they do not intend to work continuously full-time and therefore they choose employment sectors and occupational positions where labour-force interruptions are less penalized (Polachek 1975). Spending less time in employment and accumulating less human capital results in lower wages and less stable jobs (Blau and Ferber 1986) as well as low levels of authority (Wolf and Fligstein 1979). All in all, women have more chance of being segregated and employed in 'women's occupations' rather than 'men's occupations' because employers hire them under conditions of incomplete information and gender-specific generalization, as the theory of the economics of discrimination posits (Becker 1971).

The economic approach also implies that members of the family have different comparative advantages and the common goal is to utilize these resources and benefits for the efficient functioning of the family. In this view, the division of labour is gender-specific and based on comparative advantages: men usually have stronger resources for maximizing the gains of labour-force participation and money-making activities, providing the necessary financial support for the family; women usually have stronger resources for maximizing the gains of household activities, ensuring the cohesion and stability of the family. In other words, based on their different investments, men have material capital and women have cultural capital. This means, they have something different to offer in the 'marriage market' where men and women—behaving as trading partners—consider and evaluate the advantages and resources of the other partner and decide about marrying or not through the process of assortative mating. After getting married, spouses will specialize according to their comparative advantages and this specialization will increase the utility of the marriage.

The concept described above is frequently called conservative and discriminatory against women. Indeed, segregated gender roles can better contribute to the dependence of wives on their husbands than to the cohesion and stability of the family or to the equality of partners within the family. Although the economic theory predicts that husbands and wives pool all of their resources for the benefit of the family, empirical evidence demonstrates that this is not the case (see e.g. Edwards 1982; Pahl 1983). However, Sørensen and McLanahan (1987) show that wives' economic dependency has declined over time between 1960 and 1980. As a consequence of females' increasing educational attainment and labour-force participation, women's comparative advantages seem to have much greater variation than previously and they are able to compete with men in many professions. Since industrialization theory (Treiman 1970) argues that a shift occurs from ascription to achievement in status attainment processes, women are able to benefit from their increasing educational investments. In fact, the process of post-industrialization, with the emerging significance of services in modern societies, also increases females' labour-force participation (Esping-Andersen 1993). All this means that, on the one hand, assortative mating becomes a more complex process and, on the other hand, decisions throughout the whole marriage about issues related to family life, like number of children, continuation of education, wife's labour-force participation, change of job, etc., are subject to more and more calculations and negotiations between husband and wife. Moreover, against the expectations of the New Home Economics, marriage partners do not always behave and decide on the basis of full rationality. Attitudes and values influence the calculations and negotiations and—in addition to this— even preferences are not stable during the life course. Women's ambitions can change in respect of childbearing and professional career, and men's expectations can change about their wife's role in the family (Hakim 1996).

Theories related to the combination of employment and childbearing are also considered. Researchers agree that gainful work activity and childbearing compete in females' life histories, but the causal direction of this relationship is not discussed. The micro-level decision-making model developed by Bernhardt (1993: 34) assumes mutual causality between fertility plans and work plans, fertility behaviour and work behaviour, and between plans and behaviour. Cramer (1980) states that fertility affects employment in the short run, while employment affects fertility in the long run. The short-run relationship between employment and fertility is influenced by age: as women get older they limit their fertility plans in order to fulfil their employment plans (Stolzenberg and Waite 1977). Elder and Rockwell (1976) distinguished four employment patterns for married women: conventional, interrupted, double-track, and unstable. The conventional pattern means that wives left the labour force after marriage or first birth and did not return. The interrupted type means role specialization: wives stayed at home between the time of first birth until a certain age of their last child. Women with the double-track pattern did not interrupt employment due to childbearing at all or, if they stayed at home for some time, they returned to the labour market before the birth of their last child. Cases which did not fit into these types were classified as unstable. Re-examining these patterns, Sørensen (1983) found an increase in the double-track type of wives.

The core of this type of research is that spouse's resources are also taken into account. Previous analyses indicated that the higher the status of husband (measured by his education or occupation), the higher the probability that of the wife leaving the labour market (see e.g. Ferber and Huber 1979; Bernasco 1994). This finding is based on the fact that husbands with higher educational and occupational status can provide better financially for their family and that wives' contribution to the family budget is less necessary in these households.[4] However, it is possible to argue in another way. As a consequence of increasing homogamy in assortative mating, men with higher education marry women with higher education (Kalmijn 1991). Then, higher educated wives— in accordance with the human capital investment theory—tend to stay in the labour force because they have higher career ambitions and employment is more beneficial for them. In this case, husbands' resources will have a negative effect on labour-force exit and a positive effect on labour-force entry. The latter assumption refers to the cultural homogamy of spouses, whereas the first one considers their economic heterogeneity.[5] Partly in this line, Bernasco *et al.* (1998) suggest to distinguishing between husbands' cultural resources (education) and financial resources (occupation and/or income). These two resources are expected to correlate positively but to have effects with opposite signs on wives' employment. Husband's occupation (income) has a positive impact, husband's education has a negative impact, on wife's labour-force exit.

In the Hungarian context, the rapid industrialization programme, the strong labour-force demand of the economy, the centrally determined low wages left less opportunities for families to decide about wives' labour-force participation. In case of childbearing, the possibility of maternity leave was offered by the state. Consequently, the danger arises that the family decisions we are investigating relate to fertility and not to employment. However, the conditions of maternity leave—like length of leave or financial compensation during the period—have changed over time, and the costs and benefits varied accordingly. Thus, we expect that factors which usually influence the decision about women's labour-force transitions, like human capital investments (education), market capability (occupation), labour-force experience, as well as husbands' social characteristics, will have explanatory power for the Hungarian families, too. Previous research on the Hungarian stratification system proved that general mechanisms of the process of stratification, like increased social openness, decline in the effect of social origin, and an increase in the impact of education, basically work in a similar way to other modern industrial societies (Ganzeboom *et al.* 1991)—although the process does not indicate a linear trend (Luijkx *et al.* 1998). No doubt, specific features of the general mechanisms are present in Hungary, such as the fundamental role of cultural inequalities and cultural capital in determining social status (Kolosi 1988) and in reproducing social inequalities (Róbert 1984; Ganzeboom *et al.* 1990).

---

[4] Using longitudinal data, Long and Jones (1980) show that it is less the absolute amount of husbands' and wives' income which influence women's labour-force exit or entry, and much more the change in income over time.

[5] Another aspect we do not test directly but which affect wives' employment are gender-role identities. In couples where both partners are better educated, traditional gender roles are followed to a lesser degree, husbands are less conservative and more likely to accept their wives' career ambitions. Conservative gender-role stereotypes are more typical for working-class families (Hakim 1996: ch. 4; Thornton *et al.* 1983).

In analysing females' employment transitions we apply human capital theory. Accordingly, higher investments in education and training imply more ambition with respect to the professional career, and provide better market capability and higher income potential. Women with higher human capital investments and/or longer labour-force experience before marriage or childbirth tend to remain in employment and not to leave the labour market. Controlling for longer labour-force experience, older age at time of marriage increases the hazard of employment interruption (these women are in 'delay') as well as the hazard of (re-)entry into employment. In addition to educational investments, the returns on them as expressed by occupational status influence the decisions on employment transitions in the same direction. In sum, better social origin, higher level of education, and occupation increase social status, as postulated by the general expectations of status attainment research. The effect of these variables is assumed to be negative on exits from work and positive on (re-)entry into labour force. The impact of education and occupation will probably eliminate the effect of social origin due to the fact that family background influences educational and occupational attainment. If social origin has an impact on employment transitions net of education and occupation, this may be the effect of childhood socialization in the family where husband or wife grew up.

The analysis deals with the short-term impact of fertility on wives' employment, assuming that childbirth—if it occurs—tends to lead to an interruption of employment. We expect both number of children and age of children to influence the labour-force participation of women. Having a child younger than 3 years old increases the odds of entry into maternity leave and decreases the odds of (re-)entry into the labour force. A large number of children also decreases the chances of returning to the labour market.

For spouses' effects on wives' labour-force transitions we expect cultural homogamy (assortative mating based on similar education of spouses) to matter more than economic heterogeneity (husbands' financial contribution to the family budget higher than wives' contribution) in Hungary. Considering the general pattern of dual-breadwinner families in Hungary in connection with low income levels, we do not expect a significant impact of husbands' financial resources on wives' employment decisions. However, we assume that husbands' education will be the significant predictor of labour-force exit and (re-)entry. The cultural homogamy assumption implies that the lower the educational level of the husband, the higher the probability that the wife will leave employment, and the higher the education of the husband, the higher the probability of the wife's (re-)entry into the labour force. On the other hand, the distinction between husbands' cultural resources (education) and financial resources (occupation) will probably not work in Hungary due to the strong collinearity between these measures. The stronger impact of education on occupational status in state-socialist societies compared to Western market economies has been proven in several previous studies (see e.g. Kolosi *et al.* 1985; Ganzeboom *et al.* 1990).

Since the option of maternity leave was offered by the state and was a regular practice for wives in Hungarian families, analysing females' labour-force transitions in connection with childbearing cannot be restricted to the fact of employment exit or (re-)entry. However, it makes sense to focus on the duration wives spend in marriage before leaving the labour force and especially the length of interval they spend out of the labour force before returning to employment. We assume that the period which women spend in or out of the labour force before employment transitions is related to the status characteristics of wives and husbands. For example, wives with higher educational investments and occupational status will spend less time in maternity leave and will return to the labour force earlier. This means that the hazard rates for labour-force transitions are not expected to be proportional.

All these expected effects are controlled for cohort and age effects. Due to the influence of industrialization and modernization, members of younger marriage cohorts have a higher occupational status. Wives in younger cohorts have higher odds for exit into maternity leave because this option did not exist for older cohorts in Hungary. Wives in older cohorts have higher odds for (re-)entry into the labour force because they are already in the life-cycle stage where their children are getting older and need less time from the mother. Exits from the labour force decrease, and (re-)entry into labour force increase with age.

Data, Measurements, Methods

In this chapter we use data from the 1992 Social Mobility and Life History Survey conducted by the Hungarian Central Statistical Office (Harcsa 1992). The survey is based on a household sample of the Hungarian population where all members of the household aged over 14 were interviewed ($N = 29,006$). The data-collection methods employed in the survey were a standardized questionnaire and face-to-face interviews. We selected couples in their first 'marriage', living together and with the wife younger than 55 and the husband younger than 60 (age of retirement in Hungary). Both legal marriages and cohabiting couples were considered ($N = 5,472$ couples). We distinguish cohorts married between 1953 and 1962 ($N = 528$); between 1963 and 1972 ($N = 1,620$); between 1973 and 1982 ($N=1,928$); and between 1983 and 1992 ($N = 1,396$).[6]

In preparing an event-oriented dataset we followed the method in Blossfeld and Rohwer (1995). First, all jobs in the occupational history of both marriage partners were considered as separate episodes. Second, the method of episode splitting was applied, where the job episodes were divided into the smallest time unit in the dataset: years. Each of the original episodes is replaced by a

---

[6] Since these couples live in their first marriages, older marriage cohorts are biased by the fact that shorter marriages which ended with divorce or death of one of the partners before the data were collected are not included in the analysis.

contiguous set of splits with appropriate values of the covariates. The unit of observation is not the individual or couple anymore but the splits (years) derived from the job episodes separately for husbands and wives. In the next step these person-period files of the partners were matched together to facilitate a dynamic approach to couples' careers. The analysis is carried out on this person-year dataset of the couples.

The dataset includes time-independent measures, like social origin of wife and husband, age at time of marriage, as well as time-dependent measures which may vary with the job spells. We distinguish four outcomes for measuring transitions in the wife's employment history: (1) exit from employment into maternity leave; (2) exit from employment into housekeeping; (3) (re)entry into employment from maternity leave; (4) (re)entry into employment from housekeeping. All four outcomes are dichotomous measures. As explanatory variables we include information about marriage cohort, age at marriage, ageing, status of both spouses, and family characteristics. These variables are presented in the appendix to this chapter. In addition, we provide an overview of husbands' and wives' occupational status at time of marriage and at time of survey, as well as of couples' fathers' occupational statuses in Table 13.1. Wife's labour-force participation at time of marriage by cohorts is shown in Table 13.2.

For estimating the models Cox-regression is applied. This method estimates continuous hazard models, taking into account the length of the risk period (Yamaguchi 1991). This risk period (duration) varies: for example, years spent by wife in the labour force until exit to maternity leave, or years spent by wife in maternity leave until (re)entry into the labour force, etc. The risk period ends if any of the events investigated occurs. The dependent variable in the model is the hazard rate or transition rate which expresses the risk of experiencing the specific event at time t, given that the event did not occur before time t. Cox's hazard model can take into account the fact that we have so-called censored cases in which the event does not occur, for example, the wife did not exit into maternity leave, or did not return from maternity leave.

Table 13.1. Husbands' and wives' status characteristics (mean values)

	Marriage cohort			
	1953–62	1963–72	1973–82	1983–92
Husband's job at time of marriage (ISEI score)	31.6	35.5	35.8	36.0
Wife's job at time of marriage (ISEI score)	26.9	34.1	39.0	40.5
Husband's job at time of survey (ISEI score)	33.7	36.7	36.3	36.2
Wife's job at time of survey (ISEI score)	31.3	37.7	39.6	40.4
Husband's father's job (ISEI score)	28.2	29.2	30.5	32.5
Wife's father's job (ISEI score)	28.2	29.5	30.2	32.1

Table 13.2. Women's employment status at time of marriage (%)

	Marriage cohort			
	1953–62	1963–72	1973–82	1983–92
Employment	70.3	84.4	90.3	87.8
Housekeeping	29.4	14.2	7.5	7.8
Other	0.3	1.4	2.2	4.4
N	528	1,620	1,928	1,396

In the analysis we estimate the main effects of the explanatory variables as well as interaction terms of certain explanatory variables with the episode duration. These interactions make it possible to test for the proportionality of the hazard rate (Yamaguchi 1991). At the same time, this test is applied for verifying the assumptions of specific functions between explanatory variables and the interval wives spend in or out of the labour force.

Analysis

1. Labour-Force Exit

In Table 13.3, the analysis of the transition from employment to maternity leave and housekeeping is presented. The exit to maternity leave has been a more frequent event for wives than the exit to housekeeping. This is not surprising considering the employment and family policy measures which tried to restrict housekeeping in Hungarian families and accepted only maternity leave as an option for wives in leaving the labour force. Model 1 displays the marriage cohort effects. The results for the transition into maternity leave and into housekeeping go in completely opposite directions. The hazard of transition to maternity leave increases, while the hazard to housekeeping decreases, if the wife belongs to a younger cohort. This is in line with the fact that maternity leave was not an option for women in older marriage cohorts.[7]

In model 2, the other explanatory variables are added. The age effects present a curvilinear pattern, indicating a negative linear trend that levels off for both types of employment transitions. Cumulative work experience has a negative impact on the labour-force exits. Higher career investments apparently decrease the hazard of leaving employment for either maternity leave or housekeeping. Age at marriage, however, positively affects both employment transitions.

[7] In fact, the model for the transition rate from work to maternity leave is estimated only for the period after 1967 because this transition could not legally occur before this date.

Table 13.3. Effects on transition rate from work to maternity leave and housekeeping (Cox regression estimates based on person-period dataset, standard errors in parentheses)

	From work to maternity leave[a]			From work to housekeeping		
	Model 1	Model 2	Model 3	Model 1	Model 2	Model 3
Marriage cohort [b]						
1963–72	1.8013***	0.2440	2.2069***	-0.5495***	-0.6094***	-0.6749***
	(0.1271)	(0.1326)	(0.2277)	(0.1113)	(0.1171)	(0.1643)
1973–82	2.9356***	0.7485***	2.2313***	-0.4743***	-0.8559***	-0.0022
	(0.1257)	(0.1338)	(0.2362)	(0.1352)	(0.1509)	(0.2154)
1983–92	4.3590***	1.0440***	2.2673***	0.1249	-1.1729***	0.3152
	(0.1293)	(0.1395)	(0.2717)	(0.2410)	(0.2493)	(0.5664)
Age	—	-0.1453***	0.0461***	—	-0.1952***	-0.1385***
		(0.0147)	(0.0123)		(0.0174)	(0.0169)
Age sq.	—	0.0028***	-0.0009	—	0.0052***	0.0039***
		(0.0007)	(0.0007)		(0.0010)	(0.0010)
Cumulative work experience	—	-0.4539***	-0.2216***	—	-0.4709***	-0.3646***
		(0.0098)	(0.0101)		(0.0237)	(0.0247)
Age at time of marriage	—	0.4130***	0.0903***	—	0.4005***	0.3105***
		(0.0142)	(0.0141)		(0.0236)	(0.0245)
Social origin	—	-0.0008	-0.0012	—	0.0014	0.0009
		(0.0016)	(0.0016)		(0.0053)	(0.0053)
Education	—	-0.0939***	-0.0379	—	-0.1337***	-0.1809***
		(0.0102)	(0.0218)		(0.0262)	(0.0355)
Occupation	—	-0.0101***	-0.0022	—	-0.0238***	-0.0203**
		(0.0017)	(0.0035)		(0.0049)	(0.0076)
Number of children	—	-0.0219	-0.0366	—	0.0301	-0.0433
		(0.0494)	(0.0508)		(0.0762)	(0.0797)
Child aged 0–2	—	3.0022***	3.3517***	—	-0.2336	0.0050
		(0.0869)	(0.0884)		(0.1362)	(0.1413)
Child aged 3–6	—	-0.1023	-0.2286**	—	-0.1732	-0.0471
		(0.0712)	(0.0715)		(0.1462)	(0.1507)

	(1)	(2)	(3)	(4)	(5)
Child aged 7–14	—	0.7268*** (0.0971)	0.3158** (0.0982)	0.7593*** (0.1686)	0.7289*** (0.1753)
Child aged 15–18	—	0.7253*** (0.2069)	−0.0039 (0.1931)	0.4122 (0.2304)	0.3126 (0.2334)
Child aged 19 and over	—	−1.1146* (0.4479)	−1.5848*** (0.4427)	1.1791*** (0.2783)	1.0367*** (0.2793)
Husband's social origin	—	−0.0002 (0.0015)	−0.0003 (0.0015)	−0.0010 (0.0053)	−0.0009 (0.0052)
Husband's education	—	0.0142 (0.0096)	−0.0293 (0.0192)	−0.0663** (0.0246)	−0.1244*** (0.0347)
Husband's occupation	—	−0.0035* (0.0018)	−0.0047 (0.0037)	−0.0093 (0.0059)	−0.0477*** (0.0094)
Interaction terms with duration					
Marriage cohort × time					
1963–72	—	—	−9.6705*** (0.3571)	—	0.0049 (0.1124)
1973–82	—	—	−9.9992*** (0.3615)	—	0.8653*** (0.1607)
1983–92	—	—	10.1558*** (0.3737)	—	1.1324** (0.3595)
Education × time	—	—	0.0249 (0.0166)	—	−0.0540* (0.0254)
Occupation × time	—	—	0.0047 (0.0027)	—	0.0023 (0.0051)
Husband's educ. × time	—	—	−0.0479** (0.0152)	—	−0.0633** (0.0244)
Husband's occup. × time	—	—	−0.0020 (0.0029)	—	−0.0282*** (0.0058)
−2 Log likelihood	60,773.825	49,121.436	45,409.138	7,609.913	7,434.046
Sig. of improvement	0.0000	0.0000	0.0000	0.0000	0.0000
No. of events	2,335	2,335	2,335	360	360

[a] Estimates are based on events which occurred after 1967 because maternity leave was not an option before this date. [b] Reference category: 1953–62.

*** $p \le .001$, ** $p \le .01$, * $p \le .05$.

The wife's social origin (father's ISEI score) is not a significant predictor for the employment exits, but human capital investments (education) and higher market capability (occupation-ISEI) decrease the hazard rate of exit from the labour force. The number of children has no significant impact on the hazard rate but the age of the children matters. The effects differ markedly for the two types of labour-force exit. Not surprisingly, the presence of a child aged less than three years is the strongest predictor for hazard of exit into maternity leave, while this is not the case for the transition into housekeeping. Having a primary-school or secondary-school child also increases the hazard of exit into maternity leave. This is a consequence of the related family policy measures: when maternity leave was introduced in Hungary many women decided to have a second or a third child although they already had older child(ren). The presence of an adult child in the family aged 19 or over decreases the hazard rate of exit into maternity leave. The transition to housekeeping is, however, affected positively by this fact. An adult child in the family can act as a new breadwinner and this makes it economically possible for the wife to stay at home.

Husbands' occupation and education have a significant impact on wives' employment exits. The effects are negative, which means that the lower the status of the husband the higher the hazard that the wife moves out of the labour force. The difference between the two models for the two employment transitions is that, for maternity leave, the significant predictor is husband's occupation, while for housekeeping it is husband's education. This result seems to be related to marriage homogamy in the family.[8]

In model 3, interaction terms are added to the model. The strong negative estimates for the interaction between the cohorts and the duration up to exit into maternity leave indicates that the interval between date of marriage and this event decreases from the oldest to the youngest cohort. This is probably due to the increasing age at time of marriage. The same estimates are positive for the transition into housekeeping: the interval between date of marriage and this event increases. If wives in younger cohorts exit into housekeeping then they do so later because this employment transition is less connected to childbearing.

Further interaction terms reveal that, the more educated the husband, the shorter the time interval between marriage and exit into maternity leave. Similarly, the higher the education of the wife or the better the status of the husband, the shorter the time interval between marriage and transition to housekeeping.

2. (Re-)entry into Labour Force

(Re-)entry into the labour force occurs more regularly from maternity leave than from housekeeping. Employment transitions from maternity leave into

---

[8] In an early stage of the analysis, we distinguished a model with only the wife's characteristics and one in which the husband's characteristics were added to it. Because the effects of wife's characteristics remained almost unchanged when controlling for the husband's characteristics, we decided only to present the last model (model 2 in Tables 13.1 and 13.2).

the labour force are almost entirely re-entries. However, moves from house-keeping into employment contain both re-entries and new entries. The results are shown in Table 13.4. Model 1 shows the difference in the occurrence of the events by marriage cohorts.[9] The hazard for (re-)entry from maternity leave is lower for wives in the youngest marriage cohort because these couples still have small children. (Re-)entry into employment from housekeeping, how-ever, is most probable for wives in the second to youngest marriage cohort.

The age effects, controlled for only the impact of marriage cohorts (not shown in the table), also display different patterns. Wives return to employ-ment from maternity leave at an older age, when the child is getting older. However, (re-)entry into labour force from housekeeping—if it happens—occurs at a younger age. The age effect for the transition from maternity leave to work becomes negative when other predictor variables are controlled for, indicating that wives with longer work experience, more human capital investments, and better market capabilities return to employment at a younger age. Cumulative work experience has a positive impact on (re-)entry into the labour force. Higher labour-market investments increase the hazard rate of return into the labour market. Age at time of marriage negatively affects the (re-)entry into employment from maternity leave or from housekeeping.

Both human capital investments (years of education) and higher market capability (occupation) positively influence the hazard of (re-)entry into employment. For returning from maternity leave, even social origin is a sig-nificant positive predictor. The higher the wife's father's occupational status, the greater the hazard that she will return to work from maternity leave.

A large number of children decreases the hazard for (re-)entry into the labour force from maternity leave but does not significantly influence the transition from housekeeping. Returning to work from maternity leave is strongly affected by the age of the children. The presence of a child younger than 3 has a negative impact on the hazard rate of this transition. Having chil-dren older than 3, however, positively influences the hazard of (re-)entry into work from maternity leave. This confirms again that the legal time limit of maternity leave has a strong effect on families' employment decisions. The hazard for (re-)entry into employment from housekeeping is affected by the age of children in a similar way, but the magnitude of the estimates is smaller.

Spouse's effects are weaker for (re-)entry into the labour force compared to exit from work. The husband's social origin is the only significant positive pre-dictor. The higher the husband's father's occupational status, the greater the hazard that the wife will return to work from maternity leave or housekeep-ing. As in the case of wife's social background, this result indicates that family decisions are influenced by values and attitudes, gender-role preferences, and other different characteristics of family climate which may be influenced by husbands' and wives' socialization and role models they experienced in their childhood from their parents.

---

[9] The model of the transition rate from maternity leave to work is also estimated only for the period after 1967.

Table 13.4. Effects on transition rate from maternity leave and housekeeping to work (Cox regression estimates based on person-period dataset, standard errors in parentheses)

	From maternity leave to work[a]			From housekeeping to work		
	Model 1	Model 2	Model 3	Model 1	Model 2	Model 3
Marriage cohort[b]						
1963–72	−0.1586	0.0546	2.5549***	0.5568***	0.3864**	0.4724***
	(0.1233)	(0.1286)	(0.2277)	(0.1177)	(0.1321)	(0.1357)
1973–82	−0.3694**	−0.0989	2.4792***	1.2759***	0.9493***	0.3188
	(0.1216)	(0.1314)	(0.2288)	(0.1489)	(0.1765)	(0.2214)
1983–92	−0.5953***	−0.2692	2.2551***	1.1108*	0.7882	−0.1916
	(0.1331)	(0.1470)	(0.2392)	(0.4598)	(0.4703)	(1.1294)
Age	—	−0.1960***	−0.0170	—	−0.3842***	−0.2372***
		(0.0146)	(0.0146)		(0.0239)	(0.0248)
Age sq.	—	0.0017	−0.0013	—	0.0001	−0.0012
		(0.0009)	(0.0010)		(0.0013)	(0.0014)
Cumulative work experience	—	0.1853***	0.0658***	—	0.3905***	0.2407***
		(0.0113)	(0.0114)		(0.0222)	(0.0229)
Age at time of marriage	—	0.0058	−0.0523***	—	−0.0478	−0.0738*
		(0.0122)	(0.0118)		(0.0294)	(0.0293)
Social origin	—	0.0047*	0.0034	—	0.0011	0.0047
		(0.0019)	(0.0019)		(0.0059)	(0.0064)
Education	—	0.1102***	0.0638***	—	0.1668***	0.0440
		(0.0122)	(0.0128)		(0.0350)	(0.0301)
Occupation	—	0.0094***	0.0071***	—	0.0238***	0.0077
		(0.0019)	(0.0020)		(0.0055)	(0.0059)
No. of children	—	−0.2137***	0.1146**	—	0.0832	−0.0214
		(0.0427)	(0.0412)		(0.0800)	(0.0795)
Child aged 0–2	—	−1.5659***	−1.9131***	—	−0.6879***	−0.7076***
		(0.0598)	(0.0609)		(0.1705)	(0.1725)
Child aged 3–6	—	0.3216***	0.8362***	—	0.3311**	0.1874
		(0.0635)	(0.0640)		(0.1260)	(0.1260)

Child aged 7–14	—	0.7567*** (0.0731)	-0.2375** (0.0764)	—	0.2928* (0.1381)	0.3019* (0.1425)
Child aged 15–18	—	0.4918** (0.1749)	-0.2306 (0.1700)	—	0.0558 (0.1915)	0.1673 (0.1910)
Child aged 19 and over	—	-0.2305 (0.3182)	-0.5334 (0.3158)	—	-0.2919 (0.3009)	-0.4877 (0.3245)
Husband's social origin	—	0.0039* (0.0019)	0.0025 (0.0018)	—	0.0163* (0.0069)	0.0050 (0.0068)
Husband's education	—	0.0036 (0.0108)	0.0121 (0.0109)	—	0.0502 (0.0262)	-0.0134 (0.0277)
Husband's occupation	—	-0.0029 (0.0022)	-0.0028 (0.0022)	—	-0.0004 (0.0050)	-0.0057 (0.0060)
Interaction terms with duration						
Marriage cohort × time:						
1963–72	—	—	-5.9321*** (0.3161)	—	—	-0.0299 (0.2084)
1973–82	—	—	-5.5445*** (0.3143)	—	—	-0.2099 (0.2960)
1983–92	—	—	-5.4663*** (0.3415)	—	—	-0.8127 (1.0541)
Education × time	—	—	-0.1402*** (0.0243)	—	—	-0.3130*** (0.0359)
Occupation × time	—	—	-0.0145** (0.0044)	—	—	0.0084 (0.0075)
Husband's educ. × time	—	—	-0.0557* (0.0237)	—	—	-0.1089*** (0.0331)
Husband's occup. × time	—	—	-0.0030 (0.0047)	—	—	-0.0175* (0.0077)
–2 Log likelihood	37,525.264	35,582.505	32,573.827	5,699.553	4,971.626	4,642.298
Sig. of improvement	0.0000	0.0000	0.0000	0.0000	0.0000	0.0000
No. of events	1,927	1,927	1,927	377	377	377

a Estimates are based on events which occurred after 1967 because maternity leave was not an option before this date. b Reference categoy: 1953–62

*** $p \le .001$, ** $p \le .01$, * $p \le .05$.

In model 3, the interaction terms are added. The significant negative estimates for the interaction between marriage cohorts and time spent out of labour force reveal that wives from younger cohorts spent a shorter time in maternity leave compared to the older cohorts. The same interactions are not statistically significant for the hazard rate of (re-)entry from housekeeping.

Furthermore, model 3 shows significant interactions between the time interval spent out of labour force and wives' and husbands' educational level as well as wives' occupational status. Accordingly, wives' higher human capital investments and market capabilities, as well as husbands' higher educational level, decrease the length of time she spends in maternity leave. Wives' and husbands' education decrease the duration of time she spends in housekeeping, too.

Discussion

Two types of employment transitions have been analysed in this chapter for Hungarian wives living in couples: the move into and out of maternity leave, and the move into and out of housekeeping. Unlike many other market economies, part-time jobs are not widely available to Hungarian women. Since our data are from 1992, the transition to unemployment was quite rare, too, it was only a two to three-year-old phenomenon in Hungary at that time. Consequently, none of these latter possibilities of employment exit could be considered and investigated.

Maternity leave and housekeeping seem to be different alternative employment exits for Hungarian women. The results reveal strong period effects in the occurrence of these events in the marriage cohorts applied in the analysis. Frequencies for exits into maternity leave and housekeeping indicate opposing trends from the oldest to the youngest cohort; the former increases, the latter declines. Maternity leave was not an option for the older cohorts because it did not exist until 1967. However, as general living conditions improved in the 1960s, the socialist welfare state was developed and offered this possibility for mothers of new-born babies. The length of maternity leave increased, the level of financial compensation improved, and the majority of the younger cohorts stayed at home on maternity leave for a shorter or longer time. Conversely, as full-time employment became the rule for females in Hungary, housekeeping became more and more irregular from the older to the younger cohorts.

While the exit into maternity leave as such is strongly related to childbirth and entry into motherhood, housekeeping status is a more complex phenomenon with varying 'meanings'. It can be a functional equivalent of maternity leave for older cohorts. It can be a traditional status for females of older cohorts who stayed at home as housekeepers between completing their education and getting married. It can represent another traditional family lifestyle when women leave employment after getting married without waiting to give birth to a baby. It can be a kind of 'pre-retirement' when working women leave the labour force some years before the regular pension age. Finally, it can be a 'forced' situation for wives in the youngest cohort. When entry into the labour force became more difficult for young people in Hungary at the end of the 1980s and especially after 1990, young females with low human capital investments could not find a job and stayed at home as housekeepers because they were not eligible for unemployment benefit since they had never been employed.

Data indicate that the exit into maternity leave is most probable at age 20–2 because this is the most typical age for entry into motherhood for the younger cohorts of Hungarian women. Entry into housekeeping status, however, is characteristic for wives at a younger age (most likely at age 18) and women spend a shorter time in housekeeping compared to maternity leave. This result also makes sense because entry into marriage or motherhood occurred at a younger age in older cohorts (where housekeeping is a functional equivalent of maternity leave or represents the traditional family lifestyle); alternatively, those females who are housekeepers because they are not able to find a job are usually young school dropouts.

Although we did not intend to compare the Hungarian case in a strict way to the American typology developed by Elder and Rockwell (1976) and Sørensen (1983), the majority of Hungarian wives seem to follow the double-track pattern. Table 13.5 indicates that more than half of the wives in Hungarian couples return to work before they give birth to their youngest child. This double-track pattern is stable over marriage cohorts (except the youngest one). The unstable pattern is also typical, which means that wives move frequently between employment and non-employment. The conventional type is characteristic for the oldest cohort married in 1953–62, when Hungarian families were more traditional. A large proportion of wives in the youngest cohort can be found in the conventional type, too, but women in this cohort are mostly censored cases who will belong to some other type (most probably to the double-track or unstable type) at some later point in time.

As expected from the economic approach to the family proposed by Becker (1981), human capital and labour-market investments (better education,

Table 13.5. Employment pattern after marriage by marriage cohort (%)

Employment pattern	1953–62	1963–72	1973–82	1983–92	Total
Conventional	19.3	7.8	7.9	37.3	12.2
Interrupted	1.6	9.0	15.8	9.1	9.7
Double-track	50.3	56.1	51.8	38.1	52.4
Unstable	28.8	27.1	24.5	15.5	25.7
N	528	1,620	1,928	1,396	5,472

longer labour-force experience, higher occupational status) decrease the hazard rate for exits from employment into maternity leave. However, net of these effects, women with professional status seem to follow another strategy of economic logic, namely that they 'invest in their child(ren)'. This means a kind of role specialization is characteristic for professional women in Hungary, namely that they devote time for childbearing at the cost of interrupting their work career. Indeed, as Table 13.6 displays, wives who belong either to the double-track or the interrupted types have higher occupational status and educational level compared to wives in the conventional or unstable types. The strategy is definitely family-based. Husbands' occupational status and educational level is also higher for those couples where the wife belongs to the interrupted employment pattern.

On the other hand, wives in professional jobs do not use childbearing as a legal opportunity to escape from work and stay at home, as other Hungarian women with less education, lower human capital investments, and lower career motivations used to do under communist conditions of females' forced full employment. Wives in professional jobs usually had fewer children and tended to return earlier from maternity leave and continue their gainful employment. This is also shown by Table 13.6, where the age at marriage is highest for wives with the interrupted pattern and they (together with wives in the double-track pattern) have the lowest number of children, too. As mentioned earlier, maternity leave in Hungary was not a real exit from the labour force, as average women had practically no risk of not finding a job again because employers had no right by law to fire a female employee on maternity leave. This interruption was a true risk for those females who had more professional motivations and who jeopardized the continuation of their career plans and not of their employee status.

Given the specific situation of full employment under communism and the system of low wages and families with two breadwinners, it is not surprising that spouse's effects have special features as well. Since the labour market was not organized by an economic rationality, husband's occupation (financial resources) did not have the impact on wife's employment transition predicted by the New Home Economics. In fact, there is only one model of the four

Table 13.6. Employment pattern after marriage by wife's and husband's characteristics (mean values)

	Conventional	Interrupted	Double-track	Unstable	Total
Wife's ISEI score at marriage	30.74	36.50	36.37	32.96	34.87
Wife's education at marriage	8.85	10.86	10.38	9.65	10.05
Husband's ISEI score at marriage	31.65	36.85	35.41	33.43	34.58
Husband's education at marriage	9.50	11.45	10.89	10.27	10.62
Wife's age at marriage	20.40	21.08	20.39	19.88	20.32
Number of children	1.72	1.43	1.63	1.80	1.63

where husband's occupation has a significant impact. This is the exit to maternity leave and even in this case the sign of effect is negative, which contradicts the hypothesis of economic heterogeneity. However, if the interactions between the duration at risk and husband's characteristics are considered, results of the analyses for spouse's effects support the cultural homogamy hypothesis.

We assumed that husband's education would affect the wife's employment exit negatively and (re-)entry into work positively because the higher the husband's education, the higher the wife's education and the two measures were expected to have an influence in the same direction. Our assumption turned out to be less true for the direct effects but it is verified by the interaction terms.

Our final estimates (model 3) indicate the same pattern for effects of wives' and husbands' status on employment transitions (negative interaction terms with duration) and this is in line with the cultural homogamy hypothesis. We can conclude that, on the one hand, wives with a higher social status tend to invest in childbearing but are also inclined to combine fertility and career plans. Dual-breadwinner family strategies are influenced by the husbands, too. In the case of wife's exit into maternity leave, we found a negative interaction term between husband's education and duration, indicating that wives spend less time in employment and take maternity leave within a shorter period, given that they marry at an older age, give birth to a child at an older age, and that their husbands have a higher educational level. On the other hand, wives with more human capital investments and market capabilities, as well as with better educated husbands, return earlier to work from maternity leave. This is interpreted as an influence of family climate with non-traditional gender-role identities. The fact that husband's better social origin has a positive net influence on wife's (re-)entry into work also underlines the importance of men's socialization and gender-role attitudes in the process.

Analysing employment transitions under communist labour-market circumstances has specific features which make comparability to Western market economies difficult. Maternity leave as an employment interruption does not endanger further work opportunities for the average wife under full employment; only women with a high level of education and in high occupational status risk their professional career. Housekeeping is closer to the employment interruption in a Western sense, but it has lost its significance and changed its character over the decades. Hungary is a modern industrial society where meritocracy is an important driving force, and human capital investments and labour-market capabilities influence employment decisions, especially for wives with professional status. However, in consequence of the non-rational and less market-oriented allocation of labour power under communism, economic principles do not work in the same way as in Western economies, for example, resource-bargaining in a financial respect does not make sense under the system of low wages determined centrally by the state. Decision-making in Hungarian families and trading between husbands and wives seem to be more strongly embedded in partners' cultural capital and families' cultural climate, and are influenced by education-based changes in traditional role expectations. These mechanisms affect wives' employment patterns and prove that women's behaviour in the labour market can be better understood by considering couples as the relevant unit of stratification instead of as individual family members.

References

Becker, G. S. (1971). *The Economics of Discrimination* (Chicago: University of Chicago Press).
——(1981). *A Treatise on the Family* (Cambridge, Mass.: Harvard University Press).
Bernasco, W. (1994). *Coupled Careers: The Effects of Spouse's Resources on Success at Work* (Amsterdam: Thesis Publishers).
——P. M. de Graaf, and W. Ultee (1998). 'Coupled Careers: Effects of Spouse Resources on Occupational Attainment in the Netherlands', *European Sociological Review*, 14: 15–31.
Bernhardt, E. M. (1993). 'Fertility and Employment', *European Sociological Review*, 9: 25–42.
Blau, P. M., and O. D. Duncan (1967). *The American Occupational Structure* (New York: Wiley).
Blau, F. D., and M. A. Ferber (1986). *The Economics of Women, Men, and Work* (Englewood Cliffs, NJ: Prentice-Hall).
Blossfeld, H.-P. (1986). 'Career Opportunities in the Federal Republic of Germany: A Dynamic Approach to the Study of Life Course, Cohort and Period Effects', *European Sociological Review*, 2: 208–25.
——(ed.) (1995). *The New Role of Women: Family Formation in Modern Societies* (Boulder, Colo.: Westview Press).
——and K. U. Mayer (1988). 'Labor Market Segmentation in the Federal Republic of Germany: An Empirical Study of Segmentation Theories from a Life Course Perspective', *European Sociological Review*, 4: 123–40.
——and G. Rohwer (1995). *Techniques of Event History Modeling. New Approaches to Causal Analysis* (Mahwah, NJ: L. Earlbaum).
Cramer, J. C. (1980). 'Fertility and Female Employment: Problems of Causal Direction', *American Sociological Review*, 45: 167–90.
Csernák, J. (1992). 'Házasság és család: a demográfiai változások újabb irányvonalai és összefüggései' (Marriage and Family: Recent Trends and Connections in Changes in Demography), *Demográfia*, 35: 87–112.
Drobnič, S. (1997). 'Part-Time Work in Central and Eastern European Countries', in H.-P. Blossfeld and C. Hakim (eds.), *Between Equalisation and Marginalisation: Women Working Part-Time in Europe and the United States of America* (Oxford: Oxford University Press), 71–89.
Edwards, M. (1982). 'Financial Arrangements Made by Husbands and Wives: Findings of a Survey', *Australian and New Zealand Journal of Sociology*, 18: 320–38.
Elder, G. H., and R. Rockwell (1976). 'The Timing of Marriage and Women's Life Patterns', *Journal of Family History*, 1: 34–54.
Erikson, R., and J. H. Goldthorpe (1992). *The Constant Flux* (Oxford: Clarendon Press).
————and L. Portocarero (1979). 'Intergenerational Class Mobility in Three Western European Societies', *British Journal of Sociology*, 30: 303–43.

Esping-Andersen, G. (1993). 'Post-Industrial Class Structures: An Analytical Framework', in G. Esping-Andersen (ed.), *Changing Classes. Stratification and Mobility in Post-Industrial Societies* (London: Sage).

Ferber, M., and J. Huber (1979). 'Husbands, Wives and Careers', *Journal of Marriage and the Family*, 41: 315–25.

Frey, M., and I. Gere (1994). *Part-Time Employment: The Unutilized Possibility. Summary Research Report on Individual Needs for Part-Time Work and its Employers Receptiveness* (Budapest: Research Institute of Labour).

Galasi, P., and G. Sziráczki (eds.) (1985). *Labour Market and Second Economy in Hungary* (Frankfurt: Campus Verlag).

Ganzeboom, H. B. G., P. M. de Graaf, and P. Róbert (1990). 'Reproduction Theory on Socialist Ground: Intergenerational Transmission of Inequalities in Hungary', in A. L. Kalleberg, (ed.), *Research in Social Stratification and Mobility*, ix (Greenwich: JAI Press), 79–104.

——— and D. Treiman (in collaboration with Jan de Leeuw) (1992). 'A Standard International Socio-Economic Index of Occupational Status', *Social Science Research*, 21: 1–56.

—— R. Luijkx, and P. Róbert (1991). *Trends in Intergenerational Occupational Mobility in Hungary between 1930 and 1989* (Tilbury: Department of Sociology, Tilburg University, Working Paper Series, 58).

Glass, D. V. (ed.) (1954). *Social Mobility in Britain* (London: Routledge & Kegan Paul).

Hajnal, J. (1965). 'European Marriage Patterns in Perspective', in D. V. Glass and D. E. C. Eversley (eds.), *Population in History* (London: Edward Arnold), 101–43.

Hakim, C. (1993). 'The Myth of Rising Female Employment', *Work Employment and Society*, 7: 97–120.

—— (1996). *Key Issues in Women's Work: Female Heterogeneity and the Polarisation of Women's Employment* (London: Athlone Press).

Harcsa, I. (1992). *Hungarian Social Mobility and Life History Survey 1992* [MRDF]. Budapest: Central Statistical Office.

Hout, M. (1982). 'The Association between Husbands' and Wives' Occupations in Two-Earner Families', *American Journal of Sociology*, 88: 397–409.

Kalmijn, M. (1991). 'Status Homogamy in the United States', *American Journal of Sociology*, 97: 496–523.

—— (1994). 'Assortative Mating by Cultural and Economic Occupational Status', *American Journal of Sociology*, 100: 422–52.

Kamarás, F. (1997). 'Ifjúság és népesség' (Youth and Population), in *A gyermekek és az ifjúság helyzete* (Situation of Children and Youths) (Budapest: Central Statistical Office).

Klinger, A., and I. Monigl (1981). 'Népesedés és népesedéspolitika Magyarországon az 1970-es és 1980-as évtizedben' (Demographic Situation and Population Policy in Hungary in the 1970s and 1980s'), *Demográfia*, 24: 395–433.

Kolosi, T. (1988). 'Stratification and Social Structure in Hungary', in W. R. Scott and J. Blake (eds.), *Annual Review of Sociology 14* (Palo Alto, Calif.: Annual Review Inc.), 405–19.

—— J. Peschar, and P. Róbert (1985). 'On Reduction of Social Reproduction: A Hungarian–Netherlands Comparison on the Changing Effects of Social Origin and Education on the Occupational Position', in M. Kaiser, R. Nuthmann, and H. Stegmann (eds). *Berufliche Verbleibsforschung in der Diskussion*, ii (Nuremberg: IAB), 3–28.

Lipset, S. M. and H. L. Zetterberg (1970 [1956]). 'A Theory of Social Mobility', in M. M. Tumin (ed.), *Readings on Social Stratification* (Englewood Cliffs, NJ: Prentice-Hall).

Long, J. E., and E. B. Jones (1980). 'Labor Force Entry and Exit by Married Women: A Longitudinal Analysis', *Review of Economics and Statistics*, 62: 1–6.

Luijkx, R., P. Róbert, P. M. de Graaf, and H. B. G. Ganzeboom (1998). 'From Ascription to Achievement: The Status Attainment Process in Hungary from 1910 to 1992', in P. Nieuwbeerta and H. B. G. Ganzeboom (eds.), *Conference Proceedings Transformation Processes in Eastern Europe* (The Hague: ESR), 93–120.

Mayer, K. U., D. L. Featherman, L. K. Selbee, and T. Colbjørnsen (1989). 'Class Mobility during the Working Life: A Comparison of Germany and Norway', in M. L. Kohn (ed.), *Cross-National Research in Sociology* (Newbury Park, Calif.: Sage), 218–39.

Pahl, J. (1983). 'The Allocation of Money and the Structure of Inequality within Marriage', *Sociological Review*, 31: 313–35.

Polachek, S. W. (1975). 'Discontinuous Labor Force Participation and its Effect on Women's Market Earnings', in C. B. Lloyd (ed.), *Sex Discrimination and the Division of Labor* (New York: Columbia University Press), 90–122.

——(1981). 'Occupational Self-Selection: A Human Capital Approach to Sex Differences in Occupational Structure', *Review of Economics and Statistics*, 63: 60–9.

Róbert, P. (1984). 'A Multidimensional Approach to Social Mobility', in R. Andorka and T. Kolosi (eds.), *Stratification and Inequality* (Budapest: Institute of Social Sciences), 223–44.

——(1991). 'Educational Transition in Hungary from the Post-War Period to the End of the 1980s', *European Sociological Review*, 7: 213–36.

——and H.-P. Blossfeld (1995). 'Hungary', in H-P. Blossfeld (ed.), *The New Role of Women: Family Formation in Modern Societies* (Boulder, Colo.: Westview Press), 211–26.

Shavit, Y., and H.-P. Blossfeld (eds.) (1993). *Persistent Inequality: Changing Educational Attainment in Thirteen Countries* (Boulder, Colo.: Westview Press).

Simkus, A., and R. Andorka (1982). 'Inequalities in Education in Hungary 1923–1973', *American Sociological Review*, 47: 740–51.

Sørensen, A. (1983). 'Women's Employment Patterns after Marriage', *Journal of Marriage and the Family*, 45: 311–21.

——and S. McLanahan (1987). 'Married Women's Economic Dependency 1940–1980', *American Journal of Sociology*, 93: 659–87.

Stolzenberg, R. M. and L. J. Waite (1977). 'Age, Fertility Expectations and Plans for Employment', *American Sociological Review*, 42: 769–83.

Thornton, A., D. F. Alwin, and D. Cambrun (1983). 'Causes and Consequences of Sex-Role Attitudes and Attitude Change', *American Sociological Review*, 48: 211–27.

Treiman, D. J. (1970). 'Industrialization and Social Stratification', in E.O. Laumann (ed.), *Social Stratification, Research and Theory for the 1970s* (Indianapolis: Bobbs-Merill), 207–34.

Wolf, W. C., and N. D. Fligstein (1979). 'Sex and Authority in the Workplace: The Causes of Sexual Inequality', *American Sociological Review*, 44: 235–52.

Wright, E. O. (1979). *Class Structure and Income Determination* (New York: Academic Press).

——(1985). *Classes* (London: Verso).

——(1997). *Class Counts: Comparative Studies in Class Analysis* (Cambridge: Cambridge University Press).

Yamaguchi, K. (1991). *Event History Analysis* (Newbury Park, Calif.: Sage).

APPENDIX TO CHAPTER 13: EXPLANATORY VARIABLES USED IN THE ANALYSIS

Cohort effects
- three dummies for the marriage cohorts (1963–72, 1973–82, 1983–92); the oldest cohort is the reference category;

Demographic characteristics
- age at marriage;

Age effects
- age measured by years in linear and quadratic form as a time-dependent covariate;
- work experience during the career: cumulative duration of full-time employment until the next year in the job episodes, measured in years;

Status variables
- wife's social origin, measured by father's occupational status (ISEI score; for this measure of occupational status see Ganzeboom *et al.* (1992).) at age of 14;
- wife's education as time-dependent covariate, measured by years of schooling;
- wife's career resources, measured by her occupational status (ISEI score) as time-dependent covariate;

Family characteristics
- number of children as time-dependent covariate;
- new-born child: time-dependent dummy variable indicating the presence of at least one child under 3 years of age in the family;
- pre-school child: time-dependent dummy variable indicating the presence of at least one child between 3 and 6 years of age in the family;
- primary-school child: time-dependent dummy variable indicating the presence of at least one child between 7 and 14 years in the family;
- secondary-school child: time-dependent dummy variable indicating the presence of at least one child between 14 and 18 years in the family;
- adult child: time-dependent dummy variable indicating the presence of at least one child over 18 years in the family;

Spouse's status
- husband's social origin, measured by father's occupational status (ISEI score) at age of 14;
- husband's education as time-dependent covariate, measured by years of schooling;
- husband's career resources, measured by his occupational status (ISEI score) as time-dependent covariate.

14

Job-Shift Patterns of Husbands and Wives in Urban China*

XUEGUANG ZHOU AND PHYLLIS MOEN

Introduction

THIS chapter examines the workplace location and labour-force experi-ences (especially job shifts) of husbands and wives in urban China. As the theme of this book indicates, there has been increasing interest in considering the family (or couple) as the unit of analysis in studying patterns of labour-market participation and social stratification processes. Curtis (1986: 168) has argued that 'attention to family household is essential in the understanding of the social organization of inequality in complex societies', noting how the redistribution of resources and power within a family is structured by the larger social processes in the broader society. Following this line of argument, we treat the family, and especially the husband–wife dyad, as a critical inter-vening process in social stratification, examining how the spousal dyad medi-ates stratification processes and affects changes in individuals' life chances.

Two key concepts are the *family economy* and *family adaptive strategies*, both sensitizing scholars to the role of the family as a role budgeting and resource allocating unit (Moen and Wethington 1992; Smelser 1959). Existing theory and research in industrialized market societies have largely based the concep-tualization of the family economy on market-like processes where the division of labour and exchange among family members takes place in response to market opportunities and the structure of labour markets (see e.g. Becker 1981; England and Farkas 1986; Goode 1960; Mincer 1978; Sørensen and McLanahan 1987). But the family and spousal relationships are shaped and constrained by societal institutional arrangements. Therefore, a comparative

*This research is supported by a Spencer Fellowship, grants from the National Science Foundation (SES–9212936 and SBR–9413540) as well as from the Alfred P. Sloan Foundation (Sloan FDN #96–6–9, 99–6–3). We thank Liren Hou for his able research assistance. We thank the Departments of Sociology at Fudan University and the People's University, as well as the Institute of Sociology at Tianjin Academy of Social Sciences and, in particular, Weida Fan, Qiang Li, Yunkang Pan, and Xizhe Peng for their assistance in data collection.

approach to the role of the family and spousal resources gives us a unique lens to look into processes of status attainment and social mobility across societies.

In this chapter, we examine the role of spousal characteristics in affecting the likelihood of job shifts of husbands and wives in urban China, from 1949 to 1994. We situate our study in this unique institutional context to shed light on the link between the institutional context, the family, and the social stratification processes in a state-socialist society. In contrast to market societies in Western Europe and North America, the People's Republic of China has been organized under the state-socialist redistributive (planning) economy since the Communist Party took power in 1949. The role of family, spousal relationships, and labour-market structures were shaped by this institutional context. For instance, state policies and welfare programmes led to a large proportion of women working in the labour force. Furthermore, the large-scale economic reforms since the 1980s have led to fundamental changes in the state-socialist society, forcing individuals and families to respond to new opportunities and to cope with increasing risks. Thus, the Chinese experience reflects both the impacts of state socialism (in contrast to the market societies) and profound social changes over time. We should point out that, despite significant changes in recent years, during the period under study (1949–94) the urban areas were still heavily influenced by the existing institutional arrangements of state socialism, especially with the presence of a strong state sector. Though the experiences of couples in China are unique on a number of fronts, the high level of Chinese women's labour-force participation underscores the need for a theoretical focus on the family-based division of labour in the public domain (for example, in paid work). We pay particular attention to the unique features of the state-socialist institutional context in China and emphasize the potential impacts of the state on the role of the family through specific social policies, as well as through redistributive economic institutions.

Couples and Paid Labour: Theoretical Issues

The idea that the family is a social unit engaged in risk and resource sharing is not new. It is the premise of household economics and one of the central issues in sociological studies of family relations. In the household economics literature, the rational choice approach emphasizes the family or household as a rational actor, making decisions based on the comparative advantage of husbands and wives that maximize household utilities (Becker 1981; Mincer 1978). A household can be treated as a production unit where efficiency and overall benefits are gained through 'specialization and exchange' among family members. In this view, discrepancies in socio-economic status between husbands and wives, if indeed observed, can be explained by joint rational decisions within the household. But by treating the spousal dyad as symmetric, the economic approach suffers a major weakness in that its ideal-typical family appears as devoid of both gendered social relationships and the structural constraints embedded in the social institutions of labour markets. Historians and sociologists, on the other hand, emphasize the ideological and power differences between spouses, as well as the significance of the larger opportunity structure (see e.g. Moen 1989, 1992; Rosenfeld 1980; Tilly and Scott 1978; Tomaskovic-Devey 1993).

One way to conceptualize husbands' and wives' interlocking progression through jobs and locations in the social stratification structure is in terms of 'family adaptive strategies'. According to Tilly (1979), family adaptive strategies are a set of 'implicit rules guiding the behaviour'of the members of a family. Sociologists have found the concept of 'family adaptive strategy' a useful device, 'bringing the family back in as an active participant in the larger society, an actor responding to, reworking, or reframing external constraints and opportunities' (Moen and Wethington 1992: 234; Elder 1974; Tilly and Scott 1978).

Social scientists have developed several approaches in considering family adaptive strategies. The primary focus in this literature is on 'family power'—the bargaining and redistribution of power between spouses, with wives at a disadvantage given the gendered nature of roles and resources both within the household and within the larger society (Blood and Wolfe 1960; Curtis 1986; England and Farkas 1986; Hood 1983; McDonald 1980). Socially constructed family roles introduce asymmetry into the family decision-making process in the sense that, as long as husbands are presumed to be the family breadwinners, family decision-making will reflect not only relative resources but also gender roles. From a sociological perspective, 'rational' family adaptive strategies must be explained by the social construction of the reward systems outside the household.

For instance, gendered roles in the workplace in both state-socialist and market societies are well recognized (England *et al.* 1988; Reskin and Roos 1990; Sørensen and Trappe 1995). Gender inequality in China has also been documented (Whyte 1984; Entwisle *et al.* 1995; Lee 1995). Different rewards associated with gendered roles in the workplace provide incentives to induce a family-based division of labour in the public domain. They also sustain the cultural norms of gender roles that reproduce differential behavioural patterns between spouses in face of new opportunities (Moen 1989; Bielby and Bielby 1992). So long as male-role jobs are more rewarded than female-role jobs, they encourage men to take advantage of such gendered opportunities.

We adopt the notion of adaptive strategies as a heuristic, sensitizing device, serving as a bridge between social structures and individual biographies. This may be especially germane in the context of China; large-scale changes in state policy and/or the economy may require households to formulate new strategies of resource generation and allocation. We believe that the family plays an indispensable role in *both* risk and resource sharing and resource optimization. On the one hand, the family adopts risk-sharing strategies that generate and reinforce gender roles, inadvertently affecting women's life chances. On the other hand, couples may also engage in a 'collective project' of advancing both spouses' political and socio-economic status, through mutual resource optimization. Empirically, then, the prevalence of a risk/resource-*sharing* strategy may be reflected in a negative association between spouses' socio-economic status and economic benefits. In contrast, the dominance of a mutual resource *optimization* strategy may be shown in a positive association of socio-economic status and economic benefits between spouses. Both strategies are likely to coexist in a family. In this light, the family may generate or mediate multiple and potentially competing processes in allocating men and women into different positions in the social structure. In addition, movement across organizations or occupations may reflect the respondents' own location in the social structure, independent of any family actions.

In examining couples' adaptive strategies in the Chinese context, one needs to pay particular attention to social policies. The reason is simple: the socialist state plays a central role in family formation and structure, in women's labour-force participation, and in the unique stratification structures in which men and women are located. Thus, we begin with the relationship between the state and the family. We highlight two processes: (1) redistributive economic institutions; (2) varying state policies.

State-Socialist Redistributive Economy and Labour-Force Participation

The planning economy under state socialism implies that labour-force participation has been closely regulated in state socialist societies. Redistributive economic institutions create unique stratification structures. We first examine the unique dimensions of the social institutions that organize labour-force activities.

Occupational status: Scholars typically use occupational status as a conventional indicator of socio-economic status and class location. Different occupations are associated with different job attributes with regard to autonomy, authority relationship, and mobility patterns, as emphasized in Marxian approaches to social classes. They are also closely associated with prestige, social status, and lifestyles, as emphasized in Weberian views of social stratification. It is not surprising, then, that most studies of social stratification and social class have primarily focused on occupational position and mobility.

Scholars who study state socialism emphasize the political logic of redistribution in these societies. Szelenyi (1978) underscored the fundamental division between 'redistributors' and 'immediate producers', arguing that social inequalities under state socialism reflect the conflicts between these two groups. Empirically, this line of argument has led researchers to examine the stratification order of different *occupational groups*, with particular attention to the association between occupational status and political authority. Cadres, for instance, are bureaucrats and officials who redistribute economic resources and enjoy particular redistributive benefits. Professionals, on the other hand, often follow different career paths (Walder 1995; Zhou 1995). Other occupational groups (service workers, skilled and unskilled workers) tend to occupy a similar social status with regard to their economic benefits. Thus, although the occupational categories used in analysing state-socialist stratification systems are similar to those in industrialized market societies, the meaning of these categories and their location in the stratification structure are often qualitatively different across societies.

Organizational hierarchy: In a market economy, the distribution of economic rewards is based on an individual's market position and is carried out in everyday economic transactions in the market-place. In so far as occupational standing reflects market position, occupational groupings serve as a good indicator of a person's location in the stratification structure. In socialist societies, by contrast, the distribution of economic rewards is controlled by the state, which allocates a large proportion of resources *not* on the basis of occupational groups, but through work organizations (for example, subsidies, health insurance, and welfare programme). Therefore, a focus on occupational groups alone is inadequate to understand patterns of redistribution under state socialism. This observation points to the second dimension of stratification under state socialism: redistribution based on economic sectors (industries) and work organizations.

A major contribution of studies of social stratification in China is the identification and theoretical arguments about the importance of organizational hierarchies. Scholars (Bian 1994; Lin and Bian 1991; Walder 1992; Zhou *et al.* 1997) have shown that types of work organization are a major basis of social stratification in the Chinese context. They have demonstrated that the historical evolution of the socialist redistributive economy in China has given rise to a variety of organizational forms, with different property rights relationships to the state, and have linked the differences in redistributive benefits of employees across organizations to the hierarchical order of work organizations. In urban China, one may distinguish three broad types of work organization: (1) governmental agencies, public organizations, and state-owned firms that constitute the state sector and enjoy a larger proportion of redistribution benefits; (2) collective firms, often affiliated or sponsored by a local government, that are less privileged in the redistribution of economic resources; and (3) private firms that are excluded from benefiting from state redistribution. These types of work organizations are associated with differential economic benefits.

State Policies and the Family

The socialist state directly affects family formation and structure through policy regulations concerning the timing of marriage, number of children, and old age support responsibilities. For example, China's controversial one-child-per-family policy, implemented since the mid-1970s, has had profound impacts on family formation and family structure. Its impacts will continue to be felt for many years to come.

Since the revolution of 1949, China has adopted an ideology of gender equality (as Mao Zedong said, 'Women can hold up half of the sky'). Active social policies promoting women's educational opportunities and labour-force participation have affected not only women's life chances but also the nature of families, especially the spousal relationship. There is relative equality between men and women in educational opportunities and a high percentage of women in the labour force (Whyte 1984; Whyte and Parish 1984). China is not alone in this regard (see Sørensen and Trappe 1995 on job attainment in East Germany; Szelenyi and Aschaffenburg 1993 on educational attainment in Hungary).

One salient characteristic of the political dynamics under state socialism is the frequent shift of state policies over time. The stratification dynamics induced by shifting state policies can drastically transfer resources across sectors and social groups, altering opportunity structures and mechanisms of resource allocation (Whyte 1985; Parish 1984; Zhou *et al.* 1996). For instance, recent economic reforms have created new job opportunities for women from the rural areas (Lee 1995). In tandem with state policy shifts, the role of the family in the stratification processes also can be expected to vary over time.

Implications

The preceding discussion highlights the unique institutional context in which we explore couples and their career paths in urban China. We now draw some implications of the Chinese context for the study of working husbands and wives.

First, because of the different logics in resource allocation between markets and bureaucracy, labour-market institutions in socialist and capitalist economies are organized around different principles. The roles of the family, spousal resources, and family adaptive strategies are likely to differ in different societal contexts. Our research design needs to reflect these unique institutional arrangements as well as the unique mechanisms of resource allocation in China. Accordingly, we need to conceptualize the unique occupational and organizational hierarchies in the Chinese context. Because of the central role of workplaces in allocating resources in the Chinese redistributive economy and of their importance in the social stratification structure, we treat patterns of job shifts across types of work organizations as the primary analytical focus in this study.

Second, as a result of state policies in China, a high percentage of women is actively involved in full-time labour-force participation. This underscores the importance of looking at couples as the unit of analysis; most workers are married to spouses who also work. It also distinguishes the Chinese case from those of Western Europe and the United States (described in other chapters in this volume). While part-time employment has been a key strategy for a large proportion of women in Western and Northern Europe as well as the United States (see Blossfeld and Hakim 1997), women in China typically hold full-time jobs throughout their life courses. Therefore, our analytical focus is on job-shift patterns for spouses who both have full-time employment.

Finally, because of the considerable variations in state policies over time, there have been historical shifts in opportunities, resource allocations, and adaptive strategies. Our analysis must therefore take the historical context into consideration. This is especially important because the economic reform since the 1980s has led to fundamental changes in the labour-market structure and job opportunities. The role of the state in allocating resources and job assignment has been considerably weakened. We need to allow for and explore potential changes in mechanisms of job shifts across historical periods.

Data

The main tasks proposed above will be based on statistical analyses of a representative sample of urban residents drawn from a multi-stage scheme in twenty cities in China in 1993 and 1994. We selected six provinces (Hebei, Heilongjiang, Gansu, Guangdong, Jiangsu, Sichuan), each representing a conventional geographical region in China. Within each province, we selected the capital city of the province to represent large cities (population above 1 million) in that province. We randomly selected a medium-sized city (population between 200,000 and 1 million) and a small city (population below 200,000) based on the 1990 Chinese Urban Statistics Yearbook (State Statistics Bureau 1990). In addition, we included Beijing, the political centre, and Shanghai, the largest industrial city. The sample size in each city was proportional to the population in that size of city in the province. Within each targeted city, we selected residential blocks and households based on a systematic sampling procedure. That is, we selected every nth block and the nth household within the selected blocks. In each household, a respondent aged 25–65 was chosen, based on a random-number table. If the respondent was married, his/her spouse was also interviewed using an identical questionnaire. The dataset included a total of 9,600 individuals (including both spouses). Information about each respondent's life history was collected using a pretested questionnaire.

We obtained retrospective information on respondents' and their spouses' levels of education, workplace, occupation, and promotion, and the timing of these life events. For each married couple, we interviewed both the husband and the wife. Because of our sample frame (aged 25–65), and the cultural significance of marriage in China, a majority of respondents in our sample are married. We have complete information on over 3,500 married couples, with detailed work histories of both spouses.

In this chapter, we analyse husbands' and wives' job-shift patterns separately, conditional on their spouses' characteristics. We label the group (husbands or wives) under study as 'respondents', and refer to their partners as 'spouses'. Thus, when analysing husbands' job-shift patterns, the husbands become the 'respondents', and their wives are the 'spouses', and vice versa.

Variables

Dependent Variables

Our primary focus is on each spouse's organizational location. We focus on type of work organization, given the central role the work organization plays in redistributing economic benefits. We distinguish three broad categories of organizational destination: (1) government agencies and public organizations; (2) state firms; (3) collective and hybrid firms. It is desirable to use a more refined set of organizational destinations by differentiating types of work organizations within each category above. Because of the relative small number of job shifts, we use these combined categories to increase the statistical power in model estimation. Moreover, the redistributive benefits are similar among the types of workplaces within each category.

Independent Variables

We include the following variables to measure the respondents' characteristics:

Age and age squared: We examine the first- and second-order effects of age to measure the effect of work experience or seniority.

Education: We use education as the conventional measure of human capital. We distinguish the following educational levels: (1) junior high or below (the reference category); (2) senior high (including *Zhongzhuan*); and (3) college (including *Dazhuan*). As Bernasco *et al.* (1998) point out, education is also a measure of cultural capital, often reflecting more modern gender-role orientations.

Occupation: We distinguish the following occupational categories: high-rank cadre, low-rank cadre, professional, technician, clerk, service worker, private entrepreneur, and production worker (the reference category). Differentiating cadres and professionals recognizes the political logic of stratification under state socialism. Cadres (managers, bureaucrats) and professionals have different access to redistributive benefits. The Chinese bureaucratic hierarchy has mainly four levels: *bu* (ministry), *ju* (department), *chu* (division), *ke* (section). We classify those holding ranks at or above *chu* level as high-rank cadres and those at or below *ke* level as low-rank cadres. In the Chinese professional system there are senior engineer, engineer, assistant engineer, and technician levels (or equivalent levels in other professional occupations). We classify those at or above engineer level as high-rank professionals, and those at or below assistant engineer level as low-rank professionals.

Work organization: We use a set of dummy variables to indicate the organizational origin from which job shifts occur. To capture the specific origins, we use a more refined set of organizational categories:

1. Governmental agencies include ministries, commissions, bureaus, and offices at various levels of the Communist Party and state bureaucracies. The Communist Party and the administrative apparatus are interwoven at each level and both are included in this category.

2. Public organizations, in Chinese terminology, are non-profit organizations in the public domain. They include educational and research institutions, and organizations in the medical, publishing, broadcasting, and entertainment sectors. Although they are not the administrative organs of the state, most of these organizations are affiliated with the state or local government through financial and organizational linkages.

3. Among state-owned firms, we distinguish two categories: the central government-owned firms and city government-owned firms. Included in the first category are those work-units in manufacturing, processing, and other production firms and those in service sectors that are directly owned by the central government or the provincial government. These organizations enjoy extensive welfare programme in housing, healthcare, and subsidies.

4. City government-owned firms are firms that are state-owned but are managed by local (city or district within cities) government in this category. These firms benefit from redistribution associated with the state sector but are less prestigious compared with central government-owned firms.

5. Collective firms (the reference category) are not directly under the administration or financial support of the planning economy. Often they are sponsored by local government (such as district/county government or residential offices). Employees in this type of organization have the least favourable welfare programme and low social status in urban China. Collective firms are used as the reference category for type of work organizations.

6. Hybrid firms include private entrepreneurs, firms with mixed property rights, such as collective and private, or joint ventures.

Spousal Characteristics

To examine the effects of spouse's characteristics on the respondent's job shifts, we include the following variables in the model estimation:

Education: We include two dummy variables to indicate those cases where (1) spouse's educational level is higher than the respondent's; (2) spouse's educational level is lower than the respondent's. Those spouses with the same educational level are used as the reference category.

Occupation: Similarly, we include two dummy variables to indicate those cases where (1) spouse's occupational status is higher than the respondent's; (2) spouse's occupational status is lower than the respondent's. Those spouses with the same occupational status are used as the reference category.

Type of work organization: To examine the effect of spouse's location in type of work organization on the respondent's job shift patterns, we used the same set of categories for types of work organizations.

Couple characteristics: In some models we consider couple's conjoint workplace location. We use the following categories: (1) both spouses work in government or public organizations; (2) both work in state firms; (3) both work in collective or hybrid firms (the reference category); (4) husband in the state sector (government, public, state firms), and wife in the non-state sector (collective, hybrid firms); (5) wife in the state sector, and husband in the non-state sector.

Control variables: We include a set of dummy variables to indicate respondents' residential location (province, large, medium, or small city) in all of our statistical analyses to control for city-specific variations in labour markets. We also include a set of dummy variables to indicate those cases with missing values in education, occupation, and types of workplaces. Table 14.1 reports the attributes of the covariates in selected years.

Statistical Models and Methods

Our primary analytical focus is on patterns of job shifts, using couples as the unit of analysis. For the analysis of patterns of job shifts between spouses, we employ event-history analysis (Blossfeld *et al.* 1989; Blossfeld and Rohwer 1995; Tuma and Hannan 1984) to examine the rates of experiencing such events over the life course. The general modelling strategy is as follows. Suppose there are data over time on a sequence of life events, such as obtaining the first job or subsequent job shifts. Observed events are regarded as realizations of a latent, random process of change in individual life chances that depends on covariates of theoretical interest, $x(t)$, which may change over time. Information on spouses' socio-economic status and resources is incorporated into the model as part of the covariates. Following Blossfeld *et al.* (1989) and Tuma and Hannan (1984), we adopt a general event-history model:

$$\ln \lambda_{jkp}(t) = x(t)'\beta_{jkp}$$

where λ_{jkp} is the instantaneous rate of moving from status j to status k at time t. Here k refers to the job to which the person moves, and j refers to the job that the person leaves, in period p; $x(t)$ is the set of time-varying covariates of theoretical interest in the model and β the estimates of the corresponding parameters.

Because of our interest in the gendered aspects of job-shift patterns, we analyse husbands' and wives' job-shift patterns separately, conditional on their own and their spouses' characteristics. We then look at couple characteristics, in terms of both spouses' occupational locations.

Table 14.1. Descriptive statistics for variables used in the analysis, selected years

	1965		1975		1985		1993	
	Husband	Wife	Husband	Wife	Husband	Wife	Husband	Wife
Age[a]	31.2	28.7	37.0	34.6	39.4	37.4	42.2	40.3
Age sq./100	10.0	8.5	14.2	12.4	16.4	14.8	18.9	17.2
Education								
elementary or below	46.7	60.1	35.5	46.6	21.1	28.1	14.6	19.1
junior high	22.4	18.8	25.6	26.7	34.2	36.4	32.9	36.3
senior high	16.8	12.0	21.7	17.5	27.7	26.5	32.4	32.9
college	12.1	4.9	15.8	6.4	16.3	7.4	19.7	10.7
no information	1.9	4.3	1.3	2.8	0.8	1.7	0.5	1.2
Type of work organization								
government agency	19.0	5.1	15.1	4.9	11.1	5.6	10.6	5.9
public organization	9.6	8.4	10.6	10.1	11.3	10.1	10.8	10.2
central gov't-owned firm	29.4	15.9	31.5	18.4	29.1	19.1	26.4	18.0
local gov't-owned firm	16.7	12.0	17.5	15.3	19.4	17.3	18.6	16.9
collective firm	15.5	17.4	15.0	22.1	18.0	25.4	15.4	21.7
hybrid firm	2.1	1.2	2.0	1.9	3.3	2.9	7.4	5.6
farm	2.8	7.9	4.5	9.2	1.6	3.4	0.7	1.2

no work	2.0	8.1	1.0	10.9	0.8	7.1	1.2	6.2
no information[b]	2.9	24.0	2.8	8.3	5.3	9.8	9.1	13.6
Same workplace	6.2	6.2	7.9	7.9	8.0	8.0	7.3	7.3
Occupations								
high-rank manager	4.6	0.4	4.4	0.5	4.8	0.9	4.3	0.9
low-rank manager	17.6	4.2	16.4	5.5	16.2	6.3	14.7	6.1
high-rank professional	3.6	1.8	4.3	2.7	7.0	3.7	8.3	5.5
low-rank professional	12.8	10.7	15.6	13.8	11.7	14.2	10.6	12.3
clerk	2.8	3.5	2.9	3.2	3.6	4.0	4.4	5.3
service worker	5.5	7.7	4.7	9.4	7.2	12.4	7.9	13.3
production worker	41.0	32.0	40.5	38.3	40.1	38.8	35.2	32.9
soldier	4.7	0.3	3.4	0.4	1.4	0.2	1.0	0.1
private entrepreneur	0.3	0.0	0.2	0.4	1.1	0.9	3.4	2.2
farmer	1.8	6.7	3.2	7.7	0.8	2.3	0.3	0.6
no job	0.0	8.1	0.0	5.2	0.0	4.5	0.5	5.2
no information[b]	5.2	24.6	4.3	12.8	6.1	11.8	9.9	15.7
N	1,129	1,129	1,895	1,895	3,114	3,114	3,522	3,522

[a] Age, age sq., refer to the means. All other numbers in the table refer to the % in the designated category.
[b] The category of 'no information' includes those who are retired.

Results

The State, the Family, and Historical Contexts

We maintain that, to understand the role of the family, especially couples, in shaping patterns of labour-force participation and location in the social stratification structure, one needs to take into consideration the impacts of state policies on the family and the corresponding variations across historical periods. In this section, we illustrate this argument by examining the shifting patterns of family formation in China.

In China, family formation and family structures have been closely regulated by changing state policies. As a result, the timing of family formation varied across historical periods, depending on changes in state policies or the interruption of macro-political processes. To demonstrate these variations, we first report the age at marriage for different cohorts in our sample. We divide our sample into four cohorts: those who were born (1) before 1937 ($N = 387$), (2) in 1937–46 ($N = 722$); (3) in 1947–56 ($N = 1,239$); (4) 1957 or later ($N = 1,174$). These cohorts entered the marriage risk set in different historical periods. Figure 14.1 reports the hazard rates of the timing of marriage for these four cohorts. Because few marriages occurred once respondents reached their mid-thirties, we restrict our attention to ages between 18 and 34.

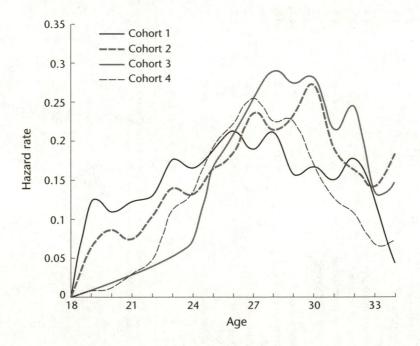

Figure 14.1. Hazard rate of the timing of marriage, by cohorts

Figure 14.1 shows that the timing of marriage did indeed vary significantly across cohorts. While these variations may be partly due to trends in the organization of the life course (as reflected in the increasing delay of marriage across advanced societies), they were mainly shaped by the effects of social policies and macro-political processes in China. For instance, the first cohort entered the risk set in the 1950s, the early period of communist rule in China. For this cohort, the hazard rate of marriage increases steadily from age 18, peaking around the mid-twenties, and then declining steadily. For the second and third cohorts, the timing of marriage was noticeably delayed, with an especially low rate of early marriage for the third cohort. This was mainly due to the political turmoil of the Cultural Revolution (1966–77), leading to the social dislocation of many families, disrupting the normal timing of marriage and other life-course events. During this period, the state also adopted policies that advocated (and forced) delays in marriage in urban areas. This policy was relaxed in the post-Mao era, as reflected in changes in the marriage patterns for the fourth cohort, when the age at marriage peaked once again around the mid-twenties.

Similarly, state policies also affected family size. In the 1950s, the government encouraged fertility. Mothers who bore more children were labelled as 'model mothers'. Since the mid-1970s, the state has adopted a restrictive one-child-per-family policy in urban areas. As a result of these policy shifts, the number of children per family in our sample varies noticeably across cohorts. The mean number of children is 2.8 for the first cohort, 2.1 for the second cohort, and 1.3 and 0.97 for the third and the fourth cohorts, respectively.

There have also been significant state policy impacts on women's labour-force participation. Since the early days of the communist state in China, the government advocated women's active participation in the labour force, before as well as after marriage and childbearing. Welfare policies and child-care facilities were established to alleviate women's burden as caregivers. As a result, there has been a high percentage of women participating in full-time paid jobs in China.

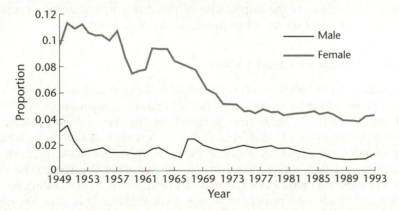

Figure 14.2. Proportion of men and women not in the labour force, 1949–1994

Figure 14.2 shows the percentage of men and women who were *not* in the labour force or only had temporary jobs in our sample, between 1949 and 1994. The percentage for men was always low, decreasing over time. For women, only about one in ten (10–12 per cent) were not in the full-time workforce in the early periods, and this proportion was further reduced over time. Figure 14.2 also captures noticeable effects of state policies. The sharp drop in women's non-employment in the late 1950s was due to the state's 'Great Leap Forward' policy that intended to accelerate economic growth. As a consequence, a large proportion of women was drawn into the labour force. The subsequent rise in non-employment in the early 1960s reflected the economic disasters of the time, which forced many women to exit the labour force. The sharp increase in non-employment for men in the mid-1960s was likely to be a result of the disruption of the initial stage of the Cultural Revolution, when millions of high-school graduates in urban areas could not be assigned a job. These patterns clearly show the importance of state policies, not only in promoting women's labour-force participation overall, but also in producing marked fluctuations due to the shifts of state policies. They also point to the importance of macro-political contexts in understanding social stratification processes in urban China.

There are significant variations between men and women in their locations in the labour force (cf. Table 14.1). Men (husbands) tend to be over-represented in high-status organizations (for example government agencies and state firms) and high-status occupations (for example, high-ranked managers and professionals), whereas women (wives) tend to be crowded in collective firms and work as service workers. For instance, in 1993, nearly 11 per cent of men worked in government agencies, while only 6 per cent women did. Similarly, nearly 20 per cent of men were managers (both high- and low-level managers), but only 7 per cent of women were. Women, by contrast, tend to have a significant presence in public organizations and work as low-level professionals. These positions are typically associated with semi-professional jobs such as nurses and technicians. Overall, there is clear evidence of gendered jobs and work organizations in the labour force in urban China. This highlights the importance of job-shift patterns among couples that may circumvent or exacerbate these gender distinctions.

Couples' Division of Paid Labour

To describe couples' patterns of occupational and organizational location, we match spouses along two dimensions of social status: occupation and types of work organization. For illustrative purposes, we arrange occupational status into eleven categories: (1) high-rank cadre; (2) low-rank cadre; (3) high-rank professional; (4) low-rank professional; (5) clerk; (6) service worker; (7) skilled worker; (8) unskilled worker; (9) private entrepreneur; (10) farmer; (11) no job. Note that these occupational levels may not be in a strictly descending order. For instance, high-rank professionals may have higher status than low-rank cadres; service workers may have lower status than skilled or unskilled workers.

We arranged types of work organization into nine categories: (1) government; (2) public organizations; (3) central government-owned firms; (4) local government-owned firms; (5) collective firms; (6) hybrid firms; (7) private firms; (8) farm; (9) no job. Again, note that the numerical number of these categories approximate but do not necessarily coincide with the descending order of the organizational hierarchy. For instance, in some periods, those working in state firms may have had a higher income than those in public or government agencies. Keep these issues in mind when inspecting the figures.

Panels A and B in Figure 14.3 show the patterns of occupational status between spouses at the time of marriage and in their most recent jobs (at the time of the interview in 1994). It appears that there is a high degree of homogamy between spouses at the time of marriage, especially among the professional and worker statuses. This is evidence of assortative mating patterns. Nevertheless, women at marriage are, not surprisingly, less likely to hold positions of high authority. Few are high- or low-rank managers (cadres) and male managers seldom marry wives who are also managers. In fact, lower rank (male) managers are more apt to marry a low-rank professional (29.7 per cent), a skilled worker (17.5 per cent), or a farmer or unskilled worker (12.5 per cent), rather than another manager (10.7 per cent). The degree of homogamy increases over the duration of marriage, as reflected in the patterns of the most recent jobs (Panel B). There, we see a higher percentage of distributions along the diagonal. By 1994, over half (53.9 per cent) of the male low-rank managers were married to either a low- or high-rank manager. This represents a remarkable move towards occupational symmetry. At marriage, 16.5 per cent of the new husbands were either high-rank (1.23 per cent) or low-rank (15.2 per cent) cadres. By the 1994 interview this had increased to 24 per cent (high-rank = 4.9 per cent, low-rank = 18.8 per cent).

At marriage, by contrast, only 4.7 per cent of wives were either high-rank (0.09 per cent) or low-rank (4.6 per cent) cadres. By 1994 this had increased to 8.3 per cent (high-rank = 1.2 per cent, low-rank = 7.1 per cent). Note that men are more likely to be married to wives in the same occupations than the reverse. For example, at the time of the interview, 56 per cent of the husbands who were high-ranking professionals were married to other high-ranking professionals, but wives who were high-ranking professionals were less likely to have a husband in the same type of occupation (only 37.7 per cent did so).

There are similar patterns in spouses' location in types of work organizations (see Panels A and B in Figure 14.4). In fact, in comparison with occupational status, there is a much higher degree of congruence between spouses in types of work organization at marriage, and the homogamy increases over the duration of marriage. Clearly, type of work organization has been a highly important dimension along which assortative mating takes place, and spouses' status changes evolve after marriage. This pattern is consistent with our previous argument that locations in particular types of work organizations are critical indicators of one's position in the social structure. This pattern may also reflect the fact that the workplace serves as a marriage market.

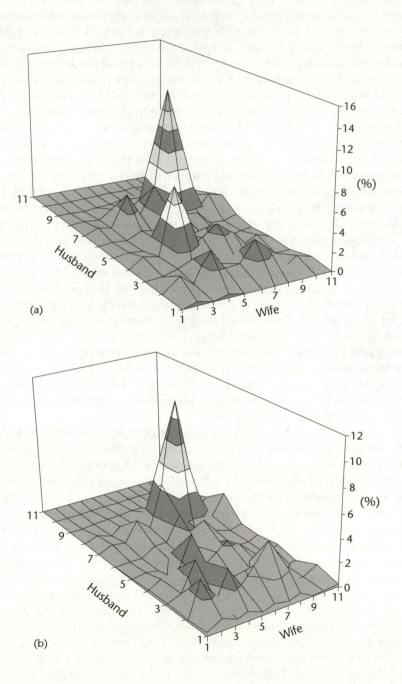

(a)

(b)

Figure 14.3. Joint distribution of occupational status between spouses during marriage

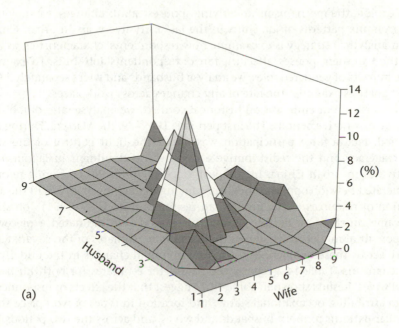

(a)

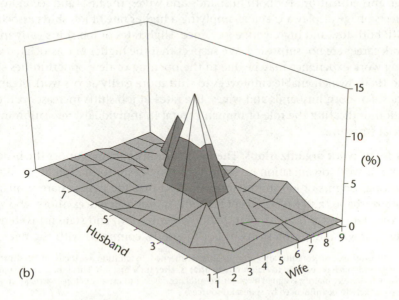

(b)

Figure 14.4. Joint distribution of organizational status between spouses during marriage

Overall Patterns of Job Shifts between Spouses

To explore the mechanisms underlying spouses' status changes, we now turn to examine patterns of job shifts in the last forty-five years in urban China. Our analytical strategy is to examine how respondents' characteristics, as well as those of their spouses, affect the rate of respondents' job shifts. To examine the impacts of gendered roles, we analyse husbands and wives separately.[1] Our first analysis examines the rate of any changes across workplaces.

Because of our emphasis on historical context, we analyse rates of job shift in two distinctive periods. The first period is 1949–79, the Mao era. During this period, labour-force participation was under the tight control of the state bureaucracy and the redistributive economy was dominant in labour-force activities in urban China. In the post-Mao era, 1980–94, economic reforms generated new job opportunities, introducing market mechanisms in the allocation of resources, including human resources (Nee 1989, 1991). Job shifts became much more flexible during this period. We estimated a piecewise exponential model which allows the parameter estimates of the covariates to vary across these two periods to capture potential changes in the underlying mechanisms. Table 14.2 reports the parameter estimates for both husbands and wives. Results shown in Table 14.2 suggest that the effects of respondents' own attributes, occupational status, and location in types of workplace show similar patterns for both husbands and wives, and across the two periods.

Age and education: For both husbands and wives, the first- and second-order effects of age display a U-shape, implying a higher rate of job shifts associated with both low and high work experience. High rates of job shifts early in the work career are not surprising. We suspect that the higher rate associated with long work experience may be due to the opening of new opportunities since the 1980s, which enable employees to shift more easily across work organizations. For both husbands and wives, the rates of job shifts increase with education, indicating the role of human capital in individuals' relocation in the social structure.[2]

Types of work organizations: The set of dummy variables under the heading 'type of work organization' in Table 14.2 provides information about organizational origins of job shifts. Again we find that the patterns are similar for both husbands and wives. Except for some minor differences, those who work in the state sector (government, public organization, and state firms) tend to have a lower rate of job shifts in both periods, compared with the reference

---

[1] We only analyse job shifts after respondents are married. In addition, we focus on job shifts after the respondents have entered the labour force, that is, after their first job. This is because first jobs in urban China were mainly assigned by governmental agencies (and usually before marriage) and they were unlikely to be influenced by spousal resources.

[2] Until recent years, most jobs in China were permanent. Therefore, most job changes reflect some 'voluntary' moves. There were exceptions, especially during the Cultural Revolution period. For instance, the send-down campaign forced millions of youth to go to rural areas. We excluded these job shifts from our analyses. Overall, the job shifts in our analyses may be interpreted as indicating a positive choice to relocate.

Table 14.2. Parameter estimates of exponential event-history model of job shifts by periods: 1949–1979, 1980–1994

	Husbands		Wives	
	1949–1979	1980–1994	1949–1979	1980–1994
Intercept	−0.82	−1.29***	0.52	−2.25***
Age	−0.15***	−0.10***	−0.23***	−0.06***
Age sq./100	0.18***	0.11***	0.31***	0.09***
Education				
senior high	0.17*	0.15**	0.31***	0.24***
college	0.40***	0.50***	0.48***	0.51***
Type of work organization				
government agency	−0.01	−0.34***	−0.37**	−0.62***
public organization	−0.50***	−0.72***	−0.57***	−0.58***
central gov't-owned firm	−0.73***	−0.51***	−0.52***	−0.43***
local gov't-owned firm	−0.81***	−0.61***	−0.62***	−0.44***
hybrid firm	0.78***	−0.51***	0.24	−0.43**
farm	0.63***	0.74***	0.18*	0.97***
Occupations				
high-rank manager	−0.19	0.22	−0.59	−0.30
low-rank manager	0.19*	0.14	−0.01	−0.06
high-rank professional	−1.27***	−0.22	−0.21	−0.60***
low-rank professional	0.29***	0.06	0.28**	0.01
clerk	0.21	−0.03	0.18	−0.23
service worker	0.07	0.13	−0.07	−0.05
soldier	0.61***	0.71***	0.72**	1.01***
private entrepreneur	0.01	−0.59*	−0.59	−0.69*
Spouse characteristics				
Education				
higher	0.09	0.06	−0.10	−0.07
lower	−0.03	−0.08	−0.10	−0.01
Occupational status				
higher	0.05	0.32***	0.18**	0.26***
lower	0.10	−0.10	−0.08	−0.11
Type of work organization				
government agency	0.17	0.21*	0.22**	0.28***
public organization	0.15	−0.24**	0.00	−0.03
central gov't-owned firm	−0.08	−0.01	−0.04	0.09
local gov't-owned firm	0.01	0.15*	0.05	−0.04
hybrid firm	0.23	0.15	0.43**	0.00
farm	−0.00	0.18	0.21	0.03
No. of events	1,198	1,528	1,140	1,557

Note: 'Junior high or below' is the reference category for education, 'collective firm' for type of work organization, and 'production worker' for occupation. For 'spouse characteristics', 'same education' is the reference category for education, 'same occupational status' for occupational status, and 'collective firm' for type of work organization. See text for the definitions of the covariates. * $p < .1$, ** $p < .05$, *** $p < .01$.

category of those in collective firms. That is, those in the state sector tend to stay in their current workplaces. This may reflect the fact that employment in the state sector was more tightly controlled by the government. It is also plausible that organizations in the state sector offer better benefits, especially latent benefits, thus both attracting and retaining employees (Zhou *et al.* 1997). For those working in hybrid firms, husbands were more apt to shift jobs in the first period. We suspect that this is because of the collectivization and nationalization policies in the early 1950s that transformed many non-state firms into state-owned or collective firms. Women's participation in this sector during the earlier period was relatively low, and thus did not show statistically discernible shifts during the Mao period. In the second period, however, both husbands and wives working in hybrid firms had a lower rate of job shifts. There tends to be a higher rate of shifts from farm to urban jobs for both spouses, mainly reflecting the effects of urbanization and industrialization in the past forty-five years.

Occupational status: Compared with the effects of organizational location, occupational status shows no systematic effects. Husbands who are high-rank professionals have a lower rate of job shifts in the first period. The same is the case for wives in high-status professional occupations in the 1980s and 1990s. Low-rank managers and professionals tended not to change their jobs in the 1950s, 1960s, and 1970s, regardless of their gender. But, regardless of gender, those who exited from the military had a *higher* rate of job shifts throughout the period of communist rule. In the 1980s and 1990s, as the economy opened up, those working as private entrepreneurs tended not to shift jobs.[3]

Spouse characteristics: Our theoretical interest centres on assessing the extent and direction to which spouses' characteristics affect respondents' job-shift patterns. We used the likelihood ratio statistic to test the null hypothesis that the inclusion of the set of the covariates measuring spousal characteristics does not contribute to the model fit. The χ^2 statistic is 42.7 for the husband model and 59.0 for the wife model, each with 20 degrees of freedom. Thus, we can reject the null hypothesis and conclude that including spouses' characteristics in our models significantly improves the model fit.

While having a spouse with more or less education does not either facilitate or constrain job shifts, spouses' work organization and occupation do matter. Husbands married to wives with higher status jobs were more apt to shift jobs in the 1980s and 1990s. For wives, spouses with higher occupational status increased the rate of their own job shifts in both periods, compared with those whose husbands had the same occupational status (the reference category). Having a spouse with lower occupational status has no significant effect on rate of job shifts (compared with the reference category), for either men or women.

---

[3] Because of the relatively small number of cases for 'soldier' and 'private entrepreneur' categories, we used them mainly for the purpose of statistical control. So we will not give substantive interpretations for their effects in our discussion.

Where their spouses work also affects respondents' rate of job shifts. Specifically, for women respondents, being married to a husband who works in a government agency has meant that they themselves are more apt to switch jobs. This has also been the case for male respondents in the 1980s and early 1990s: having a wife working in a government agency increases their rate of job shifts, while having a wife working in a public organization decreases the rate of men's job shifts. One may infer that both respondents' and their spouses' location in the social structure contributes to their rate of mobility. Their husbands' occupational and organizational location matters for women respondents in both periods. Wives' work attachments have made a difference for the rate of male respondents' job shifts only more recently (1980–94).

For this set of analyses, we did not consider the specific destinations resulting from the job shift. Yet, as noted earlier, types of work organization in urban China vary systematically in their property rights and in their relationship to the state. Accordingly, we explore patterns of job shifts, considering the destinations of the job shifts.

Husbands' Job-Shift Patterns to Specific Organizational Destinations

We estimated a set of piecewise exponential models of job shifts to three organizational destinations: (1) government and public organizations; (2) state firms; (3) collective and hybrid firms, across the two periods. We first report the set of analyses for husbands in Table 14.3.[4] There are considerable variations in the effects of the covariates on the rates of shifts to specific organizational destinations.

Age and education: We find that work experience, as measured by age, has the strongest effects on job shifts to state firms, but has little effect on job shifts to collective or non-state firms. College education has a significant effect on the rate of shifts to government and public organizations for both periods. This pattern is consistent with the general job-shift patterns reported in Zhou *et al.* (1997). Education significantly increased the rate of shifts to state firms, and collective and non-state firms, only in the second period. This may be interpreted as evidence of significant changes in the allocation of human resources in the reform era. Another contributing factor may be that rising educational levels provide more college graduates who 'spill over' to other types of organizations through job shifts.

Organizational origins: Compared with those in collective firms (the reference category), the effects of organizational origins also show some interesting

---

[4] Job shifts to each organizational destination include both job shifts from a different type of workplace to that destination, and those from the same type of organization. For instance, job shifts to government and public organizations include job shifts from state firms, collective and hybrid firms, as well as job shifts from one government agency or public organization to another government agency or public organization.

Table 14.3. Parameter estimates of exponential event history model for husbands' job-shift patterns by periods: 1949–1979, 1980–1994

	Gov't and public org'n		State firms		Collective and hybrid firms	
	1949–79	1980–94	1949–79	1980–94	1949–79	1980–94
Intercept	-5.64***	-7.76***	-2.60***	-7.74***	-1.93*	-3.75***
Age	0.01	0.11*	-0.14***	0.18***	-0.11*	0.01
Age sq./100	-0.00	-0.18**	0.13*	-0.29***	0.09	-0.06
Education						
senior high	0.35**	0.27	0.14	0.26**	0.08	0.24
college	0.57***	0.85***	0.26	0.43**	0.23	0.94***
Type of work organization						
government agency	1.07***	0.74***	0.53**	-0.00	-1.37***	-1.89***
public organization	0.98***	0.30	-0.41	-0.56*	-2.83***	-2.02***
central gov't-owned firm	-0.72**	-0.16	0.43**	0.37**	-2.68***	-1.63***
local gov't-owned firm	-0.61**	-0.17	0.31	0.53***	-2.50***	-2.09***
hybrid firm	0.82*	-0.82	1.41***	-1.32*	0.48**	-0.22
farm	1.38***	1.32***	0.89***	1.22***	-0.15	0.31
Occupations						
high-rank manager	0.36	1.28***	-0.99**	0.11	-0.35	0.31
low-rank manager	0.57***	1.05***	-0.02	-0.11	0.43**	0.06
high-rank professional	-1.13**	0.26	-1.05**	-0.44	-1.70*	-0.16

low-rank professional	0.58***	1.02***	0.12	0.01	0.49**	−0.20
clerk	0.58*	0.58*	−0.29	0.01	0.50	−0.27
service worker	0.45	−0.13	−0.37	0.19	0.23	−0.24
soldier	0.92***	1.86***	0.67***	0.67**	0.73**	0.69
private entrepreneur	1.26**	−0.60	−1.37	−5.01	0.52	−2.52**
Spouse characteristics						
education						
higher	0.39**	0.24	0.08	−0.09	−0.19	0.18
lower	−0.08	−0.02	0.01	−0.07	−0.07	−0.11
Occupational status						
higher	0.36	0.75***	0.02	0.03	−0.12	0.24
lower	0.09	−0.17	0.15	0.01	−0.09	−0.12
Type of work organization						
government agency	0.72***	0.75***	−0.21	0.29	−1.30**	−0.17
public organization	0.42**	0.22	0.19	−0.28	−0.49	−0.69**
central gov't-owned firm	0.28	0.06	0.03	0.42***	−0.49	−0.15
local gov't-owned firm	0.47**	0.58***	−0.04	0.04	−0.30	−0.03
hybrid firm	−0.24	0.74**	0.24	−0.25	−0.02	0.09
farm	0.04	−0.07	0.02	0.57**	0.30	0.37
No. of events	319	298	454	394	256	289

Note: 'Junior high or below' is the reference category for education, 'collective firm' for type of work organization, and 'production worker' for occupation. For 'spouse characteristics', 'same education' is the reference category for education, 'same occupational status' for occupational status, and 'collective firm' for type of work organization. See text for the definitions of the covariates. * $p < .1$, ** $p < .05$, *** $p < .01$.

patterns. First, those in government and public organizations have a higher rate of job shifts within the public sector in the two periods, but a lower rate of shifting to collective and non-state firms. Second, those in state firms (both central and local government-owned) have a lower rate of entering government and public organizations, as well as of entering collective and non-state firms. Those from a farm origin mainly enter the state sector in both periods. These patterns are consistent with the hierarchical order of the work organizations: employees in high-status organizations (government, public) tend to move only to organizations of similar status, but not to lower-status organizations. It is also difficult for those in lower status organizations to shift into high-status organizations. The shifts from farm origins may reflect the fact that those who were sent to the rural areas during the Cultural Revolution returned to their home cities, or else the urbanization process that incorporated part of the suburban rural areas into the urban areas.[5]

Occupational status: Compared with production workers (the reference category), cadres (both high-rank and low-rank) have a higher rate of shifts to government and public organizations, especially in the second period. There is no systematic effect of these two occupational statuses on job shifts to other destinations, especially in the second period. High-rank professionals have a lower rate of job shifts to all these destinations in the first period, but there is no statistically discernible difference in the second period. Low-rank professionals have a higher rate of job shifts to government and public organizations in both periods, but no systematic effects on shifts to other destinations. With the exception of high-rank professionals, it appears that high-status occupations (cadres, professionals) tend to have a higher rate of job shifts, which may indicate the advantages of their occupational status.

Spouse characteristics: Including the set of covariates measuring spouses' characteristics in the model shows a significant improvement of the model fit. The likelihood ratio test shows that $\chi^2 = 127.7$, df = 78, leading us to reject the null hypothesis that spousal resources do not have significant effects in our model estimation.

We find no systematic effects of spouses' educational or occupational differences on the respondents' job-shift patterns. The only noticeable finding is that having wives who have a higher level of educational increases their husbands' job shifts to government and public organizations. Having wives with higher occupational status increases the rate of their husbands' job shifts to government and public organizations in the second period. The evidence, though limited, suggests that the spousal relationship is symmetrical. More resources on the wives' side, as measured by higher educational levels or occupational status, increase their husbands' job shifts to more desirable workplaces.

---

[5] In our data-collection process, we encountered cases in which the households or the residential blocks had previously been rural and become part of the urban areas only in recent years.

Having wives who work in government agencies increases their husbands' shifts in government and public organizations in both periods. Interestingly, wives working in local government-owned firms increase the rate of their husbands' job shifts to government and public organizations. However, we need to be cautious about interpreting the causal direction. It is possible that the observed patterns of association between respondents' job shifts and spouses' characteristics are the result of family adaptive strategies based on both spouses' joint characteristics. The effects of other covariates show no systematic effects.

Wives' Job-Shift Patterns to Specific Organizational Destinations

We also estimated similar models for wives' job-shift patterns. The parameter estimates are reported in Table 14.4.

Age and education: Wives' own work experience has a significant effect on their rate of job shifts in government and public organizations in the second period. There is no systematic effect of age on other destinations over time. Similar to the patterns for the husbands, the rate of shifts to the public sector increases with educational levels for both periods. Education also increases the rate of shifts to state firms in the first period, but increases the rate to collective and non-state firms in the second period. Notice also that the magnitudes of the effects for educational levels are higher for wives than for husbands, implying that women's job shifts may be more sensitive to educational qualifications. This may also be due to the relatively smaller proportion of senior high or college graduates among women.

Organizational origins: Patterns of the effects of organizational origins are very similar between the wives and husbands. In other words, locations in types of work organizations have similar effects for both spouses. These patterns offer strong evidence of similar socio-economic status for both spouses independently of each other in urban China.

Occupational status: Compared with the analysis for the husbands, the effects of occupational status are much smaller and not statistically discernible. In other words, occupational status does not appear to have systematic effects on wives' job shift patterns, other things being equal.

Spouse characteristics: The likelihood ratio test indicates that the inclusion of the set of covariates measuring spouses' characteristics significantly increases the model fit ($\chi^2 = 259.3$, df = 78). In contrast to the findings for husbands, spousal differences in educational levels and occupational status do not have systematic and statistically discernible effects on wives' job-shift patterns.

Also in contrast, husbands' workplace locations show salient effects on their wives' job shifts. Those with husbands in government and public organizations

Table 14.4. Parameter estimates of exponential event-history model for wive's job-shift patterns by periods: 1949–1979, 1980–1994

	Gov't and public org'ns		State firms		Collective and hybrid firms	
	1949–79	1980–94	1949–79	1980–94	1949–79	1980–94
Intercept	-3.80***	-1.35***	-4.15***	-5.83***	-4.60***	-3.96***
Age	-0.13	0.36***	-0.04	0.06	0.06	0.03
Age sq./100	0.16	-0.53***	-0.00	-0.17*	-0.15	-0.12
Education						
senior high	0.97***	1.00***	0.46**	0.10	0.18	0.31**
college	1.17***	1.43***	0.56*	0.24	-0.01	1.06***
Type of work organization						
government agency	0.77***	0.93***	-0.26	-0.55	-1.25***	-2.59***
public organization	0.63***	1.02***	-0.87**	-0.91**	-1.62***	-2.29***
central gov't-owned firm	-0.20	0.36	0.67***	0.49***	-1.92***	-1.79***
local gov't-owned firm	-0.77**	-0.12	0.33*	0.57***	-1.47***	-1.40***
hybrid firm	0.05	0.19	0.87**	-0.34	0.61***	-0.05
farm	0.56	2.03***	0.45**	1.01***	0.09	0.78
Occupations						
high-rank manager	0.03	0.69	-5.92	-5.24	-0.50	-0.19
low-rank manager	0.24	0.16	-0.05	0.37	0.03	-0.09
high-rank professional	-0.37	-0.62	-0.57	0.14	0.40	-1.20

low-rank professional	0.29	0.69**	0.34	0.50**	0.36	0.18
clerk	0.80**	0.49	0.01	-0.12	0.32	0.25
service worker	0.02	0.30	-0.26	-0.01	0.07	0.10
soldier	0.70	1.80***	1.54***	1.77**	-5.97	-4.57
private entrepreneur	-5.69	-5.13	-6.47	-0.57	-0.42	-6.98
Spouse characteristics						
Education						
higher	0.06	0.16	-0.05	0.08	-0.32**	0.00
lower	0.09	-0.28	-0.51**	0.04	0.00	0.13
Occupational status						
higher	-0.16	0.13	0.06	0.25*	0.29*	0.23
lower	0.05	0.02	-0.07	-0.35	0.29	-0.24
Type of work organization						
government agency	1.04***	1.19***	0.36	0.83***	0.12	0.04
public organization	1.17***	0.85**	0.04	-0.07	-0.57*	-0.24
central gov't-owned firm	0.28	-0.35	0.32	0.69***	-0.41**	-0.14
local gov't-owned firm	0.47	0.27	0.51**	0.74***	-0.58***	-0.67***
hybrid firm	1.11*	-0.48	0.30	-0.68	-0.04	-0.34
farm	0.17	-0.01	0.98***	0.91**	-0.13	0.07
No. of events	174	159	294	291	302	291

Note: 'Junior high or below' is the reference category for education, 'collective firm' for type of work organization, and 'production worker' for occupation. For 'spouse characteristics', 'same education' is the reference category for education, 'same occupational status' for occupational status, and 'collective firm' for type of work organization. See text for the definitions of the covariates. * $p < .1$, ** $p < .05$, *** $p < .01$.
T100

had a significant and higher rate of shifts to the public sector for both periods. Those with husbands in state firms also had a higher rate of entering state firms, especially in the second period. They had a lower rate of shifting to non-state firms for both periods, especially for those with husbands in local government-owned firms.

To sum up, first, location in types of work organizations has important and systematic impacts on patterns of job shifts for both husbands and wives. Second, individual attributes (for example, age, education, and occupation) have broadly similar effects for husbands and wives. Third, the differences in the effects across periods are much less salient than we anticipated.

In terms of the influence of spousal characteristics, the set of covariates measuring spousal characteristics significantly improves the model fit, based on the likelihood ratio test. Overall, husbands' status, especially their work organization location, appears to have stronger effects on wives' job-shift patterns than does wives' work location on their husbands' job shifts. By and large, the direction of these effects is *symmetric,* in that the husband's workplace status affects the wife's workplace status in the same direction as the wife's workplace status affects the husband's.

Couple's Joint Work Status

Thus far we have analysed the effects of the job locations of each spouse separately. We now consider both in tandem. In this way we can tease out possible *couple* adaptive strategies: respondents may make job choices, or have more job opportunities or constraints, depending on where both spouses are located. We therefore estimated a set of models for husbands and wives including a set of variables measuring spouses' joint workplace status. We also included variables measuring individual attributes (age, education) and occupational status in the model as controls. In interpreting the results, we focus on the effects of the spouse's characteristics and those of spouses' joint workplace status, reporting the results pertaining to the joint workplace status in Table 14.5.

Overall, there are marked consistencies in patterns of workplace location between husbands and wives. But there are also interesting contrasts between spouses. The first panel of Table 14.5 presents the analysis for husbands. The effects of couples' joint workplace status show that, during the Mao period, when both spouses work in government or public organizations, husbands are most apt to move to jobs in that same sector, and not to jobs in state, collective, or hybrid firms. In the more recent period of economic reform, they also tend to be unlikely to move to those other sectors, but are not as mobile within the public sector.

For those couples with both spouses working in state firms in the Mao era, husbands tend not to move either into the public sector or to collective or hybrid firms. But by the 1980s and early 1990s, these husbands are more apt to shift jobs within the state sectors.

When spouses work in different sectors, with the husband in the state sector and the wife not, the husbands are unlikely to move to a collective or hybrid firm. When the wife holds a state-sector job and the husband does not, in the Mao period, husbands are more apt to move to a job in a government or public organization. In the post-Mao period (1980–94) husbands of wives working in the state sector are more apt to move to jobs in state, collective, or hybrid firms, but not to the government and public sector.

Turning to the experiences of wives (the second panel of Table 14.5), we see a degree of consistency across periods, in that when both spouses hold public-sector jobs the wife is most apt to shift jobs within that sector, compared with women in couples where both spouses are in the non-state sector. When both spouses work for state firms, the wife is most likely to shift within that sector. During the period of economic reform (1980–94), wives in non-state-sector jobs married to husbands in state jobs have a high rate of job shifts, both into state firms and within the non-state sector. Comparing the effects of the spouses' joint workplace status for husbands and wives, our findings show that, for those couples where both spouses work in state-sector jobs (in government, public, or state firms), the effects of couples' joint job status has similar effects for both husbands and wives. When either spouse is in the state sector, the other spouse tends to have a higher rate of job shift to state firms. This pattern seems to suggest that working in state firms is still the preferred (and feasible) choice for couples with some affiliation already with the state sector. With regard to job shifts to (or within) the non-state sector, there are some interesting contrasts between husbands and wives. When husbands are in the state sector and wives are in the non-state sector, husbands are unlikely to leave their (good) state jobs. But in the reform era their wives are freer to move to the private sector. When husbands are working in the non-state sector and wives in state-sector jobs, we find that husbands have a higher rate of moving to non-state jobs (while their wives have a lower rate of doing so). Thus it appears that couples like to have at least one state-sector job in the family. Having one frees the other spouse to move to (or within) less secure types of employment or enables the other spouse to move to the state sector as well. These patterns are consistent with a view of couples as devising adaptive strategies that minimize the risks associated with the non-state sector. Two strategies appear to be operating. For some cases, one spouse's secure job becomes the anchor that permits the other spouse to take on less secure employment. And in other cases, having one spouse in the state sector facilitates (or increases preferences for) the other spouse's move to the state sector as well. It also appears that the state sector still has strong appeal to individuals in both the state and the non-state sector. Overall, we find that couples' joint workplace status has symmetric effects for both husbands and wives. This pattern is again consistent with our findings in the previous analyses.

Table 14.5. Parameter estimates of exponential event-history model for couples' job shifts, by periods: 1949–1979, 1980–1994

	Gov't and public org'ns		State firms		Collective and hybrid firms	
	1949–79	1980–94	1949–79	1980–94	1949–79	1980–94
Husband's job shift						
Spouse's education						
higher	0.44**	0.24	0.16	−0.08	−0.74**	−0.09
lower	−0.02	−0.10	0.15	0.01	0.12	0.11
Spouse's occupational status						
higher	0.33	0.71***	0.35	−0.02	−0.29	0.08
lower	0.03	−0.22	0.10	−0.18	−0.27	−0.00
Spouses' joint workplace status						
both in gov't or public org'n	0.66***	0.23	−0.76***	−0.76**	−1.73***	−1.26***
both in state firms	−1.14***	−0.33*	−0.12	0.48***	−2.38***	−1.31***
husband in state sector, wife in non-state sector	−0.06	−0.09	0.13	0.53***	−1.35***	−0.84***
husband in non-state sector, wife in state sector	0.78***	0.29	0.13	0.67***	0.16	0.62***

No. of events	238	260	286	340	145	227
Wives' job shift						
Spouse's education						
higher	0.16	0.17	-0.08	0.08	-0.45***	-0.09
lower	-0.20	-0.30	-0.43**	0.07	-0.19	0.26
Spouse's occupational status						
higher	0.12	0.32	0.17	0.45***	0.28*	0.23
lower	0.00	-0.29	-0.01	-0.40	0.07	-0.48*
Spouses' joint workplace status						
both in gov't or public org'n	0.88***	0.75***	-0.93***	-1.07***	-0.84***	-2.80***
both in state firms	-0.75***	-1.25***	0.31*	0.82***	-1.94***	-1.65***
husband in state sector, wife in non-state sector	0.26	0.10	-0.13	0.45**	0.09	0.39***
husband in non-state sector, wife in state sector	0.42	0.16	0.06	0.37	-0.65*	-0.49*
No. of events	160	147	259	265	259	260

Note: Husband and wife models are estimated separately. Respondents' age, education, and occupational status were also included in the model estimation. For 'spouse characteristics', 'same education' is the reference category for education, 'same occupational status' for occupational status. 'Both in collective and hybrid firms' is the reference category for spouses' joint workplace status. See text for the definitions of the covariates. * $p < .1$, ** $p < .05$, *** $p < .01$.

Discussion

Our analysis of job-shift patterns of husbands and wives in urban China reveals some surprising findings about the effects of spousal characteristics on workers' location in the stratification structure. Spousal characteristics contribute to the model fit significantly, with spouses' workplace status tending towards both symmetry and complementarity. What we see, though, is more interdependency than dependency between spouses.

This image is supported in our findings in several ways. First, respondents' own characteristics—their education, work experience, occupational and organizational status—play an important role in determining their patterns of job shifts, even after controlling for spouses' characteristics. Second, the effects of these individual attributes show similar patterns for both husbands and wives. That is, the conventional view of women's dependency on their husbands in industrialized market societies is not empirically supported in the Chinese context. Finally, our additional analyses (not reported here) show that the effects of these individual attributes are similar before and after controlling for spouses' characteristics. In other words, the effects of the respondents' characteristics are largely independent of their spouses' characteristics, as far as job-shift patterns are concerned.

But it is also the case that spouses' characteristics, especially what type of organization they work in, significantly affect respondents' job-shift patterns. In general, these effects tend to increase the degree of homogeneity between spouses. That is, spouses in state jobs tend to facilitate their spouses' job shifts toward state jobs as well, thus increasing the similarity of socio-economic status. These patterns support our view that work sector for each spouse is a crucial dimension in social stratification processes in China. The high degree of homogeneity between spouses with regard to location in type of work organization and the strong effects of organizational origins on job-shift patterns all indicate that the hierarchy of work organizations is critical in allocating men and women into the structure of social stratification. In contrast to work sector, the effects of spouses' occupational and educational resources are more muted.[6]

We found no systematic change in the determinants of job-shift patterns across the two distinctive historical periods. In other words, the state redistributive economy has perpetuated the organizational hierarchy as well as the redistributive benefits associated with particular types of work organization, and these patterns have not changed significantly in the era of economic reform. This pattern is consistent with the findings in Zhou et al. (1997). It reflects the fact that the economic reform under way in China has been controlled by the central and local governments, and the extent of marketization is still limited

---

[6] We note that these effects are evaluated in comparison with those who had the same educational, occupational, or organizational status as their spouses. Therefore, it is possible that other alternative comparison frameworks or alternative measures of spousal resources may yield findings different from the patterns reported here.

in the time span of our study. As a result, organizational hierarchy has not been fundamentally changed, and spousal division of labour in the public domain has not been affected in a significant way across these two periods.

Our study has highlighted the importance of institutional arrangements that shape and constrain the role of the family and spousal division of labour in the public domain. Family-based resource transfer has been a central mechanism in studies of status attainment and intergenerational mobility. But studies of resource sharing between spouses have been rare. In part, this analytical neglect may reflect the institutional arrangements of market economies where career patterns depend heavily on pre-labour-market endowment, which is typically provided by parental, rather than spousal, resources. Moreover, in the West there appears to be a 'substitution' effect in the earning power between the two spouses. The higher earning power of one spouse (typically the husband) decreases the family demand on the other spouse's earning power.

This is not the case in state-socialist societies. Due to the advocacy of state social policies, the majority of women are actively involved in the labour force both before and after marriage. Because both spouses work in the public domain, and because non-monetary resources (for example, positions, political, and social resources) are critical in social mobility, collective advancement of both spouses benefits the overall family welfare. As a result, in contrast to the conventional argument about wives' dependency on husbands in other societies, we find strong evidence that the effects of status characteristics on job-shift patterns are quite similar between the married couples in urban China. Family adaptive strategies in this institutional context appear to take a form in which spouses are engaged in a collective project of advancing each other's workplace status in the organizational hierarchy of the state-socialist redistributive economy or else having one 'iron rice bowl' job that permits the other spouse to take on more risky employment.

Our study has focused on couples' job-shift patterns in urban areas of China. We want to point out that there have been and still are vast differences between rural areas and urban areas in China, each with its distinctive institutional arrangements. For instance, there is much less differentiation among jobs or types of work organizations in rural areas. Therefore, a study of couples' work careers in rural China raises a new set of theoretical issues and requires a different kind of research design. The findings in our study should be appropriately confined to urban China.

China is experiencing dramatic socio-economic transformations. The transitional nature of the current economic institutions raises questions about whether the observed patterns will give way to new mechanisms of resource allocation and of social stratification, leading to patterns more similar to those observed in industrialized market societies. Indeed, efforts in recent years to reform the state sector have led to a high level of unemployment among urban residents, with women especially vulnerable. These changes have put enormous stress on family adaptive behaviours. We anticipate that new strategies will emerge in response to these new challenges. However, given the high levels of women's labour-force participation in China and the persistent role of the state in directing and regulating the current economic reform, we think that it is unlikely that the patterns revealed in our study will change significantly in the near future.

References

Becker, G. (1981). *A Treatise on the Family* (Cambridge, Mass.: Harvard University Press).

Bernasco, W., P. M. de Graaf, and W. C. Ultee (1998). 'Coupled Careers: Effects of Spouse's Resources on Occupational Attainment in the Netherlands', *European Sociological Review*, 14/1: 15–31.

Bian, Y. (1994). *Work and Inequality in Urban China* (Albany, NY: State University of New York Press).

Bielby, W. T. and D. D. Bielby (1992). 'I Will Follow him: Family Ties, Gender-Role Beliefs, and Reluctance to Relocate gor a Better Job'. *American Journal of Sociology*, 97: 1241–67.

Blood, R. O., Jr., and D. M. Wolfe (1960). *Husbands and Wives* (Glencoe, Ill.: Free Press).

Blossfeld, H.-P. and C. Hakim (eds.) (1997). *Between Equalization and Marginalization: Part-Time Working Women in Europe and the United States* (Oxford: Oxford University Press).

——and G. Rohwer (1995). *Techniques of Event History Modeling: New Approaches to Causal Analysis* (Hillsdale, NJ: Erlbaum).

——A. Hamerle, and K. U. Mayer (1989). *Event History Analysis* (Hillsdale, NJ: Erlbaum).

Curtis, R. (1986). 'Household and Family in Theory on Inequality', *American Sociological Review*, 51: 168–83.

Elder, G. H., Jr. (1974). *Children of the Great Depression* (Chicago: University of Chicago Press).

England, P., and G. Farkas (1986). *Households, Employment, and Gender: A Social, Economic, and Demographic View* (New York: Aldine).

————B. S. Kilbourne, and T. Dou (1988). 'Explaining Occupational Sex Segregation and Wages: Findings from a Model with Fixed Effects', *American Sociological Review*, 53: 544–58.

Entwisle, B., G. Henderson, S. Short, J. Bouma, and Z. Fengying (1995). 'Gender and Family Businesses in Rural China', *American Sociological Review*, 60: 36–57.

Goode, W. J. (1960). 'A Theory of Role Strain', *American Sociological Review*, 25: 483–96.

Hood, J. C. (1983). *Becoming a Two-Job Family* (New York: Praeger).

Lee, C. K. (1995). 'Engendering the Worlds of Labor in China', *American Sociological Review*, 60: 378–97.

Lin, N., and Y. Bian (1991). 'Getting Ahead in Urban China', *American Journal of Sociology*, 97: 657–88.

McDonald, G. W. (1980). 'Family Power: The Assessment of a Decade of Theory and Research, 1970–1979', *Journal of Marriage and the Family*, 42: 841–54.

Mincer, J. (1978). 'Family Migration Decisions', *Journal of Political Economy*, 86: 749–75.

Moen, P. (1989). *Working Parents: Transformations in Gender Roles and Public Policies in Sweden* (Madison, Wis.: University of Wisconsin Press).

——(1992). *Women's Two Roles: A Contemporary Dilemma* (New York: Greenwood).

——and E. Wethington (1992). 'The Concept of Family Adaptive Strategies', *Annual*

Review of Sociology, 18: 233–51.

Nee, V. (1989). 'A Theory of Market Transition: From Redistribution to Markets in State Socialism', *American Sociological Review*, 54: 663–81.

——(1991). 'Social Inequalities in Reforming State Socialism: Between Redistribution and Markets in China', *American Sociological Review*, 56: 267–82.

Parish, W. L. (1984). 'Destratification in China'. in J. Watson (ed.), *Class and Social Stratification in Post-Revolution China* (New York: Cambridge University Press), 84–120.

Reskin, B., and P. Roos (1990). *Job Queues, Gender Queues: Explaining Women's Inroads into Male Occupations* (Philadelphia: Temple University Press).

Rosenfeld, R. A. (1980). 'Race and Sex Differences in Career Dynamics', *American Sociological Review*, 42: 210–17.

Smelser, N. J. (1959). *Social Change in the Industrial Revolution* (London: Routledge & Kegan Paul).

Sørensen, A., and S. McLanahan (1987). 'Married Women's Economic Dependency, 1940–1980', *American Journal of Sociology*, 93: 659–87.

——and H. Trappe (1995). 'The Persistence of Gender Inequality in Earnings in the German Democratic Republic', *American Sociological Review*, 60: 398–406.

State Statistics Bureau, PRC (1990). *Chinese Urban Statistics Yearbook* (Beijing: China Statistical Publishing House).

Szelenyi, I. (1978). 'Social Inequalities in State Socialist Redistributive Economies', *International Journal of Comparative Sociology*, 16: 63–87.

Szelenyi, S., and K. Aschaffenburg (1993). 'Inequalities in Educational Opportunity in Hungary', in Y. Shavit and H.-P. Blossfeld (eds.), *Persistent Inequality* (Boulder, Colo.: Westview Press), 273–302.

Tilly, L. A. (1979). 'Individual Lives and Family Strategies in the French Proletariat', *Journal of Family History*, 4: 137–52.

——and J. W. Scott (1978). *Women, Work, and Family* (New York: Holt, Rinehard, Winston).

Tomaskovic-Devey, D. (1993). *Gender and Racial Inequality at Work: The Sources and Consequences of Job Segregation* (Ithaca, NY: ILR Press).

Tuma, N. B. and M. T. Hannan (1984). *Social Dynamics: Models and Methods* (Orlando, Fla.: Academic Press).

Walder, A. G. (1992). 'Property Rights and Stratification in Socialist Redistributive Economies', *American Sociological Review*, 57: 524–39.

——(1995). 'Career Mobility and the Communist Political Order', *American Sociological Review*, 60: 309–28.

Whyte, M. K. (1984). 'Sexual Inequality Under Socialism: The Chinese Case in Perspective', in J. Watson (ed.), *Class and Social Stratification in Post-Revolution China* (New York: Cambridge University Press), 198–238.

——(1985). 'The Politics of Life Chances in the People's Republic of China', in Y. M. Shaw (ed.), *Power and Policy in the PRC* (Boulder, Colo.: Westview Press), 244–65.

——and W. Parish (1984) *Urban Life in Contemporary China* (Chicago: University of Chicago Press).

Zhou, X. (1995). 'Partial Reform and the Chinese Bureaucracy in the Post-Mao Era', *Comparative Political Studies*, 28: 440–68.

——N. B. Tuma, and P. Moen (1996). 'Stratification Dynamics under State Socialism: The Case of Urban China, 1949–1993', *Social Forces*, 74: 759–96.

————and ——(1997). 'Institutional Change and Job-Shift Patterns in Urban China, 1949–1994', *American Sociological Review*, 62: 339–65.

VII

Results of Cross-National Comparisons

15

Careers of Couples and Trends in Inequality

SONJA DROBNIČ AND HANS-PETER BLOSSFELD

I N this final chapter, we attempt to give a short summary of the most important empirical findings from countries included in the study, as well as to
confront the theories that we reviewed in Chapter 2 with the range of evidence that emerged in the country-specific analyses. A further aim is to examine the impact of employment patterns of couples on inequalities between
households, and—within the specifics of welfare state regimes—consider the
implications of our findings for the system of income and social inequalities
in contemporary societies.

Asymmetric Change in Gender Roles

Research on changes in gender-specific educational attainment shows that there
has been a marked reduction in gender differences in all contemporary societies
(Shavit and Blossfeld 1993; Erikson and Jonsson 1996). In some cases, the gender gap in educational attainment has actually been reversed, with young
women on average attaining higher levels of education than men (see e.g.
Poland and Germany in Shavit and Blossfeld 1993). This higher investment in
education among each younger cohort of women has been accompanied by an
increase in women's midlife labour-force participation, although to various
degrees across the different countries (Blossfeld and Hakim 1997; Rubery et al.
1999). Yet, as the country-specific studies in this book demonstrate, the life
courses of husbands and wives continue to exhibit different patterns. In all
countries, we find a clear division between paid and unpaid work along gender
lines in families and households. This result is reflected in labour-market
research which still shows a gender-based earnings gap (Waldfogel and Mayer
1998/9; Winkler 1998/9) and (even increasing) occupational segregation
(Blossfeld 1987; Hakim 1998). In particular, housework and childcare seem to
remain primarily 'women's work' despite substantial changes in women's
employment patterns and in attitudes once thought to undergird the sexual

division of labour. Husbands do not increase their housework and childcare participation more substantially when their wives work (Brines 1994). They seem to insist on the provider role, even when their wives' income potential is substantial, as has been shown in various country reports in this volume.

From the point of view of the economic theory of the family, the resource-bargaining model, and the marital dependency model, the division of labour in couples therefore remains a puzzle (England and Farkas 1986; Brines 1993, 1994). These theories adhere to the view that the relations underlying the division of labour in the household are fundamentally gender neutral and governed by symmetric processes of change for husbands and wives. However, our research results and recent empirical studies on housework (Brines 1993, 1994) suggests that married women and men still respond quite differently to increased wives' employment. Wives respond in ways consistent with the logic of the three gender-neutral theoretical approaches: they do less housework and spend less time on childcare when they do more paid work. But the same is not true for husbands: their participation in housework has hardly changed and their increased share in total housework is largely an artefact due to less time spent by wives on household labour (see e.g. Brines 1993, 1994; England and Farkas 1986; Robinson 1988; Singelmann *et al.* 1996). Thus, gender-role change has been generally asymmetric, with a greater movement of women into the traditional male sphere than vice versa. This means that, in most countries, whether capitalist or socialist, liberal, conservative, or social democratic, the traditional role performance of women has changed considerably, while the dimensions of role specialization in dual-earner couples have not transformed to the same extent (Brines 1990, 1993; Crompton and Harris 1999; Hertz 1986; Hochschild, with Machung 1989; Hood 1983; Mintz 1998).

This conclusion is supported by a stream of case-studies which show that, even though most women do paid work, the responsibility and recognition for family provision still falls on men, and both women and men are ambivalent about women as providers (see, e.g. Szinovacz 1984). In particular, the meaning of paid work still seems to be different for husbands and wives in most families (Cohen 1987; Hakim 1998). In general, men seem better able than women to keep paid work and family as separate spheres of life, while women in part shape their participation in the market-place in response to family needs (Gerson 1985). All this results in personal as well as structural resistance to change in the division of housework and paid labour along gender lines. Therefore, when there is an increase in family responsibilities, wives and not husbands typically respond by reducing the amount of time spent in paid work (Berk 1985). Our results in the country-specific chapters show that the presence of small children is still closely related to wives' reduced participation in paid work (see also Moen 1985; Drobnič *et al.* 1999). And in many countries, like (West) Germany or the Netherlands, women find it easier to temper their husbands' opposition to their employment or to integrate paid work with family work when they can work part-time (Krüger and Born 1991; Krüger 1993; Blossfeld and Hakim 1997; Hakim 1998).

In sum, these findings clearly support 'doing gender' approaches or a gender-specific identity-formation model. These theories locate gender itself at the heart of the division of labour between women and men and also predict asymmetrical processes of change for husbands and wives. They suggest that the equalization of gender roles is a much slower process than assumed by economic and bargaining approaches and—at least in the initial stages—leads only to a modest reduction of sex segregation in the workplace and even less change in the household division of labour. Unfortunately, the country datasets used in this comparative project do not allow us to follow this line of research due to the lack of good indicators of either gender identities or gender norms.

Cross-National Differences in Couples' Careers

The distinction between paid and unpaid work can be considered the major determinant of an individual's position in a society because the labour force continues to be the arena for the major socio-economic stratification processes in modern societies. In Western societies, individuals who are excluded from participation in the labour force, traditionally among them many women, are disfavoured in terms of material standards of living as well as social rights, which are claim rights typically acquired by economic activity (Korpi 2000).

The country-specific chapters in this book addressed the division of labour in couples across the family life course, using longitudinal data and dynamic methods. This type of analysis provides an opportunity to study how patterns of the division of labour evolve in couples as well as the processes of social change over cohorts and historical times. In this way, we are better able to assess how the improved educational resources of individual women affect the employment decisions of couples and determine the role that the family and the partner play in evolving employment patterns over the life course.

In presenting the results, we grouped the countries under welfare state regimes to better assess the potential role of welfare states in shaping the careers of couples. Our extended typology of welfare state regimes is based on the seminal threefold distinction between 'liberal', 'conservative', and 'social democratic' welfare state regimes proposed by Esping-Andersen (1990, 1999). This typology has stimulated much research in the comparative study of welfare states but also provoked criticism across a wide range of problems (Lewis 1992; Lewis and Ostner 1995; Leibfried 1992; Orloff 1993; Sainsbury 1996). We extended this typology by adding the Mediterranean welfare state regime and the (former) state-socialist countries. We adhere to the view that typologies of this kind are a useful tool to conceptualize the general contours of institutional characteristics of various societies in cross-national comparison. They also provide a theoretical orientation and facilitate the interpretation of a wealth of information on differences and similarities found in cross-national comparisons. However, one should keep in mind that there is no exhaustive overlap between ideal types and existing institutions and no one-to-one relationship between welfare regimes and individual welfare states.

As outlined in Table 2.1, we distinguish five different welfare state regimes: *conservative*, represented in our study by Germany, the Netherlands, and Belgium (Flanders); *Mediterranean:* Italy and Spain; *liberal*: Great Britain and the USA; *social democratic*: Denmark and Sweden; and *(former) state-socialist countries*: Hungary, Poland, and China. Every typology is necessarily far-sighted because parsimony, which is necessary to encompass the large picture, is brought in at the expense of country-specific idiosyncratic details. In spite of a critique stating that an explicit gender-relevant typology is needed for studying gender inequalities, our classification of countries also fits a recent classification by Korpi (2000), who explicitly strives to form a theoretically based typology of broadly conceived policy institutions likely to be of major relevance for gendered agency inequality in terms of labour-force particip-ation. Korpi selected policy institutions which reflect the multiple ways in which public support to families is organized in a society, distinguishing between three broad ideal-typical models of gendered welfare state institu-tions: the model of General Family Support, Dual-Earner Support, and the Market Oriented Policies model. In Korpi's classifications, Germany, the Netherlands, Belgium, and Italy fall under the category of general family sup-port, Denmark and Sweden under the dual-earner support model, and Great Britain and the USA under a market-oriented gender policy model.

With the exception of Italy, which in our study (together with Spain) is placed in the separate category of Mediterranean welfare state regime, other countries remain in the same cluster even when more specific criteria, with an immediate relevance to our breadwinner/dual-earner household concerns, are taken into account. In contrast to a prevailing practice in social research of excluding (former) state-socialist countries from cross-national comparisons, we were also able to include Hungary, Poland, and China, and compare how resilient the gender-based division of labour is in these countries compared to those practising welfare capitalism. Data for Poland and Hungary were col-lected in 1991 and 1992, respectively, at the initial stages of the transition period. Thus, they predominantly refer to the situation under the planned socialist economy and we therefore grouped these countries together with China under the 'state socialist regime'. It is unlikely, however, that the wel-fare policy in the post-transition period in Central and Eastern European countries will develop in unison. Instead, new worlds of welfare will probably emerge, or individual countries will approach one of the models known from the Western societies, as suggested by Deacon (1992), who already in early stages of the transition to market economies ventured an attempt to position the emerging social policy developments into Esping-Andersen's threefold (1990) typology.[1]

[1] According to Deacon (1992: 181), several emerging welfare state regime types can be detected in the region: (1) a unique post-communist conservative corporatism, which may prove to be a histor-ically brief phase, but includes as diverse countries as parts of the successor states of Soviet Union, Romania, Bulgaria, Serbia, and possibly Poland; (2) social democratic welfare state regime, most likely to develop in the Czech Republic; and (3) liberal welfare state regime type, represented in his scheme by Hungary and Slovenia.

Table 15.1 summarizes the main results for all twelve countries, and presents them separately for different welfare state regimes. The first column shows the level of marriage homogamy. Due to differences in data sources, the indicators used to measure the socio-economic position of men and women around the time of formation of marital union differ somewhat among the countries; however, they all carry long-term implications for job placement and occupational and earnings attainment: educational level, occupational score, socio-economic status, income, or type of work organization. Based on these indicators, *marriage homogamy was found to be high in all countries* without exception (Table 15.1). In several countries where the data allow the study of trends in the level of marriage homogamy, such as Germany, the Netherlands, and urban China, it was found that the proportion of homogamous couples is increasing. This development is not surprising, in the light of rising educational attainment by women, which augments structural opportunities for homogamy. However, it also has to be kept in mind that educational stratification is a persistent phenomenon in modern societies (Shavit and Blossfeld 1993; Erikson and Jonsson 1996) and a mere increase in women's educational level would not automatically lead to higher marriage homogamy if the selection of a marriage partner were random.

The implication of high marriage homogamy is that more couples are emerging where there is an approximate equality of earnings. Also, the situation where women have higher earnings potentials than their partners is becoming more common. This development questions the view that the male partner should automatically be viewed as the breadwinner and should influence the decision-making process that leads to an allocation of time and effort to paid and unpaid work between the partners. In other words, an increasing symmetry in occupational chances and earnings potentials should also lead to a more symmetric allocation of time by husbands and wives, at least within the neo-classical household production framework, as exemplified by Gary Becker's work (1965, 1993).

The neo-classical model of the family assumes that the family behaves as if it were trying to allocate the time of its members to satisfy a common set of 'family' preferences or a joint utility function. Under the gender-neutral assumptions of this model, the comparative advantage of one partner over the other drives the decisions to allocate time to market or household production. Also, the spouse-specific sources of non-earned income must exert the same effects on family allocative behaviour. However, the challenge to the neo-classical model arises if non-earned income of different family members is observed to affect differently the household's allocation of resources (Schultz 1990). When examining the allocation of time to market work and household production within couples, this restriction of the neo-classical model of family behaviour has not been supported in any of the countries studied here. Specialization in unpaid work—scheduling work and family roles sequentially over the life course—is so uncommon among men that no parallel analysis for men and women is feasible. Therefore, dynamic empirical analyses of transitions between paid and unpaid work were limited to women.

Table 15.1. Summary of main results

Country	Marriage homogamy	Effects of wife's resources on her labour-foce participation	Effects of husband's resources on wife's labour-foce participation	Consequences for pre-tax, pre-transfer income inequality between couple households
Conservative welfare state				
Germany	high	positive	negative	reduced
The Netherlands	high	positive	negative	reduced
Belgium (Flanders)	high	positive	negative	reduced
Mediterranean welfare state				
Italy	high	positive	negative	reduced
Spain	high	positive	negative	reduced
Liberal welfare state				
Great Britain	high	positive	no effects	no effects
U.S.A.	high	not studied	not studied	not studied
Social democratic welfare state				
Denmark	high	positive	positive	increased
Sweden	high	positive	positive	increased
(Former) state-socialist countries				
Hungary	high	positive	positive	increased
Poland	high	positive	negative	reduced
Urban China	high	positive	positive	increased

Note: Results for China refer to the 'preferred' job-shift patterns in organizational hierarchy.

The impact of women's occupational resources on their participation in the labour market is presented in the second column of Table 15.1. The estimates presented are summarized net effects of occupational resources, such as education, occupational score, income, or type of work organization in the case of China. That is, these are estimated effects when other factors, such as social origin, number and ages of children, work experience, husband's/partner's characteristics, and marriage cohorts are controlled. The prevailing pattern is that *women with higher occupational resources have a higher participation rate in the labour market*. Their risk of employment exit tends to be considerably lower and the re-entry rate higher. Or, in the case of Flanders and Sweden, women with higher occupational resources tend to move from full-time into part-time jobs instead of leaving the labour market. Furthermore, the country-specific analyses show that the family cycle—in particular the age of the youngest child—and historic periods have a strong impact on the participation of women in paid employment.

However, when the impact of partners' resources on women's work careers is examined, a significant diversity across countries can be detected (Table 15.1, third column). In the Netherlands, Germany and Belgium—grouped under the conservative welfare state regime—the tendency is for men with higher occupational resources to suppress spouse's participation in paid employment. Due to the diversity of data sources and indicators, it is not possible to make precise quantitative comparisons between the countries; nevertheless, it seems that this effect is strongest in (West) Germany. Here, the simulated examples show that even when the wife has substantial own resources at her disposal, high career resources of the husband can override her career potential and drive her out of the labour market. The consequence is the traditional division of labour in couples, a growing gap between male and female careers over the course of the marriage, and an increasing dependency of married women on their spouses over the life course.

In the Netherlands, there are two significant effects of the husband's characteristics on the wife's labour-market transitions. The longer the husband is unemployed, the less likely the wife is to leave full-time employment, and the higher the husband's earnings potential, the less likely the wife is to re-enter the labour market once she has children. In other words, husband's occupational and economic difficulties are compensated for in couples by a higher full-time employment of women, while high occupational resources of husbands lower the participation rate of the wives. Similarly, in Flanders women married to husbands with a higher educational level are more likely to reduce their paid employment by switching from full-time to part-time work. Overall, the general tendency in these countries is asymmetry in couples: the higher the occupational resources of the male partner, the lower the economic activity of the women.

The Mediterranean welfare state regime countries—Italy and Spain—also exhibit the patterns found in Germany, the Netherlands, and Flanders. In Italy, husband's resources affect the wife's career trajectory in two stages; in the decision to quit the labour market and in suppressing re-entry. In Spain, higher husband's resources increase exit rates while the effects on re-entry are mixed. In general, the higher the occupational position of the husband, the lower the employment participation of the wife.

In Great Britain, placed under the liberal welfare state regime, no effects of husband's occupational resources on their wives' employment transitions have been found (Table 15.1, third column). In the US study, this particular question was not examined in a way that would allow a straightforward answer. However, we know from previous research that the situation in the USA has undergone a major change in recent decades. Until the 1980s, a number of studies demonstrated that men with high earnings tended to be married to women with relatively good earnings prospects but these wives participated less in the labour force than women married to less well-paid men (Mincer 1974; overview of studies in Treas 1987). By the end of the 1980s, however, the correlation between spouses' earnings became positive, implying that highly paid husbands had wives with above-average earnings (Karoly and Burtless 1995). It might well be that an examination of the long-term employment patterns of American couples, without taking the changes in historical periods into account, would have produced a similar effect for the USA as in Great Britain.

In the social democratic welfare state regime, male's occupational resources have an opposite effect on their partner's participation rates from that in the conservative and Mediterranean welfare state regimes: husbands'/partners' resources increase women's labour-market activity. Women married to well-educated husbands in Denmark as well as women with high-income partners in Sweden are less likely to leave the labour market than women with low-resource partners.

Finally, the (former) socialist countries tend to exhibit a similar pattern as the social democratic welfare state regime countries. In Hungary, wives with husbands that have more resources are less likely to exit employment and thus manifest a higher labour-force attachment. In China, the spousal effects are symmetrical. The 'preferred' workplace status of one partner tends to facilitate the job shifts of the other, thus increasing the homogamy of the couple's socio-economic status. Poland, however, deviates from this model. Here, women with better educated husbands show a higher tendency of exiting employment and specializing in household production. We interpret this as reflecting the specific role of religious values and church influence in the country. More traditional family values and a lower female employment rate than in other Central and East European countries make Poland in this respect more similar to countries belonging to the conservative and Mediterranean welfare state regime.

In sum, cross-national analyses portray the following dynamic picture of couples' careers: the majority of couples are fairly similar in terms of their occupational resources when they enter the union. However, over the course of the marriage the paths of men and women diverge in spite of high marital homogamy. Husbands follow the traditional career patterns and only in exceptional cases interrupt employment for family reasons. These cases are so few that no separate analysis of husbands' employment transitions was possible in any of the countries included in the study. Women, however, exhibit a great diversity across countries. On the one hand, there are common patterns across countries: women's higher occupational resources increase their participation in paid employment. These results support the human capital arguments, which explain the increase in female labour-market supply in terms of the increase in women's market wage opportunities or the opportunity cost of women's time in non-market production. On the other hand, there are distinct differences in the impact of husbands' resources on their spouses' employment behaviour and these differences in broad contours correspond to the welfare state regimes. In countries associated with the conservative and Mediterranean welfare state regime, the career paths over the course of the marriage are clearly gendered, leading to an increasing division of labour within couples, specialization of spheres, economic dependency of wives on their partners, and the prevalence of a breadwinner family model. Women's paid employment is negatively correlated with the occupational position of their husbands. In the social democratic welfare state regime and generally in (former) socialist countries, the trend is reversed. There is a symmetry in couples' careers; high occupational resources cumulate in couples and get translated into more symmetric employment career paths over the life course and the dual-earner family model. Finally, there are countries where no impact of husbands' resources is detected, such as Great Britain, or where other studies indicate that a country rapidly moved from a typical breadwinner to a modern dual-earner family type, such as the USA.

What is the relevance of these findings? First, the contributions in this book show how asymmetrical the developments in gender roles have been and how important it is to take the dynamic perspective and changes over time into account. Second, this cross-national comparison demonstrates that theories which try to explain the decision-making processes concerning the division of labour within couples as independent of institutional constellations and cultural traditions within which these decisions are made, can only to a certain degree explain the actual outcomes. They might fit the specific historical periods or class-specific relationships but start losing explanatory power in another historical time or in another country context.

In all countries, there has been a shift from a male-breadwinner to a dual-earner model but the strength and the pace of this shift is contingent on broader structural, political, and ideological country 'packages'. Gender role specialization as predicted by the economic theory of the family seems to work well in conservative and Mediterranean welfare states where the middle-class male breadwinner is still able to earn a family wage and husbands' resources have a negative impact on their wives' labour-force participation. This can particularly be seen in Germany, where the tax system directly penalizes wives' full-time employment and protects the male breadwinner family (Dingeldey

2000; Gustafsson 1992). This of course dampens the speed of the diffusion of dual-earner families. However, also in conservative and Mediterranean welfare state regimes, role specialization in the household means that the small nuclear family is particularly vulnerable to the temporary or permanent loss of a unique individual who provides an essential function at home or in the labour market. Hence, specialization involves a potentially serious loss of flex-ibility and wives' employment becomes a highly adaptive family strategy (Oppenheimer 1997).

The increasing influx of women into the workforce diminishes the role of men as sole breadwinners and leads to a point where the whole system shifts from a family wage economy to an individual wage economy. In the individ-ual wage economy, the socio-economic status of the family is increasingly determined by two income sources. The combined income of the two-earner family comes to form the social standard; thus, the wife's employment and income is also in the interest of the husband. This can be seen in the positive effects of husbands' resources on their wives' labour-force participation, par-ticularly in social democratic and (former) socialist countries. In countries associated with the social democratic welfare state regime, the spread of the dual-earner model was particularly fast because of their steeply progressive individualized tax system and public-sector provision of family services. Also in (former) socialist countries, the dual-earner family was a social norm, sup-ported by the official gender equality ideology and economic necessity. In the liberal welfare state regimes, no clear effect of husbands' resources on their wives' labour-force participation could be detected. It seems that these coun-tries, particularly the USA, have experienced a very fast transition from the family wage economy into the individual wage economy, accompanied by the stagnation or actual decline of real male wages and the increase of job insta-bility (Mintz 1998).

Gender Inequality versus Class Inequality

The results of our study also highlight the way in which gender inequality within couples affects the process of socio-economic stratification and mater-ial inequality generated in the stratification process. Research on the develop-ment of inequalities in the distribution of household income indicate that, after the early 1980s, in many countries the tendency towards declining inequalities was halted and even reversed, most dramatically so in the United States and Great Britain (Atkinson *et al.* 1995; Gottschalk and Smeeding 1997; Gustafsson and Johansson 1999; Karoly and Burtless 1995).

Income inequality is the outcome of a set of processes, ranging from the per-formance of national economies, such as the economic development, the size of the industrial sector, international trade or macro-economic fluctuations, to the institutional structure of the labour market and demographic factors (Gustafsson and Johansson 1999). For households, the most important income source is remuneration for paid work. One important reason for the rise in family income inequality is the trend towards greater inequality in the job market, with declining earnings at the lower end of the job hierarchy and rising wages of top earners (Karoly and Burtless 1995). However, changes in the distribution of individual earnings do not necessarily produce equivalent changes in the distribution of family income. How strong this effect is depends on a number of factors: the distribution of unearned non-labour income, such as services and transfers provided by the welfare state, the composition and structure of families and households, such as family size and single-headed versus married couple households, and the employment patterns of household members, in particular participation in paid employment of husbands and wives. Only by taking all of these factors into account is it possible to understand the trends in social inequalities and the differences in this respect between the countries.

Changing family structure and patterns of income receipt directly contribute to the level of income inequality. Single-headed families, for example, only have half as many potential adult earners as families headed by a married couple. An increase in the proportion of single-headed families will then likely increase income inequalities between households. In husband–wife families, with which this book is concerned, the division of labour between husbands and wives also bears broader societal relevance. The level of women's participation in the labour force is not only likely to affect the distribution of resources within the couples, their interaction patterns, and bargaining positions within the family, but also has an impact on the inter-household distribution of economic well-being and class status. Thus, an interesting and still under-researched aspect of the diffusion of dual-earner couples in male breadwinner societies is that it will probably enhance social inequality—at least during a transition period. Since, in most modern societies, couples tend to marry homogamously with regard to traits determining earnings capacity, husbands and wives with high wages and influential social networks pool their resources and reinforce social differences between families.[2]

Column four in Table 15.1 presents hypothesized effects of couples' division of labour over the duration of marriage on social stratification in the countries included in the study. The general trend would seem to be that *the decrease in gender inequality in terms of labour-force participation is accompanied by an increase in social class inequalities*. In countries where husbands' occupational resources facilitate wives' labour-force participation, we can expect a cumulation of pre-tax income and other social advantages within households. Again, with few anomalies, the predictions concerning the effects of couples' career trajectories on socio-economic inequalities between the households fit the welfare state regime scheme. The conservative and Mediterranean welfare

---

[2] Particularly at the time of high unemployment levels, these developments are also expressed in polarization between 'work-rich' households with multiple earners engaged in various forms of work and 'work-poor' households, typically headed by the unemployed, elderly people, or single parents (Pahl 1987).

state regimes potentially reduce social inequalities between the households, the social democratic welfare state regime and (former) socialist countries with less gendered patterns of labour-force participation increase inter-household inequalities, and the liberal welfare state regime can be expected to fall somewhere in between.

How are we to understand these developments and—in spite of a general trend—considerable differences between the countries? As long as wives are secondary earners, their earnings have a generally equalizing effect on inter-household income. Wives most likely to be employed in such a situation are those married to low-income husbands. The wife's pay cheque can considerably raise the total family income and in this way reduce inter-household inequalities.[3] But this effect would be reversed if a major increase occurs in the proportion of wives entering the labour-force, particularly with the influx of well-educated, high-earning women who are also more often married to men with high earnings. As working women become more ubiquitous, other household members' income becomes less and less of a predictor of who works and who does not. The working and non-working groups encompass more socio-economic diversity and resemble one another more in terms of other income (Treas 1987). This can double the advantage of couples at the upper end of the income scale. So, when women married to men with high earnings enter the labour force, this can increase the inequality between spouses and households.

These developments again have important consequences for the distribution of male breadwinner families and dual-earner families across social classes in a society and for the systems of social inequalities. First, male breadwinner families in relative terms lose ground in the pyramid of social inequality of a society; especially at the lower end, low-income male breadwinner families are likely to fall below a (relative) poverty line. Thus, the advantage of dual-earner families compared to traditional male breadwinner families is likely to stimulate the further diffusion of dual-earner families. Only in countries where the tax system penalizes wives' employment and the state provision of welfare services is meagre, such as Germany, are male breadwinner families to some extent protected, and the speed of the diffusion of dual-earner families is dampened. Secondly, since working-class families traditionally had a higher proportion of dual-earner couples after the Second World War (Esping-Andersen 1999), the diffusion of dual-earner couples in middle-class and upper-middle-class makes them relatively poorer. Thus, part of the increasing inequality observed in many contemporary societies might in fact be attributed to a changing composition of male breadwinner and dual-earner families across social classes.

---

[3] In a rare systematic overview of research on the impact of labour-force involvement of married women on family income in the USA, Treas (1987) finds a surprising consistency in the findings from the 1960s and 1970s: women's greater participation in paid employment has had an equalizing effect on household income—at least among the white population. Also, Karoly and Burtless's results for the USA show that the increasing proportion of women in the labour force first reduced inequality. However, by the end of the 1980s, much of the increase in income inequality could be traced to the increased earnings of women in affluent families.

The implication is of course not that the integration of women into paid employment and an increasing gender equality in this respect is undesirable because it can increase income inequality and poverty in underprivileged classes. Indeed, such an outcome is not unavoidable, as demonstrated by the countries associated with the social democratic welfare state regime. The extent to which the equalization of the position of women in the labour market and the diffusion of dual-earner families affect class inequalities, with lower-income families as losers, depends largely on the redistributive role of the welfare state through a broad spectrum of mechanisms, particularly the tax system, insurance institutions, and family-related policies.

The conservative and Mediterranean welfare state regimes still provide a shelter for the traditional breadwinner family model and at the same time a certain protection against rising income inequalities.[4] But the trend towards a dual-earner family model can also be detected in these countries and will continue in the future. In market-oriented societies, it can be expected that the trend towards a dual-earner family model will have a strong and direct impact on social stratification and increasing income inequalities, particularly in the USA with a comparatively unprogressive tax system and few government transfers to the families. In the social democratic welfare state regime, however, the prevalence of the dual-earner family model does not have the same strong impact on class inequalities, due to the equalizing effects of state policies. In Sweden, for example, in spite of a recent increase in income inequality (Gottschalk and Smeeding 1997), the tax system with steeply progressive taxes produces considerably less inter-household inequality than in countries associated with the liberal welfare state regime.[5]

Finally, we expect that in the (former) socialist countries the dual-earner family model will continue to remain a prevailing societal norm. However, our results also show that the developments in these countries might go into disparate directions and generate a diversity of outcomes, as is already the case in Western capitalist countries. Results for Hungary and Poland support Deacon's (1992) projections of disparate evolution of welfare policy in Central and Eastern Europe. At least in the medium run, however—because of the underdevelopment of a comprehensive system of insurance institutions and the erosion of state legitimacy—the outcome in these countries will probably be increasing inter-household inequality.

---

[4] Also, in countries belonging to these two regimes, divorce rates are in general lower, and non-marital births and single-parent families less common, than in liberal and social democratic welfare states, which again reduces the impact of demographic factors on income inequalities.

[5] In a recent cross-national research study on the level of and trends in income distribution, Gottschalk and Smeeding (1997) compared the trends in disposable income inequality in the 1980s and found the largest increase in inequality in the UK, USA, and Sweden, though Swedish income distribution remained considerably more equal than in the USA or UK. In Denmark, the upward trend over the 1980s was less extreme. Among other countries included in our study, inequality rose only slightly in the Netherlands and Belgium, remained unchanged in Germany, and even decreased in Italy.

References

Atkinson, A. B., L. Rainwater, and T. M. Smeeding (1995). *Income Distribution in OECD Countries: Evidence from the Luxembourg Income Study* (Social Policy Studies, 18; Paris: Organisation for Economic Co-operation and Development).

Becker, G. S. (1965). 'A Theory of the Allocation of Time', *Economic Journal*, 75: 493–519.

——(1993). *A Treatise on the Family* (Enlarged edn. Cambridge, Mass.: Harvard University Press).

Berk, S. F. (1985). *The Gender Factory: The Apportionment of Work in American Households* (New York: Plenum Press).

Blossfeld, H.-P. (1987). 'Labor Market Entry and the Sexual Segregation of Careers in the Federal Republic of Germany', *American Journal of Sociology*, 93: 89–118.

——and C. Hakim (eds.) (1997). *Between Equalization and Marginalization. Women Working Part-Time in Europe and the United States of America* (Oxford: Oxford University Press).

Brines, J. (1990). 'Beyond the Terms of Trade: Wives, Husbands, and Housework', Ph.D. dissertation, Dept. of Sociology, Harvard University.

——(1993). 'The Exchange Value of Housework', *Rationality and Society*, 5: 302–40.

——(1994). 'Economic Dependency, Gender, and Division of Labor at Home', *American Journal of Sociology*, 100: 652–88.

Cohen, T. R. (1987). 'Remaking Men: Men's Experiences Becoming and Being Husbands and Fathers and their Implications for Reconceptualizing Men's Lives', *Journal of Family Issues*, 8: 57–77.

Crompton, R., and F. Harris (1999). 'Attitudes, Women's Employment, and the Changing Domestic Division of Labour: A Cross-National Analysis', in R. Crompton (ed.), *Restructuring Gender Relations and Employment: The Decline of the Male Breadwinner* (Oxford: Oxford University Press), 105–27.

Deacon, B. (1992). 'The Future of Social Policy in Eastern Europe', in B. Deacon, M. Castle-Kanerova, N. Manning, F. Millard, E. Orosz, J. Szalai, and A. Vidinova, *The New Eastern Europe: Social Policy Past, Present and Future* (Newbury Park, Calif.: Sage), 167–91.

Dingeldey, I. (2000). 'Einkommensteuersysteme und familiale Erwerbsmuster im europäischen Vergleich' (Systems of Income Tax and Family Employment Patterns in Europe), in I. Dingeldey (ed.), *Erwerbstätigkeit und Familie in Steuer- und Sozialversicherungssystemen* (Opladen: Leske + Budrich), 11–47.

Drobnič, S., H.-P. Blossfeld, and G. Rohwer (1999). 'Dynamics of Women's Employment Patterns over the Family Life Course: A Comparison of the USA and Germany', *Journal of Marriage and the Family*, 61/1: 133–46

England, P., and G. Farkas (1986). *Households, Employment, and Gender: A Social, Economic, and Demographic View* (New York: Aldine).

Erikson, R., and J. O. Jonsson (eds.) (1996). *Can Education be Equalized?* (Boulder, Colo.: Westview Press).

Esping-Andersen, G. (1990). *The Three Worlds of Welfare Capitalism* (Cambridge: Polity Press).

——(1999). *Social Foundations of Postindustrial Economies* (Oxford: Oxford University Press).

Gerson, K. (1985). *Hard Choices: How Women Decide about Work, Career, and Motherhood* (Berkeley, Calif.: University of California Press).

Gottschalk, P., and T. M. Smeeding (1997). 'Cross-National Comparisons of Earnings and Income Inequality', *Journal of Economic Literature*, 35: 633–87.

Gustafsson, B., and M. Johansson (1999). 'In Search of Smoking Guns: What Makes Income Inequality Vary over Time in Different Countries?', *American Sociological Review*, 64: 585–605.

Gustafsson, S. (1992). 'Separate Taxation and Married Women's Labor Supply: A Comparison of West Germany and Sweden', *Journal of Population Economics*, 5: 61–85.

Hakim, C. (1998). *Social Change and Innovation in the Labour Market* (Oxford: Oxford University Press).

Hertz, R. (1986). *More Equal than Others: Women and Men in Dual-Career Marriages* (Berkeley, Calif.: University of California Press).

Hochschild, A., with A. Machung (1989). *The Second Shift: Working Parents and the Revolution at Home* (New York: Viking).

Hood, J. (1983). *Becoming a Two-Job Family* (New York: Praeger).

Karoly, L. A., and G. Burtless (1995). 'Demographic Change, Rising Earnings Inequality, and the Distribution of Personal Well-Being, 1959–1989', *Demography*, 32/3: 379–405.

Korpi, W. (2000). 'Faces of Inequality: Gender, Class and Patterns of Inequalities in Different Types of Welfare States', *Social Politics*, 4: 127–91.

Krüger, H. (1993). 'Die Analyse ehepartnerlicher Erwerbsverläufe: Ansatzpunkte für modernisierungstheoretische Überlegungen' (The Analysis of Marital Employment Careers: Reference Points for Theorizing Modernization), in C. Born and H. Krüger (eds.), *Erwerbsverläufe von Ehepartnern und die Modernisierung weiblicher Lebensführung* (Employment Careers of Spouses and the Modernization of the Female Life Course) (Weinheim: Deutscher Studien Verlag), 209–26.

——and C. Born (1991). 'Unterbrochene Erwerbskarrieren und Berufsspezifik: Zum Arbeitsmarkt- und Familienpuzzle im weiblichen Lebensverlauf' (Interrupted Employment Careers and Occupations: Towards the Labor Market and Family Puzzle of Female Life Courses) in K. U. Mayer, J. Allmendinger, and J. Huinink (eds.), *Vom Regen in die Traufe* (From Bad to Worse) (Frankfurt a.M. and New York: Campus), 142–61.

Leibfried, S. (1992). 'Towards a European Welfare State: On Integrating Poverty Regimes in the European Community', in Z. Ferge and J. E. Kolberg (eds.), *Social Policy in a Changing Europe* (Frankfurt a.M.: Campus), 245–80.

Lewis, J. (1992). 'Gender and the Development of Welfare Regimes', *Journal of European Social Policy*, 2: 159–73.

——and I. Ostner (1995). 'Gender and the Evolution of European Social Policy', in S. Leibfried and P. Pierson (eds.), *European Social Policy: Between Fragmentation and Integration* (Washington, DC: Brookings Institution).

Mincer, J. (1974). *Schooling, Experience, and Earnings* (New York: National Bureau of Economic Research).

Mintz, S. (1998). 'From Patriarchy to Androgyny and Other Myths: Placing Men's Family Roles in Historical Perspective', in A. Booth and A. C. Crouter (eds.), *Men in Families: When do they Get Involved? What Difference does it Make?* (Mahwah, NJ: Erlbaum), 3–30.

Moen, P. (1985). 'Continuities and Discontinuities in Women's Labor Force Activity', in G. H. Elder (ed.), *Life Course Dynamics: Trajectories and Transitions, 1968–1980* (Ithaca, NY: Cornell University Press), 113–55.

Oppenheimer, V. K. (1997). 'Women's Employment and the Gain to Marriage: The Specialization and Trading Model', *Annual Review of Sociology*, 23: 431–53.

Orloff, A. S. (1993). 'Gender and the Social Rights of Citizenship: The Comparative Analysis of Gender Relations and Welfare States', *American Sociological Review*, 58: 303–28.

Pahl, R. E. (1987). 'Does Jobless Mean Workless? Unemployment and Informal Work', *Annals of the American Academy of Political and Social Science*, 493: 36–46.

Robinson, J. P. (1988). 'Who's Doing the Housework?' *American Demographics*, 10: 24–8.

Rubery, J., M. Smith, and C. Fagan (1999). *Women's Employment in Europe: Trends and Prospects* (London and New York: Routledge).

Sainsbury, D. (1996). *Gender, Equality, and Welfare States* (Cambridge: Cambridge University Press).

Schultz, T. P. (1990). 'Testing the Neoclassical Model of Family Labor Supply and Fertility', *Journal of Human Resources*, 25: 599–634.

Shavit, Y., and H.-P. Blossfeld (eds.) (1993). *Persistent Inequality* (Boulder, Colo.: Westview Press).

Singelmann, J., Y. Kamo, A. Acock, and M. Grimes (1996). 'Dual-Earner Families and the Division of Household Labor: A Comparative Analysis of Six Industrial Societies', *Acta Demographica (1994–1996)*, 159–78.

Szinovacz, M. E. (1984). 'Changing Family Roles and Interactions', in B. B. Hess and M. B. Sussman (eds.), *Women and the Family: Two Decades of Change* (New York: Haworth Press), 164–201.

Treas, J. (1987). 'The Effect of Women's Labor Force Participation on the Distribution of Income in the United States', *Annual Review of Sociology*, 13: 259–88.

Waldfogel, J., and S. Mayer (1998/9). 'Differences between Men and Women in the Low-Wage Labor Market', *Focus*, 20: 11–16.

Winkler A. E. (1998/9). 'Earnings of Husbands and Wives in Two-Earner Families', *Focus*, 20: 17–19.

Subject Index

altruism, altruist 17–8, 54
assortative mating 18, 22, 57–9, 68, 98,
    100–1, 105–7, 114, 127, 130–31, 136,
    151–2, 168, 182, 188, 195, 235–8,
    245–6, 248, 254, 269–70,277,
    296, 308, 311–4, 327, 347–9,
    375–9
  intergenerational aspect 59, 66, 107,
    269–70, 277, 307n., 316

Belgium 10, 11, 37, 39–41, 78, 98–118, 374,
    376–7, 383n.
breadwinner family model 6, 17, 19, 21–3,
    41–3, 61, 73, 100, 146, 161, 177,
    201–3, 285, 379–83
  dual breadwinner strategy 161, 314,
    326–7
breadwinner-homemaker, see breadwinner
  family model
breadwinner role 33, 77
breadwinner wage, see family wage
Britain 6, 10, 11, 37, 39, 41–3, 177–200,
    246, 374, 378–80, 383n.
British Household Panel Study 182,
Bulgaria 374n.

CEC (Commission of European
    Communities) 99–100, 115
childcare leave 44, 69n., 124, 126, 141, 179,
    188, 191, 195, 198, 202, 239–41,
    247–8, 251, 254, 265, 287–8, 295,
    308–310, 313–27
  fathers taking 198, 265
China 10, 11, 37, 39–41, 44–5, 332–67,
    374–8
Chinese Urban Statistics Yearbook 338
CIDE-Instituto de la Mujer (Spain) 152, 169
comparative advantage 17, 19, 22–3, 53–4,
    60–1, 72, 106, 123–4, 133, 136, 140,
    152, 168, 204, 207, 222, 236, 283,
    293, 311–2, 333, 375
Cornell Retirement and Well-Being Study
    207
coupled careers 9, 10, 201, 206, 225, 228
Cultural Revolution 345–6, 356
Czech Republic 374n.

Danmarks Statistik 263–6, 269, 278
Denmark 7, 10, 11, 21, 37–41, 43–4, 100,
    244, 261–280, 374, 376, 378, 383n.
discrimination 25, 148, 168
  statistical 5, 34, 207
division of labour 4, 16–20, 22–3, 26–7,
    31–7, 44–5, 54, 60–1, 64, 66, 72, 77,
    80, 124, 140, 146, 151, 168, 197,
    202–4, 225, 237, 248, 289–91,
    311, 332–3, 365, 372–3, 377, 379,
    381
divorce 20–1, 23, 26–7, 29, 31, 44, 121,
    148–9, 218, 220–2, 264, 288
doing gender 30–7, 373
domestic work, see household work
dual-career couples 177, 227
dual-earner families/couples/marriages
    28–9, 32–5, 38, 42–3, 80, 155, 180–2,
    201–2, 204–5, 372, 374, 380–1, 383
dual-earner family model 11, 29, 34, 42, 44,
    379–80, 383

earnings capacity 16–23, 27–8, 36–7, 54, 59,
    65, 68, 72, 179, 195, 235, 283, 314,
    372, 381
economic theory of the family 16–23, 26–8,
    33, 53–4, 58, 72, 80, 104, 168, 285,
    293, 296, 301, 303, 311, 325, 333,
    372, 379
educational attainment 19–22, 27, 36–7,
    54, 63, 104, 149, 152, 158–9, 165,
    168, 213, 291–3, 296, 309, 312, 371,
    375
  sex-specific 5, 17, 19–20, 27, 371
educational expansion 5, 19, 22
endogamy 58, 152
European Commission Network on
    Childcare 170, 173
Eurostat 108, 115
event-history analysis/models 10, 53, 56,
    63, 77, 81, 83, 87, 90, 94, 206, 209,
    296, 341
exchange theory 27

family adaptive strategy 24, 332, 334–5,
    338, 357, 360–1, 365, 380

family formation 10, 53n., 77, 98–102, 104–6, 114, 123, 149, 154, 263, 288, 304, 307–8, 336–7, 344
family head 3–4, 8, 57, 148, 150–1
family life cycle 8–9, 11, 30, 53, 77, 83–4, 88–95, 109, 197, 300, 303–4, 377
family solidarity 6, 8, 126
family system 6, 17, 19, 21–2, 101
family wage 36–7, 42–44, 147, 150, 203, 379
family wage economy 380
fertility 21, 27, 42, 44, 54, 78, 98, 100–1, 146, 148, 162, 184, 263–5, 288, 309, 312–4, 327
Fertility and Family Survey (Belgium) 104
Flanders see Belgium

game theory 27
gender roles 7, 23, 29, 31–2, 137, 146, 152, 158, 168, 208, 227, 292, 303, 311, 313, 321, 327, 334, 339, 371–3, 379
gender identity 30–4, 71, 104, 124–6, 133, 141, 313n., 327, 373
German Democratic Republic 20, 337
German Socio-Economic Panel 53–5
Germany 6, 10,11, 21, 22, 37, 39, 40–2, 53–76, 78, 95, 136, 182, 184, 197–8, 202, 266, 292, 303, 371–2, 374–7, 379, 382, 383n.
Great Britain see Britain
Greece 6

homogamy, see assostative mating
household head, see family head
Households in the Netherlands 81
household work 6, 7, 11, 17, 25–6, 28–31, 33, 43, 45, 53–4, 60, 66, 72, 78, 102–4, 106–7, 109, 112–114, 123–4, 136–7, 151, 168, 186, 189, 191, 203–205, 236, 284, 289, 371–2
human capital 4, 80–1, 84–5, 91, 95, 158, 185, 188, 191, 193, 207, 213, 293, 296, 303, 311, 313, 339, 350, 379
    accumulation of 21, 79, 243, 251
    investment in 17, 54, 60–1, 104, 106, 113, 122, 131, 139, 161, 168–9, 236, 311–4, 320–1, 324–327
human capital theory 64–5, 72, 122–3, 132–3, 206, 303, 311, 314
Hungary 10, 11, 37, 39, 41, 44, 277, 301, 307–331, 337, 374, 376, 378, 383
Hungarian Central Statistical Office 315

identity-formation model 32–4, 373
income potential, see earnings capacity
IDA database (Denmark) 266, 279
identity-formation model 32–34, 373
INE (Spanish National Bureau of Statistics) 148–9, 152n., 153, 170
inequality 3, 4, 28, 30, 57, 131n., 149, 227, 291, 332, 334, 374, 380–3
ISTAT (Italy) 126–7, 143
Italy 6, 10, 11, 21, 37, 39, 41–2, 121–145, 303, 374, 376–7, 383n.

labour-market studies 4, 5, 36, 39
linked lives 227
longitudinal approach 8–10, 20, 53, 55–6, 121, 179, 182, 195, 236, 313n., 373

Mao Zedong, (post)-Mao era 337, 345, 352, 360–1
marginal employment 6, 33, 42, 79, 80
marital dependency model 26–9, 372
marital dissolution, see divorce
marriage homogamy, see assortative mating
maternity leave, see childcare leave
Ministerio de Trabajo y Asuntos Sociales (Spain) 150n., 170
Ministry of Economic Affairs (Denmark) 274, 278
motherhood 20, 21, 155, 169, 309, 324, 225

Netherlands 6, 10, 11, 37–42, 77–97, 202, 372, 374–7, 383n.
Netherlands Family Survey 81
New Home Economics 122, 161, 206, 283, 326, see also economic theory of the family
New York, upstate 10, 207, 227

occupational attainment 3, 5, 7, 8, 104, 314
occupational ranking
    EGP class scheme 307
    Hope-Goldthorpe occupational score 180–2
    ISEI score 320
    SEI score 211–2, 217
    Wegener score 58, 64
OECD 29, 48, 78, 96, 125, 143, 150, 150n., 170

parental leave, see childcare leave
patriarchy 24–5
Poland 10, 11, 37, 39, 41, 44, 283–306, 371, 374, 376, 378, 383

Polish Family and Fertility Survey 284, 288, 291, 294

provider 19, 23, 25–6, 28, 31–2, 34–6, 38–9, 42, 54, 57, 59, 88, 158, 203–5, 285
role 17, 36, 372

religion 78, 86, 88, 90, 93, 95, 98, 101–2, 106, 114, 236, 244–5, 292, 295, 300, 302, 378
religious homogamy, see religion
religious values, see religion
resource-bargaining model 25–27, 372
reverse causation 10, 56
Romania 374n.

SCP (Sociaal en Cultureel Planbureau/NL) 80, 97
Second National Fertility Survey (Italy) 127
sex roles, see gender roles
Serbia 374n.
Slovenia 374n.
social capital 36, 104, 158, 165
social class 3, 8, 11, 16, 30, 34–7, 43–4, 53, 57, 69, 73, 123, 152, 158, 168, 182n., 307, 335, 380–3
social mobility 3, 72, 104, 333, 365
Social Mobility and Life History Survey (Hungary) 315
socialization 3, 17, 314, 320, 327
Socio-Demographic Survey (Spain) 149, 153
Soviet Union 374n.
Spain 6, 10, 11, 21, 37, 39, 41–2, 136, 146–173, 303, 374, 376–8
specialization of roles 16–9, 23–4, 28, 73, 103, 152, 168, 235–8, 246, 248, 254, 283, 311–2, 326, 333, 372, 379–80
standard of living 24, 29, 36–7, 43, 72, 151, 293, 373
State Statistics Bureau (China) 338, 367
statistical discrimination 5, 34

stratification 3, 4, 7, 53, 57, 98, 127, 307–8, 313, 328, 332–9, 344, 346, 364–5, 373, 375, 380–1, 383
Sweden 7, 10, 11, 21, 37, 39, 40–1, 43–4, 88, 235–260, 277, 374–8, 383
Swedish Family Survey 236, 239

tax system 42, 44, 80, 198, 259, 379, 380
traditional family, see breadwinner family model

United Kingdom, UK see Britain
United States 7, 10, 11, 22, 34, 37–43, 63n., 150n., 201–232, 292, 338, 376, 380, 382–3
U.S. Bureau of Labor Statistics 201, 231
U.S. Bureau of the Census 201, 231
USA, see United states
Urban China, see China
utility function
joint, family 17, 18, 24, 54, 375

Warsaw School of Economics (SGH) 294
welfare state 6, 37, 40, 42–3, 100, 123–4, 141, 202, 373, 379, 381, 383
welfare state regime:
conservative 11, 40–2, 123, 373–4, 376–7, 379–81, 383
liberal 11, 40–1, 43, 123, 373–4, 376, 378, 382
Mediterranean 11, 40–3, 129, 373–4, 376–81, 383
social democratic 11, 40–1, 43–4, 123, 373–4, 376, 378–80, 382–3
state socialist 11, 40–1, 44–5, 324, 373–4, 376, 378–80, 382
West Germany, see Germany
work-family interface 9, 202–5, 225
Wright's class scheme 307
WRR (Wetenschappelijke Raad voor het Regeringsbeleid/NL) 80, 97

Author Index

Abbate, C. 141–2
Abbott, A. 206, 209–10, 210n., 228
Abbott, P. 74
Acker, J. 4, 12, 26, 45
Acock, A. 15, 386
Adam, P. 161, 169
Addabbo, T. 6, 12
Alabart, A. 169
Alcobendas, M. P. 150n., 169
Alden, E. 198
Aldous, J. 49
Allison, P. D. 83, 96, 247, 259, 271, 278, 296, 304
Allmendinger, J. 14, 385
Alwin, D. F. 330
Andorka, R. 310, 330
Arber, S. 180, 198
Aronsson, T. 239, 259
Arrow, K. 5, 12
Arthur, M. B. 228
Aschaffenburg, K. 337, 367
Ashenfelter, O. 260
Ashworth, J. S. 180, 198
Atkinson, A. B. 380, 384
Aytac, I. A. 9, 12

Bales, R. 17, 49
Bane, M. J. 216, 230
Barbagli, M. 122, 142
Barley, S. R. 206, 209, 228
Barnett, R. 202, 204, 228
Barr, N. 305
Bassi, L. 229
Bax, E. H. 78, 96
Bearman, P. 231
Becker, G. S. 16–24, 45, 54, 60, 73, 104, 106, 122–4, 133, 136, 136n., 139–40, 142, 152, 161, 168–9, 204, 207, 213, 225, 228, 236, 259, 283, 302, 304, 311, 325, 328, 332–3, 366, 375, 384
Beechey, V. 247, 259
Beer, J. de 115
Bel-Adell, C. 150, 169
Bellotti, V. 137, 142
Bem, S. L. 226, 228
Bendix, R. 14
Berk, S. F. 30, 45, 372, 384

Bernasco, W. 9, 12, 36–7, 45, 65, 65n., 73, 77, 81, 86, 96–7, 104, 115, 121, 123, 127, 132, 140, 142, 205–6, 223, 227–8, 308, 312–3, 328, 339, 366
Bernardi, F. 98, 104, 121–2, 125n., 136n., 142
Bernhard, J. S. 220, 228
Bernhardt, E. M. 7, 12, 40, 45, 308, 312, 328
Bettio, F. 21, 42, 45
Bian, Y. 336, 366
Bielby, D. D. 6, 12, 32–4, 46, 225–8, 334, 366
Bielby, W. T. 6, 12, 32–4, 46, 225–8, 334, 366
Biesbrouck, W. 48
Birkelund, G. E. 38, 49
Bison, I. 139, 142, 143
Bitter, R. G. 98, 115
Björklund, A, 246, 259
Blair-Loy, M. 209, 228
Blake, J. 329
Blaschke, D. 49
Blau, F. D. 5, 12, 237, 259, 311, 328
Blau, P. M. 3, 8, 12, 26–7, 46, 307, 307n., 328
Blood, R. O. 25, 46, 334, 366
Blossfeld, H.-P. 3–6, 9–16, 20–2, 30, 38–40, 42, 46–9, 53–4, 56–9, 63, 68–9, 71, 73–4, 96, 99, 101, 104, 115–6, 125, 127–8, 132–3, 142, 171, 182, 185, 186n., 198, 206, 209, 228, 246, 259, 265, 268, 278, 292, 295–6, 304–5, 307–9, 315, 328, 330, 338, 341, 366–7, 371–2, 375, 384, 386
Blumberg, R. L. 47
Bock, E. W. 116
Boney, N. 49
Bonke, J. 150n., 169, 261, 266, 278
Booth, A. 385
Born, C. 9, 14, 372, 385
Bosch, K. van den 116
Bouma, J. 366
Bracher, M. 244–5, 259
Bradshaw, J. 170
Bragg, R. 204, 228
Brekel, H. van de 115, 117
Brines, J. 6, 12, 30–1, 46, 372, 384

Brinton, M. 216, 228
Brüderl, J. 53n., 74
Bukodi, E. 307
Burchell, B. J. 6, 12
Burchett, B. M. 230
Burkhauser, R. V. 213, 228–9
Burtless, G. 235, 260, 378, 380–1, 382n., 385

Cabré, A. 149, 169
Cain, G. G. 5, 12
Callan, T. 198
Callens, M. 99–102, 104–7, 115
Cambrun, D. 330
Cancian, M. 238, 259
Capel, R. M. 151n., 169
Carrasco, C. 151, 169
Carrasquer, P. 171
Castle-Kanerova, M. 46, 384
Castro, T. 148, 161, 169
Chan, T. W. 209, 209n., 229
Chodorow, N. 124, 142
Christoffersen, M. N. 262, 264–5, 269–70, 275, 278
Chudacoff, H. P. 227, 229
Cigno, A. 283, 305
Clark, A. 198
Clark, J. 13, 48
Clark, R. 216, 230
Clarkberg, M. 201
Clipp, E. C. 231
Cobalti, A. 130, 131n., 142
Cohen, T. R. 372, 384
Colbjørnsen, T. 330
Coltrane, S. 31, 46
Cooke, K. 180, 198
Corijn, M. 98, 101, 106, 115–6
Coser, L. 3, 12, 204, 229
Curtis, R. F. 4, 8, 12, 25–6, 46, 332, 334, 366
Cramer, J. C. 308, 312, 328
Crawford, D. 229
Crompton, R. 47, 49, 372, 384
Crosby, F. J. 49–50
Crouter, A. C. 385
Csernák, J. 309, 328

Daelemans, I. 105, 115
Dale, A. 6, 12
Dasko, F. 46
Davies, H. 237–8, 259
Davis, K. 3, 13
Deacon, B. 44, 46–7, 305, 374, 374n., 383–4
Delgado, M. 149, 169

de Lillo, A. 127, 127n., 142
Dempster-McClain, D. 231
DeRose, A. 46
Deschamps, L. 116
Deven, F. 115, 117
DeViney, S. 209, 213, 228–9
Dex, S. 4, 13, 177–80, 182, 195, 198–9
Diekmann, A. 53n., 74
Dijk, L. van 80, 96
Dingeldey, I. 40, 46, 379, 384
Ditch, J. 148, 170
Dou, T. 366
Dressel, W. 49
Drobnič, S. 3, 6–7, 13, 16, 29, 39, 44, 47, 53, 68–9, 74, 283–5, 293, 304–5, 307n., 310, 328, 371–2, 384
Duncan, O. D. 3, 12, 307, 307n., 328
Durán, M. A. 150–1, 170
Durkheim, E. 3

Eardley, T. 170
Edwards, M. 311, 328
Eggebeen, D. J. 29, 47
Eijkhout, M. P. 77, 96
Einhorn, B. 6, 13, 44, 47, 284, 289, 305
Elder, G. H. jr. 206, 227, 229–31, 312, 325, 328, 334, 366, 385
Ellingsæter, A. L. 40, 47
Engelbrech, G. 49
England, P. 18, 23, 26–8, 47, 49, 125, 142, 332, 334, 366, 372, 384
Entwisle, B. 334, 366
Erikson, R. 5, 8, 13, 20, 39, 47, 307, 328, 371, 375, 384
Erzberger, C. 9, 13, 65, 74
Esping-Andersen, G. 6, 13, 20, 40, 42–4, 47, 122–4, 142, 312, 329, 373, 374, 382, 384
Even, W. E. 66, 74
Eversley, D. E. C. 329

Fagan, C. 5, 15, 49, 386
Farkas, G. 18, 23, 26–8, 47, 125, 142, 332, 334, 366, 372, 384
Farrell, S. A. 124, 143, 144
Featherman, D. L. 330
Fendrich, M. 35, 47
Fengying, Z. 366
Fenstermaker, R. 30, 47
Ferber, M. 65, 74, 237, 259, 311–2, 328, 329
Ferge, Z. 44, 47, 284, 305, 385
Ferree, M. M. 34–5, 47
Filenbaum, G. G. 230
Fligstein, N. D. 216, 231, 311, 330

Foner, A. 230–1
Forest, K. B. 7, 8, 11, 15
Foschi M. 48
Fowlkes, M. R. 35, 47
Fox Harding, L. 147, 170
Frątczak, E. 283, 289, 294, 305–6
Freeman, R. B. 259
Frey, M. 310, 329

Galasi, P. 310, 329
Gambetta, D. 125, 125n., 142
Ganzeboom, H. B. G. 81, 97, 313–14, 329–31
Gardner, W. 57n., 74
Garrido, L. J. 151n., 152, 152n., 170
George, L. K. 209, 229–30
Gere, I. 310, 329
Gershuny, J. 182, 198
Gerson, K. 121, 125, 133, 142, 372, 384
Gerstel, N. 47
Giesen, D. 86, 96
Gilligan, C. 124, 142
Ginn, J. 180, 198
Glass, D. V. 307, 329
Glick, P. C. 8, 13
Goffman, E. 30, 47, 209, 229,
Goldthorpe, J. H. 3–4, 7–8, 13, 39, 47–8, 57, 74, 182n., 198, 227, 229, 307, 328
González-López, M. J. 21, 42, 47, 146, 171
Goode, W. J. 332, 366
Gornick, J. C. 40, 42, 47, 100, 116, 124, 126, 143
Göting, U. 44, 48
Gottschalk, P. 380, 383n., 383–4
Graaf, N. D. de 116
Graaf, P. M. de 6, 13, 42, 45, 48, 77–8, 85, 96–7, 115, 142, 228, 307n., 328–30, 366
Griffin, W. A. 57n., 74
Grimes, M. 15, 386
Grimshaw, D. 49
Gronau, R. 66, 74
Groot, W. 97
Gross, H. E. 47
Gustafsson, B. 380, 385
Gustafsson, S. 198, 380, 385

Hajnal, J. 309, 329
Hakim, C. 4, 5, 6, 12–5, 21, 30, 33–4, 38–40, 42, 45–8, 73, 96, 121, 125, 133, 141n., 142–3, 178–9, 198, 265, 278, 305, 309n., 312, 313n., 328–9, 338, 366, 371–2, 384–5
Hall, D. T. 228
Halpin, B. 209n., 229

Hamerle, A. 74, 228, 305, 366
Han, S.-K. 7, 9, 13, 201, 209–10, 229
Handl, J. 4, 13, 57, 74
Hannan, M. T. 56, 75, 206, 209, 231, 296, 306, 341, 367
Hansen, E. J. 270, 278
Harcsa, I. 315, 329
Hareven, T. K. 227, 229
Harkess, S. 49
Harris, F. 372, 384
Hartmann, H. 5, 14, 24–5, 48
Hauser, R. M. 3, 15
Hawkins, A. J. 29, 47
Heckman, J. 235, 260
Heinz, W. 49, 227, 229
Henderson, G. 366
Hendrickx, J. 77
Henkens, K. 102, 116
Henretta, J. C. 206, 209–10, 229–30
Henz, U. 88, 235, 237n., 245–8, 259–60
Hertz, R. 372, 385
Hess, B. B. 386
Hiller, D. V. 25, 48, 58, 74
Hinde, P. R. 180, 198
Hochschild, A. R. 31, 48, 202, 204–5, 226, 229, 372, 385
Hoem, B. 11, 14, 245, 260
Hoem, J. M. 46, 240, 245, 260
Hogan, D. P. 209, 229
Holzer, J. Z. 284n., 288, 291, 305
Hope, K. 182n., 199
Hooghiemstra, B. T. J. 78, 96
Hood, J. C. 205, 225, 229, 334, 366, 372, 385
Houle, R. 171
Hout, M. 308, 329
Hrycak, A. M. 209, 228
Huber, J. 4, 5, 8, 14, 25, 48, 65, 74, 312, 329
Hughes, E. C. 209, 229
Huinink, J. 14, 20, 21, 46, 48, 54, 63, 73, 98–9, 101, 116, 268, 278, 385
Hunt, J. G. 49
Hunt, L. L. 49
Hyman, H. 3, 14

Iglesias, J. 152, 170
Impens, K. K. 101, 116

Jackman, R. 284, 305
Jackson, M. 44, 48
Janssen, J. 75
Jäntti, M. 238, 259
Jasso, G. 25, 48
Jensen, A.-M. 46, 49

Joesch, J. M. 66, 74
Johansson, M. 380, 385
Jones, E. B. 313, 330
Jones, G. 57, 74
Jong Gierveld, J. de 115–6
Jonsson, J. O. 5, 13, 20, 47, 237n., 246,
    259–60, 371, 375, 384
Joshi, H. 6, 12, 177n., 179–80, 198–9, 259
Jurado, T. J. 6, 14, 147, 170–1
Juster, F. T. 208, 229

Kahn, R. L. 230–1
Kaiser, M. 329
Kalbfleisch, J. D. 296, 305
Kalleberg, A. L. 7, 14, 123, 143, 226, 230,
    329
Kalmijn, M. 85, 96, 98, 101, 116, 308, 313,
    329
Kamarás, F. 309, 329
Kamo, Y. 15, 386
Kanter, R. M. 213, 226, 230
Kaplan, H. B. 229
Karoly, L. A. 235, 260, 378, 380–1, 382n.,
    385
Kempkens, L. 77, 96
Kilbourne, B. S. 366
Killingsworth, M. R. 80, 96, 235, 260
Klerman, J. A. 239, 260
Klijzing, E. 74
Klinger, A. 309, 329
Knoke, D. 230
Knudsen, L. B. 265, 278
Kohli, M. 227, 230
Kohn, M. L. 330
Kolberg, J. E. 385
Kolosi, T. 313–4, 329–30
Koltay, J. 48
Korpi, W. 373–4, 385
Kotowska, I. E. 285, 289–91, 305
Kotter, J. P. 213, 226, 230
Kowalska, I. 284n., 288, 291, 305
Kreps, J. M. 216, 230
Krishnan, V. 98, 101, 116
Krüger, H. 9, 14, 372, 385

Laumann, E. O. 330
Lauterbach, W. 9, 14
Lawrence, B. S. 228
Layard, R. 260
Lee, C. K. 334, 337, 366
Lee, G. R. 9, 14, 25, 48, 116
Leibfried, S. 373, 385
Leibowitz, A. 239, 260
Lence, C. 149, 171

Liefbroer, A. C. 98n., 101, 106, 115–6
Lijphart, A. 78, 96
Lin, N. 336, 366
Lippe, T. van der 78, 80, 96
Lipset, S. M. 14, 308, 330
Leth-Sørensen, S. 7, 14, 261–2, 278
Lew, V. 116
Lewis, J. 373, 385
Lloyd, C. B. 14, 330
Long, J. E. 313n., 330
Lorber, J. 124, 143, 144
Luijkx, R. 97, 307, 313, 329–30
Lüscher, K. 229–30

Maassen van den Brink, H. 97
Mach, B. W. 286, 292, 293, 305
Machung A. 31, 48, 372, 385
Macran, S. 179, 197–9
Madden, J. F. 5, 14
Manning, N. 46, 384
Marcum, J. P. 98, 101, 116
Mare, R. D. 237, 260
Marsden, P. V. 230
Marshall, V. W. 230
Marx, K. 3
Mascie-Taylor, C. G. N. 98, 100, 116
Masnick, G. 216, 230
Mayer, K. U. 13–4, 20, 48, 57, 74–5, 227–8,
    230, 305, 308, 328, 330, 366, 385
Mayer, S. 371, 386
Mayordomo, M. 169
McCulloch, A. 177, 198
McDonald, G. W. 25, 48, 334, 366
McLanahan, S. 4, 8–9, 15, 23, 25, 49, 225,
    227, 231, 311, 330, 332, 367
McRae, S. 25, 28, 48, 57, 75, 179,
    199
Meil-Landwerlin, G. 147, 170
Merton, R. K. 206, 230
Meulders, D. 125–6, 143
Meyers, M. K. 47, 116, 143
Milkman, R. 124, 143
Millard, F. 46, 384
Mincer, J. 4, 14, 16–7, 48, 213, 230, 332–3,
    366, 378, 385
Mintz, S. 372, 380, 385
Miret-Gamundi, P. 152, 170
Modgil, C. 48
Modgil, S. 48
Moen, P. 6–9, 11, 13–6, 30, 35, 48, 201–6,
    209–10, 216, 226, 229–32, 332, 334,
    366–7, 372, 385
Mol, P. W. 78, 96
Moltó, M. L. 150, 160, 165, 170

Monigl, I. 309, 329
Montagut, T. 169
Moors, H. 100, 117
Müller, R. 49
Müller, W. 13, 227, 230
Murphy, M. 9, 15

Nakao, K. 211, 230
Naldini, M. 6, 14, 147–8, 170–1,
Nassisi, A. M. 143
Nee, V. 350, 367
Nieuwbeerta, P. 330
Niphuis-Nell, M. 78, 96
Noom, M. 97
Nuthmann, R. 329

O'Connor, J. 124, 143
Ofek, H. 4, 14
O'Higgins, M. 143
Oneto, G. 141, 143
Oppenheim Mason, K. 46, 49
Oppenheimer, V. K. 23–4, 27, 48, 63, 75,
    98, 116, 151–2, 168, 171, 380, 385
O'Rand, A. M. 206, 209–10, 213, 229–30
Orloff, A. S. 124, 143, 373, 385
Orosz, E. 46, 384
Osterman, P. 226, 230
Ostner, I. 373, 385
Ours, J. C. van 96

Pahl, J. 8, 15, 311, 330
Pahl, R. E. 381n., 386
Palmore, E. B. 213, 230
Pananek, H. 35, 48
Parish, W. L. 337, 367
Parsons, T. 16–7, 49
Pascal, A. H. 12
Pauwels, K. 102, 116
Pavalko, E. K. 206, 209, 209n., 230–1
Payne, G. 74
Perkins, T. 247, 259
Peronaci, R. 259
Peterson, G. W. 15
Pfau-Effinger, B. 40, 49, 68, 75, 161n., 171
Phelps, E. 5, 15
Philliber, W. W. 58, 74
Piccone, S. S. 142
Pierson, P. 385
Pisati, M. 142
Plasman, O. 143
Plasman, R. 143
Pohl, K. 74
Pohoski, M. 305
Polachek, S. 4, 14–7, 48, 311, 330

Pollaerts, H. 85, 97
Polonko, K. A. 306
Portocarero, L. 328
Pötter, U. 56, 57n., 75, 296, 305
Prentice, R. L. 296, 305
Presser, H. B. 7, 15
Preston, S. H. 238, 260
Price, A. 199
Procidiano, M. E. 98, 116
Puhani, P. 285, 288, 305

Qian, Z. 238, 260
Quinn, J. F. 213, 228–9
Quinn, R. P. 208, 231

Rainwater, L. 143, 384
Ramioul, M. 99, 116
Ramos, R. 151, 171
Rantalaiho, L. 161n., 171
Ray, J. C. 100, 116
Reher, D. S. 149, 171
Rella, P. 133, 143
Rennermalm, B. 245, 260
Reskin, B. F. 5, 15, 24–5, 334, 367
Requena, M. 148n., 171
Rhodes, M. 6, 14–5
Rijken, S. 97
Riley, J. W. jr. 202, 204, 227, 231
Riley, M. W. 202, 204, 227, 230–1
Rindfuss, R. R. 209, 231
Risdon, A. 199
Rivers, C. 202, 204, 228
Róbert, P. 104, 307, 309–10, 313, 329–30
Robinson, J. P. 372, 386
Rockwell, R. 312, 325, 328
Rogler, L. H. 98, 116,
Rohwer, G. 6–7, 9–10, 12, 14, 42, 46, 53,
    56–7, 57n., 68, 73–5, 106, 116, 128, 142,
    185, 198, 246, 259, 261, 296, 304–5, 315,
    328, 341, 366, 384
Roman, C. 8, 15
Romero, A. 171
Rønsen, M. 240, 260
Room, G. 121, 143
Roos, P. A. 5, 15, 334, 367
Rosen, E. I. 34–5, 49
Rosenfeld, R. A. 7, 14, 38, 49, 53n., 75, 231,
    334, 367
Rosenzweig, M. R. 260
Ross, K. E. 47, 116, 143
Roussel, L. 147, 171
Rubery, J. 5, 15, 40, 49, 170, 371, 386
Rutkowski, J. 291, 305
Rutkowski, M. 284, 305

Sainsbury, D. 124, 143, 373, 386
Saltzman Chafetz, J. 39, 49
Santow, G. 244–5, 259
Saraceno, C. 42, 49, 126, 128, 142–3
Savage, M. 231
Scanzoni, J. 306
Schizzerotto, A. 127, 127n., 130, 131n.,
    139, 142–3
Schmähl, W. 228
Schor, J. 205, 231
Schultz, T. P. 375, 386
Schultz, T. W. 16, 49
Scott, J. W. 334, 367
Scott, W. R. 329
Selbee, L. K. 330
Sewell, W. H. 3, 15
Shanahan, M. J. 229
Shavit, Y. 5, 15, 20, 46, 54, 74, 307, 330,
    367, 371, 375, 386
Shaw, Y. M. 367
Shehan, C. L. 98, 116
Sheng, X. 49
Sherrod, L. R. 230
Shore, R. P. 206, 230
Short, S. 366
Siegers, J. J. 78, 80, 96, 116
Siemie(ska, R. 285, 305
Simkus, A. 310, 330
Simó, C. 171
Simpson, I. H. 28, 49
Singelmann, J. 7, 15, 372, 386
Skiadas, C. H. 75
Skolnick, A. 25, 49
Sly, F. 178, 199
Smeeding, T. M. 121, 143, 380, 383n.,
    383–4
Smelser, N. 143, 332, 367
Smith, M. 15, 49, 386
Smith, N. 198, 274, 278
Socha, M. W. 284n., 306
Sokoloff, N. 24–5, 49
Solsona, M. 149, 171
Sørensen, A. 4, 8–9, 15, 23, 25, 49, 63n., 75,
    225, 227, 231, 292, 306, 311–2, 325, 330,
    332, 334, 337, 367
Sørensen, A. B. 123, 143, 230
Sorenson, A. M. 99–100, 116
South, S. J. 7, 15
Spilerman, S. 227, 231
Spitze, G. 4, 7, 14–5
Staines, G. L. 208, 231
Stanley, S. C. 35, 49
Stark, O. 260
Stegmann, H. 329

Steinmetz, S. K. 14–5, 306
Stockman, N. 40, 45, 49
Stolzenberg, R. M. 312, 330
Stovel, K. 209, 210n., 227, 231
Stromberg, A. H. 49
Sussman, M. B. 14–5, 48, 306, 386
Sundström, M. 7, 15, 88, 235, 239, 240,
    245–8, 260
Swedberg, R. 143
Swedenborg, B. 259
Sweeney, M. M. 4, 15
Swicegood, G. 231
Symeonidou, H. 6, 15
Szalai, J. 46, 384
Szelenyi, I. 335, 367
Szelenyi, S. 337, 367
Szinovacz, M. E. 372, 386
Sziráczki, G. 310, 329
Sztanderska, U. 284n., 306

Taylor, M. 198
Teachman, J. D. 9, 12, 286, 306
Teckenberg, W. 57, 75
Theeuwes, J. J. M. 96
Thoits, P. A. 34, 49
Thompson, L. 35, 49
Thomson, E. 101, 117
Thorne, B. 147, 171
Thornton, A. 313n., 330
Tijdens, K. 80, 97
Tilly, C. 227, 231
Tilly, L. A. 334, 367
Timm, A. 22, 46, 49, 259
Tomaskovic-Devey, D. 216, 231, 334, 367
Topel, R. 259
Torns, T. 151, 171
Townsley, E. 124, 143
Trappe, H. 53n., 75, 334, 337, 367
Treas, J. 211, 230, 378, 382, 382n., 386
Treiman, D. J. 162, 171, 312, 329–30
Treviño, R. 149, 171
Triest, M. 100, 117
Tuma, N. B. 56, 75, 206, 209, 231, 296, 306,
    341, 367
Tumin, M. M. 330
Tzeng, M. S. 98, 117

Ulph, D. T. 180, 198
Ultee, W. C. 45, 81, 96–7, 115, 116, 142,
    228, 328, 366

Valero, A. 149, 171
Van Dongen, W. 100, 102–3, 116–7
Van Hoof, K. 100, 117

Van Peer, C. 100, 117
Vermeulen, H. 6, 13, 42, 48, 77–8, 96
Vidinova, A. 46, 384
Villa, P. 21, 42, 45
Vogler, C. 8, 15

Wachter, M. de 116
Waite, L. J. 216, 231, 312, 330
Walby, S. 8, 15, 24–5, 50
Walder, A. G. 336, 367
Waldfogel, J. 371, 386
Wales, T. J. 180, 199
Walker, A. J. 35, 49
Walker, H. 231
Walker, J. R. 239, 259
Wallman, L. M. 230
Walsh, E. 204, 231
Walters, P. 198
Watson, J. 367
Weber, M. 3, 24, 50
Webster, M. 48
Weesie, J. 81, 97
Wegener, B. 58, 64, 75
Weinert, F. E. 230
Weiss, R. S. 35, 50

Weiss, Y. 237, 260
West, C. 30, 47, 50, 124, 144
Wethington, E. 332, 334, 366
Weygold, R. 97
Whyte, M. K. 334, 337, 367
Wilensky, H. L. 207, 209, 226, 231
Winkler, A. E. 28, 50, 371, 386
Wiśniewska, A. 289, 306
Wittig, I. 7, 13
Wolf, W. C. 216, 231, 311, 330
Wolfe, D. M. 25, 46, 334, 366
Woodland, A. D. 180, 199
Wright, E. O. 307, 330

Yalom, M. 147, 171
Yamaguchi, K. 83, 97, 296, 306, 316–7, 330
Yu, Y. 204–5, 230

Zanatta, A. L. 121, 144
Zavella, P. 34–5, 50
Zetterberg, H. L. 308, 330
Zhou, X. 332, 336–7, 352–3, 364, 367
Zimmerman, D. H. 30, 47, 50, 124, 144
Zoppè, A. 143